INDIA AND SOUTHEAST ASIA
Introspection for Future Partnership

INDIA AND SOUTHEAST ASIA
Inrospection for Future Partnership

GANGANATH JHA

ANAMIKA PUBLISHERS & DISTRIBUTORS (P) LTD.
4697/3, 21A, Ansari Road, Daryaganj, New Delhi-110 002
Phones: 23281655, 23270239; Fax: 011-27868035
e-mail: anamikapublishers@yahoo.co.in

First Published: 2010

ISBN 978-81-7975-240-1

PRINTED IN INDIA

Published by Anamika Publishers & Distributors (P) Ltd., 4697/3, 21A, Ansari Road, Daryaganj, New Delhi - 110 002, Laser Typesetting by Arpit Printographers, Shahdara, Delhi - 110 032 and Printed at Nagri Printers, Delhi.

To My Parents

Tokheswari Devi

(1916-2002)

and

K.N. Jha

(1905-1949)

Preface

Foreign Policy has been defined as the system of activities evolved by communities for changing the behaviour of other states and for adjusting their own activities to the international environment. Great Britain and France competed against each other during the colonial period to change the behaviour of Southeast Asian countries in their favour, till the end of the Second World War. The United States and erstwhile Soviet Union competed against each other after the end of the World War to bring Southeast Asia on their sides. Hence Southeast Asians were divided along ideological lines into communist and anti-communist camps. Vietnam, Laos and Cambodia belonged to communist whereas ASEAN to anti-communist camp. There were sharp divisions between the two who indulged in tirades and hostilities. This situation changed after the end of the Cold War in 1991, when all the nations in the region began to pursue the policy of rapprochement, confidence-building and regionalism to work together. Now India and China are competing against one another to win the confidence and support of Southeast Asians. In that endeavour, India lags behind due to certain reasons and it is in order to mention some of them.

India, geopolitically connected to Southeast Asia, pursued socialistic drives under the stewardship of Mrs. Indira Gandhi (1966-84). With a view to remove poverty and unemployment and establish that India was secular and socialist, her government abolished right to property from the section of fundamental rights and pursued the policy of nationalization. She supported the policy of controlled economy. Her government ignored the ongoing structural changes in the economic system of ASEAN countries as it was viewed capitalistic steps. India remained ideologically committed to socialism even under the stewardship of Rajiv Gandhi (1985-90) when drastic structural reforms were being introduced in the socialist world, namely the Soviet Union, Vietnam and Laos. When the Soviet Union disintegrated in 1991, India felt the need of structural reforms in the economic system, which ultimately opened India to the outside world. India became attuned to globalisation and forget the socialist rhetorics and populism. Our Prime Minister P.V. Narasimha Rao proved dynamic and visionary by introducing reforms to cope with the challenges of globalisation. As our reforms were late, our economic and strategic relations faced setbacks. India took its own time to build institutions to lay a solid foundation of relationship with Southeast Asian countries.

India evolved a policy of "Look East", to nurture our relations with Southeast Asia. Narasimha Rao (1991-96) and Atal Bihari Vajpayee (1999-2004) attached top priority to our relations with ASEAN and evolved suitable initiatives to strengthen our strategic and economic linkages, which were reciprocated by ASEAN. The present study, containing 22 articles, has made an effort to analyse them. In the beginning multi-lateral issues in India-Southeast Asia relations are examined. There are chapters on India-ASEAN, Sectoral partnerships, dialogue partnership, BIMST-EC, ARF, and followed by articles on bilateral relations between India and countries of Southeast Asia, namely Thailand, Vietnam, Indonesia, the Philippines, Cambodia, Laos, Myanmar and Malaysia. The last chapter has reflections of the author on community building between India and Southeast Asia.

Many scholars and experts have helped me to develop my understanding of Southeast Asia and it is my pleasure to acknowledge them. Professor Parimal Das as my teacher and guide used to inspire me for my writings. When my book, *Southeast Asia and India—A Political Perspective*, was published in 1986, he expressed his deep appreciation and I remember his inspiring kind words. The present volume may be considered an expansion of that study. Besides Professor Das, I acknowledge the academic support of Prof. Vishal Singh,

Prof. V.M. Reddi and Prof. J.K. Ray for giving me primary insights about our relationship with Southeast Asia. I have been writing on India and Southeast Asia in the past three decades in journals and edited volumes and now I have put them together. I express my gratitude to Anamika Publishers for the publication. Finally, I am beholden to my colleagues in the centre, especially Prof. Man Mohini Kaul for sustaining my academic pursuits. However, I accept sole responsibility for the views expressed or errors committed in the book.

GANGANATH JHA

Contents

1

India and Southeast Asia

Introduction

Southeast Asia is comprised of ten countries, namely, Burma, Brunei, Cambodia, Indonesia, Laos, Malaysia, the Philippines, Singapore, Thailand and Vietnam. Burma (Myanmar) shares a contiguous land and sea frontier with India and it was integrated to India during the colonial period. Thailand, Indonesia and others also share common maritime frontiers. Needless to say that they are our close neighbours, with whom our relations dates back to time immemorial. The history of the ancient Southeast Asian Kingdoms, i.e. Funan, Champa, Cambodge, Pagan, Dwarabati, Srivijaya and Majapahit indicates our intimate cultural ties. The art, architecture, epic and language have had similarities and their origin and growth cannot be understood in proper perspective without understanding Indian counterparts. Ashoka, the Great, had sent his emissaries, Sona and Uttara to spread the gospel of Buddhism in the region and Burma, Thailand, Laos and Cambodia still declare Buddhism as their state religion. The impact of Hinduism still remains as the part of their indigenous culture and religion. Although ethnic Malays accepted Islam as their religion but the Muslims in Java have not yet disowned their Hindu traditions. Some of them still believe in animism and worship spirits in different names. Bali remains a Hindu dominated society.

Malacca, Sunda and Lombok are the important sea-lanes linking East Asia with the rest of the world and Singapore, Malaysia and Thailand are industrially advanced. Singapore has an effective service sector in the field of finance, airlines, computer and shipping. Mainland Southeast Asia has diverse mountain ranges and rivers running from North to South, and most of them originate in Tibet. The main rivers are Mekong, passing through Laos, Thailand, Cambodia and Vietnam. Other rivers are Irrawadi, Chindawin and Salween in Burma, Menam Chao Phraya in Thailand, Song Koi (Red River) and Song Bo (Black River) in Vietnam. These rivers bring rich alluvial deposits regularly to make the land fertile. Most fertile areas created by these rivers are lower Burma, Central Thailand, Tongking and Mekong deltas. Thailand and Vietnam are the largest rice exporting countries in the world.

Natural Resources

Southeast Asian region is richly endowed with natural resources. The region produced 90 per cent of world's natural rubber, 50 per cent of tin, 75 per cent of world's copra, 55 per cent of palm oil and 20 per cent of tungsten. The gold mines are located in the Philippines and Indonesia and rubies in Burma and Cambodia. Timber and other hard woods are available everywhere in Southeast Asia. Oil deposits are found in Indonesia, Vietnam, Malaysia, Burma and South China Sea.

The land in Southeast Asia is extremely fertile. Rice, Sugarcane, Maize, Papaya and Banana are grown in abundance and the area is important fishing zone. Soil is mostly alluvial and the climate is Tropical. This region is thus richly endowed by nature and it is fertile. The vegetables can be grown even on hilltops.

Foreign Policy Determinants

India attaches great importance to pursuing good neighbourly relations with the countries in Southeast Asia. The policy of "Look East" is the strategy of Indian diplomacy ever since 1991 and its major thrust has been to improve our existing ties with the ASEAN region, and promote, trade, investment, tourism, Science and Technology relations. Indian policies are endeavoured to resurrect close historical and cultural ties, which were marred during the colonial period. Cold war paradigm in the past prevented India to attend various issues in our bilateral relations but the situation changed only after the termination of the cold war. Various initiatives have been taken to rejuvenate our economic, cultural and security connections.

Total bilateral trade with ASEAN countries have shown increasing trends from US $5.98 billion in 1998-99 to US $7.98 billion in 2002-03 to US $38 billion in 2007-08.

ASEAN investments which were dismal before the cold war, started growing and confidence was displayed on both sides. Various packages for the promotion of tourism were mooted and now it is not limited only to visit at Buddhist sites in Bodh Gaya. India is willing to attract investments from the ASEAN region and they have been advocating liberalization and free trade. ASEAN is trying to reciprocate Indian gestures. They recognise the importance of India as a great market where they find the existence of middle class people in millions. Besides, they have common historical, religious and security interests. Both of them support the policy of more democratization, liberalization and free trade. Both are opposed to the rise of fundamentalism and terrorism and both are supporting human rights to be universally respected.

Contemporary History

The history of colonization and de-colonization of India and Southeast Asia coincided with each other. European colonial masters scrambled amongst one another to occupy different parts of India and Southeast Asia. The Great Britain colonised India, Burma, Malaya, Sri Lanka, Singapore and Brunei. The Dutch colonized Indonesia and the French occupied Vietnam, Laos and Cambodia. Spain colonised Philippines but after the Spanish-American war, the US occupied Philippines. Anti-colonial struggle started after centuries of colonization and there were collaboration and support between Indians and Southeast Asians in anti-colonial crusades.

A great chunk of the areas in Southeast Asia were considered part of Indian sub-continent, which were arbitrarily occupied. Indian people were made to understand that in case of de-colonization, most of the separate areas would rejoin India. Notwithstanding the urge for unity, it was found that India herself was partitioned and lost territories on Western frontier (Pakistan) and eastern frontier (Bangladesh) as a result of Mountbatten plan.

However, the nationalist leaders understood the importance of a common strategy and struggle for de-colonization. They supported one another in the crusade for de-colonization. Indian National Congress regularly passed resolutions to express solidarity for support of the freedom struggle in different countries of Southeast Asia in the 20th century. Prominent Indian leaders, and intellectuals, such as Jawaharlal Nehru and Rabindranath Tagore, travelled in the region and spoke about our cultural, linguistic and religious ties. On the other hand, Ho Chi Minh (Vietnam), Sukarno (Indonesia), Tunku Abdul Rahman (Malaya) and Bogyoke Aung San (Burma) complimented India and reciprocated the feeling of common solidarity against colonial rulers.

Japanese Conquests

Japanese conquest of Southeast Asia started in the beginning of the Second World War. They occupied Thailand and forced her to sign offensive/defensive pact in June 1940 and thereafter swiftly moved to Saigon to force the French governor to permit use of ports and airports in Indochina States. The military action of the Japanese were very meticulous in defeating the British, the Dutch, the American and the French forces in Southeast Asia and give the slogan of "Asia for the Asians." The Japanese adopted "the policy of co-prosperity", and promoted local leaders to govern the country. Thus Sukarno (Indonesia), Phibun Songgram (Thailand), Emmanuel Roxas (the Philippines), Bao Dai (Vietnam), Bogyoke Aung San (Burma) and Netaji Subhas Chandra Bose (India) were groomed to provide leadership to their respective countries.

The Indian National Army of Netaji Subhas Chandra Bose had been organised and based in Southeast Asia. Its funding were solely mobilized in Malaya, Singapore, Siam and Burma. The Southeast Asians with the support of Japan solidly backed the volunteers and training of the INA. The sympathy and support for the INA volunteers in Southeast Asia were so deep that none of them were forcibly repatriated even after the defeat of Japan. A large number of INA volunteers from India preferred to stay back in Thailand and Singapore in the post-colonial period.

The Japanese conquest of Southeast Asia had exposed the vulnerability of Indian security. The British rulers were alarmed so much so that they sent Sir Stafford Cripps to India to find out constitutional means to liberate. The Congress Party advocated that the Britishers should Quit India without any pre-conditions. They believed that Indian security was interlinked with Southeast Asia and if the latter had fallen, there was every possibility of India meeting the similar fate. The history is testimony to the fact that when India was colonized, Southeast Asia too was colonized. When Southeast Asia faced Mongol invasion a little earlier, the geopolitical implications on India was substantial. Today if China is assertive of its territorial rights over every nook and corner of the South China Sea, including the Spratlys, it is a matter of concern equally for Southeast Asians and Indians. If one region is in crisis, another is bound to follow the suit.

Cold War Era

The end of the Second World War was preceded by the beginning of the cold war wherein the world was divided into Western block led by the US and the communist block led by the Soviet Union. Greater parts of Southeast Asia were under the influence of the US, which had a substantial military presence in the region. The US had Subic Bay naval base and Clarke air base in the Philippines, Can Ranh Bay naval base in Vietnam, Sattahip naval base in Thailand and several air bases in Thailand and adjoining areas. It was the main destination for military training and CIA was active in different parts of Southeast Asia. The US had organized Southeast Asia Treaty Organisation (1954) and had adopted the policy of containment against communism. It was determined to fight against communist movement in Vietnam and was militarily involved from 1964-75 to crush Communism. It was the main party in Vietnam War and can be accused of sabotaging Geneva Accord (1954), and Paris Peace Accord (1973). It was opposed to any solution wherein communists could gain power.

India was opposed to the formation of SEATO and containment drive. It had adopted socialist postures and criticized American bombing of Vietnam. Although India supported democracy and human rights at the global level, it did not understand American ethics of fighting communism.

Again it was not comfortable with Pakistan, which as a member of SEATO used American support in crusade against India. Most of the arms used by Pakistan in the wars against India in 1965 and 1971 had been acquired through the US under SEATO arrangements and the US was not ready to address legitimate concerns of India. It was, therefore, that India had to sign Indo-Soviet friendship treaty in 1971. This treaty proved a solid foundation for Indo-Soviet cooperation. On the other hand, the US was annoyed to find growing trend for Indo-Soviet relations. It projected India as a satellite of the Soviet Union and constantly worked for isolating India at the global level. As it was influential in the ASEAN region, it was successful substantially in isolating India along with Vietnam.

The situation was complicated after Vietnamese military invasion in Cambodia in 1978. Vietnam overthrew the Khmer Rouge regime and installed a new government led by Heng Samrin. India was one of the few countries, which accorded diplomatic recognition to Vietnamese installed regime in Cambodia. Japan, China, the EU, the US and the ASEAN were critical of Indian recognition and the United Nations continued to recognize the overthrown Khmer Rouge regime of genocidal Pol Pot.

The regional environment was full of polemics and rhetorics against Vietnam, India and the Soviet Union. They were projected as hegemonic powers. On the other hand, although China was a communist country, was portrayed positively. It was viewed as an actor fighting against hegemonic powers. China utilized this opportunity in its favour by strengthening its naval presence in South China Sea and Indian Ocean. It installed military outposts at Burmese territory of Coco and Hangii Islands and thus established its strategic presence in Indian Ocean region. China had never got its foothold in the Indian Ocean, but political and strategic developments during 1978-91 helped it to fulfil strategic objectives. The ASEAN became fully aware of the Chinese strategies only after the end of the Cold War. They were alarmed indeed after the Chinese forces captured Mischief Reef from the Philippine possession in 1992. China further asserted its position by publishing a Chinese map showing entire group of the Spratlys under its sovereignty, and derecognising the possession of Vietnam, Philippines, Malaysia and others.

The dissolution of the Soviet Union in 1991 saw the rise of a new world order in which the preponderance of the US was recognized. The US emphasized the importance of democracy, human rights, free trade and patent laws. Thus new issues emerged and collective regional response was required. The ASEAN subsequently felt the need to cultivate partnership with both Vietnam and India because global interests of all the Third World countries were complimentary.

India and ASEAN

ASEAN, which was born in 1967 and was aimed at promoting regional trade, investment and joint ventures, proved the main nucleus of regional cooperation, was booming and looking for new markets and investment opportunities. It found India and Vietnam complimentary now attracting investment opportunities. It also perceived India and Vietnam complimentary for strengthening regional political and security profile. Vietnam had started the process of *Doi Moi* (Renovation) aimed at liberalization, privatization and globalization. India, on the other hand, adopted the policy of economic liberalization under the stewardship of Manmohan Singh and Narasimha Rao in 1991. The new government of India also started initiating the process of liberalization, privatization and globalization. India too announced tax-free incentives for foreign investors. These policies were sufficient to attract ASEAN for further consolidation of the co-operation.

ASEAN offered sectoral dialogue partnership to India in 1992. Accordingly four core sectors of co-operation were recognized, namely trade, investment, tourism, science and technology. Sectoral partnership was instrumental in establishing institutional linkage between India and ASEAN and the partnership proved so useful that the ASEAN upgraded it within two years to full dialogue partnership in 1995. This facilitated the growth of relationship in different areas with economic, security and political implications. India was invited to participate in post-ministerial conferences of the ASEAN and also in ASEAN Regional Forum (ARF) subsequently. Both India and ASEAN began to talk of a common vision and shared destiny.

ASEAN-India co-operation committee was established to function as a key institutional mechanism to provide substantive content to different sectors of co-operation. ASEAN-India working group was also established to find out the areas for co-operation in science and technology, trade and investment, human resource development and culture. Joint co-operation committee recognized Indian expertise in the field of science and technology especially in biotechnology and IT (Information Technology). Proposals were given to co-operate in food processing, healthcare, agriculture, engineering, electronics, communication and services.

Meeting of the ASEAN-India co-operation committee decided to set up an India-ASEAN fund to develop co-operation in trade, investment, tourism, computer, solar energy and environmental protection. This fund was placed at the disposal of ASEAN Secretariat and administrated by a joint management committee. Joint co-operation committee also agreed to set up an ASEAN-New Delhi committee consisting of the heads of diplomatic missions of the ASEAN countries. Indian foreign Secretary J.N. Dixit announced the scheme of scholarship and said that each side could offer six post-doctorate fellowship upto six months in the area of science and technology. India and ASEAN also started ASEAN lecture series from eminent persons under which prominent ASEAN leaders and intellectuals delivered their lectures in India and were reciprocated. This has proved useful in confidence building and objective understanding of issues in the foreign policy and diplomacy of the ASEAN *vis-à-vis* dialogue partners.

Trade and Investment

Economic paradigm is the main thrust of co-operation with the ASEAN. India has one billion population of which a major section is comprised of the middle class. As India believed in socialistic drives and nationalization for decades, relationship with ASEAN was limited. In 1991-92 when India embarked on the policy of liberalization, the ASEAN group accounted for six percent of India's total exports but for ASEAN it was less then 1 per cent of their global trade. This situation started changing in the post-cold war era. Indian expertise in I.T., software development, small and medium enterprises and development of infrastructure, particularly in the area of power generation, transportation and construction were appreciated. Certain areas on the border of Southeast Asia were planned to be included in growth areas. These included Andamans and Northeast part of India. Of course, these proposals have not been operational so far, but potentials for future cooperation are streamlined.

Trade turnover and growing investment between India and ASEAN display confidence in each other and scope for closer partnership. India's trade with Thailand has touched more than $1 billion per year. India exports gems, precious stones, cotton and fabric, urea and fertilizers, etc. and imports pulses (urad and moong), rubber, synthetic fibre and inorganic chemicals.

Two-way trade between India and Malaysia which amounted to $772 million in 1994, increased to more than US$ one billion. It is one of the ten top investors in India. India imports palm oil, petroleum, crude rubber and non-ferrous base metals and exports engineering goods, building materials, textile, yarn, chemicals and pharmaceuticals, molasses, fruits and vegetables.

India's trade with Singapore, which accounted for nearly $44 million in 1984 rose to $1.5 billion in 1992 and it, is increasing at the rate of 10 per cent per year. India imports engineering goods, oil rigs, palm oil, organic chemicals, glass and telecommunication equipments and exports textiles, spices, fodders, inorganic chemicals, jute, fruits and vegetables.

Trading figures with Indonesia, Philippines, Vietnam, Laos and Cambodia have also shown increasing trends. Burma is also emerging as an important trading partner after the opening of Tamu-Moreh border. India is supporting constructive engagement policy *vis-à-vis* the military regime and it is treated as an important gateway of trade especially with the ASEAN region. India and Burma signed MoU on 20th May 2001 concurring the maintenance of Tamu-Kalemyo-Kalewa road. Multimode transport projects concerning upgradation of Sittwe port, navigation on the river Kaladan, and highway development from Kalewa to India-Burma border in Mizoram were other areas of co-operation. Energy related projects including solar, fossil fuel and hydroelectric energy remained items of future co-operation.

Bilateral trade figures between India and Burma stood at US $7 million, with Indonesia at $1,186 million, and with Malaysia $1,544 million in 1996-97. Indian export to ASEAN region has been largely in the areas of animal feed, cotton, rice, groundnut, synthetic fibre, machinery and bio-chemicals. There is a great potential for trade in a range of products such as auto parts and components, electronic components, railway equipment, computer and software, synthetic and organic. Indian steel textiles and yarns are in great demand in the region.

Bilateral trade with Indo-Chinese countries is also increasing. In 1997-98 bilateral trade with Cambodia amounted to Rs.10.3 crores. India donated medicines worth Rs.5 lakhs for humanitarian assistance and evinced interest in assisting agricultural development. On the other hand, bilateral trade with Laos increased to Rs.2.9 crores compared to Rs.1.3 crores earlier. Several Indian companies such as Kirloskar, Tata, B.H.E.L., Pec, etc. showed interest in exploring the market. Kirloskar exported irrigation pumps valued at US $30 million in 1998. Again bilateral trade with Vietnam registered a marginal increase of 12.5 per cent over the 1996-97 volumes of Rs.425.2 crores. As far as Indonesia was concerned bilateral trade amounted to Rs.4330.3 crores as compared to Rs.4226.2 crores in 1996-97. However, trade with the Philippines showed a downward trend in 1998. India's export to the Philippines at $90 million was down by 31 per cent from the period last year.

BIMST-EC

BIMST-EC is a sub-regional grouping involving Bangladesh, India, Myanmar, Sri Lanka and Thailand. This is the first grouping of its kind in which two ASEAN partners have come together with the three South Asian countries for economic cooperation. Established in 1998, this grouping has already identified important areas for cooperation such as communications, infrastructure, energy, trade and investment, tourism and fisheries. Each country has assumed a specific responsibility for coordination and important projects under consideration of the forum has been Asian Highway Link, Asian Railway Network and a Natural Gas Pipeline Grid. Constituted on the Bay of Bengal Rim, BIMST-EC aims at tapping vast potential of resources, both natural and human in this sub-region.

BIMST-EC is endeavoured to provide an economic forum with both private and public sector participation from member countries to promote a high level exchange of views relating to trade, investment and economic cooperation. The primary emphasis is on exchange of views on sectors such as textiles and clothing, drugs and pharmaceuticals, gems and jewelleries, horticultural and floricultural products and information technology. ESCAP hosted an expert group meeting in March 1998 at Bangkok to promote private sector participation in the BIMST-EC process. There were more than 80 participants at the meeting from all five countries. The meeting urged the private sector to play a key role in enhancing economic cooperation and concluded with a series of general and specific recommendations.

A BIMST-EC Chamber of Commerce and Industry was established and was resolved that there would be annual meetings of BIMST-EC Economic and Trade Ministers to follow up on the implementation of economic cooperation initiatives. A BIMST-EC Senior Economic Officials Committee (SEOC) was also established. The responsibilities for the various sectors identified for cooperation were delegated amongst the five countries, as follows:

Country		*Sector*
Bangladesh	-	Trade and investment
India	-	Technology
Thailand	-	Transport and Communication
Myanmar	-	Energy
Sri Lanka	-	Tourism and Fisheries.

It is remarkable that the economic ministers agreed that BIMST-EC should aim and strive to develop into a free trade arrangement. The new sub-sectors were added to the aforementioned five sectors for future cooperation and they were the following:

(*i*) Commodities such as rubber, tea, coffee, coconut and spices.
(*ii*) Automotive industries and spare parts.
(*iii*) Processed food.

BIMST-EC Ministerial meeting in Dacca on 19 December 1998, "we emphasize the need for establishing a BIMST-EC economic forum which will work as an important engine of greater economic cooperation and progress within the BIMST-EC sub-region. We reiterate our resolve to take all necessary steps to making the BIMST-EC economic forum operational for convening at the next ministerial meeting. It stated further that, "conscious of the important role that can be played by transport and communication linkages in enhancing commercial, industrial, cultural and social interaction and tourism, we reiterate the emphasis that we place on developing rail, road, multi-modal transport, stripping and air-linkages. This would reinforce complimentarities arising out of the Bay of Bengal rim identity of BIMST-EC.

BIMST-EC meeting in Burma in December 2001 emphasized the desirability of strengthening linkages among think-tanks of member countries. They also agreed to explore external financing of Mekong-Ganga Co-operation (MGC), a programme of action involving India and Indo-China states. It was hoped that the flexible nature of the co-operation agenda, ranging from culture and tourism to transport and communication could enable speedy progress. MGC involves India with five ASEAN countries, namely Cambodia, Laos, Myanmar, Vietnam and Thailand. It is endeavoured to build a road linking from Thailand to India through Myanmar. MGC wants to go a long way in developing infrastructure for transnational trade involving India's northeast border, Myanmar, Mekong region and beyond. Located between India and China, Mekong region is very important for India's security, peace and trading with East Asian countries.

The first India-ASEAN Summit, which took place in Phnom Penh in November 2002, had focused attention on relations with countries in Mekong region. Prime Minister A.B. Vajpayee on this occasion had spoken about common vision and designs with the ASEAN. India extended $10 million credit to

Cambodia and signed three agreements in the areas of trade, technical education and maintenance of the 1000-year-old Tom Pram Temple. India also conceded greater tariff concessions to Myanmar, Laos, Vietnam and Cambodia.

Security Cooperation

Security cooperation between India and Southeast Asia had started during the Second World War. Indian National Army of Netaji Subhas Chandra Bose had been strongly backed by the Southeast Asians and INA headquarters were based in Singapore. The INA volunteers infused the sense of patriotism and independence and it had a great appeal in mobilizing the people in anti-colonial struggle. INA had conquered territories near Assam and Meghalaya but it had to withdraw after the sad disappearance of Netaji and defeat of Japan. Had INA been successful in its objectives, the strategic ties with Southeast Asians, would have been impregnable.

When India became independent it signed defence treaties with Burma and Indonesia. Accordingly the defence forces of Indonesia and Burma were given advanced training in India and it was reciprocated. But defence relations with both Burma and Indonesia were halted. When Burma came under military rule in 1962 and Indonesia became radical under President Sukarno in the beginning of 1960s, the defence ties were diluted. The cold war of the two super powers had created an environment which was edged in favour of other regional powers. Moreover India became deeply embroiled in its domestic affairs after the Chinese aggression in 1962. India's influence had started receding in the region when ASEAN was born.

When ASEAN was established it was viewed as anti-communist organisation and therefore India was not ready to associate with ASEAN activities. Neither ASEAN countries wanted to involve India in any of its activities.

India-ASEAN relationship began to improve only after the end of the cold war when India became a sectoral partner of ASEAN in 1992 and subsequently Indian Navy was invited to join in the joint exercises with ASEAN countries.

Southeast Asia has been facing substantial threat to its security and its stability. Security threat in the past was posed by the threat of communist subversion but now the threat of fundamentalism and terrorism are substantial. The external threat that they perceive emanate from the northern neighbours. Japan had invaded Southeast Asia during the Second World War and now China is the potential aggressor.

China has a presence in the Pacific and Indian Ocean and its Navy is impregnable compared to ASEAN states. It is keen to fill up vacuum in case of the American withdrawal and in that endeavour it has established Naval installations at Pescadores (Pengshu), Pratas (Dongsha), Paracels (Xisha), Spratlys (Nansha), Coco and Hangii (Myanmar).

ASEAN states are afraid of China and willing to strengthen security profile by allowing the United States to have bases in the region. Malaysia offered Lumut Naval Dockyard, Thailand offered Sattahip naval base and similarly, Indonesia and Philippines offered strategic facilities to the United States.

In this context ASEAN countries preferred collaboration with India. Malaysia, Indonesia and Singapore looked for security connection with India. Initially India agreed to give training to Royal Malaysian Airforce pilots on MIG-29 aircraft. Malaysian Navy showed interest in buying Indian fast petrol craft boats. ASEAN states were ready to share Indian expertise in Marine Commando training, postal surveillance, and anti-piracy operation, weather observation, coastal search and rescue operation, defence of ports and harbours and shallow water mining, etc. India also offered coastal surveillance Radars and L-70 guns.

India took part in UNTAC activities in Cambodia along with the ASEAN countries and the subsequent contribution in strengthening defence system in Southeast Asia proved effective in confidence building and therefore India became a member of ASEAN regional forum (ARF). The objective of ARF has been the promotion of confidence building, development of preventive diplomacy mechanism and conflict resolution mechanism. ARF had 24 members in which ASEAN has the leading role. It is mainly aimed at resolving political and security problems. The style of ARF is musyawarah dan Mufakat (consultation and consensus). ARF has promoted Track-I and Track-II diplomacy to resolve regional security problems. Track-I is conducted at the institutional levels such as ARF or at the level of respective governments but Track-II aims at mobilising non-governmental organizations, business groups and strategic institutions in the region. In Track-II, preventive diplomacy is preferred so that the belligerent is restrained. The preventive diplomacy creates an environment in which the concern of each partners are expressed and the decisions are taken after wide consultations. The evolutionary rather revolutionary approach is preferred for conflict resolution.

Principal objectives of ARF as earlier stated was to foster constructive dialogue and consultation on political and security issues of common interest and concern. India was associated with this organisation so that it could contribute to regional understanding, confidence building, and suggest ideas for preventive diplomacy in the Asia-Pacific. India has been supporting regional consensus and the constructive engagement policy with Myanmar. It has invited ASEAN for joint exercises in the Andamans and attaching importance to China despite border problems.

ARF achievements are not impressive so far. Much talked about transparency in defence matters has yet to materialised. Many members of ARF do not publish defence white papers and those who do so, reveal nothing. At the same time official defence spending figures are not trusted. Earlier plan to create a regional arms register for conventional arms transfer has remained really on papers. It has done nothing to curb drug trafficking or rapid spread of light weapons to criminal and rebel groups. Again it failed to take any initiative on the issue of East Timor and rise of terrorism.

The problem of terrorism is substantial in the region and they are of different types. First of all, Southeast Asia is the biggest producer of opium and opium related products. There are connections between drug peddlers and insurgent groups in Northeastern part of India comprising Assam, Meghalaya, Arunachal Pradesh, Nagaland, Manipur and Tripura. The drug peddlers have a network and collusion with politicians, terrorists and police and they supply narcotics inside and outside the region. American President Bill Clinton highlighted the threat of narco-terrorism before the UN General Assembly by saying that:

"no one is immune, not the people of Latin America or Southeast

> Asia, where drug traffickers wielding imported weapons have murdered judges, journalists, police officers and innocent passers-by."

Cox Bazar provides an important market for the sale of M-16, different types of Kalashnikovs, AK-47, and Chinese guns. The weapons left by insurgents during the Vietnam War and Cambodian civil war are cheaply available through arms dealers in Southeast Asia. The insurgents in the region are in liaison with arms merchants and rebels in Acch, Ambon, Mindanao and West Irian are constantly getting their supplies. This problem has been very chronical, which eludes an effective solution.

Islamic terrorist outfits cause the most important and immediate threat to Southeast Asian security. They are spread in different parts of Southeast Asia and have linkages with terrorist organizations at the global level. Al Qaida has supporters in Indonesia, Malaysia and the Philippines and they have their secret cells in Singapore, Bangkok, Jakarta and other areas.

Islamic terror groups are striving for Darulah Islamiah Raya (DIR) aimed at creation of a union of the Malay world. The areas comprising DIR are Malaysia, Singapore, Indonesia, Rakhine, (Burma), Mindanao (Philippines) and Patani (Thailand). They have trained militias and modern weapons. They want to overthrow the existing order and establish Taliban type of regime in the region. Thus unity in diversity (Bhinekka Tunggul Ekka) and Panchshila principles, which were the guiding principles of governance in Indonesia, has been threatened. Brunei and Malaysia are constantly reviewing their policies to cope with the demands of fanatic groups. Although both Brunei and Malaysia had to declare Islam as the state religion, it is not sufficient to please the terrorists.

A new history of terror and bloodshed started in Indonesia on 12th Oct. 2002 when Jemaah Islamiyah (JI) bombed tourist resorts at Bali. This event had international ramifications. In this bombing 190 people died and 300 became injured. Majority of the victims were from Australia, Britain, France, Germany and Sweden. India was alarmed and it was one of the first countries to express its anguish. American ambassador in Jakarta, Ralph Boyce met President Megawati and told her to wrap up the terrorist cells, block it and demonstrate that they were serious. US emphasized that Indonesia has been a terrorist heaven after the bombing in Bali and ordered 350 Americans connected with US embassy to leave the country.

The US denounced bombing by calling it a despicable act of terror. Abu Bakar Bashir was projected as the main leader of the crime and JI was declared a terrorist organization. Hence it is a crime to contribute funds to JI. Members of JI were debarred to enter the United States.

Terrorist outfits are disliked because of their inhuman attitudes. They are propagating Jihad for their adversaries and they kill their fellow Muslims for offering opposite opinion. They do speak of Shariat laws and Islamic ethos for governance but it is theocratic in nature.

India is also facing the threat of Islamic terrorism in Kashmir. Kashmiri Pandits have been driven out of their homes and their properties have been usurped. The terrorists are killing innocent people in the valley regularly and the terrorist outfits are strongly backed by Pakistan and some other Islamic countries. The government of India has been trying to resolve the dispute but bloodshed and dispute remains.

Indians, generally, thought that the dispute was due to two-nation theory or because of clash of two religious groups in India. However, the experiences in Indonesia show that terrorism thrives even under one religion. Islam by all means are given due importance in Indonesia, but Islamic terrorist organizations are not ready to recognize this reality. They talk of Darul Islam, or Islamic raya or Al-Qaida. Thus both India and Indonesia are facing similar problems and they have many ideas to share for conflict resolution. Other partners in the ASEAN are feeling too much concern for political developments in Indonesia especially after the Bali massacre. They have a consensus to fight terrorism and enlist the cooperation of India to the extent possible.

To conclude it can be stated that India's relations with Southeast Asia has been deep-rooted and integrated with one another. Indian influence in Southeast Asia is visible to such an extent that some Indians commit the error of projecting them as "further India".

India's relations with Southeast Asia got disturbed during the cold war period because of three factors. Firstly, it opposed

American policy of containment and formation of SEATO. Secondly, it expressed its solidarity with communist forces in Vietnam. It upgraded its diplomatic relations with North Vietnam in 1972 and exchanged ambassadors. But it did not offer the same privilege to South Vietnam.

Another issue, which came in the way, was India's diplomatic recognition to Vietnamese installed regime in Cambodia in 1979. The ASEAN was unhappy with India's decision.

Thirdly, India became friendly with the Soviet Union and Vietnam, which were disliked by the Americans and pro-American leaders in the Asia-Pacific. Adversarial environment changed only after the end of the cold war.

India became a sectoral partner of the ASEAN in 1992 and dialogue partner in 1995. It was thereafter that the relations began to improve. The core sectors for cooperation became trade, investment, tourism, science and technology, IT, biotechnology and human resources.

India is a member of ARF and thus India and ASEAN are cooperating in security matters. India has been participating in ASEAN post-ministerial meetings and ARF meetings and has contributed to confidence building and peace-making.

When Pokharan-II was conducted in 1998, America, Japan and Australia expressed great reaction but some of the ASEAN leaders expressed appreciation of India as a nuclear power.

India and ASEAN have similar views on the threat of terrorism. They believe that terrorists are inhuman and devilish. They have no respect for religion as they are inhuman and unethical and they are devils to be decimated. ASEAN countries have displayed better understanding of India's problem in Kashmir and seven states of the Northeast. Unlike the cold war period; they are not supporting polemics against India. ASEAN in fact, accord prime importance to India as an essential wing of ASEAN zumbo.

To conclude, India's endeavour of conducting good neighbourly relations with Southeast Asia are paying dividends in economic and strategic terms. This has the support of Indian Parliament and of all the countries in the region in the hope that with Indian support, Asia-Pacific might emerge as an important centre for democracy, free trade and globalization.

2

Netaji in Southeast Asia

Netaji Subhas Chandra Bose was in Southeast Asia for merely two years (1943-45) but the heroic role that he played during this period would always be written in the letters of gold. He introduced revolutionary dynamics in our freedom struggle, which had been avoided so far. He led our freedom movement to a great height by defeating the British forces at the battlefront in 1944 and making Assamese frontier vulnerable. This was the first victory of the Indians in an open battle, which transmitted great hopes of success against the British in the forthcoming liberation war. This had greatly boosted the morale of the nationalists and it had shaken the foundations of the British colonial system. It is a reality that Netaji's endeavours were strongly backed by the nationalist leaders in Southeast Asia and we must acknowledge their support in those days. In order to have a proper understanding of Netaji and his role in Southeast Asia, it is necessary at the outset to know him as a person and his ideologies.

Netaji was born at Cuttack on 23 January, 1897. His father's name was Janaki Nath Bose and mother's name was Probhabati. His school education was completed in Cuttack and college education in Calcutta and Cambridge. He was brilliant and had been selected for Indian Civil Services (ICS) in 1920. He, however, resigned from the ICS in 1921, and established contacts with Deshbandhu Chittaranjan Das. He joined Indian National Congress under his influence in 1921. He believed then that Mahatma Gandhi's truth and non-violence to promote freedom movement was the best, because it was generating new forces and new activities to promote socio-political conditions leading to open revolt against the British rule by the people of India.[1] But he was doubtful that Gandhi's non-violent struggle alone would bring freedom. He always visualized the need for the emergence of Garibaldi or George Washington to defeat the enemy forces at the battlefront in order to gain independence.

Netaji firmly believed that without a revolutionary struggle, it was impossible to force the British to withdraw from India. His own conviction reached after much reflection and study of history, was that British rule in India was a military occupation which could not be expected to wither away without a bitter struggle.[2] But as an astute strategist, he believed in creating suitable conditions to confront the Britishers, and in that endeavour he found his association with the Congress quite useful. He worked devotedly to fulfil Congress resolutions and whenever he found opportunities for innovative actions, he performed it with immaculate skills. When he raised a volunteer corps in 1928 on military lines for the purpose of maintaining law and order at the site of the Congress session, it had been appreciated even by Motilal Nehru, the then Congress President.[3] The Volunteer Corps were clothed in military uniforms and were also trained in military manners under the leadership of Netaji, who had been declared its Commanding Officer General. The Western press felt great concern at this development and was highly critical that being a civilian, Netaji had dressed himself in military uniform.

Netaji attached importance to mobilization of public opinion while in the Congress Party (1921-38). When he was elected the President of the Congress at Haripura Session of the party in 1938, he found suitable international environment to develop military capabilities to throw out the colonial yoke. The background of the Second World War was ready and Great Britain was sure to be embroiled and weakened. Mahatma Gandhi, Pandit Nehru and some others did not approve of the changes in the methods of the Congress movement. They opposed the course of action suggested by Netaji.

Nevertheless, Netaji was convinced that no country could free itself from foreign domination without military revolt and without efforts to destroy the military strength of the colonial power. He emphasized that the Congress movement must come out of its stagnation and be realistically dynamic to defeat the military forces militarily. On the other hand, proponents of the non-violent struggle argued against it on moral grounds. They also suggested that the military confrontation idea was impractical and unrealistic.

Despite powerful opposition of his ideas in the Congress Party, when Netaji contested for the post of Presidentship for the second time in 1939 (Tripuri Session), against Mahatma Gandhi's candidate, Pattabhi Sitaramaiya, he became victorious. This proved his popularity, but Netaji was not allowed to function thereafter. Netaji found unfriendly atmosphere for himself in the Congress and therefore he resigned from its membership. He returned to Calcutta and established Forward Bloc to implement his ideas. But soon he was put under house arrest by the Britishers and it looked as if he had been immobilized. However, Netaji escaped and disappeared from his confinement on 16 January 1941 and stories of his heroic escape is quite well known. Thereafter, he went to Germany via Kabul, because it was then the only European Power interested in extending support to Indian nationalists. France, Holland, Portugal and the United States had colonial possessions in the region and their interests were bound to be disturbed if British interests in India were adversely affected.

When Netaji reached Germany, he established 'Free India Centre' in Berlin, which had a semi-diplomatic status. The German Foreign Office was monitoring its activities and Netaji was talking regularly on Berlin radio. His activities were supported by the Germans and he was not allowed to contact other agencies. Though he felt restrictions on his activities, but he was hopeful that the Germans would march on victory campaign to India through West Asian routes. However, the Germans under the euphoria of its success against all European powers, decided to march towards Moscow. This was a strategic blunder and Nataji lost all hopes of German march against British India.[4] It was, therefore, that when he was contacted to come to Southeast Asia to lead a war for national liberation, he readily agreed. As Southeast Asia was contiguous to India, he found it strategically suitable to launch military operations. Moreover, overseas Indians were ready to support his quest for military campaign, and he was assured of absolute liberty to decide his strategies for future course of actions.

Here it is in order to analyse Southeast Asian situation on the eve of Netaji's arrival. In case of the European powers, they had been defeated by the Germans and were mortally afraid of the German subjugation, but Southeast Asia was getting sufficient rays of hopes to gain their self-government. Most of the nationalist leaders—Sukarno, Sihanouk, Bao Dai, Phibun Songgram, Aung San and Emmanuel Roxas—were supported by the Japanese, and as a result the nationalist movement in the region had reached its crescendo. By mid-1942, the Japanese had defeated the Western colonial forces everywhere in Southeast Asia, and had shattered the myth of Western supremacy. Most of the countries had got indigenous rulers and the colonial administrators had been sacked. All the countries were supporting "Greater East Asia Co-prosperity Spheres", and they were expected to fight western colonial powers under Japan's leadership. Thus, they popularized the slogan of "Asia for Asians", to foster the feeling of regional solidarity. President Sukarno's three slogans, "Japan—the Liberator of Asia", "Japan—the Protector of Asia", "Japan—the Light of Asia", (Three A Movement), had been propagated to acknowledge the Japanese contribution in defeating the Western colonial powers,[5] but at the same time Indonesia was attaching prime importance to strategic preparations to confront the Dutch forces eventually.

Southeast Asian leaders knew very well that the Japanese protection and dominance were temporary and they themselves have to fight for their sovereignty. They had to be prepared to prevent the come-back efforts of the former rulers. Thus they were strategically trying to strengthen the nationalist forces to cope with the emerging threats. Any activity that helped in weakening the western colonial yoke was appreciated and they sought to assist them. As Netaji was determined to fight against British forces, Southeast Asians felt these endeavours quite complimentary. It was logical to think that if India is liberated, it would strengthen nationalist causes in the Southeast Asian region. If British colonialism is thrown out of India, it is bound to have chain reactions. It would be impossible thereafter to maintain their colonial structure in Malaya, Burma and Singapore. Other colonial masters in the region—the Dutch in

Indonesia, France in Indo-China, and the US in the Philippines would be forced to go out.

The Japanese, on the other hand, were already equipping the nationalist resistance forces so that in case of their absence, Southeast Asians would be in a position to fight. In this sphere, the Japanese found in Netaji some potentialities and encouraged the idea to bring him to Southeast Asia. Japan had thousands of prisoners of war (POWs), whose services were being sought now to defeat the Western colonial powers. Many of the POWs were Indians who were caught fighting for Great Britain. They were now to be given nationalist lessons to work for the nationalistic cause. However, to convert their loyalty from British to nationalist cause and channelise their energies in the desired direction, it was necessary to have a leader with nationalist credentials, who could prove charismatic, inspiring and dashing. Netaji had all those qualities and thus Japan viewed him as a strategic partner.

The Japanese took the assistance of Ras Behari Bose to invite Netaji to come over to Southeast Asia from Germany. Ras Behari had organized India Independence League in Japan and had revolutionary credentials. His name had first hit the headlines for throwing a bomb at Lord Hardinge, then India's Viceroy, while the viceregal procession was passing through Chandni Chowk in Delhi in 1912. Again during the First World War, he was involved in a plot to organize a rebellion of Indian soldiers in the army on similar patterns as in 1857, and had made arrangements for arms and ammunitions from Germany. The plot, however, was discovered and arms shipments were captured. There were great search for Ras Behari's arrest and therefore he fled and took shelter in Japan. He stayed there for decades and worked for India's liberation.

Ras Behari held Netaji in great esteem and he welcomed the idea to invite Netaji to take over the leadership of India's independence movement. He called for a meeting of India Independence League in Bangkok in June 1942, where the landmark decision to invite Netaji to come over to Southeast Asia was taken. Thus contacts with Netaji in Germany was established with the help of Japan and arrangements were made to bring him to Southeast Asian front. Netaji came to Japan in

June 1943, where he was briefed about the ground realities. Netaji was honoured to attend the session of the Diet in Japan where General Hideki Tojo, the then Premier, declared that:

> "Japan is firmly resolved to extend all means of support in order to expel and eliminate the Anglo-Saxon influences from India, which are the enemy of Indian people, and to enable India to achieve full independence, in the true sense of the term."[6]

Netaji was introduced to military officers in Japan and he got fresh insights. Japan expressed full support to India's liberation war and assured to provide arms and equipments.

Netaji thereafter came to Singapore on 2 July 1943, where Ras Behari had called for a conference of the Indian Independence League. On this occasion the representatives of ethnic Indians in the entire Southeast Asian countries had assembled. All of them enthusiastically welcomed Netaji and it was on this occasion that Ras Behari formally handed over the leadership of freedom movement to Netaji. The Indians, assembled on this occasion, expressed their devotion to the nationalist struggle. Thus Netaji was handed over the leadership of Indian Independence League, and in order to start war for independence he announced on 5 July 1943 the formation of Indian National Army (INA). While announcing the formation of INA, he addressed his volunteers by saying:

> "Soldiers of India's army of liberation, today is the proudest day of my life of announcing to the whole world that India's army of liberation has come into being in Singapore—which was once the bulwark of British empire. This will emancipate India from British colonial yoke under Indian leadership. He further added, "Comrades! My soldiers, let your battle cry be—To Delhi! To Delhi!"[7]

Both the League and the INA subsequently proved indispensable parts of the same organization, functioning with the sole objective to liberate India.

General Tojo was happy at the formation of INA and was gracious enough to come to Singapore on the occasion of the birth of the INA and he was presented a march-past by the INA volunteers. Netaji expressed profound appreciation of the great honour that the Japanese Premier had done to the INA, by spending so much of his valuable time in order to inspire Indian army. He further said that:

> "This day will ever remain a red-letter day, in the history of the newly organized Army of Free India. Your excellency's presence among our soldiers today, immediately after sending an inspiring message to the Indian Independence League Conference yesterday, has given a powerful impetus to our revolutionary struggle."[8]

The announcement of the formation of the INA had electrifying impact on the course of the independence movement. But here it is appropriate to say that the INA was not born in a vacuum. It had been evolved through the active cooperation of the overseas Indians. Ras Behari in Japan and Swami Satyanand Puri in Thailand had prepared the groundwork for it and Indian Independence League offices in Singapore, Bangkok and Kuala Lumpur had worked tirelessly to organise it. After 1942, Baba Amar Singh and Giani Pritam Singh in Bangkok had established close contacts with the Japanese officials in the region, including Field Marshal Terouchi and General Sugiyama. They had attracted the support of a section of Indians in the British army to work for the liberation war. Captain Mohan Singh of the 1/14 Punjab Regiment, who devoted himself for the nationalist cause, did extraordinary work to assure the welfare of Indian prisoners of war in the Japanese Camps to lure them on the nationalist side. Whenever the life of any Indian in the region was endangered or their property was to be usurped, Captain Mohan Singh was there to provide protection. The Japanese avoided to disturb the interests of ethnic Indians in the region whereas they were harsh against ethnic Chinese. Indian Independence League was responsible for favourable attitudes of the Japanese. The League was also publishing a newspaper, *Azad Hind*, and had mobilized public opinion for war of national liberation.[9]

Netaji proved successful in mobilizing them under the banner of INA. After assuming its leadership, he undertook visits to various parts of Southeast Asia to mobilize moral and material support and appealed to overseas Indians to make sacrifices. He also tried to establish rapport and friendly relations with indigenous leaders of Southeast Asia and response of his appeals in Thailand, Burma, Malaya, Cambodia and Vietnam was extremely enthusiastic. Thousands of people thus volunteered to work for the INA and assured to make their humble contributions for the INA.

On his return to Singapore, he restructured Indian Independence League and seven new departments were introduced to suggest ideas in the different areas—security, war, propaganda, finance—and others. He also opened its new offices in different parts of Southeast Asia for better coordination and networking. He attached utmost importance to the information media and besides publication of *Azad Hind*, radio broadcasts was given importance. Radio was the only means through which the messages could go to the common people. Hence Azad Hind Radio was regularly broadcasted from Singapore, Tokyo, Bangkok, Saigon, Rangoon and other places.

It is pertinent to point out here that Netaji gave due importance to enlist the support of women to make the liberation struggle successful. He established Rani of Jhansi Regiment as a branch of the INA and the arrangements were made to establish training camps for them at Singapore, Thailand and Burma. While speaking at Rani of Jhansi Camp in Singapore, Netaji said:

> "The history of great women in India is as ancient as the Vedic period. The greatness of Indian womanhood had its roots in those early days when India had its Sanskrit culture. The same India which produced great women in the past produced Rani of Jhansi, Lakshmi Bai, at a grave hour in India's history. And today when we are facing the gravest hour in our history, I have confidence that Indian womanhood will not fail to rise to the occasion."[10]

It is understood that the Indian women in Southeast Asia and the Far East were so overwhelmed and influenced by Netaji's leadership that many of them not only volunteered to work for the INA, but also offered their precious jewelleries and ornaments to Netaji to make freedom movement successful.

When Netaji was satisfied that necessary arrangements for his revolutionary endeavours had been made, he formally announced the formation of the provisional government of India with headquarters in Singapore on 21 October 1943. This was subsequently known as the government of the Azad Hind.

While forming this, Netaji was emotional and gave enthralling speech. He said that the provisional government is entitled to, and hereby claims, the allegiance of every Indian. It guarantees religious liberty as well as equal rights and equal opportunities to all its citizens. It declares its firm resolve to pursue the happiness and prosperity of the whole nation and all its parts, cherishing all the children of the nation equally and transcending all the differences cunningly fostered by an alien government in the past."[11]

This government became a matter of world headlines. The nationalists in general welcomed it but the Britishers were extremely alarmed. The government of the Azad Hind was given diplomatic recognition by Japan, Germany, Italy, Crotia, Burma, Thailand, nationalist China, Manchuria and the Philippines.[12] In short, the government of the Azad Hind generated nationalist euphoria as never before.

Japan was very happy with the activities of the Azad Hind government and they invited Netaji to get his insights for the success of Greater East Asia. When Netaji went to Japan in November 1943, the emperor of Japan received him with all the honours due to the heads of states. Netaji attended Greater East Asia Conference in Tokyo in November 1943 and proved himself a subject of star attraction amongst the invitees. It was here that the Japanese Premier, Tojo handed over the Andaman and Nicobar islands to India. These two islands had been under the Japanese occupation ever since 1942. Netaji took them for Azad Hind government and undertook tour of that area in December 1943. It was on that occasion that he had renamed them Shahid and Swaraj respectively, and listened to the problems of the people on those islands.[13]

Now Netaji focused his attention on Burma to launch liberation war against British forces. With that objective in mind, Netaji established second headquarters of the INA in Rangoon in the beginning of 1944. Netaji wanted Burma to be a base through which the INA could launch operation. He tried to establish strong foothold there so that INA forces could enter Indian territory safely and establish its authority. The INA came into action on 4 February 1944 when it successfully challenged the British forces on the Arakan Front. On 18 March 1944, the

INA crossed the Burma border and for the first time, stood on the soil of India. Netaji was so overwhelmed with this victory that he proclaimed March 21st to be a national day, for it was on this day that the Indian soldiers for the first time conquered a piece of Indian territory from the British hands.[14] The liberation war, however, was halted within three miles of Imphal because of the inclement weather and the lack of air cover. The strategic retreat of the INA proved very costly, but it did not affect its morale.

In the meanwhile, the balance of power in the European hemisphere started changing. The Germans began to face reverses and Japan too faced gloomy situation. They began to concentrate their forces at the home front and the dynamics of the war changed. On 11 August 1945, the United States dropped atom bomb on Hiroshima and Japan was forced to surrender. Netaji was in Saigon at that time to negotiate the purchase of strategic weapons. He boarded a plane in Saigon on 17 August 1945 which unfortunately crashed at Formosa on 18th August 1945.[15] Thus one of the brightest sons of India died and became immortal for good.

Conclusion

In retrospect, we find that Netaji had successfully identified himself with the nationalist aspirations of Southeast Asia and the leaders in the region viewed him as their own. They offered him assistance to the extent possible and Netaji could travel any time in any corners of Southeast Asia as natives. Netaji was successful in his missions and the people offered active cooperation. It is a historical reality that his INA was comprised not only of ethnic Indians but also ethnic Thais, Burmans, Malayans and Cambodians. The credit goes to him that even in the Rani of Jhansi Regiment, there were volunteers of different countries of Southeast Asia. This was possible because leaders like Field Marshal Phibun Songgram, Aung San, Sihanouk, Roxas, and others projected Netaji as their own crusader against western colonialism. One of the surviving ministers of the war time in Thailand, Sunthorn Hongladarom (then Information Minister) told me in a personal interview in April 1974 that Subhas Bose wielded enormous influence on Field Marshal

Phibun Songgram (1938-45), so much so that he needed no prior appointment to see him. He used to come everyday to the Radio Station to record his voice and he was extremely punctual in his time. Thailand viewed his activities as their own and showed great commitments for its success. It had given Bankhen for military training to the INA and Sanam Ruan for recruiting volunteers to the INA. It had also offered cultural forums to Indians to promote the feeling of Indian nationalism. The commitments of Thailand towards INA was so deep-rooted that even after Phibun Songgram was replaced by Seni Pramoj as the Premier, it treated surviving INA people in a great esteem, and did not repatriate them as desired by the Britishers. Britain had declared that the INA activists should be treated as war criminals and necessary arrangements were made for their trial in Delhi. Thailand then was facing internal turmoil, yet they remained sympathetic to the INA. A number of people associated with the INA like Karuna Kusalalaya, H.L. Sachdeva, Dev Nath Das and G.D. Narula, to whom I very often talked at Thai-Bharat Cultural Lodge (Bangkok) in 1974, were full of praise for the government of Thailand for the help in rehabilitating them and treating them as their own nationals. Though the impact of the INA phenomenon in other countries of Southeast Asia was also quite strong but today they are forgotten heritage of our endurable relations. In short, it can be observed here that the success of the INA phenomenon was also due to Southeast Asia and we must acknowledge and pay tributes for their assistance in our freedom struggle.

Indonesia and Vietnam maintained the legacy of the INA and continued to pursue revolutionary path. They became victorious against the Dutch and the French forces respectively. Though they too had similar historical background as India, and were less resourceful, they were not deterred to pursue their revolutionary path. Both fought bravely against colonial forces in their own ways and this battle gave them a rallying point to promote their common nationalism. They are firmly united despite innumerable challenges. Indians, on the other hand, sacrificed their revolutionary path and expressed faith in non-violent methods to tackle the Britishers. The result was partition of the country and disorder, communal riots and mass migration of people from India to Pakistan and vice versa. Though the country was decolonised but the cost of discarding revolutionary path was too high. This development in itself proved the relevance of the ideals preached by Netaji Subhas Chandra Bose.

REFERENCES

1. Girija, K., Mookerjee, 1975, *Subhas Chandra Bose,* New Delhi, Publications Division, p. 31.
2. *Ibid.,* p. 30.
3. *Ibid.,* p. 22.
4. Subodh Markandeya, 1990, *Subhas Chandra Bose: Netaji's Passage to Immortality,* Bangalore, Arnold Publishers, p. 177.
5. D.G.E. Hall, 1968, *A History of Southeast Asia,* London, Macmillan, p. 820.
6. N.G. Jog, 1967, *In Freedom's Quest: A Biography of Netaji Subhas Chandra Bose,* Bombay, Orient Longmans, p. 235.
7. Text of the speech of Netaji Subhas Chandra Bose to Indian National Army, Singapore, 5 July 1943.
8. Text of the speech of Netaji to welcome H.E. General Hideki Tojo, Prime Minister of Japan in Singapore on 6 July 1943.
9. See the Chapter "Waiting for the Leader", in N.G. Jog, n. 6, pp. 219-233.
10. See the text of "Netaji's address to Rani of Jhansi Regiment", in K.M. Tamhankar, 1946, *On to Delhi, 23 Enthralling Speeches of Subhas Chandra Bose,* Bombay, Phoenix Publications, pp. 96-97.
11. For details regarding the provisional government, see N.G. Jog, No. 6, pp. 240-249.
12. *Ibid.,* and also see Mookerjee, No. 1, p. 86.
13. Mookerji, No. 1, p. 86.
14. *Ibid.,* p. 87.
15. *Ibid.,* p. 89. For a comprehensive analysis of this aspect see, "The Last Flight", in Subodh Markandeya, No. 4, pp. 267-284.

3

India's Relationship with Southeast Asia

India is geo-strategically linked to Southeast Asia and culturally an integral part as explained by G. Coedes (France) and B.R. Chatterji (India) in their writings. The religion, epic, literature and architecture of different countries in Southeast Asia speaks about intimate historic and geo-strategic connections but they are considered part of separate regions. The colonial interlude for centuries interrupted our traditional links. The independence was followed by politics of the cold war in that India is not an integral part of Southeast Asia. Although it was not a digestible proposition that India is not an integral part of Southeast Asia, but it was accepted inadvertently even by our Ministry of External Affairs. Annual Report that it published did not include Southeast Asia in the section of "India's Neighbours". Similarly the yearbook or handbook published by some countries in Southeast Asia did not mention India as one of their closest neighbours. Their text-book did not attach much coverage to understanding history of Angkor, Dwarawati, Champa, Pagan, Sri Vijaya or Majapahit which may explain Indian connections in the historical past. Their think-tank referred importance of ASEAN + 3 (China, Japan, Korea) for evolving strategies in economic and security affairs culminating in the formation of East Asian community. An assessment of the overall opinion of Southeast Asia indicate that the cold war mindset in which India was referred to as poor, underdeveloped and camp follower--has changed only to a limited extent.

Although the attitudes of ASEAN leaders and intellectuals are changing but their strategic thinking have yet to understand India as a serious partner. To quote Jusuf Wanandi.

> "India, which has a potential in the future of having a security role in the region is mainly confined to the subcontinent and

> still has to go through her structural changes economically before she can really play a greater role in the region."[1]

India was neglected by the ASEAN during cold war years. The major thrust of the domestic policies of India and ASEAN were entirely different. India endeavoured to establish socialistic pattern of society and thus nationalisation, democratisation, secularisation became the prevailing norm. On the other hand, ASEAN countries supported privatisation and open market system. They provided incentives to investors and welcomed transnational corporations and technologies. The ASEAN growth rates were high at 6 to 8 per cent and it was projected as a trojan horse of success. The ASEAN model attracted their former adversaries like Vietnam to join it. Vietnam's admission was followed by Laos, Myanmar and Cambodia and hence all the ten countries of Southeast Asia became partners in ASEAN. Promotion of free trade was welcomed and rapid steps were taken to hasten the face of globalisation. However, the economic development of the region was suddenly jolted after the financial crisis of 1997-98. The investors started withdrawing their deposits and thus there was acute shortage of foreign currencies. This crisis taught the value of state control on financial institutions and also that of constant monitoring over it. Hence Indian economic system proved relevant in the changed context.

India and Southeast Asia admit convergence of interests in economic, political and security matters. It faced reverses in the SAARC and ASEAN regions initially. It evolved new initiatives to strengthen partnership with countries in Southeast Asia and Far East in the post-cold war era and called it "Look East" policy. The concept of Look East was advocated by P.V. Narasimha Rao, I.K. Gujral and Atal Bihari Vajpayee, the three Prime Ministers of India respectively. Although Sukarno, Phibun and Roxas also advocated "Look East" in 1940's but their emphasis and objectives were different from India. "Look East" for an Indian is connected with their traditions that they offer prayers to the rising sun in the morning. Southeast Asia is geographically located in the East and an important component of our traditional folklores. It was identified as central to India's foreign policy in the entire Asia-Pacific. India's Look East had three-pronged approach. First, to renew political contacts with the ASEAN partners; second, to increase economic interaction (trade, investment, science and technology, tourism etc.) and third, to forge defence links with ASEAN partners as a means to enhance political and strategic interests and understanding.[2] Indian think-tanks are reviewing the notion of economic security, self-reliance and national interests in the light of developments in the post-cold war era. As a nation of one billion people, India cannot afford to remain a marginal player in the global economy, as measured for instance by our share in world trade or income. Commensurate with her size and civilizational characteristics, India is willing to assume greater role in global affairs and world economy. Look East policy is endeavoured to fulfil those aspirations and it has evoked positive response in the ASEAN region.

The meaning and contents of Look East policy was decided by Narasimha Rao himself during his tenure as the Prime Minister of India (1991-95). His speech delivered on 8 September 1994 in Singapore was a milestone to influence the opinion of Southeast Asians where he spoke about endogenous and exogenous nature of the problems, which were a matter of common concern and common interests, and they were:

(*a*) interpretations of sovereignty, whether over the oceans, in outer space, over territory, resources etc.;
(*b*) frictions arising out of differing cultural perceptions—as we witnessed in the case of Michael Fay;
(*c*) massive needs and demands of relatively under-developed populations and migratory tendencies, with no respect for national boundaries;
(*d*) confrontational postures on a broad range of fundamental issues related to trade barriers, currency stabilisation, international aid and investment flows;
(*e*) intensification of the debate over linkages between issues such as human rights, labour-laws, environmental protection and resource management, liberal information flows, etc. in political and economic relationships.[3]

Southeast Asian countries were also looking for suitable

answers to aforementioned issues but Indian Premier pointedly articulated:

> the increasing tendency on the part of dominant powers to assume that they cannot only define the means, but even the ends of collective international endeavour. This has been revealed in the form of intrusive prescriptions in the areas of social regulation, dissemination of knowledge, technological development and even domestic administration. The worst part of this tendency is that on closer scrutiny, it can be easily shown to be based on unsympathetic half-knowledge, and not unoften even total ignorance. He further stated that worldwide criminal networks of drug trafficking: smugglers, terrorists, money launderers and other such elements who have no stake in peace and real prosperity but manage to suborn Governments to ensure the furtherance of their own interests.[4]

The opium growing Golden Triangle is located in Southeast Asia and clandestine sale of illegal drugs and narcotics are endemic. The issue of human rights record in Indonesia, Burma, Vietnam, Laos and the Philippines are very often criticized and the demands for more democratization are advocated. The Spratlys are being claimed by the Chinese and the possession of Vietnam, Malaysia and the Philippines in that region are questioned. Besides there are some religious groups sponsoring terrorism. The organisations like Jemaah Islamiyah are inspired by Al Qaida, and they have trained terrorist groups in the name of Islam. They have suicide squads and sophisticated weapons to attack their targets. Aceh in Indonesia, Mindanao in the Philippines and Patani in Thailand are in the grip of Islamic terrorists but people in certain areas in Malaysia are also supporting fanatics. There has been attacks on public places and various governments are faced with a dilemma on how to tackle them. As they take the help of religion to legitimate their violence (Jehad), they are supported by some of their co-religionists. Indeed it is delicate to address the issue of terrorism based on religion and this is a pretext for the United States to advise them about certain measures. India and Southeast Asia are sensitive to prescriptions given by the western world to tackle their domestic problems. They have their indigenous way to address them and show full faith in dialogue and negotiations for conflict resolution. They believe that the problem of terrorism is a temporary phenomenon and it would wither away in due course. However, there is consensus on the fact that terrorists are inhuman and enemy of the civilised world. They are bound to be contained effectively in due course because the people in general demand peace and development.

Indian perspective of outstanding problems of common concern for the region complimented Southeast Asian opinion. India was invited to be a sectoral partner of ASEAN in 1992 and full dialogue partner in 1995. The sectoral partnership was to promote trade, investment and tourism relations, but dialogue partnership had a broad agenda for cooperation. It had security, political, economic and cultural areas of cooperation. In 1996, India became a member of ASEAN Regional Forum (ARF) aimed at confidence building, conflict resolution and preventive diplomacy. It was guided by ASEAN stand on the question of East Timor during 1998-99.

India had been an active member of the ARF and has worked together with ASEAN in several areas including search and rescue, sea piracy and disaster relief, helping to further advance the ARF process. India has acceded to ASEAN's Treaty of Amity and Cooperation (TAC) in October 2003, which further promotes regional peace and stability. India shares ASEAN's fundamental principles of non-interference, respect for each other's territorial integrity and sovereignty and resolving disputes in a peaceful manner. Signing TAC promoted India to the inner circle of ASEAN. Collaboration in the international fora to realise the aspirations of the developing world increasingly features as another facet of ASEAN-India relations, given India's leading role in supporting the cause of the developing world.[5]

Economic relations too have significantly improved. In so far as India is concerned, in less than four years from 1992, our two-way trade has more than doubled; in 1996-97, it stood at US $6 billion and crossed the target of US $10 billion in the year 2002. From negligible figures in 1992, investment approvals from ASEAN upto 1997 were in excess of US $5 billion. In the reverse direction, ASEAN accounted for a significant proportion of Indian investments abroad. Significantly, the region has emerged as a promising growth area in trade, investments, joint ventures, tourism, etc.[6]

The two-way trade constitutes about 6 per cent of India's total trade. India's principal ASEAN trading partners are Indonesia, Singapore, and Malaysia. With others, the trade is gradually picking up. India's exports to ASEAN grew by 37.9 per cent in 2002-03 and the value stood at US $4.65 billion. The main items of Indian exports comprise of gems and jewellery, drugs and pharmaceuticals, electronic goods, meat and meat products, sugar, cotton yarn fabrics, wheat, spices and finished leather.

India's imports from ASEAN stood at US $4.8 billion in 2002-03 witnessing a rise of 18 per cent since 2001-02. The main items of Indian imports include vegetable oils, electronic goods, newsprint, natural rubber, pears and precious stones, and wood and wood products.

The FDI inflow into India from ASEAN in 2002 stood at US $85 million. Over the period from 1992-2003, ASEAN accounted for about 3.55 per cent of the total FDI inflow into the country. Sectorwise, power and oil refinery, telecom, electrical equipment, and IT have received the largest share of ASEAN investments. Now, pharmaceuticals, biotechnology, and the Info Tech are turning out to be the promising areas for ASEAN investments. Statewise, Singapore, Malaysia and Indonesia are the top three investors. The total FDI inflow to the ASEAN countries from India during 2002 stood at US $182 million. The main recipients of the funds were Indonesia, Malaysia, and Singapore.[7]

An obvious and natural extension of India's economic space, it was perceived, was ASEAN, which had emerged as a significant and promising growth area of the world. With a combined population of nearly 400 million and a land area larger than India's, ASEAN's GDP is in the region of US $400 billion; its exports, already significant, have grown steadily and are in the region of US $220 billion; it is an important destination for foreign investments and a major source of investments abroad.[8]

India is exploring communication routes from New Delhi to Hanoi through construction of railways and highways.

Tamu-Kalewa-Moreh road has been constructed and direct trade and transit facilities have been increased with the ASEAN. India is a member of BIMST-EC (Bangladesh, India-Myanmar-Sri Lanka-Thailand Economic Cooperation) in which Nepal and Bhutan have recently joined. BIMST-EC is endeavoured to promote close cooperation of South Asian with Southeast Asian region. India is also supporting Mekong-Ganga cooperation in which India and five ASEAN countries, namely Cambodia, Laos, Vietnam, Burma and Thailand are associated. The decision of India, Thailand and Burma to build a road linking Thailand to India through Myanmar is bound to promote Indian trade with the countries in the Mekong region and beyond.

Table 5.1: India's Trading Ties with ASEAN Countries
(Figures for 2002-03 in US $ million)

Country	*Exports*	*Imports*	*Total*
Singapore	1434.32	1445.31	2879.63
Malaysia	752.90	1477.14	2230.04
Indonesia	832.70	1391.86	2224.56
Thailand	716.60	22.76	739.36
Philippines	475.80	124.67	600.47
Vietnam	339.90	29.35	369.25
Myanmar	75.60	338.77	414.37
Cambodia	19.99	0.61	20.60
Laos	1.58	0.14	2.73
Brunei	4.48	0.32	4.81
Total	4653.88	4830.92	9484.80

Source: Commerce Ministry of India.

The ASEAN-India Business Council (AIBC) and India-ASEAN Economic Cooperation Committee (AIECC) are exploring trade and investment relations and they indicate a large potential for future cooperation. The trading ties with ASEAN countries are increasing but it is not commensurate with the vast potentials as focused in India-ASEAN summit meetings, which has been held yearly so far.

The first summit was held in Cambodia in 2002 and the second was held in Indonesia in 2003. The ASEAN has reiterated the faith that partnership with India has been conceived as an ongoing effort to create interdependence and linkage with a country with a large and liberalising market as well as democratic and pluralistic polity which could respond positively to ASEAN's aspirations.[9]

Indian Prime Minister, Atal Bihari Vajpayee attached great importance to emerging relations with the ASEAN and had participated in the summit meetings with a range of ideas to promote cooperation in economic and strategic areas. Some of the recognised sectors that India has advocated for cooperation are science and technology, biotechnology, information technology, space technology application, financial services, human resource development and education, etc. Indian Prime Minister, while attending the second India-ASEAN summit, had projected shining India in the following words:

> Over the last 12 years, the Indian economy has maintained an average annual growth of over 6 per cent, which is better than that of most other countries. Our interest rates are falling, inflation has been kept down, and foreign exchange reserves are growing rapidly. India remained unaffected by the Asian financial crisis a few years ago. We have targeted an 8 per cent growth over the next five years. As our economic base is large, there is considerable untapped potential for India's continued—and even accelerated—economic growth.
>
> Perceptions shape decisions. Often they are flawed. Sometimes, they are incomplete. The rich cultural diversity and spiritual traditions of India are well known, but they constitute only one aspect of India. There is another India, the India of the 21st century, which is still not so well known, with its many strengths:
>
> > One, an inherently strong economy driven primarily by indigenous skills and domestic enterprise.
> >
> > Two, a growing and accessible domestic market, with import and investment barriers falling away. To take just one random example of the growth of the market: in the last few months, it has been absorbing about 2 million mobile phones a month. Import duties are moving towards ASEAN levels, and sectorial caps on foreign investment are rising.
> >
> > Three, a rich pool of human resources—English speaking, with R&D skills, technological training and managerial capabilities.
> >
> > Four, some special capabilities in state-of-the-art technologies. India is one of only three countries—the others

> are USA and Japan—to have indigenously designed and manufactured super computers. It is one of only 6 countries, which can build and launch its own satellites.
>
> Five, global leadership in technologies of the knowledge Economy. India's pre-eminent position in IT and IT enabled services has led global companies to set up captives in India or to outsource their operations to quality Indian service providers.
>
> Six, a sound and transparent financial system, with well-managed banking and insurance sectors, and vibrant capital markets. Our paperless, computer-driven National Stock Exchange is the third largest in the world, in terms of number of annual transactions.
>
> India is today a country on the move. We are experiencing many revolutions simultaneously. There is, of course, the IT revolution. This in turn has unleashed a socio-cultural revolution, which has empowered hundreds of millions of our citizens, strengthening our democracy and stimulating our creativity.[10]

Vajpayee stated further that:

> It is this India that seeks to partner ASEAN in this era of globalisation. India's trade and economic interaction with the ASEAN countries has been steadily growing, but not fast enough. A year ago at the First India-ASEAN Business Summit, I had said that the India-ASEAN trade of less than 10 billion dollars does not do justice to our combined population of one and a half billion people, producing a trillion and a half dollars worth of goods and services annually. Our trade has since grown by about 25 percent, but my comment remains valid.[11]

He said that:

> Non-Asians view Asia as the principal market of the future. But it will also emerge as a manufacturing hub and, global provider of services. In the next 10 years, as the population of the developed world ages, a younger and better-educated work-force will emerge in Asia to fill the breach. This generation will drive the future growth of the global economy. Asian countries should work towards strengthening their mutual synergies, so that they are strategically placed to derive maximum benefit from emerging opportunities. The India-ASEAN partnership should energise this process to move us closer to our shared goal of making this truly the Asian century.[12]

India's position at the intersection of Asia's main cultural and geopolitical zones has implications for ASEAN since developments in India would have an impact on the region. India shares maritime borders with Thailand and Indonesia, and with the enlargement of ASEAN, India is now the immediate neighbour of ASEAN countries, sharing a 1600 kilometre border with Myanmar.

India possesses nuclear capabilities and a modern naval force. With its dynamic economic growth and superiority in engineering and sciences, India is expected to play an important role in maintaining the peace, stability and prosperity of Asia.

India is committed to its relations with ASEAN since it believes in a shared destiny with the region and wants to identify with it. The strengthening of its relations with ASEAN and East Asia is seen as a success of its "Look East" policy promulgated in 1991. The realisation of the ASEAN-India Summit in November 2002 was an important milestone in its "Look East" policy.[13]

Mr. S. Pushpanathan, Head of External Relations Cell in ASEAN Secretariat (Jakarta) has stated that:

> "Medical research and pharmaceuticals have been identified as areas for closer cooperation between ASEAN and India. In medical research, cooperation could focus on the prevention of communicable diseases. In pharmaceuticals, ASEAN would be keen to work with India on strengthening ASEAN's capacity and competitiveness in the manufacturing of pharmaceuticals, traditional medicines and biological products, facilitating access to affordable medicines".[14]

India's pharmaceutical market is expected to grow from US $6 million in 2002 to about 25 billion in 2010 with the reduction in manufacturing costs, the introduction of new technologies, a growing middle class, competitive markets and better research and development. India is expected to gain a substantial global generics market share. ASEAN investors could take advantage of the opportunities by investing in this sector, focusing on joint manufacturing of pharmaceutical products, which could help reduce the import costs of such products.[15]

Tourism cooperation holds great potential given the historical, religious and cultural affinities between India and

ASEAN, and the growing purchasing power of the Indian middle class. There were some 750,000 Indian visitors to ASEAN in 2000, making up only 2 per cent of total visitor arrivals in our region, while ASEAN visitors accounted for less than 5 per cent of India's total visitor arrivals. Considering the projected demand and opportunities, the private sectors of both sides could look at better promotional and marketing activities to boost tourism, including pilgrimage tourism.[16]

Besides economic interaction, a range of activities in cultural, political and strategic areas are projected. Southeast Asia has emerged as another hub of terrorism. There are a number of terrorist groups in the region which has had links with Al Qaida formed in 1987 by Osama bin Laden. Their way of thinking and style of operation are inhuman and violent. Their act of bombing tourist resorts in Bali in 2002 shocked the people everywhere. Their network in Indonesia and the Philippines are adversely affecting the image of ASEAN as a heaven for peace and stability. The bombing of Davao airport in March 2003 and Bali blast in October 2002 were masterminded by Abu Sayyaf group in the Philippines and Jemaah Islamiyah in Indonesia, respectively. Kumpulan Militan Malaysia (KMM) has also got assistance from Al Qaida to support terrorist activities. Laskar Jihaad under Jaafar Umar Thalib in Indonesia has been actively supporting the rise of radical Islam and has been responsible for several incidences of violence in Ambon. Moro Islamic Liberation Front (MILF) and Abu Sayaff group in the Philippines are supporting terrorist activities in Mindanao.

Jemaah Islamiyah under Abu Bakar Bashir, is believed to have command, control and communication structures to guide their trained militia, and they are keen to force the creation of Islamic state in different parts of Southeast Asia. India, on its part, is witnessing the menace of terrorism in Kashmir and areas in the border regions adjoining Burma. Most of them have transnational support and they are posing substantive threat to the issues of peace and development. India and ASEAN have collectively resolved to sign Declaration for Cooperation to Combat Terrorism on 8 October 2003. The declared objectives of the declaration are two-fold:

(*a*) The participants reaffirm the importance of having a framework for cooperation to prevent, disrupt and combat international terrorism through the exchange and flow of information, intelligence and capacity-building.

(*b*) The participants emphasize that the purpose of this cooperation is to enhance the efficacy of those efforts to combat terrorism.[17]

International terrorism would increasingly figure as an important area for ASEAN-India cooperation due to developments in India and ASEAN. Both sides want to ensure a peaceful and stable region to conduct economic activities and cooperation besides contributing to the international fight against terrorism. A declaration was concluded subsequently to formalise ASEAN-India cooperation in addressing terrorism and related crimes.

India-ASEAN cultural relations have also improved. Being the birth place of Lord Buddha, India is an area of intense academic mythological and religious interests. There are various places in India connected with Southeast Asian literature and there are a number of people who want to visit them. ASEAN understanding of India and vice versa have increased. Indian Council of Cultural Relations (ICCR) is offering fellowship to students from ASEAN countries and ASEAN-India Fund in supporting lecture series from eminent persons in India and vice versa. The government agencies at the ASEAN level are sincere in promoting understanding and partnership feeling. However, it would prove strategically useful if the Department of Southeast Asian Studies at Jawaharlal Nehru University, which has produced hundreds of M.Phil. and Ph.Ds., is promoted as an important think-tank, strengthened on the pattern of Singapore Institute of Southeast Asian Studies, which will ultimately provide crucial and better perspectives for new ideas and initiatives.

To conclude India-ASEAN relations are bound to grow if Asia-Pacific will be the hub of economic activities in the 21st century. They have to work together closely to face the challenges of 20th century and revive the affluence of the Subarnabhumi, wherein both were closely connected.

REFERENCES

1. Jusuf Wanandi, "The Regional Role of 'Track Two' Diplomacy: ASEAN, ARF and CSCAP" in Hadi Soesastro and Anthony Bergin (Eds.), 1996, *The Role of Security and Economic Structures in the Asia-Pacific Region*, CSIS, Jakarta, p. 166.
2. S. Viswam, 1997, "India's Look East Policy", *World Focus*. v. 18. No. 6, June, p. 5.
3. Sanjaya Baru, 1999, *National Security in An Open Economy*, New Delhi, p. 2.
4. See the Text of speech by P.V. Narasimha Rao, 1994, "India and the Asia-Pacific Forging a New Relationship", Singapore, 8 September 1994, *Strategic Digest*, October 1994, p. 1413.
5. *Ibid.*
6. S. Pushpanathan, 2004, *ASEAN and India: A Partnership for Success*, India-ASEAN 2003, Jakarta, p. 33.
7. *Ibid.*, p. 28.
8. *Ibid.*, p. 29.
9. *The Hindu*, Madras, 12 November 2002.
10. Text of the speech, Atal Bihari Vajpayee, India-ASEAN Summit, Bali, Indonesia, 2003.
11. *Ibid.*, p. 8.
12. *Ibid.*
13. Pushpanathan, No. 6, p. 32.
14. *Ibid.*, pp. 33-34.
15. *Ibid.*
16. *Ibid.*
17. See the text of ASEAN-India Joint Declaration for Cooperation to Combat International Terrorism, Bali, Indonesia, 8 October 2003.

4

Northeast India as Gateway to Southeast Asia

India's Northeast is geographically and ethnologically linked to Southeast Asia, and it is an important element in abridging the ties between the two. Needless to say that close ethno-cultural ties between the two can facilitate relations, and it has very often been viewed negatively. The ethnic Ahoms, Burmans, Thais, Laotians and Viets have similar history, and for an outsider it is difficult to distinguish their facial features. Sanjoy Hazarika has rightly observed that:

> "the girls of Imphal in Manipur who ride cycles and scooters, resemble their Thai and Lao counterparts. They could easily be placed either in Bangkok or Vientiane. The seductively swaying Manipuri dances are similar to the gentle rhythms of Khmers and Laotians as well as Thais and Indonesians. The distinctive shawls of Nagaland, Manipur and Mizoram, each colourful strand proclaiming a tribe, a lifestyle and an identity, share commonalities across the borders in Myanmar and Thailand".[1]

India is embarked on seeking closer economic and security relations with this region as concomitant to its "Look East" policy. It was accepted as the Dialogue Partner of the Association of Southeast Asian Nations (ASEAN) in 1995, in which all countries of Southeast Asia, including Myanmar, is represented. Our friendly gestures are reciprocated by the ASEAN, yet the volume of Indo-ASEAN trade and investment flows are much below that of Sino-ASEAN trade and investment. There is much scope to enhance our commercial relations and in that context, Northeast can play a vital role, subject to the conditions that there is a proper and effective coordination amongst its contiguous neighbours.

Northeast is an ideal place to establish growth areas on the pattern of Johore Bahru on Singapore-Malaysia border or Riau on Indonesian-Singapore border. Although conducive environment is yet to emerge and serious initiatives yet to be taken, it needs to be emphasized that cooperation in this area would benefit not only India or ASEAN, but a great part of Asia. It is our assumption that Northeast can act as a catalyst in promoting regional cooperation and provide gateway to all the countries in the subcontinent wishing to enter ASEAN or Asia-Pacific market and vice versa.

Geographical Location

It is necessary at the outset to understand the geographical situation of the Northeast, which is regarded as a part of great tropical rain forest that stretches from the foothills of the Himalayas to the tip of the Indochina Peninsula and the mouth of the Mekong River as it flows into the Gulf of Tonkin.[2] However, today Northeast generally connotes that part of Asia, where India's seven states—Arunachal Pradesh, Assam, Manipur, Meghalaya, Mizoram, Nagaland and Tripura—are located. It is spread over 255,000 square kilometres of which only few kilometres are contiguous to India, which comprise only two per cent territories. This is also known as Chicken's neck and located across Siliguri in Assam. The rest of the Northeast frontiers are contiguous to Bangladesh, Myanmar, China and Bhutan and that comprise 98 per cent of the total length of the borders.[3] Bangladesh indeed divides the territories of Northeast with Indo-Gangetic plains. Bangladesh is sovereign, independent country, with which relations have not always been cordial. However, developments in that country have impinging impact on Northeast and vice versa.

Bangladesh, known as East Bengal in the historical past, had been the centre of Indian civilization for centuries. When Northeast was integrated with British India after the first Anglo-Burmese war in 1824, it was apparently on the pretext to secure the frontiers of East Bengal from external aggression. The Britishers not only grabbed Assam, encompassing the entire Northeast, but also Burma to strengthen their defence postures. It would be appropriate here to analyse historical developments that prompted Britain to annex India's Northeast along with Burma.

It is believed that Burmans at the end of the 18th century developed geo-political ambitions to expand their territories over Ahom areas. The rulers in Cachar, Assam and Manipur were weak and they were playing subservient role to the Kings of Amarapura. The Burmese rulers were in a position to influence the selection of Kings in various palaces of the Northeast. When the influence of the Ahom rulers in Assam declined due to palace intrigues, revolt and disorder, Burma became assertive over Cachar, Manipur and Arakan and when Bagyidaw succeeded Burmese throne in 1819, he adopted chauvinistic policies for territorial expansion. His Commander-in-Chief, Maha Bandula was reputed warrior and nationalistic. Hence Burma adopted a "forward policy" *vis-à-vis* Assam and Maha Bandula led military forces to attack and annex it with Burma in 1822. He fought bravely and became victorious. Burma then sent an envoy to Calcutta to demand the surrender of Assamese princes—Chandrakant Singh and Purandar Singh—who had sought protection from the British crown.[4] Burma thereafter asserted its rights over Manipur, where the King was dethroned on the ground that he had failed to attend King Bagyidaw's coronation. Again Burma dispatched its forces to Cachar because its ruler had sought British protection.[5]

Burmese moves alarmed the British, who believed that with the passes of Cachar in their possession and Assam and Manipur under their control, Burmese would be strategically facilitated to attack Eastern Bengal too. There were consensus amongst British strategists that Burma after taking control of Assam, were directing the frontier moves from the Brahmaputra to the Naaf Rivers as a coordinated plan for the conquest of Bengal. Lord Amherst, the Governor General of British India decided to retaliate. Hence British protectorate over Cachar was announced and the military was alerted. Britain thus declared war on Burma on 5 March 1824 and used large scale sea-borne invasion of Lower Burma by stationing expeditionary forces at Andamans. Its navy quickly moved and occupied Rangoon on 10 May 1824, but it had to face stiff resistance in ground warfare. Maha Bandula fought bravely but the news of the fall of

Rangoon forced him to retreat. The British forces, led by Sir Archibald Campbell gradually proved stronger because of better arms and powerful navy. When Maha Bandula was killed and Burmese withdrew, the Britishers imposed reparation from the Burmese King and demanded the cession of Arakan, Tenasserim, Assam and Manipur, together with an indemnity of a million sterling in rupees for ceasefire.[6]

The Burmese wanted peace and therefore, they agreed to British terms and conditions. Although the Burmese had little resources and were unable to pay one million sterling, they were left with no alternative. Besides they promised to refrain from all interference in northeastern frontier of India. The Britishers with its foot hold over lower Burma, too developed geo-political ambitions and fought two more wars in 1852 and 1885 against Burma and turned them as part of British India.

The annexation of Burma and its merger with British India was not in good taste. It was disliked and Britishers themselves realized it. Hence Government of India Act (1935) was passed five decades later which bifurcated Burma from India and both got their political independence in 1947 and 1948, respectively.

Strategic Overview

Though all the countries situated on Northeast frontiers are equally important for maintaining stability and order in the region, but Myanmar's role in that context is crucial. Myanmar is of security importance, has been proved more than once in history. The British colonial masters felt their colonial order in India secured only after the annexation of Burma. In the Second World War, the Japanese occupation of Burma and the attack along the Northeast border posed a direct threat to our security. The fall of Burma to the Japanese alerted our freedom fighters to accelerate their activities. The British colonial masters on the other hand, envisaged danger from that quarter. India had lost some territories in the Northeast and the Andamans to the Japanese, and the Britishers were feeling shattered and concerned. There were strategic projections that India would fall ultimately and Britishers would have to withdraw.

K.R. Narayanan has observed that geographically, Burma is a bridge between China and India which, with development of modern communications, will become a strategic thoroughfare. He has further stated that Jawaharlal Nehru had an understanding of all this in his mind when he tried to forge intimate relations with Burma and together with Prime Minister U Nu strove for wider Asian cooperation, including friendship and cooperation with China as a key factor.[7]

It is worthwhile to recall that when U Nu's government was facing internal rebellion and fall of Rangoon was possible, Nehru took initiative to organise Commonwealth economic assistance. He also allowed the Burmese government to acquire arms from India in view of the Chinese threats. Besides these strategic assistance, India had stationed three troops carriers in the Bay of Bengal for rushing military aid for the defence of Rangoon in case of necessity at the request of Burmese Prime Minister, U Nu.[8]

India could not maintain her cordial relations with Myanmar after the downfall of U Nu, and this generated constraints for regional cooperation. The ideological factors came in the way and thus both sides suffered immensely.

Besides Myanmar, China is another powerful actor, which considers Northeast, along with Myanmar, under its area of influence. China has strengthened its strategic profile by providing US $1.4 billion worth of military assistance to Myanmar to curb or control insurgencies in Shan, Karen, Arakan and other areas.[9] According to reports published by the *Nation* in Bangkok, dated 29 January 1994, China has supplied some 100 T-63 and T-69 tanks, 150 armoured personnel carriers, 30 107-mm battery rocket launchers, about 100 five-ton trucks as well as some 122 mm howitzers and 130 mm field guns to Myanmar. The air force has taken delivery of 24 F-7 interceptors and 12 more promised. Besides 10 Hainan-class fast attack patrol boats were delivered to the navy and a naval base at Hainggyi Island in the mouth of Irrawady River has just been completed. China has also helped to set up a long range radar station in Coco Island, just 30 km away from India's Andaman Islands. China and Myanmar have consolidated their strategic ties and it is sought to be used for regional cooperation.

China has tried to fortify her position in the Northeast also. It does not accept the MacMahon Line and has enforced its territorial claims over NEFA (Arunachal Pradesh). In fact, it had attacked Indian positions militarily in 1962 and annexed a good chunk of the territories. This continues to remain a sensitive area and it is ritual for the Chinese to repeat its claims over Arunachal Pradesh whenever the occasion arises. Despite this, the imperatives of trade, investment and regionalism have diluted the militancy of the Chinese particularly in the post-cold war period. Most of the countries in the region are interested in forging closer economic ties with the emerging East Asian tigers, and this has the support of regional associations. The Chinese as pragmatic people cannot ignore the regional consensus, and advertently does not play any obstructionist role to prevent trade and other economic interaction in Southeast Asia.

Ethnic Connections

The ethnic aspect, their divergence and interrelations and ethnocentricity have been influencing the politics of the region. Many people in the Northeast share similar cultural and genealogical background with the people in Myanmar. The ethnic Burmans are generally associated with Tibeto-Burman linguistic family and so has been the case with ethnic Ahoms. Kachins situated near Chinese frontiers have Tibeto-Burman lineage. Again Mons or Nagas of Nagaland have ethnic connection and social interactions with their counterparts in Myanmar. There are more than 90,000 Nagas in Myanmar. T. Aliba, the former Chairman of Nagaland's United Democratic Front, have stated that there are as many as 600 Naga villages in Myanmar, bordering Nagaland. He also stated that the people living across the border were socially, culturally and ethnically akin to various tribes in Nagaland.[10]

Again Chins situated in western part of Myanmar and Mizos in the Northeast are bound by ethnic connections. Shans spread into Myanmar, Laos, Thailand and Northeast have ethnic bonds. Khamtis and Singpo of Arunachal Pradesh are seeking Shan identity. They are interlinked with Kachins also. All of them are Buddhists and have similarities of customs and traditions. In short, it can be stated that various ethnic groups of Myanmar have their counterparts in the Northeast.

They indeed have transnational connections and strong sense of ethnic identity. It was this reason that in 1990, Indo-Burma Revolutionary Front comprising the National Socialist Council of Nagaland, the United Liberation Front of Asom and the United Liberation Front of Myanmar had been formed.[11] Its objective was to unite the tribes of Mongoloid origin on either side of the border and to carve out an independent state of their own.

If we analyses the genesis of this phenomenon, we find that bulk of these people originated in Yunnan province of southern China. The homeland of the Tai speaking people—Shan, Lao and Thai—were also located in the southern China. They gradually migrated along rivers into Southeast Asia at the beginning of this millennium. The Mongol invasion of 1238 and destruction of the Burmese Kingdom of Pagan forced the migration to Southeast Asia massively. The territories from India's Northeast to Vietnam facilitated the migration from China to Southeast Asia. There were continuous movement of the people from Yunnan to Southeast Asia. However, the mountain ranges neither allowed similar connections to the people of the subcontinent towards Southeast Asia, nor there were any compulsions as the Chinese faced.

Shans immigrated first and settled down in northern Burma in the fertile upper valleys of the Salween, Irrawady and Chindawin Rivers. The Shans called themselves Tai Yaay, which means "Big Tai" as opposed to Tai Nauy "Little Tai" in Thailand and Laos.[12] This distinction probably refers to a period when the Shans established their state in upper Burma and Thais and Laotians were yet to migrate to their Southeast Asian homelands.

The new migrants from southern China came to an area under the impact of Indian civilization. Shans, Thais and Lao people retained the essence of their indigenous culture but at the same time adapted themselves beautifully to the areas that they had come. They took the help of Buddhism, Hinduism or animism to prove their distinctive culture. They expanded their territories at the cost of the Khmer empire and paid regular tributes to the Han rulers to strengthen their security postures.

In the post-independence era, different ethnic groups are trying to locate their missing links to promote the feeling of their nationalism. The ethnic Chinese have established their network successfully and ethnic Malays have tried to discover their commonalities in Malaysia, Indonesia, Brunei and the Philippines. The Thai people are trying to establish their missing links with the Shans and the Lao people. Again the Ahoms too are trying to discover their linkages with their people on other side of the frontier. However, we have to understand this aspect of ethnicity in Indian context.

The British colonial masters conquered most of the areas in the Northeast along with Burma and linked them into a common administration. Hence, interactions of Indians in Burma and Malaya were promoted. The routes through Patkai ranges were traversed and the Britishers developed some means of communication by constructing roads, bridges and rail links. Indians started going towards Northeastern region for trade and commerce. Britain indeed helped ethnic Indians in Southeast Asia to break the monopoly of the Chinese business and Indians were successful in Burma, Malaya and Singapore to a great extent.

The Indians simultaneously forged people to people contact in Southeast Asia. They reminded them of civilizational and religious connections. They convinced them that their war against British colonialism were connected with war against colonialism in Southeast Asia. As a result, Southeast Asians showed their complete solidarity with our nationalists. When Netaji Subhas Chandra Bose established Indian National Army (INA) on the soil of Southeast Asia, Burma, Thailand, Malaya and Singapore greatly assisted it. They provided men and material to liberate India and INA volunteers are full of praise for Southeast Asian leaders who assisted them. Although INA could not succeed and liberation came under the leadership of Indian National Congress but it had its implications. The colonial masters—France, Holland, the US and Britain—were forced to go and liberate their respective domains in Southeast Asia.

The lessons that we derive from this phenomenon is that we are interdependent. We have to fight collectively to meet the challenges of poverty, unemployment and illiteracy. We have to resurrect our culture and civilization and that can be possible if we strengthen the feeling of regionalism.

All the countries in Southeast Asia have joined through the ASEAN to make their collective voice stronger. They have a strong say in Asia-Pacific Economic Cooperation (APEC) and World Trade Organization (WTO). They have offered their membership to Myanmar despite the opposition of some western countries. They are cultivating ties with India also and have offered Dialogue Partnership, aimed at increasing trade, investment and tourism relations. Thus suitable strategic environment is a pre-requisite to be evolved on our common borders. Myanmar as an important component of the ASEAN, has to support that endeavour. However, the problem that we have faced in the recent past is that Myanmar has hardly figured in our foreign policy planning exercises. This is in spite of the fact that it is a country with which we have had the closest of historical and cultural relations, which according to K.R. Narayanan, was ruled as part of India albeit under the British empire, which had struggled along with us for freedom and which had after independence cooperated with us for building up Asian solidarity and the non-aligned movement, and which is geopolitically, of basic importance to our national security.[13]

The problems in bilateral relations erupted due to ideological and extraneous factors. However, the situation has changed now. The military rulers attach prime importance to economic development since 1990 is quite well known.[14] They are trying to prove themselves as a good partner of the ASEAN and adhering to the principles of ASEAN Treaty of Amity and Cooperation. They have resolved to support stability and development of neighbouring countries and its contribution to regional cooperation would prove substantial if it can assist the phenomenon of turning Northeast as a Gateway to Southeast Asia in economic terms.

The ASEAN had been supporting the policy of "Constructive engagement" with Myanmar and now it is upgraded into full membership. ASEAN is interested in expanding the scope of constructive engagement further to enlist the cooperation of neighbouring areas. In that context, the reference to Northeast is important. India's Northeast is the only area besides China, that ASEAN nations have contiguous land borders. The ASEAN pursuit to cultivate friendship with China started in 1975 and that have reached its optimum level. India's Northeast, though disturbed, is a new, enterprising area, which attracts attention. The proposition of trade and investment, growth triangle or quadrangle, etc. to be established in that region are very attractive. The ideas are being circulated to include the involvement of the ASEAN including Myanmar, and Bangladesh, China and India, and as and when such ideas would be realized, it would prove catalytic, and would benefit all the partners. Besides this would prove a good exercise in confidence-building and partnership for regional integration and solidarity.

Potentials of the Northeast

Northeast is potentially rich in agricultural and industrial enterprises.[15] It has both highland areas and plains, and endowed with natural resources. Arunachal Pradesh has coal and crude oil reserves. It has dolomite, limestone, graphite, marble, lead and zinc yet to be exploited. Assam has petroleum and petro-based products besides limestone and coal. It is also producing tea of best quality and exports it to the outside world. It has considerable plain areas for producing rice, fruits and vegetables. Again Meghalaya has coal mines, limestone, silica, silimanite, rock phosphates and uranium deposits. It has enormous potentials to generate hydro-electricity. Similarly Nagaland has abundance of plywood, pulp and paper. Again Tripura, Mizoram and Manipur have natural resources to support agricultural and industrial enterprises. More than half of the territories in the Northeast are covered with thick forests. It has teak and timber of superior quality and the soil is very fertile. Some areas have also started producing opium clandestinely which needs to be streamlined.

Northeast has geographical contiguity with Myanmar and Indian ocean and therefore natural and geographical problems are similar. Thus the ideas are floated to connect them through building highways, railways and bridges so that it would integrate with the dynamically growing economies of the

ASEAN. Australia helped in the construction of a friendship bridge from Bangkok to Vientiane over the Mekong River, and Thailand has plans to construct highways to connect several areas of Myanmar with Thailand. It is encouraging to hear that Myanmar has taken up development projects on a priority basis in the past five years, and is building bridges, inland water transport along the Irrawady, and it is also expanding its existing ports with the Chinese cooperation.[16] The military has undertaken a major railway construction project in Mandalaya, and rail links with India and Bangladesh are being revived. All these efforts are geared to accelerate infrastructure for development and the results are satisfactory. Myanmar's GDP growth rates are rising at 10 per cent and it is so assuring that during 1992-96, foreign investments grew significantly to US $4.3 billion.[17] The investors are gradually coming despite reservations of the western countries regarding the political system.

The Economic and Social Commission for Asia and the Pacific (ESCAP) is pleased to note about the economic development in Myanmar and adjacent areas. It has come out with a project to construct a railway network crossing through this region in the name of Trans-Asia-Railway (TAR). This railway is proposed to link Istambul to Singapore, covering a distance of 14,000 kilometres.[18]

At present, TAR is attempting to connect existing rail-lines and construct where it does not exist. The reconstruction of the missing link of 550 km in Iran between Kerman and Zahedan has already started. On the other hand, efforts are made to abridge 1400 km missing link between Bangladesh and Thailand. TAR project, if completed, would travel through the Northeast and connect Turkey, Iran, Afghanistan, Pakistan, India, Nepal, Bangladesh, Myanmar, Laos, Thailand, Malaysia and Singapore. Such endeavours would facilitate one world, one market concept. At the same time, it would facilitate integration of natural economic territories (NET) in transnational borders.

If there is a proper environment for regional cooperation and if the regional leaders initiate honest efforts, India would like to treat Northeast as gateway to Southeast Asia and remove every barrier on its part but because of the sensitive nature of the strife, and absence of confidence building, it remains a wishful thinking. India herself is to be blamed for the disturbances in the Northeast. It is, generally, believed that Indian Government did not make serious effort since the Nehruvian days to understand the region, and it was left largely to the care of civil and military bureaucracy. Mrs. Indira Gandhi and later Rajiv Gandhi signed accords that were never fully and honestly implemented. To the already existing militancy in Nagaland and Manipur, problems in Tripura, the Bodo agitation and the Gorkha unrest in Darjeeling were added during Rajiv Gandhi era.[19]

Despite disturbances in the region, India has tried to take initiatives to promote trade and transit in the Northeast. Premier Narasimha Rao, who evolved "Look East" policy, had established nine-member sub-committee to examine the feasibility of setting up export promotion centres at some strategic locations with all the infrastructural facilities like cold storage, packaging, warehousing, customs, banking, exhibition centres, transport facilities and air cargo complex.[20] The sub-committee examined various aspects of trade and business and came to the conclusion that establishment of a full-fledged trade and commerce centres for promotion of export would be highly useful. Thus Northeastern Council was advised to do the needful and start a full-fledged trade and commerce wing.

The activities of the Northeastern Council and growing interactions in the region, influenced Premier Deve Gowda to visit Northeast in 1996. He made his commitments to support economic development of the region and announced economic package of Rs.6,100 crores.[21]

Deve Gowda also supported establishment of a High-level Commission to examine the backlog in respect of Basic Minimum Services and Gaps in infrastructure sectors for development of states in Northeastern Region. This Commission was formed in November 1996 and headed by S.P. Shukla. It was assisted by B.G. Verghese, Sho Sainghoka, Jayant Madhab and Darshan Kumar as its members. The Commission submitted its report in March 1997 and offered important suggestions. The Commission has rightly observed that the people of the Northeast must feel that they are equal partners in a process of culturally friendly, equitable and sustainable development.[22]

The report has stated that Northeast is endowed with bio-diversity, hydro-potential, oil, gas, coal, limestone and forest wealth. It is ideally suited to produce a whole range of plantation crops, spices, fruits and vegetables, flowers and herbs, much of which could be processed and exported to the rest of the country and world-wide. Markets must be developed and problems of transportation, power, infrastructure, finance and services overcome.[23]

Besides giving attention to develop power, communication, railways, roads, agriculture and education, the Commission has paid ample attention to remove problems in trade and transit. It has emphasized the importance of trade and transit with Bangladesh, China and Myanmar in particular. The report has clearly stated that "Northeastern states are keen to resume their traditional trade and cultural ties with these neighbouring states and visualise great mutual benefit to all concerned".[24] All those neighbours have locational advantage in supplying their goods to the Northeast and vice versa. However, an attempt is made here to provide an overview of benefits that may be derived from our trade with Myanmar.

Trade with Myanmar

The signing of Memorandum of Understanding (MoU) with Myanmar in 1994 has opened the prospects of better trade and hopes of a revival of traditional links. As a result three trade exchange points have been designated at Moreh-Tamu in the Manipur sector, Champhai-Rhi in the Mizoram sector and at an as yet third point which could be at Ledo or Lekhapani in Upper Assam and on through the Pangsau Pass in Tirao along the famous wartime Burma Road through Myitkyina and Mandalaya to Kunming in Yunnan.[25]

The high-level commission has noted that the Moreh trade has started but considerable infrastructure needs to be developed. Myanmar has expressed its readiness to cooperate with India in upgrading the Tamu-Kalewa-Kalemayo Road (160 km) which the Border Roads Organization has undertaken at the cost of Rs.92 crores.[26] This is likely to stimulate bilateral trade because the demands for Indian goods in Myanmar to construct a railway from Kalewa towards Tamu to connect the Chindawin valley with the existing system up to the Irrawady valley from Yangon. It is interesting that a rail line has already been laid from the Yunnan border to Mandalaya with Chinese assistance. Myanmar road network is also developing links with Thailand and Laos and missing bridges are coming into place.[27]

Manipur sharing 326 km border with Myanmar is the important transit point. Agricultural products and consumer items are being exchanged here. It is reported that the western region of Manipur up to Chindawin valley provides a natural market for Indian goods and it may prove the most important gateway to Southeast Asia.[28]

Indian Institute of Foreign Trade (IIFT) did a survey of export opportunities in Myanmar in 1995 and found great potential for trade between the two sides. It projected that the volume of informal trade through Moreh was up to Rs.2,000 crores and through Champhai up to Rs.500 crores and through Lungwa (Nagaland) up to 100 crores.[29] A wide range of goods are exported through Moreh, including cycles and cycle parts, motor accessories, tyres, drugs and pharmaceuticals, cotton yarn, branded foods, edible oils, petroleum products, cement and other construction material. The items coming into the country are timber, fruit and vegetables and host of third country manufactured goods including electronics and synthetic items.[30]

Taking the aforesaid economic interactions in mind, S.P. Shukla Commission has recommended that an inter-ministerial task force be set up to review the entire Northeast border and inter-country trade issue, with reference to Bangladesh, Myanmar, Southeast Asia and Southwest China, and to report on trade opportunities, related manufacturing possibilities in the Northeast, required infrastructure and communication links, banking and warehousing facilities, necessary customs and security arrangements.[31]

The economic cooperation with Myanmar and other adjacent neighbours and continued dialogue would certainly bring positive environment for peace and prosperity and remove the haze caused by insurgents in the past few decades.

Drug Trafficking

The meeting point of Myanmar, Laos and Thailand borders comprise core areas of Golden Triangle, where opium is produced. Its control and supervision can be facilitated only with the joint collaboration of the neighbours. It is very well known that as the rainy season ends in October, hundreds of hill farmers come to the golden triangle to clear their fields and plant opium poppies. The opium producing areas are spread into 40,000 hectares of land and there have been 20 or more heroin refineries to make them refined and exportable.[32] The opium growing areas are mainly under the control of the Wa, Kokang and Shan ethnic groups. In 1945 Burma produced 45 tons of opium but when General Ne Win came to power in 1962, the production increased to 300 tons per year. William Beachner, Regional Director of the UN International Drug Control Programme says that it is impossible to give accurate estimate of opium production in golden triangle. The Myanmar rulers put it at between 300 and 400 tons, while the Americans are saying that it is around 2,600 tons at present.[33] However, Rupa Chinai of *The Times of India* reported in April 1997 that more than half of world's illicit opium is produced in Myanmar.[34] While opium production in Burma was estimated to be from 450 to 600 metric tons in 1985, it increased to 1470 to 200 tons in 1989. As the number of opium edicts in the region are rapidly rising, the growth is booming.[35]

The opium poppy has not been indigenous and it was introduced by the British colonial masters in the Shan state in 1850s as an export crop.[36] As the climate was ideally suited and opium yielded high profits, the production expanded into adjoining areas of Thailand and Laos. Gradually drug mafia with international connections supported opium growers and the government exercised little control.

However, curbing opium production is a challenging task today. The international community would like to regulate it. Although the governments in the region are assuring the outside world to curb it and has indulged in opium burning occasionally, attended by international observers, the endeavour looks elusive. Myanmar has been signing various anti-drug accords and receiving financial and technical assistance but it has not proved successful. Before 1988, the US alone provided $86.6 million worth of drug suppression assistance to Burma, which included helicopters for use in locating and destroying opium fields, but these efforts have ultimately failed.[37]

Again the economics of drug trade is staggering. A kilo of no. 4 heroin costs a minimum of US $1500 in the Shan state border and five times a few kilometres away in China. If Myanmar produces only 200 tons of heroin, it would fetch at least US $2 billion, before it crosses the border and up to $10 billion more if it goes down further.[38] Myanmar remains the principal source of heroin to the outside world. The number of drug addicts have grown in Myanmar along with India, Thailand, Nepal and Bangladesh.

Bertil Lintner recently reported that the site of the opium refineries are being shifted now along Indo-Myanmar borders. A refinery facility is available at Tahan quarter of Kalemyo, a garrison town in southern Sagaing Division. This produces pure no. 4 heroin to be smuggled through India-Bangladesh borders. Lintner has also reported that such refineries have been newly established at Singkaling Hkamti and Homalin along the Chindawin River in Sagaing and at Paletwa in Chin state.[39] The smuggling route is also changing now. Earlier it was through Thailand, but now it is through India's Northeast to Bangladesh and from there to different destinations in the world. The UN International Narcotics Control Board reported in March 1997 that India is a major transhipment point for heroin from the golden triangle, with observation that lower level of officials, particularly in the border regions, are involved in taking bribes for ignoring drug smuggling.[40] Indian government feels concerned that its territories are used as a conduit to smuggle heroin.

According to World Health Organization (WHO) and the UN, there are close to 500,000 drug addicts in Myanmar itself and their number might be more in India, Bangladesh and Nepal. A coordinated joint effort is needed to control the evils of drug trafficking, and in that endeavour, the initiative and role of Myanmar may prove crucial.

There seems to be a vicious circle in resolving the menace of drug trafficking. Some of the insurgent groups have liaison with drug lords in the Northeast. Though it is not difficult to find their complicity, but it has proved hard to encircle them. There are several extremist outfits in the Northeast and there are many underground operations. The state of Manipur, an important gateway to Southeast Asia, has as many as 17 different groups, namely All Manipur Students' Union, Manipur People's Party, Manipur Congress, People's Liberation Army, Revolutionary People's Front, National Socialist Council of Nagaland, United National Liberation Front, Red Guards, Meitei State Committee, People's Revolutionary Party of Kangleioak, the Poirel Liberation Front, Kangleioak Communist Party, the Red Brigade, Kanglei Yawol Kanna Lup, Kuki National Army, Kuki National Front and Kuki Defence Front.

Similarly, there are several political parties and insurgent organisations in other states of the Northeast. For instance, All-Bodo Students' Union, Bodo Security Force, United Liberation Front of Asom (ULFA) in Assam, National Socialist Council of Nagaland (NSCN), Naga National Council of Nagaland, Achick Liberation Matgrik Army (ALMA) in Meghalaya, All-Tripura Tribal Force and Tripura National Volunteer Force, and Karbi Anglong, Darbi Darbar Party and Hmar People's Convention (HPC) in Mizoram, and United Liberation Movement of Arunachal Pradesh. Most of the above mentioned groups identify their interests in protecting the rights of their own communities which is divided on ethnic lines. Their goals are parochial and therefore controversial. The Bodo, the Karbis and the North Cacharis in Assam are demanding autonomous Council or a separate statehood to fulfil their tribal aspirations. The Ahoms who ruled over the Northeast for centuries in the past, cannot digest the demands of either Bodos or Karbis and the government has to think in terms of national interests.

As the militants in the region are always in need of arms and to procure arms, they have to mobilise resources, they have supported the growth of mafia dons for abduction, ransom and forced donation. At the same time, they extend their support in drug trafficking and it goes on and on.

There is unrest in the Northeast which disturbs developmental outlook and political stability. The government of India is anxious and former Prime Minister Deve Gowda paid personal attention to the Northeast by initiating a serious dialogue. His successor Inder K. Gujral also showed his concern equally and tried to reinforce and compliment the task left by his predecessors. He undertook five-day visit to the Northeast in May 1997 and announced several socio-economic development plans to be pursued.[41] Besides news bulletins in Tripuri language on All-India Radio and establishment of Central Universities in Mizoram and Nagaland, Government of India also announced approval for Dimapur to Dibrugarh railway connection and Kohima to Agartala railway lines. These links might emerge as an important part of Asian Super highway in the 21st century. These efforts would certainly create right atmosphere for peace, but the dilemma of the Northeast has rightly been expressed by Ved in the following words:

> "Over half a century, two contrasting images of Northeast have got etched in the public mind. One is a picture postcard of colourful tribals with their quaint customs leading sedate lives in Sylvan surroundings. The other is the militant with the gun and the explosives, feared at home, despised by Delhi and wooed by the Western media and Christian missionaries."[42]

Recent Developments

It is understood now that integrated development programmes in the Northeast can be promoted with the support and coordination of Bangladesh and Myanmar, and to enlist their cooperation, communication needs to be developed. The construction of roadways, railways and riverways, and above all regional perspective is to be emphasized. During the stewardship of Gujral Rs.11,000 crores have been allocated to connect the missing communication links with neighbouring countries of the Northeast and it is regarded as a positive development.

The government is proposing to declare the region of Northeast a tax-free zone and offer a host of incentives as part of a new deal in this golden jubilee year of independence. The plan aims at encouraging relocation of industries and establishment of entire spectrum of industries based on locally available raw material and local consumer demand. Other proposals in the new deal include central investment subsidy of 15 to 25 per cent, interest subsidy on working capital, concessions in excise levies and extension of the transport subsidy beyond 2005 AD.

The efforts are made to give emphasis on agro-based processing units such as milk and milk-based products, fruits and vegetable processing, meat and poultry products, cattle poultry fisheries feed, processing of edible oil and plantation crops. It also wants to assist the growth of decaying handloom industries and protect the interests of indigenous traders. Above all, the government would like to generate employment conditions, prevent drug abuses and ensure regional cooperation.

It might be stated at the end that the success of various deals and proposals are dependent on trust and cooperation of the people in the Northeast. The opinion of tribal and local leaders can tilt the balance in favour of one side or another. The tribal and local leaders can be possibly influenced if they are given profits in business and trade and assured access to increased interaction with their ethnic groups in trans-border areas. This can be arranged with the support of the neighbouring countries with a regional approach. If Myanmar as the Dialogue Partner of India under the ASEAN framework, agrees and cooperates, it can provide important inputs. Myanmar indeed has potential to facilitate peace making in the Northeast, provided incentives are given for regional cooperation.

REFERENCES

1. Sanjoy Hazarika, 1995, *Strangers of the Mist: Tales of War and Peace From India's Northeast*, New Delhi, Penguin Books, p. xviii.
2. *Ibid.*, p. xv.
3. Notes on Development of commerce in North Eastern Region for Export to neighbouring Southeast Asian countries, Federation of Industries of North Eastern Region, Guwahati, 29 January 1997, p. 1.
4. For better analysis of this aspect, see D.G.E. Hall, 1968, *A History of Southeast Asia*, London, Macmillan, pp. 596-600.

5. *Ibid.*
6. *Ibid.*
7. K.R. Narayanan, "India Indifferent to Burmese Struggle", *Sunday Economic Times*, 8 January 1991.
8. *Ibid.*
9. Dipankar Banerjee, "Need for New Ties", *Hindustan Times*, 15 October 1996.
10. *The Times of India*, 7 December 1992.
11. *Sunday Economic Times*, 8 January 1991.
12. Shan and Tai Yaay refer to the same geographical and cultural areas. For details see, Stephen Sparkes, "On the Shan Borderlands in Mae Hong Son", *NIA Snytt*, *Nordic Newsletter of Asian Studies*, No. 4, December 1995, p. 1.
13. *Sunday Economic Times*, 8 January 1991.
14. For details about Economic transformation see, Burma Peace Foundation, Selected Documents on the Burmese Economy, Geneva, 1996.
15. For details about economic potentials, see *Competition Success Review Yearbook*, New Delhi, 1997, pp. 569-604.
16. *Hindustan Times*, 15 October 1996.
17.
18. *The Hindu*, 16 October 1996.
19. *The Times of India*, 27 May 1997.
20. For details see the Report of Industries of North Eastern Region, No. 3, pp. 1-2.
21. *The Times of India*, 21 May 1997.
22. High-Level Commission Report to the Prime Minister, *Transforming the Northeast*, New Delhi, Planning Commission, Government of India, p. 2.
23. *Ibid.*
24. *Ibid.*, p. 62. Arunachal Pradesh has had clandestine trade with China and the traders used to barter rice, handloom articles, chilli, ginger, meat and gold with Indian yarn, woollen blanket, salt and medicine and so was the case with Myanmar and Bangladesh.
25. *Transforming Northeast*, pp. 92-93.
26. *Ibid.*
27. *Ibid.*, p. 93.
28. *The Times of India*, 21 October 1997.
29. Quoted in *Transforming Northeast*, No. 25, pp. 93-94.
30. *Ibid.*
31. *Ibid.*, p. 94.

32. *The Nation,* 3 March 1992 and 5 March 1992.
33. *Bangkok Post,* 28 November 1992.
34. Rupa Chinai, "The Myanmar Connection", *The Times of India,* 24 April 1997.
35. *The Times of India,* 24 April 1997.
36. *The Nation,* Bangkok, 3 March 1992.
37. *The Nation,* 3 March 1992.
38. *Bangkok Post,* 5 February 1992.
39. Bertil Lintner, "Opium Refineries in Burma", *Far Eastern Economic Review,* 5 November 1992, p. 5.
40. *The Times of India,* 21 April 1997.
41. Mahendra Ved, "Northeast could do with dose of Gujral Doctrine", *The Times of India,* 27 May 1997.
42. *Ibid.*

5

BIMST-EC and India's Look East Policy

BIMST-EC is a regional grouping aimed at economic and cultural cooperation amongst the partners and it is comprised of Bangladesh, India, Myanmar, Sri Lanka, Thailand, Bhutan and Nepal. It is working towards evolving a mechanism for co-operation amongst the partners to establish growth areas and if it becomes successful, it will certainly assist the pace of globalization, confidence-building and development in the region.

BIMST-EC came into existence on 27 December 1997 with the membership of Bangladesh, India, Myanmar, Sri Lanka and Thailand, but Bhutan and Nepal also joined it subsequently. The main areas of co-operation as identified by BIMST-EC included co-operation in trade, investment, industry, transportation, infrastructure, science and technology, human resource development, energy, fisheries, agriculture, natural resources and tourism. The responsibility for promoting economic co-operation in different sectors has been delegated, and it may prove a landmark initiative for regional co-operation between South Asians.

Although the proposal of establishing BIMST-EC emanated from Thailand but it could be a reality only when India and others responded positively. India used to be apprehensive against Thai proposals during cold war years. As Thailand was the headquarters of SEATO and actively engaged in "bleeding Vietnam white", its foreign policy initiatives were regarded pro-American but the global situation changed after the end of the cold war in 1991.

India began to review its old policies and supported globalization and liberalization in the post-cold war era. There were growing emphasis on promoting ties with countries of

Asia-Pacific and in that endeavour came out with initiatives in the name of "Look East" Policy. Thus there were increasing dialogues with People's Republic of China, Australia, Japan, Korea and Southeast Asia. As a result, India became the dialogue partner of ASEAN and a member of ASEAN Regional Forum. It also became the important driving force in Mekong-Ganga co-operation, BIMST-EC and in the politics of Asia-Pacific. The trade, investment and tourism ratio have increased and Indian credibility in strategic and economic spheres are substantial. In fact, the old mindset is changing rapidly and suitable environment emerging for regional co-operation and partnership.

In this chapter the effect will be made to examine the evolution of BIMST-EC, its significance and role in regional co-operation. We shall also examine why India could not play its role in the regional co-operation in the past and shall also examine the compulsions to evolve "India's Look East" Policy and how that was reciprocated by "Look West" Policy of Thailand and ASEAN, etc.

BIMST-EC covers a geographic area, which has been important for India strategically, economically, culturally and politically and it is of crucial importance for success of India's "Look East" Policy. Bangladesh, Bhutan, Myanmar, Nepal, Sri Lanka and Thailand are neighbouring states with which our frontiers are contiguous. The cultural and economic interaction with all of them have been deep-rooted historically but the level of understanding and cooperation have not been satisfactory in the contemporary past. BIMST-EC was mooted to address the issues bedevilling cooperation and evolve a new environment which could take care of the needs of globalisation, and generate the feeling of togetherness and cooperation.

BIMST-EC is still at the evolutionary stage to indicate spectacular results, but potentials for future cooperation are projected which may benefit all the partners immensely. South Asians were especially enthusiastic in the beginning about this organization because they felt that this grouping would succeed in doing where SAARC had failed. There were many who felt that BIMST-EC was an alternative of SAARC. They viewed BIMST-EC as an important instrument for regional cooperation, understanding and confidence building. However the Asian financial crisis (1997-98), and the rise of terrorism in the region dampened initial spirit of cooperation.

BIMST-EC geographically connects India with ASEAN countries, and to East Asia through ASEAN. The ancient routes, which provided a passage to China and which were disrupted during the colonial era, are also located in BIMST-EC region. Besides geo-economics, it has geo-strategic significance for India as BIMST-EC is required to address the issues of insurgency in India's Northeast, the proliferation and smuggling of narcotics through golden triangle and political consensus of cooperation in the region. If the gas-pipeline, hydro-power connection, Asian highway or rail network are to be constructed or transport linkages are to be restored, the guarantees against sabotage and peaceful environment are required. It is a reality that groups of pirates, smugglers, terrorists and drug peddlers are active on India-Myanmar and India-Bangladesh frontiers. There are certain pockets where secessionists and terrorists are active and they have transnational support. BIMST-EC, while evolving infrastructure for cooperation, are worried about it.

When ASEAN was evolved, contentious bilateral and multi-lateral issues were kept under the carpet. All the partners gave priority to economic cooperation and politically contentious issues were kept locked. On the other hand, SAARC insisted on resolving political issues at the outset. Pakistan argued the resolution of Kashmir dispute as a pre-requisite for cooperation. India argued that the existing frontiers between India and Pakistan should not be disputed. The political debate was so volatile at the SAARC summits, that the agenda of cooperation were ignored. Thus South Asia remained the poorest region in terms of economic development. The lack of understanding and trust were dominating and political leaders promoted ethnic, territorial and separatist tendencies. The western world always exploited the existing political turmoil in their favour and the region remained in perpetual backwardness. The situation started changing only after the end of the cold war. South Asians began to talk of sorting out bilateral disputes but the mindset was difficult to change. On the other hand, ASEAN, which was developing rapidly, was interested in promoting ties with South Asians. They had already nurtured their commercial ties with ASEAN+3 (Japan, China and South Korea) and new areas were to be explored. Moreover, the challenges posed in the evolving new world order were to be faced collectively and neither India nor ASEAN could ignore this reality. It is in this context that Sino-Indian dialogues were promoted and East Asian Community concept evolved. BIMST-EC agenda is to facilitate such an understanding along with business and trade. The construction of transnational highways and railways would promote cultural and economic interaction. Whether the endeavour of BIMST-EC will be achieved or not, are indeed linked with the projections as to whether Asian resurgence will be a reality.

The credit for establishing BIMST-EC belongs to Thailand, which had played a leading role in the establishment of ASEAN in 1967. India, which had been isolated in the politics of ASEAN during cold war years, was viewed as an important regional actor in the post-cold war era. It was, therefore, that India was offered sectoral partnership of the ASEAN in 1992 and full dialogue partnership in 1995. Thailand was especially interested in cultivating India. It had earlier given priority to improving ties with Vietnam and Laos in the name of changing Indo-China from "battleground to market place". Now it viewed India as large market with potentials for enhancing the level of cooperation. But India would not be cultivated without taking into consideration the geopolitical and regional factors. Other South Asians in-between were also to be cultivated. Bangladesh, Myanmar, Nepal, Bhutan and Sri Lanka were important because they too were looking for windows for regional cooperation.

Thailand took the formal initiative to propose BIMST-EC in 1995 but formal launching was delayed till 1997. Being strategically located in the middle of Southeast Asia, Thailand was endowed to play a key role in the success of BIMST-EC. However, the Asian financial crisis coinciding with the establishment of BIMST-EC diluted the attention of Thailand in attending the needs of this grouping for some time. It was embroiled in coping with the financial crisis along with South Korea, Indonesia and others. India, on the other hand, was coping with internal issues in the Northeast. Although initiatives were taken to improve relations with Myanmar and build infrastructure of cooperation, but it was not sufficient. It succeeded in the construction of Tamu-Kalemyo road which was flagged off on 29th October 1997, but many such roads[1] are needed to establish transportation network. However, it was a good beginning to connect India with Myanmar, the two important partners in BIMST-EC.

BIMST-EC Agenda

The Bangladesh, India, Sri Lanka, Thailand Economic Cooperation (BIST-EC) was born in Bangkok on 6 June 1997 with the objective of creating an environment for cooperation in various fields between the member countries in order to enhance the livelihood of the peoples in the region and promote the feeling of togetherness. This regional group resulted first and foremost from Thailand's initiatives. In keeping with its "Look West" Policy, Thailand had been advocating the concept of Bay of Bengal Community and expanding relations with countries in the Indian sub-continent. In October 1994, Mr. Surin Pitsuwan, Thai Deputy Foreign Minister proposed to create a "growth triangle" between India, Sri Lanka and Thailand in the Andamans. Neither India nor Sri Lanka took serious note of the proposal. Thailand articulated the proposal once again in January 1995, when Supachai Panitchpakdi visited India. New Delhi then showed appreciation for the concept and Bangladesh, India, Sri Lanka and Thailand began to give it a concrete shape. The foreign ministers of the four countries met in Bangkok to decide the aims, purposes and principles of the grouping. The Bangkok Declaration of 6 June 1997 laid the foundation for Bangladesh-India-Sri Lanka-Thailand Economic Co-operation (BIST-EC). Subsequently in the special ministerial meeting convened in Bangkok on 22 December 1997, Myanmar was admitted to the grouping where it was decided to rename BIST-EC and make it BIMST-EC (Bangladesh-India-Myanmar-Sri Lanka-Thailand Economic Co-operation).[2] At the ministerial meeting in December 1998 Nepal was welcomed as an observer and in 2003, both Nepal and Bhutan were admitted as members.

The aims and purposes of the BIMST-EC, identified by the Ministerial Declaration are to create an enabling environment for rapid economic development through identification and implementation of specific cooperation projects in the sectors of trade, investment and industry, technology, human resource development, tourism, agriculture and infrastructure and transportation. Secondly, to accelerate the economic growth and social progress in the sub-region through joint endeavours in a spirit of equality and partnership. Thirdly, to promote active collaboration and mutual assistance on matters of common interest in the economic, social, technical and scientific fields. Fourthly, to provide assistance to each other in the form of training and research facilities in the educational, professional and technical spheres. Fifthly, to cooperate more effectively in joint efforts, that are supportive of and complementary to national development plans of member states, which result in tangible benefits to the people in raising their living standards, including generating employment and improving transportation and communication infrastructure. Sixthly, to maintain close and beneficial cooperation with existing international and regional organizations with similar aims and purposes. Finally, to cooperate in projects that can be dealt with most productively on a sub-regional basis among the BIMST-EC countries and that make best use of available synergies.[3]

BIMST-EC had a co-operative work programme in six key sectors, namely trade and investment, technology, transport and communications, energy, tourism, and fisheries. Activities under each sector were to be co-ordinated and monitored by a BIMST-EC country nominated as head country for the sector. Under the six key sectors there were several sub-sectors, e.g. gems and jewellery, drugs and pharmaceuticals, horticulture, food processing, automobiles, coconut and spices, etc. The cooperation framework involved networking and information building in the preliminary stages. The members shared information on possibilities of future co-operation, including specific joint ventures.

BIMST-EC was the organization in which for the first time two Southeast Asian countries and three South Asian countries came together to foster economic cooperation in the specified areas. Since all the BIMST-EC member countries are washed by Bay of Bengal, some wanted it to be expanded to rope in

Indonesia, Malaysia and Singapore and form a wider 'Bay of Bengal Community' so as to harness the full potential of the region. BIMST-EC was given importance as the SAARC had failed in promoting the ethos of regional cooperation. There were serious differences between India and Pakistan, and consensus on regional issues were elusive. But BIMST-EC provided them an alternative in which India, Bangladesh, Nepal, Bhutan and Sri Lanka from SAARC, and Myanmar and Thailand from ASEAN came together.

This regional grouping provided a bridge between five SAARC and two ASEAN countries to interact and cooperate. BIMST-EC should be a greater potential to increase trade among member countries by taking advantage of their geographical location in the region of the Bay of Bengal and the Eastern Coast of the Indian Ocean. Discussions have already been held with regard to building a Trans-Asia Highway linking the five countries and also setting up a BIMST-EC Airline connecting the capitals and important cities of the member countries. Cooperation within the BIMST-EC is based on respect for the principles of sovereign equality, territorial integrity, political independence, non-interference in internal affairs, peaceful co-existence and mutual benefit. The unique feature of BIMST-EC is that it establishes a link between ASEAN and SAARC. The official declaration states that "....cooperation within BIMST-EC will constitute an additionally to and not be a substitute for bilateral, regional or multilateral co-operation involving member-states".

Member countries of the BIMST-EC share a primary responsibility for strengthening the economic and social stability of their sub-region and ensuring peaceful and progressive national development. The member-states have also confirmed that the group would be committed to the principle of open regionalism. BIMST-EC is thus consistent with India's other regional projects. Moreover, it supplements its partnership with ASEAN since it aims at interesting interactions with two ASEAN members—Thailand and Myanmar. In this regard, BIMST-EC is a stepping stone to the India's "Look East" Policy. BIMST-EC aims at creating a sub-regional role of growth between South and Southeast Asia. In fact, it is inspired by the innovative model of growth triangles that has emerged in Southeast Asia. Indeed, BIMST-EC Concept Paper starts with the following observation, "....Successful economic co-operation at the sub-regional level has been a new and encouraging feature of the dynamic growth of the Asia-Pacific Region."[4]

BIMST-EC applies many characteristics of the East Asian sub-regional co-operative schemes. First, sub-regional Asian co-operative arrangements often try to enhance co-operation among countries at varying stages of economic development. But, the fact is that sub-regional co-operation emphasizes the complimentarities of the resource bases of the different partners. It helps to increase economies of scale in the production bases and facilitates the spill-over of growth across national borders. Moreover, in sub-regional economic zones, the focus is not only on trade, but also on the promotion of tourism, natural and human resources development and infrastructure. This is the case with BIMST-EC, as one of its priority goals is to build up infrastructure linkages among member countries, especially transportation linkages. At the inaugural ministerial meeting on 6 June 1997, the representatives of the member-states decided to consider the feasibility of setting up a regional airline.[5] This would provide the required network for enhancing business and tourist links between the member-countries. The objectives of BIMST-EC are also to enhance intra-regional energy co-operation through an action plan for development and utilization of natural gas, wind, solar and water/tidal wave energy sources. Thus BIMST-EC is a dynamic process of co-operation that tries to expand the resources of the Bay of Bengal sub-region as well as the growth of its future output. This project has benefited from the support of international institutions, such as the Asian Development Bank and ESCAP, which have conducted preliminary studies.

In the area of maritime transport, experts suggested that possibilities of forming joint ventures between shipping lines of member countries be explored along with cooperation in the Human Resource Development (HRD) of seafaring manpower. As for HRD, India has offered to organize training programmes under the aegis of the National Institute for Highway Engineers. In communication linkages and networking, it has been proposed that each country will identify national focal points for establishing linkages between regional and national activities.

BIMST-EC holds frequent meetings, participated by the stake holders of BIMST-EC. The main objective of the meetings is to bring the economic and technical cooperation among member countries by suggesting recommendations, policies and decisions with common agreement. They adopted the criteria for admission of Observers and Guests in future meetings of BIMST-EC and welcomed all countries and international organizations satisfying the criteria, principles and procedures which they have adopted and who may wish to participate in the activities of BIMST-EC as Observers or Guests, and are desirous of contributing to the realization of the goals of social, economic and industrial cooperation and progress within the BIMST-EC.

The leaders emphasized the need for establishing a BIMST-EC Economic Forum to work as an important engine of greater economic co-operation and progress within the BIMST-EC sub-region which will serve to promote Government-Private Sector cooperation among the member-countries.[6] The formation of the BIMST-EC Business Forum by the representatives of private sector of BIMST-EC countries which was organized by ESCAP in Bangkok in March 1998 was appreciated by the delegates and they hoped that the BIMST-EC Business Forum will enhance private sector cooperation among the member-countries in identified sectors, sub-sectors and projects.

They reaffirmed the significant potential for cooperation in tourism sector in promoting people to people contact and reinforcing the historical, cultural and economic synergies of the BIMST-EC sub-region. The initiative of India was appreciated, taken in pursuance of the decisions of the Special Ministerial Meeting of December 1997, in convening the Tourism Summit in Kolkata in October 1998 and note the Action Plan adopted at the meeting. The delegates welcomed the recommendation to declare the Year 2001 as 'Visit BIMST-EC Tourism Year' and called upon the concerned authorities and private sectors to take tangible steps towards this.[7]

Conscious of the important role that can be played by transport and communication linkages in enhancing commercial, industrial, cultural and social interaction and tourism in the BIMST-EC region, they reiterated the emphasis that they place on developing rail, road, multi-modal transport, shipping and air linkages. This would reinforce complimentarities arising out of the Bay of Bengal rim identity. In this context, they recognized the importance of the speedy implementation of BIMST-EC component of Trans-Asian Railway and Asian-Highway Projects.

It was decided that the energy sector being another important dimension of BIMST-EC cooperation will receive priority attention. Efforts will be made to draw up appropriate action plans and to work out arrangements for the enhancement of cooperation in the areas of natural gas, wind, solar and water/tidal wave energy resources. They reiterated the need for the promotion of cooperation in fisheries through the conduct of a comprehensive study on marine resources, processing and marketing to be conducted in coordination with the relevant international organizations and acknowledged the important contribution of ESCAP towards furthering economic cooperation among the BIMST-EC countries. The delegates requested that ESCAP should continue to play an active role in the BIMST-EC projects by assisting the various sectoral committees, specially in the aspects of providing background information for cooperation, technical support, seeking funding and participating in other required areas and it was realized that member countries should seek to forge stronger links with development partners and international organizations, including the World Bank, the Asian Development Bank and the UNDP.[8]

The faith in the importance of Asian solidarity, enhancing South-South cooperation among developing countries in the face of opportunities and challenges that are being presented by globalization and liberalization of the international trade and financial systems was reiterated. The belief in the need to coordinate the positions and policies on major issues relating to international flows of goods, services and capital within the framework of international institutions such as the World Trade Organization and other was reaffirmed by the Joint Statement.

In addressing the future directions of BIMST-EC, it was resolved (*a*) to fully exploit the complimentarities within

BIMST-EC region; (*b*) to exert combined political will for the success of the organization; (*c*) to ensure that each of the member-countries individually is able to reap adequate benefits from BIMST-EC cooperation, with special attention to those at lower stages of development; (*d*) to develop short, medium and long-term plans and strategies and to implement them in a systematic and coordinated manner, (*e*) to act as a bridge between the South Asian and Southeast Asian Regions; (*f*) to aim and strive to develop BIMST-EC into a free trade arrangement and to focus on activities that facilitate trade, increase investment and promote technical cooperation among member-states; (*g*) to act as a vehicle for making the international economic and trading system more favourable to developing countries; (*i*) to remove constraints and facilitate trade in goods and services and in people to people contacts; (*j*) to vigorously pursue sub-regional energy cooperation; (*k*) to work towards transport and communication network and linkages, etc.

The third BIMST-EC ministerial meeting was held in New Delhi on 6 July 2000. This ministerial meeting was attended by the ministers of BIMST-EC countries and their respective delegations. At the conclusion of the meeting, the leaders of delegation issued the joint statement. It was realized that the global economy is now on a path of recovery after the financial crisis. Therefore, it is the right time to provide momentum to BIMST-EC by enhancing economic, commercial and technical cooperation among the member countries, both at the government and private sector levels.[9]

They welcomed the inputs provided by the deliberations of the second meeting of BIMST-EC Trade and Economic Ministers which was held in New Delhi in April 2000, towards the regional cooperation in the trade and investment. They recognized the significance of their discussions pertaining to trade facilitation and investment promotion, which were also taken up at the first meeting of the Sectoral Committee on Trade and Investment. It was appreciated that the private sector is taking keen interest in pursuing business opportunities and developing linkages in the region under the auspices of the BIMST-EC Business Forum comprising representatives of national/designated chambers of commerce and industry of member-countries.

The recommendations of the Economic Forum, which met formally for the first time in New Delhi on 3 July 2000, relating to trade facilitation both in the context of establishment of a Free Trade Area (FTA) in future and/or a Preferential Trade Arrangement (PTA) in the intermediary stage was welcomed. They also commended the proposal for setting up of a joint BIMST-EC Chamber of Commerce.

The delegation agreed to strengthen and rationalize the institutional mechanisms of BIMST-EC, and to evolve necessary guidelines and organizational rules in respect of all BIMST-EC partners, so as to better streamline and co-ordinate BIMST-EC activities. With a view to further strengthening the BIMST-EC institutional mechanisms and ensuring regularity in the schedule of Ministerial Meetings for the effective implementation of the Bangkok Declaration, they agreed that future annual ministerial meetings should be held in the month of February each year.[10]

They reaffirmed the importance of 'Visit BIMST-EC Tourism Year 2001' and urged the member countries to raise the profile of this region by considering measures such as joint marketing strategies and promotional efforts including through pooling of airline resources. In order to encourage intra-regional travel, member countries could also consider special air-fare and other promotional arrangements.

In the fisheries, technology, transport and communications sectors, already identified for cooperation under BIMST-EC, it was urged that the sectoral committees meet as soon as possible to identify areas of cooperation and draw up the related plans of action. The critical role which cooperation in the energy sector can play in the future development of the region was reaffirmed. In this context, BIMST-EC countries should enhance cooperation in such areas as sharing energy-related information and data, sharing of technology and expertise, and cooperation in energy-development programmes. It was recommended that the enhancement of awareness about BIMST-EC be intensified to involve people from all circle in order to strengthen the spirit of BIMST-EC cooperation and to elevate BIMST-EC's profile in international fora. The contribution of ESCAP to BIMST-EC's ongoing programme of cooperation was acknowledged. The need to foster networking arrangements and stronger links with development partners and donors, relevant international organizations and the private sector, in order to provide impetus to BIMST-EC's current and proposed regional cooperation activities was reiterated.

It was recognized that the twin processes of globalization and trade liberalization bring new opportunities and challenges for countries of the BIMST-EC. In order to better harness the potential benefits arising from such developments and at the same time to overcome the adverse effects of such global trends of common concern to developing countries, member countries need to cooperate and coordinate their efforts for addressing these issues at relevant regional and international fora. In realizing the primary objective of BIMST-EC to promote economic cooperation in the region and facilitate trade and investment opportunities, the threat posed by terrorism to peace, stability and economic development was discussed, and the need for cooperation to address this problem expressed.

At the first meeting of BIMST-EC Economic/Trade Ministers Meeting, termed as the retreat, held in Bangkok on 7 August 1998 decided that BIMST-EC would initially begin co-operation efforts in six areas. It was agreed that each country would play the lead role in planning and implementing programmes in each of the areas for a period of approximately three years.

The lead country for trade and investments was Bangladesh, for technology was India, for transportation and communication was Thailand, for energy was Myanmar, and for tourism and fisheries was Sri Lanka.

Since some of the sectors are very big, for greater efficiency in achieving the aims and objectives of BIMST-EC, the six sectors have been further divided into sub-sectors with each sub-sector having a chair country responsible for co-ordinating activities of that sub-sector reporting to the lead country.

The meeting imparted a new dimension to economic cooperation between the member states. It was agreed that BIMST-EC should aim and strive to develop into a Free Trade

Arrangement, and should focus on activities that facilitate trade, increased investment and promote technical cooperation among member countries. It was further reiterated that BIMST-EC activities should be designed to form a bridge linking ASEAN with SAARC.

The second meeting of the BIMST-EC Economic/Trade Ministers was held in New Delhi on 27 April 2000. The ministers met to review the progress on the initiatives agreed to in their first meeting in Bangkok, to take stock of recent developments in the global economic system, and to decide the action agenda for economic cooperation.

The ministers took note of the recommendations of the Senior Trade/Economic Officials Meeting (STEOM) which had met on 26 April 2000. The ministers accepted the recommendations of STEOM on the action agenda for economic co-operation and it was decided that the countries affected by the global financial crisis were now well on the road to recovery. It was important to push ahead the momentum of recovery through close economic cooperation between the member countries by taking advantage of the complimentarities that existed. The action agenda formulated by the STEOM should be implemented by all countries effectively and within agreed time frames. The private sector should be closely involved in the implementation of the action agenda.[11]

The rapid changes in the global economic environment driven largely by technological developments and deregulation and often adversely impacting on fragile economies necessitated close cooperation and frequent consultations to facilitate appropriate responses and policy changes. It was agreed that the ministers would hold regular consultations on various issues in the multilateral agenda, especially in the WTO.

The ministers stressed importance of establishing a clear work programme to implement the shared vision for a free trade arrangement in BIMST-EC region. The ministers decided to constitute an inter-governmental group consisting of officials dealing with international trade to prepare a concept paper on possible approaches towards a preferential trading arrangement leading to the Free Trade Area on the basis of inputs from all member-countries within a period of 6 months for consideration of the ministers.[12]

Transport and communication issues are critical to the development of economic cooperation in the region. A cohesive and well-coordinated approach to these issues is essential to ensure early implementation of the agreed projects. It was agreed that India would be the lead country for this sector and would convene a meeting of experts to examine the feasibility as well as the funding options for early implementation of the BIMST-EC component of the Southern Corridors of the Trans-Asian Railway and Asian Highway Projects.[13]

Intellectual Property Rights are a major area of concern for developing countries. The ministers emphasized the need for joint initiatives on the basis of the Phuket Action Plan and the New Delhi Action Plan to intensify cooperation between the member countries and to enable sharing of experiences. Issues such as protection of indigenous knowledge and bio-diversity should be especially addressed in such initiatives.

Electronic commerce is another area at the forefront of technological change in international business. It is important that member countries keep abreast with developments in this area. It was agreed that India would be the focal point for possible initiatives in this area including the launch of E-BIMST-EC and India will prepare a concept note identifying the issues and potential for cooperation between member countries.

The first meeting of Senior Trade/Economic Officials of BIMST-EC was held on 26 April 2000 in New Delhi. Member countries exchanged views on the progress in the six identified sectors of cooperation. Bangladesh, the lead country for Trade and Investment Sector, reported that the sectoral meeting on trade and investment had been held in Dhaka in November 1999. It was decided that steps should be taken to hold meetings in various sub-sectors pertaining to trade and investment before 2000. India mentioned that it would be organizing a technical workshop for discussing ways and means of combating diseases and enhancing productivity in the coconut and spices. A conference for identifying possibilities of collaboration in the automotive sector will also be hosted by India. Sri Lanka reported on the Tourism Sector, for which they are the lead country. Sri Lanka said that the Expert Group meeting on Tourism was held in August 1999 in Colombo. Myanmar reported on the energy sector and mentioned that they had set up a national level committee to oversee this cooperation.

The meeting noted with interest the potential for cooperation in new and renewable sources of energy. India made a presentation in this regard covering wind energy; photovoltaic, solar water heating, bio-mass and bio-gas energy as well as Ocean Thermal Energy Conversion (OTEC). Other areas discussed in the energy sector included industrial energy efficiency. It was decided that aquaculture will also be included in the cooperation in the fisheries sector.

India, the lead country for the technology sector, made a presentation on the possibilities of cooperation in high technology areas such as remote sensing satellite communication, composite material technology, computer-aided design and manufacture, etc. India agreed to prepare a few areas of cooperation from which a selection would be made by member countries. India also made a presentation on the setting up of a portal for BIMST-EC countries.

The meeting noted that the World Customs Organization (WCO) has adopted the Kyoto Convention for modernizing customs procedures and practices with a view to make the functioning of customs procedure efficient and effective. It was felt that there is a need to harmonize the customs procedures and practices within the BIMST-EC. Member countries, identify the impediments to the trade at the field level and seek uniformity in classification of products at 8 and 10 digit HS level in respect of items, which are highly traded between the member countries.

The meeting recommended that Working Group on Customs be formed to examine the possible areas of cooperation as well as identify and eliminate the various impediments to trade relating to customs procedures and formalities. The meeting agreed that the common objective should be to strive to achieve international standards. This will help in retaining and enhancing competitiveness of the products of BIMST-EC countries in international markets. The meeting recommended that there should be a mechanism for exchanging information on standards. A networking arrangement should also be put in place within the member countries so that information on conformance assessment procedures in respect of international standards can be exchanged. The modalities of mutual recognition of laboratories should also be explored.

The member-countries exchanged views on strengthening the banking arrangements to facilitate trade and investment as well as tourism. The meeting recommended that a meeting of the central banks of the member countries should be held to identify banking problems including the opening of Bank branches, speeding up and simplification of procedures of banking transactions and flow of foreign exchange remittance.

The meeting noted that the member countries of BIMST-EC are also signatories to the World Trade Organization (WTO) and are thus obliged to adhere to the TRIPS Agreement which stipulates the minimum standards for the protection and enforcement of intellectual property rights in the member countries. The meeting further noted with satisfaction the Phuket Action Agenda and the New Delhi Action Plan relating to issues pertaining to institutional linkages between national IP offices, promotion of HRD, networking of enforcement agencies and promotion of public awareness.

The issue of mobility of business people was discussed, particularly in the context of facilitation of visas. The meeting recommended that multiple long-term business visas should be issued as far as possible to businessmen of BIMST-EC countries. Ever since its inception, BIMST-EC has been keen to take up regional initiatives to gain optimally from the emerging trends of globalization, especially in the context of liberalization of international trade and investment. As has already been observed, throughout the world the private sector is gradually playing an increasingly prominent role and providing the driving force for economic development. It is expected that the private sector of the BIMST-EC member countries would play a leading role, in partnership with governments to help attain the goal of economic prosperity in the region.

Recognizing the fact that sub-regional co-operation can progress only under the aegis of inter-governmental co-operation and co-ordination, and also recognizing the private sector as the engine of growth, for the purposes of enhancing interaction between government bodies and the private sector representatives of the BIMST-EC countries, the BIMST-EC Economic Forum was conceptualized at a meeting in Dhaka in 1999.

A special BIMST-EC Senior Officials meeting held on 19-20 December 1997 in Bangkok recommended the establishment of the Economic Forum, to serve on a platform for enhancing interaction amongst high-level public and private sector representatives. This was later formally agreed upon by the member states, as stated in the joint statement of the BIMST-EC special ministerial meeting on 19 December 1998 in Dhaka reiterated its resolve to take all necessary steps for making the BIMST-EC, to take preparatory steps for establishing the Economic Forum. Accordingly, Bangladesh hosted the preparatory meeting on the formation of the Economic Forum in Dhaka from 9-10 November 1999. The BIMST-EC Economic Forum is a representative group of both the public and private sectors. Their role is to discuss matters pertaining to achieving the objectives of BIMST-EC and suggest recommendations to be taken up at the ministerial meetings each year.

The aims and objective of the BIMST-EC Economic Forum are as follows:

(*i*) To promote economic cooperation and trade between BIMST-EC member countries.

(*ii*) To provide a forum for high-level exchange of views between representatives of governments and the business community, including experts on trade and development issues.

(*iii*) To identify and assist in the implementation of cooperative work programmes in the fields of trade, investment and infrastructure.

(*iv*) To assist in generating increased volume of intra-BIMST-EC trade together with enhanced investments from other countries of the world.

(*v*) To provide inputs in formulating effective strategies to prepare the BIMST-EC member countries to face the challenges of globalization.

(*vi*) To sensitize government mechanisms to respond appropriately to the needs of the private sector of the BIMST-EC member countries.[15]

The Economic Forum could consist of two to six high-level representatives of the public and the private sectors from each member country and the Chairman of the BIMST-EC Business Forum or his representative. So far as role and functions of BIMST-EC Economic Forum are concerned, endeavour is to:

(*i*) provide strategic leadership in initiating economic activities to benefit the group as a whole;

(*ii*) facilitate the implementation of development projects undertaken by the group;

(*iii*) develop mechanisms for greater private sector involvement in BIMST-EC activities;

(*iv*) enhance quality of information flow and promote institutional linkages and networking;

(*v*) generating increased participation by the business community in the identified sectors of BIMST-EC.

It was decided that the meeting of the BIMST-EC Economic Forum would be held over two days annually, prior to the BIMST-EC Senior Official and the Ministerial Meeting. The country hosting the ministerial meeting will also be responsible for making all necessary arrangements for convening the Economic Forum meetings.

The first meeting of Economic Forum of BIMST-EC member countries took place in New Delhi on 3 July 2000. Government and private sector representatives from Bangladesh, India, Myanmar, Sri Lanka and Thailand participated in the meeting. India chaired the meeting. At the commencement of the meeting, delegates recalled the earlier discussions held in Bangkok and Dhaka for finalizing the concept, role and functions of the Economic Forum. Delegates discussed measures to facilitate private sector-government interaction in order to increase trade and investment among the BIMST-EC countries. The Economic Forum adopted the concept paper as its terms of reference.

It was also decided that the national committees will be formed at the nodal focal points in the each country to identify the problems in tariff and non-tariff areas, logistic difficulties and recommend specific proposals for remedy to the BIMST-EC Business Forum at the regional level. The national committees in this respect may be assisted by the sectoral committees. The national committees shall send three representatives to the BIMST-EC Business Forum to deliberate on these recommendations, and formulate a final set of recommendations for placement to the BIMST-EC Economic Forum. The nominees of the national committees to the regional BIMST-EC Business Forum may be accompanied by the members of the sectoral committees.

It was understood that the Economic Forum had to link, in respect of trade and investment issues, with the trade and economic ministers meeting as well as with the meeting of the BIMST-EC ministers at the national level. It should be ensured within each member country that there are both effective private sector exchanges as well as government-private sector exchanges. It was stressed that recommendations relating to the private sector of the BIMST-EC sectoral and sub-sectoral meeting in respect of the six sectors identified for co-operation should be examined by the Business Forum and the Economic Forum for implementation/submission to the Senior Official Meeting and dialogue and co-operation of the private sector of the BIMST-EC countries should be through the Chambers of Commerce and the Industry Associations of the BIMST-EC countries.

It was decided that efforts should be made to promote the establishment of downstream and value-added industries within BIMST-EC countries. There should be a mechanism evolved for technology transfer among small and medium enterprises (SMEs). The Economic Forum would deliberate on issues relating to e-Commerce among the BIMST-EC. In this connection, the offer of India to set up the BIMST-EC portal was noted.

The Economic Forum recognized the importance of close co-operation in agro-industries, food processing, dairy farming, horticulture, floriculture, animal husbandry, etc. In area of fisheries, cooperation should be soon launched in the area of trade and investment in fish and fisheries products, as well as research and development and technical cooperation for mutual benefit.

It was stressed that in the drugs and pharmaceutical sectors, cooperation can take place in areas such as inclusion of Ayurveda/traditional medicine systems into the general category of drugs and pharmaceuticals, establishment of mechanisms to safeguard intellectual property rights for traditional remedies, establishment of a universal standard for prepared traditional medicines, exploration of possibilities for joint ventures in manufacturing of pharmaceuticals and drugs, introduction of a compulsory health insurance scheme, exchange of information on companies engaged in counterfeit drug trading and smuggling activities. Cooperation in the pharmaceutical sector should also include R & D in diseases such as TB, malaria, etc. common to our region; joint work in traditional systems of medicine, as well as in biotechnology; between the universities and R & D institutions in the sphere of intellectual property rights relating to the drug sector.

A number of sectors, such as drugs and pharmaceuticals, textile and clothing, information technology, gems and jewellery, horticulture and floricultural products and processed food and tourism were identified as areas in which initial collaborative efforts could be undertaken by the Economic Forum to promote trade and investment. As a first step, promotion of business should be started in these sectors by studying and simplifying tariffs link measures, rules of origin, non-tariff barriers, import licensing, quantitative restrictions, customs procedures including pre-shipment inspection, customs nomenclature, customs valuation, etc. evaluating market disruption criteria such as dumping, subsidies, countervailing duties, safeguards, etc. that prevail in each of the member states.

The Economic Forum felt that it would be useful to have countries volunteering to take a lead on the issues in respect of Trade Fair participation, SME development and related employment creation activities. The lead country should give its report within a year on what has been achieved. It was suggested that information technology cooperation can take place in areas such as establishment of an IT Training Institute for member countries, joint ventures to set up IT Parks, improving communication links, setting up of independent BIMST-EC Software Quality Assurance Testing and Certifying Labs, creation of public awareness of IT through common TV programmes, etc.

In the gems and jewellery sector, cooperation can take place in many areas, i.e. setting up of training programs amongst the BIMST-EC countries for the training of gem and jewellery personnel, exchange of technical personnel, exchange of trade missions to promote gems and jewellery trade, setting up of joint ventures in mining, cutting and polishing of gemstones, and jewellery manufacture, etc. In textiles and clothing sub-sector, cooperation can take place in areas such as promotion of intra-regional trade, intra-regional investments, human resource development, research and development and information dissemination.

In tourism sector, cooperation in areas such as facilitation of travel formalities, human resource development, strengthening of transportation networks, development of new tourism products, marketing and promotional strategies, incentives for tourism investment opportunities, environmental management of tourism and cultural preservation, exchange of information on regulatory issues, clearing bottlenecks that impede growth, etc. were discussed.

In the area of tourism, the following recommendations were also made:

1. Task Force to study and recommend measures to expand air-sea capacity and frequency to remove bottlenecks to enhance tourism, trade, investment and growth.
2. Aim to visa-free travel ultimately, with the interim facility for visa-on-arrival for businessmen of the member countries.
3. Countries to collaborate on areas of joint promotion for the awareness and the publicity of BIMST-EC tourism.
4. Areas of possible tourism collaboration identified were:
   (*i*) Buddhist circuit
   (*ii*) Brahmaputra circuit
   (*iii*) Spice route circuit
   (*iv*) Coastal circuit (of the Bay of Bengal)
   (*v*) Cultural circuit.[16]

In March 1998 at a meeting organized by UNESCAP in Bangkok the businessmen from the five BIMST-EC countries formed an expert group known as BIMST-EC Business Forum. The aims of this group were to enhance private sector co-operation among member countries in the BIMST-EC region, in the identified sectors and sub-sectors.

A BIMST-EC Tourism Conference was organized in Kolkata from 30-31 October 1998. The BIMST-EC tourism ministers and leaders of the delegations adopted an Action Plan for cooperation in tourism. It established targets for cooperation in the area of BIMST-EC corridors and infrastructure, including roads, railways-air telecommunication, and in the areas of facilitation HRD, new products and joint marketing promotion.[17]

India hosted a WIPO sub-regional Forum for Intellectual Property Rights (IPR) among BIMST-EC countries in New Delhi on 18-19 November, 1999. The participating delegates noted the excellent potential for intensifying cooperation in the areas of IPR in BIMST-EC countries. In order to give greater impetus to such cooperation, the meeting proposed that it would be desirable to officially include cooperation in the area of IPRS as a sub-sector of cooperation under the trade and investment sector in BIMST-EC. The meeting stressed the critical role that information technology could play in facilitating IPR related cooperation under BIMST-EC and emphasized the importance of sharing information on IPR-related issues.[18] In this context, it stressed the need to intensify linkages between IPR-related institutions in member countries. The importance of close networking between patent and trademark offices in BIMST-EC countries for facilitating collation of information at a regional level was also discussed.

The initial trade between member countries of BIMST-EC was not very large. The intra-regional trade of BIMST-EC countries during 1999, was around 3 per cent of their global imports and 2.9 per cent of their total exports. The imports of Bangladesh and Sri Lanka were dependent on other BIMST-EC countries to the extent of more than 12 per cent in 1999. The corresponding import share of other countries of BIMST-EC (India, Myanmar and Thailand) is significantly low in the range of 1.16 to 2.67 per cent. The export basket of Myanmar was dependent on other BIMST-EC countries to the extent of around 18 per cent in 1999. Similarly, India's export basket was dependent on other BIMST-EC countries to the extent of around 5 per cent (its total exports). Other members' (Sri Lanka, Bangladesh and Thailand) export share to BIMST-EC was small to the extent of around 2.8, 1.7 and 1.2 per cent, respectively. India is a major exporter in the region, as far as total intra-regional exports is concerned. Out of total amount of US $3245 million of intra-BIMST-EC trade, India exported US $2016 in 1999. At the same time, intra-regional import was not concentrated to one country.[19]

So far as India's trade with BIMST-EC member countries is concerned, India's major trading partners with respect to exports in the BIMST-EC region are Bangladesh followed by Sri Lanka. India imports mainly from Thailand followed by Myanmar in the BIMST-EC region. Major items of exports to BIMST-EC countries include: cotton yarn, fabrics, gems and jewellery, transport equipments, machinery and instruments, drugs, pharmaceuticals and fine chemicals, manufactures of metals etc. India's imports from BIMST-EC countries included commodities such as made-up of textiles, raw jute, electronic goods, machinery, spices, etc.

While summing up, we find that BIMST-EC provides India an effective gateway to nurture partnership with Asia-Pacific. It can provide opportunities to the partners to establish political, economic and strategic linkages. It can assist in constructing road and port networks and facilitate construction of trans-Asian highway, railway and joint ventures. India and other South Asians are bound to be benefited if they cooperate with ASEAN countries in projects such as hydro-carbon, hydro-electric, gas pipeline, mining, power and tie-up in infra-structural development. Again the cooperative environment amongst the BIMST-EC countries will enable in controlling drug-trafficking, piracy and illegal trade in the region.

If BIMST-EC objectives are achieved, the vision of Asian resurgence will be possible. It may facilitate the notion of 21st Century as "Asian Century", but if it is unable to infuse cooperative environment, the region will continue to remain impoverished. Indian leadership has given due importance to partnership with BIMST-EC, which can be understood properly if we peruse through the following statements of former Foreign Minister, Jaswant Singh. He spoke the following on 6 July 2000:

> When we meet here today for discussions of BIMST-EC matters, we in effect, reaffirm the warm and close ties that the people of our countries have shared for centuries. Not too long ago, traders from our lands travelled on camel or horseback, or by boats and dhows, to sell and buy goods from each other. Some of them even settled outside and married abroad. The active contacts maintained in earlier times created a rich backdrop for intensifying people-to-people contacts between our countries. Surely, in the present age of jet travel, satellite communications and the internet, this should not be difficult to achieve....[20]

Foreign Minister stated further that:

> Decidedly, in the current global economic scenario, regional cooperation assumes a special role and significance. In this era of interconnectivity and mutual economic interdependence, the phenomenon of globalisation is perhaps inevitable. However, as the recent East Asian crisis established beyond doubt, globalisation does nothing to address our immediate problems of poverty, malnutrition, unemployment or absence of basic amenities and infrastructural facilities. In order to survive in this highly competitive world, developing countries such as ours will have to learn to fend for themselves. We will also have to develop our own strengths and expertise.[21]

He further emphasized that:

> Indeed, the economic foundation of this grouping can scarcely be overemphasized. Located in close proximity of each other, with large common borders and close linkages, the members of this grouping have come together to create an island of prosperity in the region. Some of us have strengths and expertise in many areas—whether food processing, information technology, infrastructural industry, agriculture or human resources. Given this potential, it is essential that we reinforce it. To do this, our countries will have to increasingly rely on domestic and indigenous resources and technology. Sourcing of technology and technical manpower would be economical, but could, in the long term, also train and orient our people for competing outside this region. Again, because of our immense population, our region itself constitutes a very large market for products and services produced

> by this region. Understandably, there will be tremendous competition from countries outside the region. However, with joint pooling of resources and technologies, we would create highly competitive economic conditions in many sectors.

He added that:

> Given these parameters, I find that BIMST-EC's current focus on sectors like transport and communications, energy and technology is most timely. In the current era of knowledge-based skills and expertise, it is most essential for all economies to have sound infrastructural conditions. Without adequate facilities in core areas of the economy, no economic development efforts can succeed. Since all these areas require massive investments and expertise, collaboration at a regional level would seem highly desirable. In any case, some of the BIMST-EC proposals, e.g. BIMST-EC project pertaining to the establishment of multimode transport linkages, are being concurrently pursued under other multilateral initiatives such as the Asia Highway and Railway project of ESCAP. Intensification of efforts in this regard will, thus, be rendered easier. However, creation of such infrastructural facilities cannot occur overnight. It also requires arranging for massive funds and investments. To the extent that BIMST-EC acquires speed and cohesion in its various cooperative ventures, outside agencies and even our own private sector will be encouraged to invest in such areas. I trust that the deliberations of this meeting will facilitate efforts in this direction.[22]

The statements of Jaswant Singh clearly indicate the relevance of BIMST-EC for India, but it can be observed that this grouping has so far not been able to fulfil its targets. There are some irritants which act as stumbling blocks such as insurgency in India's Northeast. Some political issues which worked against SAARC are also active; and historical, ethnic and religious matters are raised. At the same time, the region is facing political turbulence. Maoists in Nepal are engaged in anti-monarchy drives. Islamic fundamentalists are active in Bangladesh, and ethnic insurgencies in India's Northeast and parts of Myanmar remains unresolved. The insurgents know that if BIMST-EC cooperation is successful and if there is rapid development of the region, it will give birth to those forces which will dilute the identity and rationale of their activities. Thus, the insurgents are in search of a scenario which makes the debate over "who gets what, when and how" unending. There are some elements which articulate their share in the projects even before it is launched. It is, therefore, that suitable cooperative environment are elusive. Again the investors are not fully assured that their investments will pay dividends if they invest in BIMST-EC region. Despite the existing problems, we cannot overlook the forces of globalisation. BIMST-EC is bound to be successful, and as and when it will achieve its objectives in letter and spirits, the dream of Asian resurgence will be a reality. At the same time, it will help India to fulfil the objectives of "Look East" Policy, and greater regional integration with Asia-Pacific.

REFERENCES

1. Ministry of External Affairs, Government of India, Annual Report, 1997-98, p. 17.
2. Declaration on the Establishment of BIST-EC, Bangkok, 6 June 1997.
3. *Ibid.*
4. Concept Paper of BIST-EC, 6 June 1997, introduction.
5. *Ibid.*, also see V. Suryanarayan, "Prospects for a Bay of Bengal Community", *Seminar*, No. 487, March 2000, pp. 58-62.
6. Joint Statement of the BIMST-EC Ministerial Meeting, Dhaka, 19 December, 1998.
7. *Ibid.*
8. *Ibid.*
9. Joint Statement of BIMST-EC Ministerial Meeting, New Delhi, 6 July, 2000.
10. Second Meeting of the BIMST-EC Economic Ministers, Dhaka, 27 April, 2000.
11. Report of the First Senior Trade/Economic Officials Meeting of BIMST-EC, New Delhi, 26 April, 2000.
12. *Ibid.*
13. *Ibid.*, also see BIMST-EC experts Meeting on Transport and Communications, New Delhi, 23 April, 2001.
14. www.bimstec.org.
15. Concept Paper of the BIMST-EC Economic Forum, Dhaka, 9-10 November, 1999.

16. Meeting of the BIMST-EC Economic Forum, New Delhi, 3 July, 2000.
17. *Ibid.*
18. *Strategic Digest*, New Delhi, Vol. 34, No. 5, May 2004, p. 675.
19. *Ibid.*
20. Prakash Nanda, 2003, *Rediscovering Asia: Evolution of India's Look East Policy*, New Delhi, Lancer Publishers, pp. 498-500.
21. *Ibid.*
22. *Ibid.*

6

India's Sectoral Partnership with the ASEAN

India is in geographical proximity to the original members of the Association of Southeast Asian Nations[1] (ASEAN), i.e. Thailand, Malaysia, Singapore, Indonesia, Brunei and the Philippines. India shares common maritime frontiers in the Indian Ocean with Thailand, Malaysia, Singapore, and Indonesia. India's Andaman and Nicobar islands are located at the distance of 112 miles from Indonesia and have historical and cultural links with all the ASEAN countries. Geopolitically, India has had intimate connections with the ASEAN region and whenever the security of India or Southeast Asia was threatened in the past, both of them suffered equally. The British colonisation of India in the eighteenth century had adverse implications for the sovereignty and independence of the Southeast Asian countries. Southeast Asian states were colonised by either Britain, France, Holland, the US, or Spain and later, in the twentieth century, when Japan moved in pursuit of the co-prosperity and occupied Southeast Asia during the period of 1942-45, it had its repercussions on India's security. Some parts of Indian territories, i.e. the Andaman and Nicobar islands, had already fallen and Japan was poised to conquer India. There were fears of India's imminent fall to the Japanese but that did not happen. Japan started facing reverses and its military expedition towards India was somehow averted. After the end of the Second World War, Britain was unable to sustain its colonial hold over India and thus there was a transfer of power and India became independent. The realization of India's independence on 15 August 1947 had a positive impact on the freedom movement in the region of Southeast Asia. Southeast Asian countries became independent subsequently.

Thus the strategic developments of the past prove that the momentous events in India and Southeast Asia have intimate connections and these events have long-term implications for each other. They cannot ignore each other's geo-strategic concerns without jeopardising their national or regional interests.[2]

Presently India and the ASEAN countries are faced with similar security concerns. The Chinese naval build-up in the South China Sea and its incursions into the Indian Ocean through Burma, have been accelerated. China's intention of projecting itself as a major maritime power of the region is quite disturbing. After the dismantlement of the Soviet Union and the emergence of a new world order, a number of states in the region are faced with new challenges. They are trying to adjust themselves to a new world order and India and Southeast Asia are feeling similar security and economic concerns. It is in this context that the leaders in India and Southeast Asia believe that the current need is to have good relations between India and the ASEAN member countries.

Moreover, this area requires peace and development. Development is possible with the acquisition of new technologies. These technologies can be acquired if there is no diversion of resources for security related expenditures. That will be possible only if the country does not perceive a real threat to its security. To bring about that situation, every country should show its peaceful intentions through words and actions. If the countries in the region respect each other's sovereignty and security concerns, there will be opportunities for peace and prosperity.

India and ASEAN had differences of opinion and they were on opposite sides during the Cold War. Though India tried to improve its regional relationships and its leaders paid visits to the ASEAN countries, it had limited success. In that endeavour, a firm step was taken by ASEAN when it accepted India as a "sectoral dialogue partner" in its Fourth Summit Meeting at Singapore on 27-28 January 1992. Thus India was able to have a dialogue with ASEAN on promoting trade, investment, scientific and technological cooperation, etc. This certainly helped the two sides to arrive at common perspectives. When

Singapore's Prime Minister, Goh Chok Tong, announced that India's application to become a "sectoral partner" was approved by ASEAN, it was occasion for rejoicing in India. South Korea had also been a "sectoral partner" of ASEAN before becoming a full-fledged "dialogue partner" in 1992.

It is worth noting that Pakistan and other South Asian countries were also lobbying to become a "dialogue partner" of ASEAN. Pakistan pleaded that it was a former ally of non-communist Southeast Asia. It was one of the eight members of the Southeast Asia Treaty Organisation (SEATO) and had committed its forces for anti-Communist crusades. Pakistan withdrew from SEATO in 1972 after its debacle in Bangladesh. SEATO became defunct subsequently after the communist takeover of South Vietnam in 1975. But the fact that it had committed itself to protect the security of the SEATO partners in the past and was thus an old ally of the anti-communist grouping allowed it to seek the status of a "dialogue partner". Pakistan's Minister of State for Economic Affairs, Sadar Aseef Ahmed, had gone to Singapore on the eve of the fourth summit. He sounded out several ASEAN countries about the possibility of joining the grouping in some capacity.[3] The then Pakistani Premier, Nawaz Sharif, had also visited Singapore earlier and tried to press the ASEAN countries for its inclusion. On the basis of military dominated polity and propagation of Islam they sought affinity with some of the countries and expected that these factors would support them in getting the status of a "dialogue partner". Although these factors were important, ASEAN included India as a "sectoral partner" before Pakistan. This surprised the diplomatic circles in Pakistan and India but the region as a whole appreciated the realistic appraisal of the ASEAN decision-makers.

In fact, India's case was supported because of trade, investment and geographic links with the countries in the ASEAN region. The "sectoral partnership" have ushered a new era of commercial, scientific and technological cooperation. But the most important area which has hitherto not been mentioned is strategic cooperation. As mentioned earlier, India shares maritime borders with the ASEAN countries, spreading into thousands of miles. Their joint collaboration to exploit marine resources, fishing, shipping, and conduct patrols might prove useful to the two sides. The joint naval exercises with the ASEAN countries could be a positive effect on the confidence building and boost their sense of security. Malaysia, Indonesia, and Singapore have already taken some initiatives to have strengthened security relationship with India. Their defence officials have visited New Delhi for talks and they have been reciprocated. The Malaysian Defence Minister, Mr. Najib Abdul Razak, visited India in March 1992 and there was an agreement that India would assist Malaysia in strengthening defence forces and in the maintaining of aircraft belonging to the Royal Malaysian Air Force. It was further reported that Indian experts would train the Royal Malaysian Air Force pilots on MiG-29 aircraft.[4] On the other hand the Royal Malaysian Navy was likely to purchase fast patrol craft boats. An understanding has been reached on sharing Indian expertise in marine commando training, coastal surveillance, anti-piracy operations, weather observation, coastal search and rescue operations, defence of ports and harbours, and shallow water mining capability. India has also offered its coastal surveillance radars and L-70 guns to Malaysia.[5]

Meanwhile a high level delegation led by Indonesia's naval chief of staff, Moehamad Arifin visited New Delhi to explore more effective ways to strengthen maritime cooperation. His mission was followed by the visit of the Indonesian Minister of Industries, Mr. Hartato in March 1992. During his visit India and Indonesia signed a memorandum of understanding to cooperate in the fields of small-scale industrial sector, capital goods, and newsprint industries. India agreed to set up joint ventures in Indonesia for manufacturing equipment required by that country.[6]

On the other hand, Singapore has been supporting the idea to include India as a guarantor for the Zone of Peace, Freedom and Neutrality (ZOPFAN) proposed by ASEAN in 1971. Former Prime Minister, Lee Kuan Yew, while addressing the national day rally on 20 August 1989 had stated that there was a need to include India as a guarantor of ZOPFAN because it was a significant military power in the region. India was manufacturing its own MiG-27, T-72 main battle tanks, frigates, missiles and its technologies were quite advanced.[7]

Now that India has become a "sectoral partner", there is every possibility of expanding cooperation and understanding. India will be in a position to participate in the ASEAN foreign minister's meetings and thus will understand the regional perception and demands better. India will get an opportunity to talk to ASEAN leaders more frequently and relations are bound to be strengthened.

In retrospect it is interesting to know why there was so much delay in including India as a dialogue partner. ASEAN which emerged as a non-communist grouping, did not see eye to eye with India on its policies towards Indochina. India's attitudes and perceptions differed from one another on the question of support to the Democratic Republic of Vietnam *vis-à-vis* the Republic of Vietnam from 1972 until 1975 and People's Republic of Kampuchea from 1979 to 1989. India was supporting the opposite sides of ASEAN in both cases. India and ASEAN had different motivations and objectives to support one group against another, and neither side was intending to offend each other, yet the relationship suffered. India's endeavour to maintain balanced and cordial ties with the countries in Southeast Asia suffered a real setback when on 7 January 1972 India decided to upgrade the level of its diplomatic mission with North Vietnam, from Consulate General to Embassy level. The anti-communist forces in the region became apprehensive about the Indian overtures. They did not take it kindly and thus called for dropping India from the International Control Commission (ICC), which had been established for a peace-keeping role in Indochina in July 1954. Anti-Indian propaganda was effective and India was dropped from the ICC in 1973. Thus India's stand, though realistic, was viewed as pro-communist. But the Indian prestige suffered heavily when, on 7 July 1980, the country gave its diplomatic recognition to Heng Samrin's People's Republic of Kampuchea. This time ASEAN reaction was very negative. This regional grouping, which had invited India for an observer status in June 1980, and which had been campaigning against Vietnam's military intervention and through this the creation of an illegitimate state, felt unhappy to know about India's diplomatic recognition to Kampuchea. At that time, the United

States, the European Union, Japan and China as well as the ASEAN countries opposed Vietnam-supported Heng Samrin regime. They were determined to nullify the creation of a regime illegally installed by force. Thus the United Nations also with-held recognition of the regime led by Heng Samrin, which was in control over the territories.

Recognition by India was based on three developments. First, the regime led by Heng Samrin was the *de facto* government, controlling most of the areas in Cambodia. Second, the recognition of Cambodia had the backing of India's public. Congress (Indira) promised the electorate that if the party were to win the election, the new government would recognise the Heng Samrin regime. Congress(I) was given a massive mandate in the 1980 elections and the new government was encouraged to recognise the Heng Samrin regime. Thirdly, the socialist countries (the Soviet Union and East European countries) had also recognised the Heng Samrin regime. Hence India decided to recognise the regime and it became a controversial issue instantly. The ASEAN countries were very strongly opposed to it. The then Chairman of the ASEAN Standing Committee, General Carlos P. Romulo, expressed ASEAN displeasure on 10 July 1980 by saying that the ASEAN states regretted India's untimely decision of recognition.[8] There were adverse remarks not only in the ASEAN, but also in the American and Western press. Some of them viewed the recognition as dictated or inspired by the Soviet Union and criticised India as a Soviet satellite. India's steps towards recognition were portrayed as a gambit in the Cold War game of the two super powers. There was vociferous criticism of Indian diplomacy in the West. China asserted that India was an ambitious power trying to pursue hegemonistic goals with the support of the Soviet Union. India was perceived as a major threat to the peace and security of the region, desiring to establish predominance over the Indian Ocean. There was adverse propaganda against its naval build-up and thus attempts were made to harm its geo-political interests. Some of the strategic thinkers in the ASEAN countries too expressed serious reservations about India's naval build-up and highlighted its negative impact on the security system of the region. Although India's endeavours in the Indian Ocean were aimed at providing security to its vast maritime borders and keeping watch on the trespassers, it became a subject of vicious propaganda.

Most of the anti-India propaganda was intentional and misinterpreted. China took full advantage of this state of affairs. It pushed ahead its naval build-up in the South China Sea located on the northeast side of Southeast Asia and pleaded that its endeavours were aimed at countering Indian build-up in the Indian Ocean on the Southwest of Southeast Asia. The Chinese exercises, in fact, directed at projecting its power potential to South and Southeast Asia, indeed posed a real threat to the security system of South and Southeast Asia. Such a build-up have been accelerated after the reported withdrawal of Russia and the United States from the Cam Ranh Bay naval base and Subic Bay naval base respectively. The Chinese are keen to fill up the vacuum with its increased presence in the South China Sea. Its naval installations at Pascadores (Pengshu), Pratas (Dongsha), Paracels (Xisha) and around the Spratlys (Nansha) have been menacing.[9] China has accelerated its claims of sovereignty over the entire South China Sea, which begins at the southern border of China and ends at the northern border of Indonesia. Moreover the Spratlys Islands in the South China Sea are an area of contest and confrontation. Vietnam, Malaysia, the Philippines, Taiwan, and China have claims over parts of the Spratlys. As that area has the potential oil assets and is important for the security of the ASEAN region, Southeast Asian states are apprehensive about the Chinese claims and naval build-up. But that has not deterred China from pursuing its claims. In March 1992, China passed a bill, entitled, "the Law of the People's Republic of China on its territorial waters and their contiguous areas", and arrogated to itself the power to use force to exercise its sovereignty over its far-flung territorial waters including the whole of South China Sea and much of the East China Sea. The law's purpose was to enable China to exercise control over the adjacent areas, and to safeguard state security as well as its maritime rights and interests. Harvey Stockwin[10] has commented that under this law China could militarily seek to exclude all naval vessels seeking to proceed from the Pacific to the Indian Ocean via the South China Sea.

It is estimated that about 4,000 merchant ships traverse this passage every day. China, with the support of the proposed law, could impose a surcharge on the oil tankers, which serve as Japan's energy lifeline and which pass through this sea lane.

All these developments have far-reaching implications for the security of the region, and the ASEAN countries are concerned about it. They are trying to sort out their differences over their maritime borders and the 200-mile Exclusive Economic Zone (EEZ). They are particularly concerned about the future of the Spratlys. Two of the ASEAN states, i.e. Malaysia and the Philippines, are greatly concerned about protecting their rights and ownership of the Spratlys Islands and they attach much importance to them for their integrity and security. Like Vietnam, they too are not impressed with the Chinese logic and claims over the entire South China Sea. They would prefer to have negotiated settlement and Indonesia has already organised two international workshops to discuss the problem of the Spratlys in the context of the South China Sea and to evolve solutions for resolving the dispute. The first workshop, entitled, "On Managing Potential Conflict in the South China Sea", was held in Bali on 22-24 January 1990 and the second workshop on the same subject was held at Bandung on 15-18 July 1991. The participants at the workshops in Bali and Bandung discussed every aspect of the South China Sea conflict and came to the conclusion that any territorial and jurisdictional dispute on the South China Sea area should be resolved by peaceful means through dialogue and negotiation. Force should not be used to settle territorial and jurisdictional disputes. The contesting parties were urged to exercise self-restraint in order not to complicate the situation, etc.[11]

Besides the Spratlys, ASEAN has reasons to be concerned about the security connections between Burma and China. Burma, situated on the western frontiers of the ASEAN states, has turned out to be "a strategic extension of China".[12] Beijing's military supplies to Yangon go far beyond the regime's need for small arms to put down insurgencies. Valued at $1.4 billion, its military arsenal includes F-7 jet aircraft, Hainan class naval patrol boats, light tanks, anti-aircraft guns and armoured personnel carriers. China is also developing Burma's infrastructure, giving itself an easy route from Yunnan to the Indian Ocean. It is also building a naval base at Hainggyi for its own use.[13]

These reports are disturbing for India as well as ASEAN and therefore, more and more strategic interaction with ASEAN are needed. ASEAN is evolving ways to have more dialogues with the dialogue partners in order to create better security environment. They are apprehensive about the ambitions of the regional powers and they would like to deter them in their advance. ASEAN, therefore, is trying to retain the naval presence of the United States in order to strengthen its security posture. Though the United States is planning to vacate the Subic Bay naval base by the end of 1992, the ASEAN countries are offering alternatives to retain their presence in the region. They are sure that in the event of American withdrawal, there will be a power vacuum in Southeast Asia. It is in this backdrop that Malaysia has offered its Lumut naval dockyard to service American naval ships and Singapore has permitted greater access of its facilities to the American navy.[14] It has agreed to provide facilities to repair and service American naval ships. Thailand is continuing to maintain its strategic links and is keen to offer facilities at Sattahip naval base and Indonesia is negotiating an agreement for ship repair facilities.

On the other hand, India has shown a better understanding of the ASEAN perspective and has initiated strategic interactions with the United States. It has responded favourably to the proposals of General Kickleighter, the former head of US Pacific Command, to pursue a policy of gradually strengthening ties that are intended to improve cooperation and partnership by the end of this decade, the mechanisms include high-level visits, exchanges, periodic policy reviews, Indo-US army staff talks, and cooperative work in selected areas of common interest.[15] India is trying to develop closer understanding and co-operation with the US. It has already agreed to the proposals for Indo-US joint naval exercises in the Indian Ocean. All these developments are in line with the policies and interests of the ASEAN countries.

Presently, we are witnessing the emergence of a new world order. The Soviet Union is no more and the United States is the predominant power. Thus new moorings and new challenges are emerging and they must be suitably tackled. The United States is committed to support the maintenance of world peace, protect human rights, and remove trade barriers at the global level. President George Bush, in his annual state of the union message to the US Congress said:

> But we are the United States of America, the leader of the West that has become the leader of the world. As long as I am President, we will continue to lead in support of freedom everywhere not out of arrogance, and not out of altruism, but for the safety and security of our children.

He further added that:

> We will work to break down the walls that stop world trade. We will work to open markets everywhere.[16]

These pronouncements have impacts on the global level. As liberalising trade is an important component of the new world order, the countries in this region are introducing important changes in their economic policies. The ASEAN countries have passed the resolution to establish an ASEAN Free Trade Area (AFTA) within fifteen years through the introduction of the Common Effective Preferential Tariff (CEPT). The ASEAN have identified fifteen products under the CEPT, i.e. vegetable oil, cement, chemicals, pharmaceuticals, fertiliser, plastics, rubber products, leather products, pulp, textiles, ceramic and glass products, gems and jewellery, copper cathodes, electronics, wooden and rattan furniture.[17]

These changes have their impact on India as well, where the process of economic liberalisation to attract external trade and investment are being introduced rapidly. As there is relative stability and phenomenal progress in the ASEAN region, India is keen to promote interaction with them. The ASEAN countries are endowed with vast natural resources and Singapore has already emerged as a newly industrialised country (NIC). Malaysia, Thailand and Indonesia are developing very fast. ASEAN is producing oil on a massive scale. Indonesia produces 1.189 million barrels of oil per day, followed by Malaysia that produces 510,000 barrels, and Brunei

240,000 barrels per day.[18] Besides they have rubber, tin, palm oil, rice, and pulses. Singapore is producing high-tech items, i.e. computers, and other electronic goods. On the other hand, India is producing capital and transport equipment, industrial plant and machinery for sugar, cement, textiles, and rolling mills, electrical power generating equipment, commercial vehicles, diesel engines and other electrical equipment and components for export.

Indian exports to the ASEAN countries, though very small in volume, are gradually increasing. In 1974-75, Indian exports to Indonesia were worth Rs.50 to 55 crores, to Malaysia Rs.28.09 crores, to Singapore Rs.36.79 crores, to Thailand Rs.12.32 crores and to the Philippines Rs.4 crores. The imports totalled Rs.11.20 crores from Malaysia, Rs.7.22 crores from Singapore, Rs.2.64 crores from Indonesia and Rs.9,800,000 from the Philippines.[19] India was also importing about 400,000 tons of rice from Thailand per year from 1971 to 1975. The total exports of engineering goods from India to the ASEAN countries also went up by $40 million in 1991, from $105 million in 1989-90 to $145 million in 1990-91. Singapore's imports from India were substantial reaching $59 million in 1990-91 from $44 million in 1989-90. India's exports to Malaysia were worth $35 million, followed by Thailand at $24 million, Indonesia $19 million and the Philippines $8 million.[20]

India's trade with the ASEAN countries as a proportion of its world trade was very small in 1971, standing at 1.5 per cent in terms of the value of exports and 0.39 per cent in terms of the value of imports. These shares rose to 4.2 per cent in the case of exports and 5.2 per cent in imports in 1979.[21] Though it showed an upward trend there was no appreciable rise in the volume of trade in the 1980s. However, now there is a favourable climate for increasing the volume of trade for mutual benefit. India's exports to Indonesia have been mainly in engineering goods, iron and aluminium ore, machinery and auto components, chemicals and honey. On the other hand, India imports spices, vegetable oil and cement. As far as Malaysia is concerned, India's exports are of engineering goods, manufacture of metal and machinery equipments, fruit and vegetables. The major imports are palm oil and fats, rubber and related products, tin and other non-ferrous base metals. Regarding Thailand, India's exports are of marine products, feed stuff for animals, chemicals, machinery, gems and jewellery. The imports are rice and pulses (Moong and Urad), synthetic fibres, and inorganic chemicals.[22] As far as Singapore is concerned India's exports have been non-metallic mineral manufactured items, textiles, yarn, spices, fodder, chemicals and fruits. The major imports are engineering goods, petroleum products, oil rigs for prospecting offshore oil, and certain items connected with ships and aircraft. Finally, India's exports to the Philippines have been chemicals, live animals, fodder, transport equipments and engineering goods. The major imports are vegetables, textile fibres (other than cotton and jute), and copra.

The volume of trade is increasing and that can be further improved with the understanding and cooperation of Japan and the United States. The latest figures indicate that India's trade with Singapore which was merely $44 million in 1988 now stands at $1.5 billion, and is rising at the rate of 10 per cent per year.[23] Again the value of bilateral trade with Thailand, which was worth $24 million in 1988, stood at $1 billion in 1991. The trade relations with Indonesia and Malaysia are also expanding, and their figures, which stood at $19 million and $35 million respectively in 1988, have doubled now.

Besides trade, there is a vast scope for expanding investment relations between India and ASEAN. Among the South Asian states, only India has substantial equity investments in joint ventures in the ASEAN countries. With the exception of Brunei, India has investments in all the ASEAN countries in a wide range of areas, such as textiles, cement, paper and pulp, computers, precision tools, chemicals, iron and steel, office furniture. Out of the 222 total Indian joint ventures, about eighty-six are located in the ASEAN region.[24] Indian investments in Singapore are increasingly in the sphere of high technology areas. Singapore had joint ventures with Indian concerns in the production of welding electrodes, electric fans, sewing machines and automobile accessories till 1985 and subsequently expanded to include manufacturing silicon semi-conductors, rectifiers, kitchenwares, chemical dyes and computers. Its performance has been quite satisfactory and mutually beneficial.

Indonesia has about twenty-two joint ventures with India to manufacture textiles, sugar, paper, steel pipes, tubes and rayon. After the recent visit of the Indonesian Minister of Industries, Hartato, to India in March 1992, new areas of joint ventures were explored and those selected were cotton and synthetic yarn, engineering files, billets and wire rods, steel furniture, rubber rollers, drugs and pharmaceuticals, pump sets, solar system, oil and gas and water heaters. The minister invited Indian businessmen to take advantage of the growing import market in his country, which is presently at US $4 to 5 billion, by setting up joint ventures there for manufacture of equipments required by that country.[25]

Malaysia have had the largest number of joint ventures with India to manufacture cotton textiles, steel furniture, glass bottles, electric fans, cycles and palm oil.[26] There have been about 34 joint ventures, but after the recent visit of Defence Minister Najib Abdul Razak to India in March 1992, the investment relations expanded in the area of security and defence related technologies.

As far as Thailand is concerned, India has had joint ventures in producing synthetic fibre spinning plants, steel mills and cotton piece goods for a long time. Presently, there are 20 Indo-Thai joint ventures in the area of textile manufacture, rayon, chemicals, dye stuffs, iron and steel products, construction and management. On the other hand, the Philippines also have joint ventures with India in the area of manufacturing transmission line materials, diesel engines, and yarn.[27] In recent years, the two countries extended the area of their collaboration to develop cashew plants and dairy products.

Thus we find a considerable Indian investments in the ASEAN countries but that is yet to be reciprocated by the ASEAN countries. The ASEAN investments in India have so far been insignificant. Though Singapore, Malaysia and Thailand have evinced interests in joint ventures in South Asian countries, their modest investments are confined to Bangladesh and Sri Lanka. Singapore has joint ventures with Sri Lanka for gems and readymade garments and with Bangladesh for textiles. Thailand and Malaysia have joint ventures only with Bangladesh to manufacture chemicals, electrical goods, footwear, and pencils. Malaysia and Bangladesh also collaborate in deep sea fishing but their joint ventures are yet to be expanded to India.[28] India is trying to attract ASEAN to make investments. India's Finance Minister, Manmohan Singh, recently invited businessmen from the ASEAN countries to invest in Indian capital market for which the procedures have been liberalised.[29] India is trying to integrate with the global economic system and improve the investment climate. India, with a population of 800 million, offers a big market, and its development will contribute to regional development and stability. When Brigadier General Lee Hsien Loong, the Deputy Prime Minister of Singapore, visited India in March 1992, he expressed happiness to cooperate with India in trade and investment. He hailed the recent economic reforms initiated by India and favoured more collaboration and joint ventures. It transpired during Mr. Lee's visit that Singapore will make investments in India for ship building and repairs and packaging. Lee said that India had the manufacturing capabilities while Singapore had the necessary infrastructure for ship building. In addition, there were great potentials for the development of tourism and maritime interests.[30]

These developments are considered path-breaking in Indo-ASEAN relationships. If Singapore supports joint ventures in India, it will attract other ASEAN partners as well.

India is also trying to induce non-resident Indians (NRIs) in ASEAN to invest in India. The government has already introduced appropriate changes in its economic policies in the field of Foreign Exchange Regulations Act (FERA), foreign currency deposits, complete profit repatriation regulations. Indian leaders are also endorsing dual citizenship to NRIs to attract their investments for India's progress. Thus the proper investment climate is in the offing. The Indian Investment Centre, with headquarters in New Delhi and an overseas office in Singapore, is trying to facilitate investments from ASEAN. It is pertinent to remember that the overseas Indians had sustained the activities of Netaji Subhas Chandra Bose's Indian National Army during the Second World War. Now their cooperation is required to augment the cause of peace and development of an independent India.

It is encouraging that India and the ASEAN countries now have complimentary items for imports and exports and with the economic liberalisation in India, Indo-ASEAN relations are bound to improve. India and ASEAN are on the same side in the emerging new world order and they are expected to forge a policy of partnership, greater co-operation and understanding. India has supported ASEAN in finding out peaceful settlement of the Cambodian crisis and contributed a brigade group (about 3,500 men) a medical battalion, and one army battalion (1,000 troops) for the UN Transitional Authority in Cambodia (UNTAC) for its peace keeping role.[31] India is showing a better understanding of the security situation in ASEAN and is ready to share the problems. India is keen to work together with the ASEAN countries in security and economic matters. It will be pleased if the bonds linking the age-old region's civilisations are reinvigorated. The status of a "sectoral dialogue partner", may prove a means to that end.

REFERENCES

1. For further details about the ASEAN, see Michael Leifer, 1989, *ASEAN and the Security of Southeast Asia*, London, Routledge; Alison Broinowski (ed.), 1982, *Understanding ASEAN*, London: Macmillan; Bernhard Dham and Werner Draguhn (ed.), 1975, *Politics, Society and Economy in the ASEAN States*, Wiesbaden, Otto Harrassowitch, and also see Somsakdi Xuto, 1973, *Regional Cooperation in Southeast Asia: Problems, Possibilities and Prospects*, Bangkok.
2. India and Southeast Asia have geo-strategic connections of far-reaching ramifications. Indonesia, Singapore, Malaysia and Thailand have maritime borders in the Indian Ocean and thus they are always concerned about the developments there. For an analysis of the security connections between India and Southeast Asia, see K.M. Panikkar, 1945, *India and the Indian Ocean: An Essay on the Influence of Sea Power on Indian History*, London, George Allen and Unwin.
3. "Pak Bid for Trade Links with ASEAN", *Indian Express*, 26 January 1992.

4. *The Times of India,* 17 March 1992.
5. *The Times of India,* 23 March 1992.
6. *The Times of India,* 17 March 1992.
7. *The Times of India,* 22 August 1989.
8. *Hindustan Times,* 11 July 1980.
9. Woody Islands at the Paracels are being developed as a staging area for operations in the Spratlys Islands, *The Times of India,* 24 March 1992.
10. Harvey Stockwin, "China Seeking to be Super Power?", *The Times of India,* 9 March 1992.
11. Joint Statement of the Workshop on Managing Potential Conflicts in the South China Sea, Bandung, 18 July 1991, Points 4 to 6.
12. Inder Malhotra, "Political Commentary: Unending Brutality in Burma", *The Times of India,* 19 March 1992.
13. *Ibid.*
14. Pravin Sawhney, "Malaysian Army: India to Help Modernisation", *The Times of India,* 23 March 1992.
15. "The Kickleighter Proposals", *The Times of India,* 8 September 1991.
16. "Bush Outlines New World Order", *Strategic Digest 22,* No. 3 (March 1992), 295.
17. The text of the ASEAN's Singapore Declaration of 1992, *Jakarta Post,* 29 January 1992. For an understanding of Indian perception and policies, see S.D. Muni, "India and the Post Cold War World", *Asian Survey 31,* No. 9, September 1991, pp. 862-74.
18. *The Far East and Australia,* 1989, London, 1989, Europa Publications Ltd., pp. 265, 455 and 636. Also see, R. Berthelot, "Energy Transition in South and Southeast Asia", *Natural Resources Forum* 13, No. 3, August 1989, pp. 215-26.
19. Ganganath Jha, 1986, *Southeast Asia and India: A Political Perspective,* New Delhi, National Book Organisation, pp. 132-33.
20. *The Times of India,* 17 May 1991. Intra-ASEAN trade amounted to $24 billion in 1990, and combined annual output of the ASEAN in goods and services accounted for $265 billion. For further details, see *The Times of India,* 29 January 1992.
21. Charan D. Wadhva and Mukul G. Asher (ed.), 1985, *ASEAN-South Asia Economic Relations,* Singapore: ISEAS, p. 273.
22. *Ibid.,* 274.
23. *The Times of India,* 4 December 1991 and 25 February 1992.
24. Wadhva and Asher, *Economic Relation,* p. 19. Also see Shobha

Ahuja and Bhattacharya, "Trade Complimentarities and Prospects for Regional Import Substitution among SAARC-ASEAN Countries", *Foreign Trade Review*, 23, No. 2, July-September 1988, pp. 186-99.

25. *Hindustan Times*, 17 March 1992.
26. M. Ezhilarasi, "Indo-Malaysia Relations", *Foreign Affairs Reports 40*, No. 3 and 4, March-April 1991, pp. 1-20.
27. *The Times of India*, 25 February 1992, and Jha, *Southeast Asia and India: A Political Perspective*, pp. 133-35.
28. Wadhva and Asher, *Economic Relation*, p. 262.
29. *The Times of India*, 24 March 1992.
30. *The Times of India*, 26 March 1992.
31. *The Times of India*, 29 March 1992.

7

Need for New Initiatives in Indo-ASEAN Partnership

ASEAN region is the priority area to be paid attention under the framework of India's "Look East Policy". This policy, as evolved by our policy-makers more than a decade, has assumed importance in our foreign policy, but due to economic crisis, political instability and a plethora of other issues it has not yielded the desired results. India is not included in ASEM and APEC and it is not considered top destination for investments and tourism. Hence, there is a constant need for appraisal of our policies and commitments in view of our long-term interests. However, it is pertinent to point out that two issues, which were the main areas of cooperation in the ancient past, needs innovative initiatives to make them vibrant. They are the matters connected with cultural and economic partnerships.

India's national interests in terms of culture and economy are interconnected with the ASEAN. It can play a meaningful role in the Asia-Pacific with the concurrence of the ASEAN and its efforts towards globalization can be facilitated by the ASEAN partners. The revival and resurrection of India's glorious past is impossible without the support of Southeast Asia and it is no exaggeration to say that the prosperity of India is linked to the ASEAN region and vice-versa.

It is felt that India needs a long-term partnership with Southeast Asian countries for its stability, security and development. Some of the outstanding problems like ethnic disputes, insurgency in the Northeast, narcotics trade, smuggling and border disputes, etc. can be tackled effectively if there is regional understanding and cooperation. The suitable environment for peace and development can evolve if it has the support of a regional grouping.

Although India is supporting the globalization process for trade and investment, but certain impediments hamper it. The SAARC which was established to promote regional understanding, have failed. It is unable to resolve bilateral disputes and remains a mute spectator to destabilizing trends. The stability and development, which have been the bedrock of success for the ASEAN, are totally ignored in the context of SAARC. The political leaders are mostly concerned about their cheap popularity in their own countries and ignore their long-term regional interests. Thus, they raise the issues of ethnic interests and territorial claims with emotions and appeals. Hence, the grounds for regional integration and cooperation is diluted. India has been unable to enthuse SAARC partners because economic issues are superseded by political issues. It is primarily due to failure of SAARC that India sought regional cooperation through the policy of "Look East". The general assumption being that if ASEAN China and Japan becomes friendly and cooperative, if they understand Indian position and outlook in proper perspective and if they take along India in the globalization drives, it would neutralise most of the unfriendly elements detrimental to playing its natural role in South Asia.

"Look East Policy" of India, which was adopted in the post-cold war era, is to cultivate partnership with the ASEAN, China, Japan and Korea, to enhance our position in the politics of Asia-Pacific, to promote our national interests for stability, security and prosperity and to neutralise the growing challenges at the domestic and external levels. We share contiguous territorial frontiers with China, Myanmar, Thailand, Indonesia and others and our cultural and religious past have had common features. The ethnic and trading interaction have continued from time immemorial on common frontiers. They are doubtlessly neighbouring states who are keen to restore missing links to promote our partnership to new heights of success.

However, the impediments exist *vis-à-vis* our relations with the ASEAN. India was very close to the socialist world before 1991 and it did not take any substantive decision to promote cultural or economic partnership with the ASEAN. Japan, China, the EU and the US on the other hand, attached importance to the ASEAN as favoured nations, which was aptly reciprocated by the ASEAN countries. Naturally, ASEAN became pro-Western in their outlook and projected Vietnam as their common threat (1975-89). We differed with the view of the ASEAN regarding Vietnam and Cambodia (1978-88) and there were polemics and mud-slinging and thus the relations showed downward trend. This situation created visible gaps in our understanding and perception. However, the dissolution of the Soviet Union and rapid development in the emerging new world order posed new challenges and new problems to be addressed. Thus, we discovered convergence of interests to cultivate each other.

The ASEAN boom, their independent standing and incentives of trade and investments attracted India. On the other hand ASEAN was also looking for new partners and untapped markets. The dissolution of the Soviet Union, their withdrawal from Cam Ranh Bay naval base (Vietnam) and the American decision to withdraw from Subic Bay naval base (the Philippines) and the fear of withdrawal from entire region created the syndrome of a security vacuum. On the other hand, the Chinese attempts to occupy the Spratlys, and Mischief Reef incidents and their foothold in the Indian Ocean compelled ASEAN for new thinking. China began to claim sovereignty over South China Sea and it had shattering impact on some of the ASEAN countries. Now the ASEAN felt positive role for India in the changed situation and thus, India was invited as a sectoral partner of the ASEAN in 1992 and subsequently it was offered full dialogue partnership status in 1995. Several committees and working groups sprang up to give inputs to the growing partnership and naturally bureaucrats in the MEA are suggesting ways and means, but they always tend to be slow in proving themselves innovative and timely.

An objective appraisal of the existing relations indicate that the level of cooperation have increased substantially but it will take years to be at par with that of Japan, China, Korea or Australia. It is a reality that some of the dialogue partners are considered more important than India. Some of them might not agree with the philosophy of ASEAN vision and spirits, but because of some other reasons they exercise more influence. Although India is adjusting its policies in tune with ASEAN vision and prove herself a reliable partner, but it has not been allowed participation in ASEM or APEC. This has not stopped India from wholeheartedly supporting ASEAN stand on Cambodia, Myanmar and East Timor. However, the experiences suggest that there is a need for self-introspection. We must evaluate our "Look East Policy" to find out whether these policies are dated or relevant. Whether there is a scope for new inputs or does it require new priorities for better output? Policy-makers must be constantly in touch with entrepreneurs, journalists and academicians to bring dynamism in our partnership. We must draw some lessons from economic reforms in Vietnam and China and should be quick to adjust in the changing environment.

India's trade and investment relations have marginally improved in the new dispensation. Indo-ASEAN trade increased from $2.9 billion in 1993 to $6.5 billion in 1996 and investments amounted to $1.8 billion (1996), but business interaction slowed down after the financial crisis. India's exports have gone up from 4 per cent (1985-91) to 8 per cent (1992-98) and imports also increased from 5 per cent to 8 per cent in the same period. In terms of ASEAN total trade with the world, the ASEAN exports in real terms were 1.14 per cent and imports were 0.91 per cent in 1992-98. The figures clearly suggest that India is yet to emerge as a major trading partner of the ASEAN.

Although people to people contacts and cultural interaction have increased, but for regional integration some new initiatives are required. The proposals for growth areas/triangles and infrastructure for service industries and tourism, for instance, should be explored. Appropriate infrastructure for promoting trade and investments should be given priority. Concrete measures should be taken for fulfilment of the ASEAN vision and Hanoi Action Plan (1998) whereby the decision was taken to evolve a network for trans-ASEAN transportation, i.e. the railway, highway, waterways and telecommunications, etc. We have already constructed a road at Tamu-Moreh Border to link India with the ASEAN and similar attempts are needed to promote the endeavour of regional integration at different places. Ganga-Mekong Project and BIMST-EC should not remain merely an accord on paper, but there should be substantive contribution from all those who cherish to develop and be the partners in the global market.

Although ASEAN sought dialogue partnership with India and expressed common understanding, but they have reservations about our economic policies and liberalization. They desire to see changes in tune with their own economic policies, but under the given situation of coalition politics, any drastic reform is difficult. The ASEAN views India as a big market, but not as a favourite place for investments. Though the ASEAN faced constraints due to the economic crisis (1997-98), but this is not the main reason for ASEAN to ignore India as their favoured investment destination. The prime constraint is the unchanged perception of investors in the ASEAN, which is yet to transform towards India.

India's economic partnership with Singapore, Malaysia and Thailand have shown increasing volumes but the remaining seven partners needs to be enthused. The areas of cooperation should be looked into so that regional integration gets a new thrust. The ASEAN partners should think about affirmative action *vis-à-vis* India and important gaps should be filled up to balance the situation. This would be in tune with the policy of constructive engagement with peripheral partners and help the endeavour of AFTA and collective prosperity.

The overall objective of the ASEAN, as understood, is to bring about collective development of the partners and foster the feeling of regional integration. If India, contiguous to Southeast Asia, is unable to keep pace with the development track of the ASEAN states or if it remains one of the poorest region, if the threat to stability and security remains substantial, the prospects for integrated development of the region would be harmed in the long-run.

Although Thailand and some others have adopted "Look West Policy" to reciprocate India's "Look East Policy", and have proposed to build roadways, railways and waterways to involve India in the economic and strategic partnership, but the visible gains are not consonant and sufficient for the requirements. India is committed to the globalization process in the hope that the benefits would percolate down at the universal level, but in the absence of that happening unpredictable development might occur detrimental to regional peace and stability.

8

ASEAN and India: Dawning of New Partnership

Trends in recent developments in relation to the Association of Southeast Asian Nations (ASEAN) indicate that India is considered important factor in the stability and development of Southeast Asia. Whether it is an issue of democracy, human rights, environment, trade or investment, there is convergence of interests. There are commonalities in Indian and Southeast Asian viewpoints and the partnership is taking firm steps for cooperation. Though there are bureaucratic hazards in the way, but that is not sufficient to dilute booming partnership.

Historical Overview

The geographic setting of Southeast Asia testify that India, China and Australia are situated on its three different frontiers. All of them have tried to project their inter-dependence with Southeast Asia and expressed their support for regional peace and stability. They have promoted increased dialogue and coordination through regional forums and thus the consensus is emerging on security and economic matters. Hence the ASEAN is emerging as a key actor in the politics of Asia-Pacific and primus interpares for the success of India's "Look-East" policy.

Though India, China and Australia have projected their importance in the stability and development of Southeast Asia but the ASEAN perception of their role have varied and it has been changing from time to time. Australia has been most successful in the beginning, from 1954 onwards in demonstrating its devotion for partnership. As an active member of Southeast Asia Treaty Organisation (SEATO) and

Five Power Defence Pact (FPDP) and through "dialogue partnership", it understood Southeast Asian interests and made consistent efforts to lay solid foundations of friendship. However its role in the secession of East Timor from Indonesia was disliked by the ASEAN as a group.

China and India, were not associated with either SEATO or FPDP and were regarded as destabilizing factors at one stage or the other. China began to review its ASEAN policies after the signing of the Shanghai Communiqué (1972). It snapped government level support to the Communist parties in Southeast Asia and looked for evolving economic partnership with the ASEAN. It accelerated government level contacts with the ASEAN countries and supported the policy of trade and commerce with the latter.

India, unlike China, was not connected to any subversive organizations in Southeast Asia and assumed that its geographic location in the middle of West Asia and Southeast Asia could not be ignored in any strategic calculations of the region. It left frustrated when it was initially ignored in the politics of the ASEAN. They under-estimated the importance of each other and were swayed by the cold war innuendos. It is felt in retrospect that India was also self-righteous and did not make any substantial effort to cultivate ties. That proved a boon for India's adversaries in the region. It is a reality that the ASEAN-Chinese relations grew by leaps and bounds especially after Vietnam's intervention in Cambodia (1978). China like ASEAN, was emphatic to propagate that Vietnam posed security threats to the stability of Southeast Asia. Vietnam's intervention in Cambodia proved a rallying point for the US, China and the ASEAN and they projected Vietnam's behaviour as hegemonistic. They also decided that Vietnam must withdraw from Cambodia or it would be internationally isolated. They inadvertently or advertently supported the policy of "bleeding Vietnam white".

India, however, did not agree with the ASEAN perception of Cambodian tangle and expressed sympathies for Vietnam. This was not appreciated by the ASEAN and therefore India was viewed a threat to regional stability. It was projected as a surrogate of the Soviet Union, a destabilizing factor in the politics of the ASEAN. India was friendly with the Soviets and they had supported each other in times of crisis, but this partnership did not nurture negative agenda for Southeast Asia. It was just a coincidence that the Soviet Union, India and Vietnam became close friends and the dynamics of the cold war proved them on opposite side of the ASEAN. It was unfortunate for all the three but India had to pay heavily in terms of economic, political and strategic calculations.

But the situation began to change rapidly in the beginning of 1990s. The ASEAN now attached priority to partnership with India. Both began reviewing their economic and foreign policies constantly and provided forceful thrust to "Look East" policy.[1] They tried to adjust and accommodate their common interests to the extent possible. Thus, India has succeeded in projecting a new image which is complimentary to the ASEAN endeavours of amity, peace and cooperation. It is also interesting now to note that both India and Russia are the full dialogue partners of the ASEAN.

It is understood that although India tried to be always friendly, but its positive image had been tarnished because of its close friendship with the Soviets. However, with the end of the Warsaw Pact, COMECON and the Soviet Union, global environment changed, and this had its impact on the power politics of the ASEAN region. Vietnam introduced economic reforms in the name of "doi moi", to cope with the existing realities and looked for partnership with the ASEAN, to which it had opposed for decades. It withdrew its forces from Cambodia and cooperated with the ASEAN to resolve the dispute. It pursued economic liberalization and market economy to woo foreign investments and supported ASEAN consensus in matters of regional, economic and security matters. It expressed total support to ASEAN Treaty of Amity and Peace, and looked for ASEAN search for conflict resolution on the overlapping sovereignty claims of the Spratlys. The ASEAN partners felt satisfied and in 1995 offered its membership to Vietnam.

However, the changes in India is always gradual and slow. The impact of the Soviet dissolution was far-reaching. This reality was unacceptable to a section of the people and the situation have not changed fully even now. Having a democratic polity, and Communist Party as a coalition partner in New Delhi, socialist and populist slogans are very often given credence. Hence policy changes cannot be introduced without creating a suitable public opinion. India, with its multi-party system and with leftist, rightist, centrist and regional parties, have always expressed divergent opinion on economic reforms and liberalization.

Nevertheless the global changes forced the government to adapt themselves in the emerging world order. India thus began to review its economic policies and reorient its system as per the demands of the global economy. In that endeavour, it felt that the ASEAN had the potentials to help her. Thus India extended cooperation to the ASEAN search for establishing peace in Cambodia and bringing warring factional leaders of Cambodia to Jakarta Informal Meet (JIM I and II), and later co-operated with the United Nations Transitional Authority in Cambodia (UNTAC) operations. Thus it contributed its share in establishing peace and democracy in Cambodia to the satisfaction of the ASEAN leaders.

In the meanwhile ASEAN also reviewed its policies and started attaching role to India in regional matters by offering "sectoral dialogue partnership" in 1992. Accordingly cooperation in trade, investment, tourism, science and technologies were promoted. ASEAN-India Business Council (AIBC), which was established to look after these matters gave their expert opinion and plans for cooperation and collaboration. Thus interaction of India and the ASEAN leaders grew and both showed understanding and goodwill for each other. India's former Minister for External Affairs, Pranab Mukherjee reiterated this and urged Indian business community in a symposium on 13 March 1996 that they should set a target for establishing two or three major impact projects every year in India, in one of the ASEAN countries, or in third countries with ASEAN collaboration. The R & D effort between India and the ASEAN should be strengthened as number of projects are on the anvil in three areas, such as information technology, advance materials and bio-technology to make them truly viable and self-sustaining enterprises by joining in the collaborative effort.[2]

In fact, there are compelling circumstances for India and the ASEAN to work together. They are facing similar challenges and feeling similar concerns in the emerging world order. They do feel a need for each other and this perception is congenial for stability, peace and progress of the region. It is this reason besides imperatives of economic paradigms that the ASEAN offered full dialogue partnership to India in its fifth summit meeting in Bangkok in 1995. India aspired to arouse friendly feeling for the ASEAN during cold war years also, but its association with the Soviets, socialistic drives at the domestic level and controlled economy, came in the way. Again India's economic performance was poor and international propaganda against its poverty was vicious. It is understandable that because of the rapid rise in population, corruption and mismanagement, economic problems were complicated. The free press highlighted negative developments with juicy tales and our regional image as "poor and impoverished" were effectively established.

The ASEAN emerged as a major actor in the politics of the Asia-Pacific after the end of the Cold War and it offered opportunities to India to come closer. Both India and Southeast Asia were facing similar challenges in the post-cold war period because the United States, the victor of the cold war and protector of the ASEAN states so far, began transforming the world order and thus emphasis was given to promoting democracy, human rights, environment, and free trade, etc. at the global level, to the advantage of western powers.

The ASEAN states did not object to the broad objectives of the emerging international order, where it was going to contribute to better and more civilized living, but did not like certain western standards that were sought to be thrust upon them. They began to articulate their responses *vis-à-vis* western concept of democracy, human rights and environ-ment and in that process India offered complimentary role.

Democracy

Although democracy is important as a civilized system of government but in order to transform any political system, some important precautions are needed. If a system is removed without a smooth transitional arrangement and without evolving conducive political institutions, it is shortlived. For instance, the Soviet Union under M. Gorbachev introduced *perestroika* and *glasnost* without assessing its impact on the unity and integrity of the nation.

Democracy should reflect the type of society, their customs, conventions and their overall moorings. It may differ from one country to another and there is no single model. Abraham Lincoln defined democracy as the government of the people, for the people and by the people and thus they vary from one region to another. There cannot be a unified code of conduct to implement it.

Thus implementation of democracy, as Jusuf Wanandi says, might be relative and dependent upon history, values, stages of development, etc. and differences in implementation cannot be avoided. Again in order to have stability and development, efficiency and "good governance" cannot be ignored. We find that most of the Southeast Asian states started with democratic system in the post-independence era, but failed because they could not provide the evidence of "good governance".[3]

It is understandable that every country has to evolve their indigenous political order, and their sovereignty demands that they should oppose imposition of values from outside. South and Southeast Asians have already imbibed western values during the colonial period. There are some who implemented a political system after modifying the colonial constitution but there are some countries which are assertive and innovative to look for indigenous models.

The ASEAN countries, for instance, are trying to articulate their different viewpoints and asserting it at international foras. India has taken note of it and is interested in supplementing it. It believes that closer ties with the ASEAN would ultimately help reassertion of Asian identity, for which it had worked through Afro-Asian Conference, Bandung Conference and non-alignment (NAM). Though the quest for Asian identity was appealing, but it was lost in the dusty winds of the cold war. Now there are positive changes in the regional environment that may prove conducive to regional integration.

Human Rights

India adheres to universal declaration of human rights (1948) and also to declaration of civil and political rights (1976) and has established its own Human Rights Commission to monitor it. However, due to certain developments, it has been subjected to criticism for human rights violations and it is a sensitive issue. Similarly some ASEAN countries are also criticized for human rights violations and thus, India and some ASEAN partners feel similar concerns.

It is a reality that there are separatists and terrorists in India and parts of Southeast Asia. They are organized and instigate people on religious, ethnic or linguistic grounds. They operate violently and vitiate peaceful communal life. They engage themselves in collecting ransom, kidnapping, looting, raping and murdering of opponents. They foment fear psychosis and violate human rights of those who are generally law abiding and innocent. The state is, therefore, forced to intervene and take "police action", resulting in omission and commission. An understanding of the developments in Kashmir, Mindanao, Patani, Arakan and Jaffna suggest that the state intervention was first to protect civil rights of the general people and secondly to prevent fragmentation of the state.

The state intervention provokes chain reactions and the communal harmony is disturbed. The right to life to all those isolated from terrorist organizations are threatened and those supporting the government are labelled enemies and forcibly evicted from their homelands or killed. Thus "police action", very often proves itself a necessary evil and sometimes counter-productive. The police tends to display brute force. If the local people obeys them, the terrorists attempt to foil them by murder and extortion. If the people support terrorists, they are projected "fifth columns" and punished by the state.

The separatists do often talk about cultural imperialism or "cultural relativism" as the compulsive factor for their militancy. The proponents of "cultural relativism" view universality of human rights helping the process of imposition of dominant culture on minorities. They understand that there is no such thing as universal rights, and the natural rights theory ignores the social basis of an individual's identity as a human being, because a human being is always the product of some social and cultural milieu. The different traditions of culture and civilization are different ways of being human; it follows, therefore, that rights which belong to all human beings at all times and in all places are rights which people have as desocialized and deculturized beings.[4]

Thus "cultural relativists" are trying to influence human right activists. It is commonly understood that each ethnic, cultural and religious groups are important within the boundaries of a nation, and the endeavour of the state is to provide similar opportunities equally to all, but majority opinion cannot be ignored in democracy or dictatorship either, and that is applicable at the universal level.

But Third World countries are very often reprimanded or subjected to queries for violating minority rights. A study of the United Nation's High Commission for Refugees (UNHCR), Amnesty International, and Asia Watch testify that they critically evaluate the performance of the Third World *vis-à-vis* minority rights. This provides encouragement to separatists inadvertently and thus, they establish contacts with those organizations and foment trouble at the local level.

There are some subtle differences in the western concept of human rights and that of the Third World. Jusuf Wanandi of Indonesia has aptly summed up these differences into four headings: (a) Universality of Human Rights (west) versus cultural relativism, (b) the stress on civil-political rights (west) versus socio-economic and cultural rights, (c) Individual rights (west) versus communal and societal rights, and (d) sanctions for human rights violations in relation to the principle of intervention. He has explained Third World dilemma and analysed the problems that may follow if the proposed sanctions by the West is implemented for human rights violations.[5]

Both India and the ASEAN countries are opposed to imposition of western standards and they advocate common approach to attend grievances connected with human rights. India's Premier, P.V. Narasimha Rao spoke in course of his visit to Thailand that:

> "international relations face fresh problems such as the inclination amongst some countries to impose their own perceptions and

values on others. Human Rights is an example. Countries like ours, committed to preserving fundamental human rights in an exceedingly difficult situation created by terrorist attacks on innocent civilians, are targeted for scrutiny and criticism. Now conditions are sought to be placed on the giving of assistance that is meant for the poor and needy."[6]

Environment

Besides human rights, environment is emerging as a contentious issue and in this context ASEAN responses reflect the opinion of the Third World. Western countries are trying to subject Third World to observe certain standards for environmental protection also. As there is a proposal to increase forest covers on at least 30 per cent of the global territory, and as the western countries have already denuded their forest covers and as they are running totally short of cultivable land, they want to supplement it by restructuring environment laws, which is detrimental for the interests of the Third World.[7]

The western countries are striving to frame laws so that the Third World is compelled to increase its forest covers. Though the western countries have mostly contributed to environmental hazards through massive industrialization and nuclear experimentation, they wish that the Third World should balance the situation through massive afforestation. But they don't intend to commit aid substantially. This issue was raised by Malaysian Premier, Dr. Mahathir Mohammad at the Earth Summit at Rio Dc Jeneiro (1992), who demanded that the western countries should part with 0.7 per cent of their GDP ($125 billion) as overseas development assistance to the south for increasing forest covers and environmental protection.[8]

Dr. Mahathir and some others believed that if the global environment is to be protected on some areas of the globe, the obligations should be shared by the north and south in cash and kind respectively. As this endeavour would benefit humanity without any discrimination, incentives should be given. Though Malaysian proposal was constructive, but it was rejected by the US on the ground that such an endeavour would overlap the functions of the Global Environment Facility (GEF).

Free Trade

India and the ASEAN find convergence of interests on the issues of free trade and patent laws. They are edged in favour of the west and they pose certain threats to the interests of the Third World. The attempts of the developed countries to introduce labour standards with issues of global trade have serious implications for the Third World. The projection of deprivation of the developing *vis-à-vis* developed nations are drawn and it is quite disturbing.[9] Mahathir has bluntly expressed his disappointment on several occasions. On the eve of the Singapore Summit of the ASEAN in 1992, he stated:

> "When Cold War was on, we all yearned to be free from this oppressive conflict. We in the ASEAN, who won the war, have a right to be more free now but it seems that we are less free. The evolving world order is full of restrictions".[10]

ASEAN decided to establish ASEAN Free Trade Area (AFTA) with a time table of 15 years. Declaring AFTA, however, did not arrest the tendencies of protectionist drives. NICs are supporting free trade but it does not mean that they ignore indigenous industries. Again the countries with weaker economies can't compete with NIC and they are less enthusiastic of free trade.[11]

India, however, is a supporter of free trade and campaigning its relevance. The proposal for preferential trade agreement (SAPTA) has been signed for South Asia upon whose success the future of free trade depends.[12] The fact that India is advocating the utility of free trade in the region has endeared ASEAN, because that would complement the endeavour of AFTA in due course. India's support for liberalization and free trade is an elixir to promote ASEAN trade and investment in South Asia.

India has more than one billion people of which one-fourth belong to the middle class, numbering about 250 million. Similarly Bangladesh with 123 million, Nepal with 22 million, Pakistan with 133 million and Sri Lanka with 19 million, have a rising population of middle class, who look for latest gadgets and technologies. They want latest cars and television sets which have attracted the attention of major entrepreneurs. They are willing to capitalize on this growing market and ASEAN as an important actor in the politics of Asia-Pacific, deserves better treatment than others because of their proximity to India.

The ASEAN is striving for collaborative relations by greater trade and investment. Their networking is being offered to facilitate our trade with East Asia and European markets and their business overtures are conducive to our economic developments.

The ASEAN extended "sectoral dialogue partnership" to India in January 1992 and to Pakistan in 1993. At that time, the ASEAN group accounted for six per cent of India's total export but for ASEAN it was less than 1 per cent of their global trade.[13] The ASEAN was satisfied with India's responses and decided various sectors for cooperation. They invited Prime Minister, P.V. Narasimha Rao to address annual Singapore lecture (1994), which is otherwise reserved for world leaders. Mr. Rao, who spoke on "India and the Asia Pacific—Forging a New Relationship", endeavoured to assure ASEAN partners that they would find in India a reliable partner, a vast market if it is given a larger role in the Asia-Pacific. The process of this development will simultaneously involve the renaissance of a great and noble civilization, which we all share in some measure.[14] Prime Minister also answered many questions and spoke in depth on reforms in Indian economy and said that it was irreversible. His visit proved good exercise in confidence building.

The sectoral dialogue between India and the ASEAN was fruitful in many ways. Dato Ajit Singh, the Secretary General of the ASEAN, took the initiative to set up a centre for trade and investment information and promotion in 1993 and supported exchange of trade missions and trade fairs. He said that strides made by India in advanced technology, particularly in the processing of primary products, could be of great use in the ASEAN world.[15] On the other hand, Mr. Dinesh Singh, the leader of Indian delegation, presented a six-point programme for cooperation including the setting up of a body of experts to identify project areas where Indian enterprise could be utilized.[16] These included software developments and marketing small and medium enterprises, institutionalized linkages in major sectors such as petroleum and natural gas, joint ventures and development of infrastructure, particularly in the areas of power generation, transportation and construction.[17]

This meeting of the sectoral partners also decided to set up India-ASEAN fund to develop cooperation in specific areas, i.e. tourism, trade, investment, computers and informatics, solar energy and environmental protection. It was decided that the fund would be placed at the disposal of ASEAN secretariat and administered by a joint management committee. They agreed to set up an ASEAN-New Delhi Committee consisting of the heads of diplomatic missions of the ASEAN countries to facilitate sectoral dialogue relations with India. It was proposed by Indian Foreign Secretary, J.N. Dixit that each side should offer six post-doctoral fellowships up to six months in areas of science and technology.[18]

The ASEAN certainly seems to be satisfied with growing economic contacts and therefore, they have decided to upgrade sectoral level relations to "dialogue partnership". As a result, the relations are not only confined to trade, investment, tourism, science or technologies but new agendas of cooperation are being mooted and confidence in each other are growing.

India has been included in ASEAN Regional Forum (ARF), and it is trying to complement the process of regional confidence-building measures, the development of Preventive Diplomacy and evolution of conflict Resolution Mechanisms. Its participation in ARF has certainly proved that it is with regional security consensus. India is also applying the wisdom learnt from ARF experiences to resolve its own disputes with Pakistan, which is the ultimate objective of the "Gujral doctrine".[19] Such changes in Indian approach are different that they pursued in the past 50 years.

It is quite interesting that some ASEAN countries have appreciated Indian stand and they believe that India and Pakistan are capable to resolve all their disputes including Kashmir. But as they have geographic proximity with India, they are promoting better interaction with it, though both are associated with the ASEAN as partners, respectively.[20]

Growth Triangle

Some of the ASEAN states have proposed "growth triangle" to provide new dynamism and momentum to India-ASEAN relations. The experiment for establishing "growth triangle" has been tried amongst Singapore, Malaysia and Indonesia and that have proved beneficial to the partners. It is a type of entrepreneurship in which the three provide different inputs, such as "A" may provide territory, "B" the capital, and "C" the expertise and management. The three partners try to supplement the efforts of one another to promote trade and business, Indonesia and Singapore have growth areas in Bantam and Malaysia and Singapore have growth triangle at Johore and all the partners have benefited in the business venture.

In October 1994, Mr. Surin Pitsuwan, Thai Deputy Foreign Minister proposed "growth triangle" relations, involving India, Sri Lanka and Thailand in the Andamans.[21] He believed that such an endeavour would augment supply of raw materials, financial goods and high technology. This proposal was once again reminded by Mr. Supachai Panitchpakdi in January 1995, who explained that "Thailand wished to build a four-lane highway between Andaman Sea and the Gulf of Thailand and envisioned construction of a deep-sea port, refineries and industrial ventures alongside the highway."[22]

It is interesting that business circles in Indonesia are interested in "growth triangle" for Andamans involving India, Indonesia and Thailand. New Delhi side of India-Indonesia Friendship Association had articulated this idea in 1993 but bureaucracy on both sides have not yet agreed to engage in this venture. India is yet to be conversant with the advantages of growth triangle. It was this reason that when India advocated trilateral co-operation in the name of *troika*, involving one or two ASEAN countries in industrial joint ventures in world third countries it had little response. It proposed "troika" to Singapore for joint ventures in Vietnam.[23] Through this venture, India proposed to produce goods urgently required in the Third World.

India and Indonesia have close geopolitical pragmatism which demands opening new vistas of trade and cooperation. Indonesian Minister, Joop Abe in his 1997 visit to India has explained this desire very clearly, but both sides are presently giving importance for improving infrastructural and communicational aspects, and growth triangle proposal is yet to be taken up for serious consideration.

Trade and Investment

The trade turn-over and growing investment between India and the ASEAN countries display the confidence of each other and increasing business vistas. For example, if we examine India's trade with Thailand, it has touched more than $1 billion per year.[24] It was negligible in the past, but now it has picked up momentum. India's export zoomed ahead of target during 1990-92, when it exported gems and precious stones, cotton and fabric, machinery and parts, urea and fertilizers, while imported pulses (urad and moong), rubber, machinery, synthetic fibres and inorganic chemicals. The trade volume rose further by 20 per cent in 1994 and there are optimistic projections. Again two-way trade between India and Malaysia during 1994 was of $772 million.[25] According to latest reports, the two way trade between the two crossed $1300 in 1995, an increase of 41 per cent over 1994.[26] India is an importer of palm oil, petroleum, crude rubber and other non-ferrous base metals and exports engineering goods, building materials, textile, yarns, chemicals and pharmaceuticals, molasses, fruits and vegetables. On the other hand, trade with Singapore which accounted for merely $44 million in 1988, rose to $1.5 billion in 1992 and it is increasing at the rate of 10 per cent per year.[27] Singapore provides the outlet not only for East Asian markets but also for the US and European Union. India imports engineering goods, oil rigs, palm oil, organic chemicals, glass and telecom equipment, etc. and exports textiles, spices, fodders, inorganic chemicals, jute, fruits and vegetables. Same trends are visible in relations to other Southeast partners.

According to Federation of Indian Chambers of Commerce and Industry (FICCI) the annual average growth rate of India's export to ASEAN countries during 1991-95 was as high as 40 per cent. As compared to this, export to the US grew by 28 per cent, to Japan by 18 per cent and to EU by 24 per cent. Similarly annual average growth rate of imports from ASEAN was up by

23 per cent as compared to 15 per cent from the US, 17 per cent from Japan and a mere 13 per cent from the EU.[28] FICCI has also projected that it would be beneficial for India to concentrate on ASEAN as a major potential market and explore the possibilities of greater interaction with the ASEAN economies.[29]

Investment ties are also giving encouraging signals. Indian entrepreneurs had been eagerly investing in the ASEAN economy, but it was never reciprocated before 1991. Now the scenario is changing and India is viewed as one of the biggest markets of the world. If we examine the investment figures of Thailand, Malaysia and Singapore in India, it may look meagre but it has potentials to attract prospective investors. Thailand agreed to invest $120 million in India in 1993 to collaborate in fishing, prawn farming, shrimp feed meal production and tourism.[30] Some Thai companies have also signed agreements with Indian companies in the telecom sector. When Bihar Chief Minister Laloo Prasad Yadav visited Thailand in August 1995, Bangkok-based Shivnath Investment Company Pvt. Ltd. as well as Usha Siam Company Ltd. signed Memorandum of Understanding (MoUs) to develop Buddhist sites in the state, including modernization of the airport and construction of a meditation centre at Bodh Gaya.[31] They strove to prepare a master plan in this regard and search out feasibilities of developing tourism.

On the other hand, Malaysia is enthusiastic to invest in India. Renong Overseas Corporation is engaged in feasibility study for building 700 kilometre superfast express highway between Calcutta and Siliguri, costing Rs.3500 crores on a build-operate transfer (BOT) basis.[32] Again Tenanga National has signed agreements to develop $800 million power plant in Bangalore and $705 million power project in Tamil Nadu.[33] The two countries signed investment protection agreement on 3 August 1995 which is first of its kind that Malaysia signed with any nation in South Asia. Malaysia has agreed to provide national treatment to companies from India. The agreement envisages construction of a 13,000 kilometre highway, at the cost of $20 billion over the next 20 years on BOT basis.[34] Again Hyderabad's Kumar Group of Industries signed a joint venture agreement with MBF Holdings and Corporate Arrow for setting up a finance company in India.[35] Khemyan Corporation signed another agreement with Bangalore-based Khoday's group to develop township, hotels resorts, commercial and industrial complexes in India.

Singapore, however, is the biggest ASEAN investor so far. It invested $30 million in 1992, $33 million in 1993 and $48 million in 1994.[36] Both countries signed 12 cooperation agreements, worth several million dollars in September 1994 of which four were in the manufacturing sector and the remaining in service sector. The joint ventures to be established in India covered a wide range of areas from aquiculture, bakery, banking commercial office complexes, LPG terminal, mini-township, restaurant chain, ship-building and telecom equipments.[37] Ganpatrai Jaigopal of Bombay signed joint venture agreements with two Singapore based companies—Thakral Investment Holdings Pvt. Ltd. to set up a state of the art ship-breaking facility with a capacity of 100,000 tonnes per annum at Sosia, Gujarat. The project cost was estimated at $5 million.[38] Again Western India Group signed joint venture agreement with M/s. Sembawang Engineering to undertake designing, engineering, building, owning and operating of liquefied petroleum gas terminal facilities in India. This project was estimated to cost Singapore $100. Again TCFC of India joined hands with M/s. Kephinance Investment Pvt. Ltd. to set up a new Banking company in Goa. This envisages an investment of $13.5 million. Yet another agreement for a joint venture was between Growth Techno Projects Ltd. (India) with M/s. CONTECH (Singapore) for a $700 million township project in Ghaziabad. Again Singapore-based SIA Engineering Company announced the project of $390 million to set up an aircraft maintenance facility in India.[39]

Reflective of the growing interest of Singapore in India, MoUs for projects worth $130 million were signed between Indian and Singapore companies on 5 January 1995 on the eve of CII centenary function in Calcutta. This included a proposal to set up a 70 acre technology park in Gurgaon and an import terminal for petroleum products at Paradip.[40] MoUs included establishment of a project for manufacturing telecom equipment and other for a shrimp plant.[41]

Conclusion

We find that ASEAN states view India significant in economic terms ever since India chose the path of economic liberalization and market economy. As the ASEAN countries are booming and expanding their business,[42] and as it has already penetrated in Chinese and other neighbouring markets, it looks towards India with eagerness. On the other hand, India is favourably inclined and attaching prime importance to the ASEAN for cultivating ties. This convergence along with changing external environment is certainly creating conducive atmosphere to project India as a factor in the stability and development of Southeast Asia and vice versa.

Both India and Southeast Asia believe that they are essential for each other in neutralizing external threats, particularly to cope with the issues of democracy, human rights, environment and free trade. They have to evolve joint strategies to protect their long-term interests.

Most of the states in this region have a plural society and there is a quest for "unity in diversity". India pursues this principle but politicization throws its own challenges. There is a need to evolve regional response to attend them and promote integrationist trends.

India and the ASEAN states have many experiences to share. The ASEAN states attach prime importance to good governance, stability and efficiency in the polity of the nation. However, political developments of the past few years suggest that there is an increasing urge for more democratization. On the other hand, India has a liberal democracy where reforms are advocated to accelerate developmental problems. Though political problems in India and the ASEAN states differ, but both have many experiences to share and policies to emulate. However, from Indian viewpoints the most important is to learn business experiences from the ASEAN partners. The ASEAN perceive India as a gateway of trade expansion in South Asian region and India views ASEAN as a gateway of trade expansion in the Asia-Pacific. They have to strike a balance to accommodate interests of each other and prove useful and complementary to one another perpetually.

REFERENCES

1. "Look-East" Policy as defined by Foreign Minister Inder Kumar Gujral, is not an attempt to detach India from sub-region of South Asia or of looking away from the West. "What 'Look-East' really means that an outward looking India is gathering all forces of dynamism—domestic and regional and is directly focusing on establishing synergies with a fast consolidating and progressive neighbourhood to its East in the mother continent of Asia". For details see the statement by H.E. Mr. Inder Kumar Gujral at the meeting between ASEAN and its Dialogue Partners, Jakarta, 24 July 1996.
2. *Hindustan Times,* 14 March 1996. Also see, D. Banerjee, "Southeast Asia and India: Emerging Opportunities", *Strategic Analysis,* New Delhi, Vol. 17, No. 6, September 1994, pp. 703-16.
3. Jusuf Wanandi, "Confrontation on Human Rights", *Indonesian Quarterly,* Jakarta, Vol. 21, No. 3, 1994, p. 246.
4. T. Mulya Lubis, "Human Rights Standard Setting in Asia: Problems and Prospects", *Indonesian Quarterly,* Vol. 21, No. 1 (1994), p. 28 and also see A.J.M. Milne, *Human Rights and Human Diversity,* Albany State University of New York Press, 1986, p. 1.
5. Jusuf Wanandi, No. 3, p. 245; also see "Human Rights and Democracy in the ASEAN Nations: Next 25 Years", *Indonesian Quarterly,* Vol. 21, No. 1, 1994, pp. 14-24.
6. P.V. Narasimha Rao in a Banquet speech in Bangkok on 7 April 1993 and *Bangkok Post,* 8 April 1993.
7. *The Times of India,* New Delhi, 27 June 1992.
8. *Ibid.*
9. For analysis of this aspect, see Muchkund Dubey, *An Unequal Treaty: World Trading Order After GATT,* New Delhi, New Age International Limited, 1996, and V.R. Krishna Iyer and Others (eds.), *Report of People's Commission on GATT,* New Delhi, Centre for Study of Global Trade System and Development, 1996, and also see S.P. Gupta and Somsak Tambunlertchai, *The Asia-Pacific Economics: A Challenge to South Asia,* Delhi, Macmillan India Ltd., 1992.
10. *Hindustan Times,* 28 January 1992.
11. "If AFTA Drops the Ball Now, Protectionists Will Pick it Up", *Asiaweek,* 3 November 1993, pp. 21-22.
12. A.S. Abraham, "SAARC Summit" *The Times of India,* 29 April 1995.
13. *The Times of India,* 19 March 1993.
14. *Hindustan Times,* 9 September 1994.
15. *The Times of India,* 17 March 1993.
16. *Ibid.*

17. *The Times of India,* 18 March 1993.
18. *Ibid.*
19. Inder Kumar Gujral, India's Minister for External Affairs, has expounded his views that in order to have confidence building with Pakistan, retort and retaliation are counter-productive. We should give a patient hearing to Pakistan and search out avenues of cooperation.
20. *The Times of India,* 6 January 1995.
21. *The Times of India,* 1 July 1995.
22. *Ibid.*
23. "India, Singapore Plan Troika to Tap Developing Markets", *The Times of India,* 9 September 1994.
24. *The Times of India,* 25 February 1992.
25. S. Rajagopalan, "Economic Ties High on PM Agenda", *Hindustan Times,* 1 August 1995 and also see, Sujatha Singh, "India's Economic Reforms and Opportunities for Malaysian Businessmen", *Strategic Analysis,* New Delhi, Vol. 17, No. 1, April 1994, p. 52.
26. Jaishree Balasubramanian, "Upstarting in Trade with Malaysia", *The Times of India,* 6 May 1996.
27. *The Times of India,* 25 February 1992.
28. FICCI Symposium on "India: Full Dialogue Partner of ASEAN—New Business Opportunities", Background Paper, FICCI, New Delhi, 13 March 1996, pp. 1-17.
29. *Ibid.*
30. Saroj Mohanty, "India Thailand Plan Trade Triangle", *The Times of India,* 1 July 1995.
31. *Hindustan Times,* 3 August 1995.
32. *Hindustan Times,* 8 February 1995.
33. *The Times of India,* 14 February 1995.
34. G. Chandrasekhar, "India, Malaysia Sign Five MoUs", *The Times of India,* 4 August 1995.
35. *Ibid.*
36. *The Times of India,* 5 August 1995.
37. *The Times of India,* 3 September 1994.
38. *Hindustan Times,* 10 September 1994.
39. Nitya Chakaraborty, "Rao: India will Soon have Dialogues with APEC", *Hindustan Times,* 10 September 1994.
40. *The Times of India,* 6 January 1994.
41. *The Times of India,* 6 January 1995.
42. For this aspect see, M.C. Abad, Jr., "Re-engineering ASEAN", *Contemporary Southeast Asia,* Singapore, Vol. 18, No. 3, December 1996, pp. 237-53.

9

The Muslim Separatist Movement in Southern Thailand from an Indian Viewpoint

The behaviour of the Muslim minorities in South and Southeast Asia has been a sensitive issue in the twentieth century.[1] Whether they are living in democracy or dictatorship, they have proved themselves to be unhappy. Though the Muslims are in minority in Burma, Sri Lanka, Nepal, India, the Philippines and Thailand in the region (for comparative overview, see Table 10.1), their politics in the latter three countries are subjects of concern. The political masters of all the three countries generally prefer to remain silent on critical issues related to them. The Muslim minorities are considered to be "vote banks" in India and therefore the ruling elites are ready to admire and offer them all possible facilities with a view to attracting their votes. Their deep interest in Islamic resurgence are generally overlooked. Their opposition to family planning perpetuates economic backwardness. But all these issues are left for the individuals to raise and debate. The national political parties in India don't touch any critical aspect related to Muslims because this may be good enough for the opposition to label them anti-Muslim. The Philippine Government, on the other hand, has pursued an aggressive policy to subdue the Muslim minority. It has invited the leaders of rebel groups of Muslims to come and negotiate and at the same time indulged in military action on a massive scale. In Mindanao and Sulu archipelago, where the Muslims were in majority in the past, there have been demographic transformations. The Christian population from other overpopulated islands have migrated into the archipelago and have been successful in reducing the numerical majority of the Muslims. Imelda Marcos, the wife of the former Philippine President shuttled from Libya to Egypt to find a negotiated settlement without accepting the major demands of the rebels. Contrary to India and the Philippines, the government in Thailand offered a somewhat different example. Here there are some groups of Muslims in Bangkok who have accepted reforms in their faith but the majority of them in the South are non-assimilative. The Malay Muslims are very conscious of their separate identity and history and the politics of those Muslims is treated as a threat to the security of Thailand.

Table 10.1: South and Southeast Asia: The Position of Muslim Minorities

Country	Total Population	Majority Community	The Muslim Minorities
1. Burma	28.89 million	Buddhists	Muslims
2. India	453.2 million	Hindus 82.7%	Muslims 61.4%
3. Nepal	11.7 million	Hindus 92%	Muslims 2.97%
4. Philippines	43.94 million	Catholics (31,169,488)	Muslims (1,584,963) 10%
5. Sri Lanka	12,711,143	Buddhists (8,567,570)	Muslims (909,941) 4%
6. Thailand	39,950,306	Buddhists 94 %	Muslims 4 %

Source: *The Statesman Yearbook*, London, Macmillan Press, 1977-78, but for Nepal, see Marc Gaborieau, "Muslims in the Hindu Kingdom of Nepal", in T.N. Madan (ed.), *Muslim Communities of South Asia: Culture and Society*, New Delhi, 1976, pp. 86-87.

A comparative study indicates a difference in the political attitudes of the government of India, the Philippines and Thailand *vis-à-vis* their Muslim minorities and in the same way the intensity and volume of the activities of the Muslim minorities in all the three countries also differ from one another. Though all the three countries are opposed to the militant activities of Muslim rebels, they are unable to contain them. It is in this sphere that some experts may find the role of these minorities as a set of elements standing in interaction. But such an opinion may be no more true than the "domino theory" in the context of Vietnam. Many factors are responsible for the restlessness of the Muslim minorities. Briefly, the problem has been on account of their social outlook, political behaviour, historical reminiscences, economic backwardness and illiteracy. The rise of Islamic fundamentalism in recent years and the support and sympathy of some Muslim countries to sustain Islamic movements in Thailand and the Philippines are certain factors which have aggravated the militancy of the Muslims in those countries. Besides this, the failure on the part of the government to transform the socio-political outlook of the minorities is a major factor for unrest.

In this Chapter, an attempt will be made to analyse from an Indian viewpoint the phenomenon of Muslim separatist movement in Thailand and its impact on the behaviour of Muslim minorities in the region.

At present, there are about two million Muslims in Thailand.[2] About four-fifths of Thailand's Muslims are Malays living in South Thailand. The smallest region, with a total land area of 72,961 square kilometres in four peninsular provinces, South Thailand contains somewhat less than 14 per cent of the country's area and about 12.3 per cent of the total population of Thailand.[3] This is the only area in Thailand where there is a large reservoir of tin and has over 90 per cent of the country's natural rubber. Besides this, rice, coconut, rambutan and durian are also produced.

The southern region in which the majority of the people are Muslims is divided into four provinces popularly known as *chaidaen paak tai*. These provinces are Pattani, Yala, Narathiwat and Satun and have a combined land area of 14,00,97 square kilometres or 19.1 per cent of the total land area of southern Thailand. The total population of these four provinces is 1,212,673 out of which 909,500 or 75 per cent are Muslims.[4] Most of these Muslims earn their livelihood through some combination of rice farming and coconut growing (This region grows two-thirds of the country's coconut palms). They also grow rubber, palm oil and remain involved in fishing, mining, forestry and cattle raising.

The pattern of society in the four southern provinces is such that the Muslims feel alienated from the Thai mainstream. They are separately situated, away from Buddhist settlements. The Buddhists and the Chinese population in this area are mainly situated in the cities, whereas the Muslims are situated in the countryside. They are mainly farmers and labourers. Their history, language, and culture are different from those of the Thai Buddhists, but match closely to those of the Malays situated across the border in the peninsular Malaysia. Their social activities, till recently, were confined to a visit to the mosque and the Islamic schools known as *Pawno* or *Pondok*.[5] Study of Islam, Malay and Arabic offered by the *Pondok* takes precedence over secular education which is run by the government schools.

The Thai Kingdom, where about 93 per cent of the population is Buddhist, has not proved sufficiently sympathetic towards the religious and linguistic differences of the Muslims in the south. Muslims are intensely interested in retaining the essence of their traditional culture and fear that the Thai government is trying to assimilate them by changing their local customs, institutions, language and religion.[6] Such a fear which is propagated by Muslim fanatics, fundamentalists and often by international Islamic associations which have driven people of the area to start a war of national liberation. In 1969 the Muslims of the four southern provinces established "Barisan Nasional Pembebsan Republik Pattani" (BNPRP), also known as National Liberation Front of the Pattani Republic (NLFPR) in order to establish an Islamic State. This organization was at first headed by Hajji Yusuf al-Tamani, a teacher of Islamic religion.[7] Again under the supervision of Tengku Abdul Jalal, the BNPRP organised "Tentera National Pembebsan Rak'yet Patani" (TNPRP) or National Liberation Army of the Pattani People. Their emblem bears an imprint of moon, stars and the words TNPRP. This TNPRP has a guerilla army and the membership of trained men who are devoted to founding an independent state of Pattani. Generally, the people from *Chaidaen paak tai* are recruited in NLF but if other Muslims are willing to join it, they are welcome.[8] BNPRP is not only flexing its armed muscle but taking other militant steps too to keep alive its existence. Pattani Liberation Front (PLF) has been making press statements and distributing messages and newsletters in the villages. It has tried to indoctrinate the inhabitants with a great spirit of nationalism and urges hostility against Thai rule.

The guerillas of PLF have made their presence felt in the Pesisir Gunong Budo Hill area in the tri-border region of Yala, Narathiwat and Pattani. PLF occasionally conducts ambushes and attacks police installations to obtain weapons and sometimes uses terrorism to remind both the government and the people of the area of their potential. The routine operations of the PLF are confined to extortion, conducting road blocks, kidnapping for ransom and closing the rubber plantations in order to get money for further strengthening of the organisation.[9]

Bapa Idris (Father Idris) is the supreme commander of BNPRP. He is a respected leader of the south, who has taken shelter in the forests to continue his activities to establish a separate Islamic State of Pattani. He does not want to accept negotiations with the government. Some of his predecessors who wanted to talk to the Central Government of Thailand were killed in this process. Haji Sulong, along with his son and some of his followers were suppressed, discouraged and eliminated in this endeavour.

Bapa Idris holds the view that the struggle to free Pattani cannot be achieved by throwing flowers but by flying bullets.[10] Bapa Idris is one of the men most hunted by the Central government. There is a huge reward of money on his head.[11]

The predecessors of Bapa Idris explored negotiated means to solve the problems in the south. Haji Sulong (Abdal-Qadir) meticulously formulated a charter of seven demands and met the central ministers in April 1947.[12] Though the Prime Minister was sympathetic to his demands, he was powerless to do anything as there was political instability in the politics of Thailand during the period, 1945-48. As Haji Sulong championed the cause of secession, he had become increasingly unacceptable to the central government. He was arrested and subsequently killed in 1954.[13] His death caused serious loss to both sides. His elimination was mourned by many people and this event took secessionist movement to a point of no-return. Haji Sulong became a martyr for the secessionists. But they have also taken revenge on the government forces in many ways. They have killed many officials and police personnel. The rebels have killed even the private secretary of the Queen of Thailand, who was on a goodwill mission to that area.

There is a striking similarity in the insurgency activities of the Muslims of South Thailand and that of southern Philippines. They are also engaged in a secessionist movement and have founded "Moro National Liberation Front" (MNLF), under the leadership of Nurulhadji Misuari to establish Bangsa Moro Islamic Region. MNLF has a Bangsa Moro Army (BMA) equipped with American made M-16s, Belgian G-2s and small rockets.[14] BMA has 30,000 men trained in guerilla warfare.[15] MNLF is the spokesman of the Muslims of the thirteen provinces[16] of the southern Philippines rich in natural resources, i.e. iron-ore, gold, palm oil, plywood and other minerals. There is a prospect of large reservoir of oil near Palawan and a big scope for enhancing the fishing industry in the area.

Like southern Thailand, there is a geographical homogeneity in the location of 13 Muslim provinces in the Philippines. However, the government has opposed the contention that the Muslims are in majority in all the 13 southern provinces. According to an estimate, the Muslims are in a majority in only five provinces of the southern Philippines, viz. Basilan, Lanao del Sur, Maguindanao, Sulu and Tawi Tawi.[17] There is the absence of geographical homogeneity and therefore, the question of autonomy for those provinces does not arise. Moreover, a plebiscite held in April 1977 under the supervision of the government rejected the demand for autonomy in the south. In this plebiscite, about 75 per cent of the 4,025,000 registered voters had used their franchise. Out of 6,500,000 registered Muslim voters in the 13 provinces, about 3,000,000 had exercised their votes and the outcome was the rejection of the demand for autonomy.[18]

Here it is pertinent to point out that Indian Muslims, though forming the world's third largest Muslim population (according to 1971 census 61.4 million), have not opted for any secessionist movement in the recent past. Though their living conditions are not far better in comparison with their counterparts in Thailand and the Philippines, they have so far adopted only peaceful means. Their socio-economic conditions are not satisfactory and they want improvements. But the democratic polity of India has proved a safety valve to understand their viewpoints. Some Muslims in India stayed back despite a large scale migration of their co-religionists to Pakistan. They are not concentrated in one area, except Kashmir. The Muslims under M.A. Jinnah were successful in partitioning the country in August 1947. They wanted to have a separate homeland, and the colonial masters favoured them. But the present situation is different. They might be in search of a climate to establish another Pakistan, but the geo-political factors are against it. Indian Muslims are gradually being politicised, but there has been little success. A person of the rank of Syed Abdullah Bukhari, Shahi Imam of Jama Masjid, Delhi, whose forefathers have been traditionally Shahi Imam since the days of Mughal dynasty, has sometimes taken interest in the cause of the rise of radical Islam, but he wants to confine himself to constitutional limits only. His appeal amongst the Muslims are also limited. The leading organisation to instigate militancy is Al Qaida inspired Mujahideen to radicalise Muslim minds.

Though the economic situation of Indian Muslims is poor, they remain antipathetic towards reform in their socio-political outlook. The academic institutions to teach Islamic religion and civilization like Madrasah, Darul Uloom of Deoband, Darul Uloom of Nahdlatul Ulama are still functioning in India in the same way as it was doing in the colonial past but their attitudes are changing now.

Roots of Discord

Thus it is a serious concern of social scientists to study the problem of Muslim minorities in Thailand to pinpoint the various factors responsible for espousing the separatist movement. In order to have a proper understanding of the separatist movement in Thailand it is necessary to go back in history and trace the developments that prevented the Muslims from joining the national mainstream.

Islam came to Southeast Asia in the mediaeval period and Pattani, Brunei, Java, Malacca, Sumatra and Malaya became some of the important centres of Muslim culture and civilization.[20] Pattani kingdom had jurisdiction over a large territory now under Thailand and Malaysia. The Kingdom of Pattani, though very resourceful, was not more powerful than the Kingdom of Thailand. Pattani which comprising Kelantan, Yala and Narathiwat in the south, Perak and Kedah in the west and Gulf of Thailand in the east, was not always on friendly terms with the Buddhist rulers of Thailand.[21] These two kingdoms engaged in fierce battles on numerous occasions. On several occasions Thai rulers subdued the rulers of Pattani, though sometimes they could not. The Sultan of Pattani sent tributes or *Bunga Mus* (Golden Flowers) to the King of Thailand, but on occasions they sent tributes to any ruler in the area who mattered in the spread of Islam.

Pattani's separate existence came to an end in 1801 but this did not fully undermine the influence of Sultan. The Britishers had come into the area and they were interested in the areas controlled by the Sultanate of Pattani. They applied pressure against Thailand and hence in 1909, the Anglo-Siamese treaty was signed. Thailand ceded its jurisdiction over Kedah, Perlis, Kelantan and Trengganu to Britain. This area, later known as the Unfederated Malay States, had no problem at all in joining with other Muslim-dominated areas. Pattani was left in Thailand whose culture and civilization was different when the four states were merged with British Malaya, Pattani's rulers felt unhappy. The division of Pattani divided the Muslim nationalist movement in the area. This partition was more or less like the partition of Bengal in British India in 1905, a calculated move to bring divisions among the leaders of the national movement.

The people and the ruler of Pattani did not sit idle on the eve of the British merger of the Unfederated Malay States. Pattani petitioned London to be placed under the British along with the unfederated Malay States.[22] Britain declined to accept such a request. British refusal to place Pattani under its rule might have been prompted to avoid tackling a strong sense of nationalism of the people of Pattani. Again, the impact of the adverse reports against it by the British residents of Bangkok, and rational policy under the supervision of British advisors of the King of Thailand might have been a factor in the rejection of Pattani's requests.

Pattani's political influence was doomed after its partition in 1909. The people in Pattani had no option but to compromise with Buddhist counterparts which they abhorred. Thus, Pattani and other Muslim-dominated areas left in Thailand adopted a common strategy to boycott Thai administration. They refused to attend national schools and preferred to study only at *Pondok*. They opposed any move towards national integration and over the years isolated themselves with the rest of the country. Barbara Whittington-Jones visited Pattani in 1947 and gave an account of the isolation of those people. The report revealed that despite more than half century of persecution and neglect, Thai rule had failed to de-nationalise the people of Pattani and nothing impressed her more than the tenacity with which they preserved their old traditions. Whittington-Jones further reported:

> As the Malays refuse to send their children to Siamese schools and have so far stubbornly refused to acquire even a rudimentary knowledge of the Siamese language (during the whole of my visit I found only one Haji, a former district officer, able to read and write Siamese), this educational starvation is retarding their entire social and economic development.[23]

The Muslims in India have more or less the same dilemma. History is testimony to the fact that they ruled over India in the mediaeval period for more than 600 years. The history of Islam indicates that whichever country they ruled, they converted the people into Islam to such an extent that they became the majority people. Indian experience however, remained an exception, where 25 per cent of the people were of Islamic faith in pre-partition India. Hindus remained in majority and thus their mission to make India Daarul Islam failed. Though India was a centre of Islamic culture and civilization and was instrumental in spreading Islam in some Southeast Asian countries, it could not be converted *en masse*. The Britishers became the colonial masters in the 18th century and provided a great relief to the Hindu community which was facing threats to its religion and way of living by the Islamic institutions.

In the beginning of 20th century it looked possible that India would become independent. This made the Muslims scared because they thought that the Hindus being a majority community would subjugate and oppress the Muslim community with a vengeance. At the same time they had not forgotten their design to rule India and therefore, under the leadership of Aga Khan, the Nawab of Dacca, founded All-India Muslim League in 1906. Muslim League was quite communal in approach and initially it seemed that it could not assume a national role for that community. But it soon rose into prominence. Indian National Congress which was nationalist by all means, was systematically opposed by the Muslim League. Though some illustrious Muslims of India, Khan Abdul Gaffar Khan, Maulana Abul Kalam Azad and Rafi Ahmad Kidwai were with the Indian National Congress, the majority of the Muslims were in the Muslim League.

The Muslim League under the stewardship of Rahmat Ali, Shoukat Ali, Iqbal and Muhammad Ali Jinnah, subsequently pursued a separatist policy and propagated that Hindus were the real enemies of the Muslims. Hindus and Muslims were entirely two different nationalities which could not work in unison. Their sentiments have been summed up by F.K. Khan Durrani in the following words:

> There is not an inch of the soil in India which our fathers did not once purchase with their blood. We cannot be false to the blood of our fathers. India, the whole of it, is therefore our heritage and it must be reconquered for Islam. Expansion in the spiritual sense is an inherent necessity of our faith and implied no hatred or enmity towards the Hindus. Rather the reverse, our ultimate ideal must be the unification of India, spiritually as well as politically under the banner of Islam. The final political salvation of India is not otherwise possible.[24]

Muhammad Ali Jinnah was thus prompted to propound "two-nation theory", to create a separate homeland for Indian Muslims. Subsequently the Lahore Resolution of 1940 was passed at the Annual Conference of the League for the division of India.[25] It said that all the Muslim-majority provinces of

British India should be united to comprise a separate nation for Muslims.

The Muslim League supported British war efforts during the Second World War but Indian National Congress wanted to bargain for its support. Winston Churchill, the British Prime Minister, was unwilling to concede anything to India which might adversely affect British morale. The Congress leaders, therefore, were persecuted and jailed for intensifying their demands for independence at that crucial period of Second World War. Taking advantage of the British mood, the Muslim League started a vicious propaganda to instigate communal riots which continued till Earl Mountbatten announced his plan for India's independence; when the Mountbatten Plan was being discussed, Muslim communalism also climaxed and thus vitiated the political atmosphere and communal harmony. The Mountbatten Plan envisaged partition of India into two parts and the granting of independence to both. The communal conflict and rioting were the immediate reasons for the leaders of the Congress to accept the partition proposal of Mountbatten. They had a simplistic notion that in case the Muslims in India would get homeland for themselves, there would be no further rioting. Thus Pakistan came into existence. The partition of India resulted in more bloodshed. About 12 million people were made refugees.[26] Many thousands of people died in the communal riots and there was an upheaval on the subcontinent.

After the partition, many Muslims stayed back in India and the government offered them the equal status *vis-à-vis* Hindus (comprising 82% of the total population). Constitutionally and practically, the Muslims were given similar privileges. Two Presidents of India were elected from the Muslim community, i.e. Zakir Hussein and Fakhruddin Ali Ahmad before 1975. The government is secular but it is very difficult to understand the minds of certain educated Muslims. They are groping in history for the grandeur which they represented while reigning in India in the mediaeval period. A searching analysis of the mind and attitudes of the Muslims in India suggests that their general outlook have yet to change to develop a common outlook towards the nation.

Again, there are some *Ulama* and *Imams*, who in order to champion the causes of their religion go so far as to be frowned upon. Even some academic institutions in India have been sectarian in approach. Aligarh Muslim University (AMU) is one of the traditional institutions of higher studies for Muslims in India. The management of the University still holds Muhammad Ali Jinnah in higher esteem than Mahatma Gandhi.

There are some Muslim intellectuals in India who are in favour of Islamic reformism, but they are branded by others as spies of Hindus. Irfan Habib, Professor in history, AMU, has been punished because the latter was advocating theories in support of secular living in India. Hamid Dalwai is another Muslim social worker from Maharashtra, who argued bonds of friendship between the two communities and bring reforms in the outlook to the orthodox elements in his community. His activities were limited to certain areas of Maharashtra. His actions were disliked by *ulamas*. The associations such as Jamaat-e-Islam and its student wing, Jamiate Tulaba were critical of Irfan Habib and Hamid Dalwai. The government is helpless as they consider interfering in matters pertaining to Indian minorities so delicate that they are unable even to delete the word "Muslim" from the Aligarh Muslim University under the impression that it would offend the sentiments of Indian Muslims. The intellectuals were in favour of erasing the word "Muslim" from that University to give the institution a secular outlook as a prelude to removing the word "Hindu" from Banaras Hindu University.

However, the government of Thailand has been consistently strict towards Muslim minorities. The military rulers, i.e. Field Marshal Phibun Songgram, Sarit Thanarat, Thanom Kittikachorm, and others have followed a policy of suppression and oppression *vis-à-vis* the Muslims in the South. They had no sympathy for these groups and they have adopted harsh measures to contain them.

Movement Divided

The Muslims in *Chaidaen paak tai* are mostly inhabitating the rural areas and their houses are situated far away from the abode of the Buddhists. The usual venue of their social congregation is the *Pondok* or the mosque. The majority of them are ignorant of Thai language and their preferred language is Bahasa Malay. They do not like their children to go to the government schools but to *Pondok,* where they study subjects like Quranic exegesis, the science of the prophetic tradition, Islamic jurisprudence and theology. The Muslim children are taught how to offer *Namaaz* five times a day and how to prove himself a noble Muslim. They also teach Malay language and the history of Pattani. They are unwilling to include any chapter about the Buddhists in Thailand and how to adopt "Thai way of life". Such an education at the primary stage have caused a conservative outlook. They imbibe a political culture which is dragging them into perpetual trouble with their government. This rift has gradually widened to the point of no return.

The Muslim rebels in the south are divided into several groups. According to Astri Suhrke, the various rebel groups could be divided into four parts, i.e. ordinary bandits, Thai terrorists, Malayan People's Liberation Army, and lastly Muslim separatists.[27] They, however, have also been classified by Nantawan Haemindra into three groups. The first favours a separate administrative unit within a federation with Thailand. The second group wants an independent state under a Sultan, and the third advocates a single independent state of Pattani.[28] The first group was popular among the older generation of the people of *chaidaen paak tai,* whereas the second and the third groups are popular among the younger generation. The majority of the people are in the third group which has founded PLF. But unlike MNLF of the Philippines, PLF has no regular army, though they have trained several groups of people for guerilla warfare.

Following the death of Tungku Yala Nasae, the grandson of the former Pattani Sultan, Tungku Abdul Kader, the strength of RNPRP has fallen steadily and a new separatist group known as "Pattani United Liberation Organisation" (PULO) has come into existence. PULO is divided into units of less than 10 persons to infiltrate, strike at civilian targets near the border and retreat into hideouts in forests to Malaysia. In 1981, the guerillas of PULO killed 26 Thai Buddhists in Betong and Bunnang Satta district.[29] The Muslim separatists have been wearing jungle fatigues and using tinned rations and equipment similar to those used by Malaysian forces. According to Paisal Sricharatchanya, PULO is led by Samaeh Thanan and has 550 armed men.[30] Another rebel group operating in South Thailand is the guerillas of CPM (Communist Party of Malaysia) whose overall strength is about 2000 (of whom 200 are in Sadao, 650 in Yala-Betong highway and 450-500 in Waeng districts).[31]

The insurgents have, by and large, three important means of income. First and most important is the generous financial aid of the Islamic countries.[32] Libya, Syria, Egypt and Saudi Arabia are some who have clandestinely and otherwise aided the insurgent groups in Thailand and the Philippines. Thai authorities have found some evidences of collusion between PULO guerillas and Malaysia. In the course of hot pursuit inside Malaysia, Thai authorities found PULO camps where there were propaganda materials and several empty cartridges. Thai authorities have also found a letter at Narathiwat written by Liaison Office in Kelantan asking the youth of the area to join at a camp at Pesir Mas (Malaysia) for guerilla training.[33]

Again, in mid-1980 in course of a battle against PULO forces near Budo Hills, some letters were found written in Bahasa Malay, sent from PULO Liaison Office, Damascus. It revealed that a group of recruits had already been trained and were on route to reach Pattani.[34] According to the information posted at Songkhla, there are several countries in the Middle east aiding and abetting the Thai Muslim rebels. In the past decade, these aids are estimated to have been 200 million (US $8.7 million).[35]

The second important source of income are through the sale and supply of narcotics. Thai rebels are involved in the smuggling of opium across the borders. The rebels get it from the Golden Triangle and send it to Australia, Asia and Western Europe. The couriers pay about 160,000 Baht (US $6,900 for one 700 grams of consignment of high grade heroin in Bangkok and sell it at the Thai border for about Baht 200,000 to Malay couriers, who get about Baht 260,000 in Kuala Lumpur.[36]

The third source of rebel fund is through ransom and voluntary contributions.

Legal Status of the Thai Muslims

Legally, the Thai Muslims have the same rights and freedoms as ethnic Thais. The Royal Act of 1947 on Islam gives recognition to the status of mosque officials, viz. the *Imam*, the *Khatib*, and the *Muezzin*. The Royal Decree on Patronage of the Religion of Islam also provides for the appointment by the King, of an important person with good education in Islamic religion, (who is elected by the Chairman of the provincial councils for Islamic Affairs) to serve as *chularajmontri*. The *chularajmontri* is to give advice to the Religious Affairs Department of the Ministry of Education in the matters concerning Islamic religion and activities and ceremonies connected with Islam. The Royal Act of 1946 had also provided for the application of Islamic laws in the four southern provinces.[37]

A perusal of the constitutional status of the Muslim minorities suggest that the Thais have provided them not less than others. In Nepal there are many restrictions on the activities of the Muslims.[38] In Sri Lanka, the Muslims, comprising six and half per cent of the total population, are conscious to prove that they are not the sub-caste of either the Sinhalese or the Tamils. Their main political organization, the Muslim League, is canvassing support to receive concessions from the majority groups in accordance with their numbers.[39] Burma has suppressed the Muslim minorities in the region of Arakan and has forced a sizable section of Rohingyas to go out of the country. The Muslims in the Philippines are not discriminated against by the law of the land, but there are some practical issues which have worked against them. In India, the Constitution and the politics have not given them any solid ground to be militant. However, the fanatic elements are rising.

The State religion of Thailand is Buddhism and the Buddhist religion is a factor in Thai politics. Though His Majesty, the King, often offers generous help for people having faith in Islam, yet the very socialisation of the Thai people is towards Buddhism.

Government's Help to *Chaidaen paak tai*

In the last decade, the government has accelerated the pace of development in the south. It is trying to improve the communication networks, and thus national highways and roads have been constructed to link the various southern districts. Provision for electricity and drinking water has been made. Some health centres have been introduced and mobile medical units have been established.[40] Recently the King initiated the establishment of thirteen irrigation projects at Narathiwat, including a 275 million Baht project to irrigate about 42,000 acres of farmland.[41] They want to do everything to raise the agricultural output and for that they want to give all sorts of help. Thai administration has even decided to erect a large mosque in Pattani at an estimated cost of US $200,000.[42] In order to bridge the communication gap between the two communities, training centres have been set up at Chulalongkorn University, Bangkok; and Songkhla University, Pattani; with emphasis on the study of Malay language and the Muslim culture.

Bureaucratic Loopholes

The behaviour of the Thai bureaucrats, who are responsible for development and nation-building has been targeted to be unjust in Pattani areas. The administrators deputed in the Muslim provinces in the south are generally ignorant of the local language, culture and customs, and as they are transferred to other provinces every three years, they care even less to know much about them.[43] The appointment of a Muslim to a high ranking position in the bureaucracy is never happily welcomed by the Thais unless the incumbent conceals all his identities and, better still, incorporates Thai identities.[44] Arong Suthasasna says that even in universities, it is necessary to have Thai names to receive the award of graduate degrees. Again the officers working at *chaidaen paak tai* are faced with a dilemma. This is very well summed up in the following words:

> Most of these officials are extremely careful of their performances and daily behaviours, otherwise they can become the victims of the official suspicion very easily. They are in a very difficult position with regard to human relation. If they are too close to the people, Muslims, they are suspected by their fellow Buddhist officials. Should this happen, their careers are in great jeopardy. By contrast, if they are close to the Thai officials, and identify

> themselves accordingly, they will be contempted by their fellow Muslims with the charge of being Buddhist oriented. This also makes life extremely difficult (sic).[45]

Such a situation has so far doomed the political settlement between the government and the secessionist forces. There may be some *ulama* seeking to bring rapprochement but they have no suitable climate to try their luck. They can assemble at the mosques only on Fridays and in many cases the Imams are accompanied by spies of both sides.[46] Thus all the efforts go in vain.

Again a policy of thc government to balance the population and culture in South Thailand has alarmed the Muslims. This policy has been practised under the programme: "Self-help Land Settlement Project", since the days of Field Marshal Sarit Thanarat. Under this scheme a number of people from the north and northeast are being encouraged to migrate to four southern provinces under the protection of the government forces. They are armed by the government forces. These migrants are generously given land and land titles, and financial and technical aids. The secessionists fear that this process will submerge the Malay population and make even the *chaidaen paak tai* a Thai majority area.[47]

In 1981, the Government of Thailand introduced a special centre to supervise the administration of *chaidaen paak tai.* Besides Border Patrol Police (BPP), there is a Special Terrorist Cell for the southern region known as the "Special Suppression Unit", to subdue the PLF, PULO, or BRN guerillas. On occasions, the military have also swung into action along with the suppression units to crush the rebels. In 1974, for example, a special war unit from Neresuen military camp, Lopburi, was in action for a brief period.[48]

In July 1980, it was felt that the existing police forces were not sufficient to tackle efficiently thc militancy of the rebels. Thus a 400-strong police task force was formed to tackle them.[49] These are certain measures which are unpopular with the people in Pattani.

Future Outlook

The secessionists may have great and pious ambitions but they suffer from certain weaknesses. First, is demographic, as they comprise less than four per cent of the total population of Thailand. Secondly, their armed forces are too ill-equipped to face the growing strength of the government. Thirdly, they are not a monolithic group but are divided into several groups each under separate leadership. Some of them are the surrogates of the different Islamic countries of the Middle-East. Fourthly, their influence has been diluted after some of them decided to attempt a liaison with the Communist Party of Thailand (CPT). Finally, they are unable to get the open support of Malaysia, because the latter is the partner of Thailand in a regional grouping, known as ASEAN (Association of Southeast Asian Nations). As Malaysia is the only country to border *chaidaen paak tai,* its open support is important for the success of the secessionists.

The territories in *chaidaen paak tai* are contiguous to Songkhla located in the middle of Pattani and Satun. Songkhla is a Buddhist majority area and the influence of the rebels in Satun have fallen in recent years. The focus of the government in recent years had been to demolish the root cause of insurgency in the south and with that objective in mind there has been demographic changes. It may be predicted that the majority status of the Muslims in *chaidaen paak tai* will not remain the same in future.

Since the end of absolute monarchy in Thailand, there has been greater drive to bring the national minorities to adopt "Thai way of life". Under Field Marshal Phibun Songgram, the government followed a policy of *Rattangiyom* (nationalism). Accordingly a Thai national was expected to pay respects to three institutions, i.e. *chart, sasna* and *pramahakasastra* (nation, religion and monarchy respectively) in Thailand. Allegiance towards these institutions is demanded even today. Whether a person belongs to Chinese or Muslim descend, they are expected to show their devotion to these three institutions. These three institutions are symbolised by three colours of the national flag. Here one must be clear to the fact that the meaning of *sasna* (religion) is not Christianity or Islam. The meaning of the word *sasna* in the context of Thailand is Buddhism. Such a notion is not congenial to harmonious living in a plural society. Islam itself is very proud of its culture and history and opposed to assimilation.

The outlook of the Muslims is being criticised as modernist approach is not favoured. The government has supported the reformist missions and the immigrant Muslims from China, India and Pakistan are increasingly adopting Thai way of life. But, the Muslims of the *chaidaen paak tai* are not ready to do anything to change their traditional outlook.[50] Such an attitude may be disturbing and hence conflict resolution is difficult.

The politics of the subcontinent has really proved a morale booster for the Muslim rebels in the region. The Muslims of India wanted a homeland for themselves on the basis of their religion. The Indian subcontinent was divided on the basis of religion before independence. The Muslim majority areas on the eastern and western flanks of India were given to create Pakistan. Both parts of Pakistan could not stay together for long. Within two decades of their existence, there was a split and Pakistan too was divided into two parts and thus Bangladesh came into existence.

There is another interesting aspect of the separatist movement in Southeast Asia. Here the Islamic rebels in particular, are aided and abetted by some Islamic countries of the Middle east. The general public attitude to such type of assistance is not favourable. If their money is used towards subversion, the donors are hated by the concerned governments as well as the public.

It is also clear that the intensity of the threat posed by the separatists to the Government of Thailand is not serious enough to threaten the sovereignty of the country. Therefore, the complicity of the Islamic countries in these movements are worthless. At present neither the rebels nor the government are in a mood to compromise but sooner or later the rebels will have to moderate their viewpoints to live and let live option.

The Malay Muslims in Thailand are continuing to be very conscious of their separate cultural identity. The basis of their separatism is their distinctiveness as a separate cultural group. They can make an effort for assimilation with the Thais, if the latter can make it possible for them to feel social security. It is a historical fact that the people of Pattani did not embrace Thai integration of their own will. It was imposed over them after their military defeat by the Kings of Thailand. Now in order to have a common national outlook, the conditions should be created by the government so that the latter may feel com-fortable. Again, their economic conditions must be improved. Should this happen, their militant postures might change. If they prosper economically, their political behaviour will certainly change for the better. Their economic development might clear the path for assimilation like their Chinese counterparts. However, the present balance is "terror versus terror", and this may not lead towards understanding and peace.

The developing countries have to understand some cues from the United States of America. Being a plural society, the U.S. had some highly conscious cultural groups, i.e. American Indians, Chicanos and American blacks. Their overall outlook has been changing over the years and none of them oppose American nationalism. Again Tamils and Bengalis in India were very proud of their distinct culture and civilisation. Their association in India was not thought to be permanent by some in the past, but they are important components of the Indian Union. However, if the Indian Government would demand a change in their regional dress, cuisine, language and culture, the outcome of the same may be disastrous.

Thailand wants solution of the problem in *chaidaen paak tai*. But it is pertinent to examine who will be the *via media* to bring rapprochement? When and how their negotiations will start? What will be the basic principles to govern the basis of their negotiation? Who will be there to enforce the terms and conditions of the negotiations? What will be the future of cultural distinctiveness of the Malay Muslims in Thailand? To what extent, the Thais will come down to adjust the demands of the insurgents? And what will be the impact of compromise on the minds of the Muslim minorities in other parts of Southeast Asia? These are certain questions to be probed in future.

REFERENCES

1. I have surveyed mostly the materials in English language and have not visited the four Muslim provinces of South Thailand. I

have interviewed some Muslim leaders of Thailand such as Nai Direk Kulsiriswasd Ibrahim Qureyshi and some others. I am grateful to Dr. Andrew D.W. Forbes, Department of Religious Studies, University of Aberdeen, Great Britain, for taking keen interest in my writing.

2. *Thai Muslims*, 1979, Bangkok, Ministry of Foreign Affairs, p. 2. But according to Bapa Idris, the head of Pattani Liberation Front, there are three million Muslims in southern Thailand alone. See Press Release of RNPRP, *Suara Siswa*, Kuala Lumpur, Vol. 2, No. 2, December 1970, p. 57.
3. According to a rough estimate in 1977, South Thailand had a population of 5,444,000. See *Thai Muslims, ibid.*, pp. 6-7.
4. *Ibid.* According to Nantawan Haemindra, the Muslims constitute 78 per cent of the total population of Pattani, 61 per cent of the total population of Yala, 78 per cent of the total population of Narathiwat and 83 per cent of the total population of Satun. Nantawan Haemindra, "The Problem of Thai Muslims in the Four Southern Provinces of Thailand (Part One)", *Journal of Southeast Asian Studies*, Singapore, Vol. VII, No. 2, September 1976, p. 198.
5. *Pawno* or *Pondok* are important institutions in teaching Islamic civilisation and religion. A *Pondok* is an Islamic school and its counterpart in India is known as *Madrasah*. In *chaidaen paak tai* there are 512 pawnos of which 335 are in Pattani, 83 in Yala, 16 in Satun and 78 in Narathiwat. See Police Colonel Ganpanat Chintavirot, *Notes on the Separatist Movement in the South*, Bangkok, 1974. Also see Nantawan Haemindra, No. 4.
6. For analysis of the politics of Thai Muslims, see, Astri Suhrke, "The Thai Muslim Case", *Comparative Politics*, Vol. 7, No. 2, January 1975, pp. 187-204, and also see, Ganganath Jha, "Muslim Minorities in the Philippines and Thailand", *India Quarterly*, New Delhi, Vol. 34, No. 3, July-September 1978, pp. 328-46.
7. *Suara Siswa*, Kuala Lumpur, December 1970, p. 54. Also see Dennis Walker, "Conflict Between the Thai and Islamic Cultures in Southern Thailand, 1948-1970", *Studies in Islam*, New Delhi, Vol. 9, Nos. 3 and 4, 1972, p. 136.
8. TNPRP is divided into several groups of 10 to 25 men, each under different leaders. For a study of their activities, see Nantawan Haemindra, "The Problem of Thai Muslims in the Four Southern Provinces of Thailand (Part Two)", *Journal of Southeast Asian Studies*, Singapore, Vol. 8, No. 1, March 1977, pp. 85-115.
9. *Thai Muslims*, Bangkok, Ministry of Foreign Affairs, 1979, p. 10.

10. *Suara Siswa*, No. 2, p. 57.
11. Dennis Walker, No. 7, p. 136.
12. On 3 April 1947, Haji Sulong along with a few Muslim leaders of the South presented a charter of demands which remains relevant even now. These demands included restructuring the bureaucratic and constitutional provisions of the Thai Government *vis-à-vis* the Muslim community, i.e. the recognition of Bahasa Malay as lingua franca of the south, the transformation of the bureaucratic set-up, the appointment of 80 per cent local people in the administration of the south, the recognition of Muslim laws and establishment of Muslim court, etc. See *Suara Siswa*, No. 2, pp. 15-16.
13. Arong Suthasasna, "Thai Political Authority and Muslim Ethnic Group", A paper presented in Thai International Seminar held in New Delhi, 24-27 February 1981, p. 7, and *Suara Siswa, ibid.*, p. 57.
14. J.S. Barry, "The Philippines: Why the Roads are not Safe any more", *Far Eastern Economic Review*, Vol. 81, No. 26, 2 July 1973, p. 22.
15. Richard Vockey, "Islands under the Gun", *ibid.*, Vol. 112, No. 20, 8-14 May 1981, p. 36.
16. The thirteen provinces of the Philippines where the Muslims are claiming to have their majority are Basilan, Davao del Sur, Lanao del Norte, Lanao del Sur, Maguindanao, North Cotabato, Palawan, South Cotabato, Sulu, Sultan Kudarat, Tawi, Zamboanga del Norte, and Zamboanga del Sur.
17. Rodney Tasker, "The Philippines: Plebiscite for the South", *Far Eastern Economics Review*, Vol. 95, No. 8, 25 February 1977, p. 23.
18. Rodney Tasker, "The Philippines: Uneasy Peace After the Plebiscite", ibid., Vol. 96, No. 17, 29 April 1977, p. 9.
19. Third World Sikh Convention (Talwandi Group) was held in April 1982 to demand greater autonomy for the State of the Punjab. An ardent advocate of Khalistan, Ganga Singh Dhillon, who stays in the United States, was to be the chief guest in it. But he was deported. Bukhari presided over the convention and spoke in favour of greater autonomy, etc. *The Times of India*, New Delhi, 14 April 1982.
20. Andrew Forbes says that the inhabitants of southern Thailand were converted to Islam during 14th and 15th centuries. For centuries the Islamic kingdom of Pattani existed as a vassal state of Thailand. The sovereignty of Pattani kingdom was finally robbed in 1801 when it was fully incorporated with Thailand. See Andrew D.W. Forbes, "Islam in Thailand: Assimilation,

Secession or Co-existence", A paper read in a seminar on 25 February 1981 at International Conference on Thai Studies, New Delhi, February 1981, p. 5.

21. The history of Pattani and their struggle against the Buddhist Kingdom of Thailand has been well elucidated in Y.B. Mathur, "Muslims in Siam, 1900-1925", *Studies in Islam*, New Delhi, Vol. V, No. 4, October 1968, pp. 220-31.
22. Lau Teik Soon, "Security Situation on Malaysia-Thai Border", *Asia Research Bulletin*, Singapore, Vol. 2, No. 1, July 1971, pp. 1-7.
23. *Suara Siswa*, No. 2, pp. 13-14.
24. F.K. Khan Durrani, 1944, *The Meaning of Pakistan*, Lahore, p. IV.
25. The following is the relevant point of Lahore Resolution which ultimately became a factor for the partition of India into two parts. The resolution said: "Resolved that it is the considered view of this session of the All-India Muslim League that no constitutional plan would be workable in this country or acceptable to Muslims unless it is designed on the following basic principles, viz. that geographically contiguous units are demarcated into regions which should be so constituted, with such territorial readjustments as may be necessary, that the areas in which the Muslims are numerically in a majority in the Northwestern and Eastern zones of India should be grouped to constitute "Independent States" in which the constituent units shall be autonomous and sovereign." See, Ziauddin Ahmad Suleri, 1944, *The Road to Peace and Pakistan*, Lahore, p. 126.
26. *Ibid.*
27. Astri Suhrke, "Thai Muslims: Some Aspects of Minority Integration", *Pacific Affairs*, Vol. XLIII, No. 4, Winter 1970-71, p. 539.
28. Quoted by Jha, No. 6, pp. 340-41.
29. Paisal Sricharatchanya, "The Muslims Move in", *Far Eastern Economic Review*, Vol. 114, No. 42, 9 October 1981, p. 23.
30. Idem, "PULO and the Middle East Connection", *ibid.*, pp. 28-29.
31. *Ibid.*, p. 24.
32. Dilip Mukerji, "Southeast Asia: Oil Financed Militancy", *World Focus*, New Delhi, Vol. 1, No. 5, May 1980, pp. 20-22.
33. Paisal Sricharatchanya, No. 29, p. 26.
34. *Ibid.*
35. *Ibid.*
36. *Ibid.*
37. *Thai Muslims*, No. 2, pp. 5-6.
38. The Royal Nepal government has declared Hinduism to be the State religion and has declared conversion illegal. The first

official document, Code 1952 says that spreading of Kabirpanthi, Christian, Islamic and other irreligious and foreign creeds, delivering for the purpose of spreading them, speeches which may corrupt the religion of the people, converting any member of the Brahman caste from whose hand water is accepted is prohibited. In case of inheritance, they have to follow Hindu laws in all cases—even where only Muslims are involved—are tried by State courts presided over by Hindu judges. Even the slaughtering of the cows is prohibited. See Marc Gaborieau, "Muslims in the Hindu Kingdom of Nepal" in T.N. Madan (ed.), *Muslim Communities of South Asia: Culture and Society*, New Delhi, 1976, pp. 86-87.

39. Mohamed Mauroof, "Aspects of Religion, Economy and Society Among the Muslims of Ceylon", in *ibid.*, p. 66.
40. The electricity distribution programmes were implemented in the 1970s at the cost of Baht 100 million. See, *Thai Muslims*, No. 2, pp. 18-19.
41. Paisal Sricharatchanya, No. 29, p. 26.
42. Andrew Forbes, No. 20, p. 11.
43. A team of Thai scholars including Dr. Chai Anan Samudvanij, Dr. Suchit Boonbongkorn and Dr. Sombat of Chulalongkorn University, spoke about this at Jawaharlal Nehru University on 20 April 1978 while answering questions about their Muslim minorities.
44. Arong Suthasasna, No. 13, p. 9,
45. *Ibid.*, p. 12.
46. Dennis Walker, No. 7, p. 147.
47 *Suara Siswa*, No. 2, p. 19. (It is pertinent to point out that the policy of balancing the population has been followed in the Philippines also by the majority community. However, the situation is different in case of India. Moradabad district is situated in Uttar Pradesh and dominated by the Muslims. Most of the lands of this area have been purchased by the Muslims and there are a few observers in India who have named this area "mini-Pakistan").
48. Arong Suthasasna, No. 13, p. 14.
49. Paisal Sricharatchanya, "The Muslims Move in", *Far Eastern Economic Review*, Vol. 114, No. 42, 9 October 1981, p. 23.
50. Raymond Scupin, "The Politics of Islamic Reformism in Thailand", *Asian Survey*, Berkeley, Calif., Vol. 20, No. 12, December 1980, pp. 1223-35 and "Islamic Reforms in Thailand", *Journal of Siam Society*, Bangkok, Vol. 68, Part 2, July 1980, pp. 1-10.

10

Indo-Thai Relations: Problems and Prospects

This article seeks to trace the roots of Indo-Thai relations and examine why Indo-Thai relations could not flourish in the post-Independence era. Was it on account of the Cold War and the Indian policy of non-alignment that Thailand could not come very close to India? Or was it due to personal differences in the outlook of our first Prime Minister, Jawaharlal Nehru, and his counterpart in Thailand, Field Marshal Phibun Songgram? Again, was it a fact that Thai-Pakistani ties obstructed bilateral relations with India? What has been the role of Indian immigrants in Thailand? What are the prospects for Indo-Thai relations?

Indo-Thai relations date back to time immemorial. Thailand is part of Suvarnabhumi, which finds mention even in the Ramayana of Valmiki written *c.* 1000 B.C.[1] Later, when Buddhism emerged, Suvarnabhumi became well known in India. In 329 B.C. (Buddhist Era 300) Ashoka the Great deputed Sona and Uttara to Suvarnabhumi to spread the gospel of Buddhism. It is believed that Sona and Uttara went to a city now called Nakorn Pathom (Nagar Pratham), in Thailand. The residents of Nakorn Pathom welcomed the missionaries and became the first people in Suvarnabhumi to accept the Buddhist religion. Situated at a distance of about 40 kilometres from Bangkok, Nakorn Pathom is today a place of national importance for the Thais. There is a huge pagoda to mark the place where Sona and Uttara gave their first discourse on the greatness of Buddhism and laid the foundation for the spread of Buddhism in the rest of Southeast Asia.

It is not only from India that Buddhist missionaries went

to Thailand. Burma, Ceylon (Sri Lanka), and Indonesia also sent their missionaries in course of time. King Jayanaga of Sri Vijaya (Indonesia) sent a missionary to spread the Mahayana cult of Buddhism in A.D. 700 (B.E. 1300).[2] Another important missionary came from King Aniruddha of Pagan (Burma) to spread Hinayana Buddhism in A.D. 1000 (B.E. 1600).[3] Most important of all were the missionaries who went there from Sri Lanka in the thirteenth century.[4] In 1253 some Thai Buddhist monks went to Sri Lanka and returned with the Pali version of the holy *Tripitaka*. They also asked some monks of Sri Lanka to visit Sukhothai. During the reign of Rama Khamheng of Thailand, some Buddhist monks of Sri Lanka went to Thailand. King Rama Khamheng requested them to settle in his capital, Sukhothai. These monks were experts in the Theravada cult of Buddhism and exercised much influence on the Thais. King Rama Khamheng embraced Theravada Buddhism and made it compulsory for all the future Kings of Thailand. He also proclaimed Theravada Buddhism his State religion. Theravada Buddhism continues to be the State religion even today.

The year 1253 is a landmark in the history of Thailand in many ways. It was during that year that the Thais finally defeated the Khmer Government and founded their own kingdom in Sukhothai. In later years King Rama Khamheng (1283-1317) of Thailand developed very cordial relations with the then ruler of China, Kublai Khan, who blessed him to expand his territories at the cost of the Khmer Empire. India was then by no means a powerful country because it was facing repeated invasions on its western frontier. It was under Muslim rule, and Islam had started spreading. Muslim rule was not conducive to the spread of either Buddhism or Hinduism. On the other hand, the Burmese, the Khmers, and the people of Sri Lanka strongly believed in and practised Buddhism. The Thais, therefore, looked to them for enriching their treasure of thought and literature regarding Buddhism. Though during the Moghul period and thereafter hundreds of Thai monks continued to visit Saranath (Uttar Pradesh) and Bodha-Gaya (Bihar) on pilgrimage. India was in no position to influence the Thais because of different state religion and the political culture.

Cultural Heritage

For many centuries cultural contacts between India and mainland Southeast Asia were disrupted because of Muslim and British rule in India. This did not, however, totally spoil the cultural influence of India already assimilated in those countries. When we observe Thai styles and practices in the field of religion and philosophy, art and architecture, sculpture and painting, dance and drama, language and literature, we can easily see this striking affinity with India's.[5]

Even today in Thailand both Brahmin and Buddhist rites are observed. The ceremonies at which the Brahmins officiate are the coronation of the King, *Piti Raek-Na-Kuan* (a ceremony connected with ploughing), the tonsure ceremony, and the swing ceremony.

The Brahmins perform most of the rituals relating to the coronation of the King. They conduct the *homa* (fire sacrifice). They also supervise the ceremonial bath, the elaborate preparation of consecrated water, purification, and anointment. Then along with men of the highest rank, they lead the King to the Octagonal Throne. During the actual ceremony of coronation, it is the chief of the Brahmins who hands the Great Crown of Victory and the royal regalia to the King. The chief of the Brahmins also takes precedence of all others in paying homage to the King.[6] The King then receives benediction from the other Brahmins, who are the first to receive his commands.[7] The Buddhist benediction follows later in ceremonies in which the Brahmins take no part.

The second important ceremony in which the Brahmins play an important role is *Piti Raek-Na-Kuan*. The King chooses the Minister of Agriculture to play the part of *Phya Raek Nah* (Lord of the Festival). The Brahmins give him a choice of three *panungs* (lower garments). If he chooses the longest, rain is supposed to be abundant during the year. *Phya Raek Nah* ploughs a number of furrows and plants rice, which the farmers eagerly gather and plant with their own paddy seeds for good luck. The bulls that pull the plough during the festival are then presented with seven varieties of grain to eat; from the variety they choose, the Brahmins foretell the year's best crop. *Piti Raek-Na-Kuan* is a national ceremony of Thailand.

Both the King and his Ministers attend it. It is usually celebrated in the month of May.

The Brahmins play a similarly important role in the tonsure ceremony. Now this ceremony is a private one for princes between eleven and thirteen years of age.

Lastly, there is the swing ceremony, which is celebrated each year during the second lunar month in the Vishnu Temple opposite Sao Ching-Cha on Dinsaw Road. Before the accession of King Mongkut (1851–68) to the throne, this was also a State ceremony. The Brahmins carry the image of Lord Vishnu and place it on a swing on this occasion. In India, too, the image of Lord Krishna is placed on a swing on the occasion of Janmashtami, the date of His birth. This ceremony is called "Palana" in Delhi and Uttar Pradesh, "Jhula Parva" in Bihar, and "Oonjal" or "Thottil" in Tamil Nadu. This ceremony is still widely celebrated all over India.

Thai architecture as exemplified in the Royal palaces and the Buddhist *wats* bears a close resemblance to the temples found in India. Archaeologists find in Thai architecture an amalgam of the style characteristic of the Gupta period (North India) and the Pallava period (South India), as also of the Khmer style (Cambodia) and the style obtaining in Sri Lanka. The Wat Arun in Bangkok has a *trishula* (trident) at its top as in the temples of Shiva in India. The image of Lord Buddha seated on a lotus in the various temples in Thailand inevitably reminds us Indians of the image of Lord Vishnu or Lord Siva seated on a lotus in the various temples in India.

Thai paintings derive their themes from the Buddhist Jataka tales and from the episodes in Ramakien (Ramayana) and the Mahabharata. The temple of the Emerald Buddha in Bangkok, which is considered to be the most sacred in Thailand, has a series of murals containing the whole story of the Ramayana. To the Thais, Rama is a symbol of goodness, virtue, and piety; Sita, an apotheosis of womanhood; and Hanuman, an embodiment of humour, ingenuity, and gaiety. Evaluating the Indo-Thai cultural links, Prince Prem Purachatra, former Thai Ambassador in India, once said:

"The hierarchy of Hindu gods and goddesses provided inspiration

> to our Thai artists, and some of them have assumed symbolic significance, such as Vishnu, the patron of engineering and science, and Ganesh, the patron of fine arts. We award guilded statues of Saraswati to the winners of Thailand's top cinematic honours."[8]

Thai classical dance and drama—the *Khon* (masked play) and *Lakorn*—derive their themes mainly from Ramakien and the Mahabharata. The folk dances of Thailand remind us strongly of the Manipuri style of dance in India.

In the field of language and literature, we find that there are many words of Sanskrit and Pali origin in the Thai language. The literature, being essentially religious, is full of mythological tales of Buddhism and Hinduism. Ramakien or Ramakirti is the most exalted of literary works in the Thai language. Though there is a slight difference in the presentation of Thailand's Ramakien and India's Ramayana, yet the basic story is the same. In India, the Hindus attach a religious significance to the Ramayana, but in Thailand, the State religion being Buddhism, such a significance is held by the holy Tripitaka.

Some Thai festivals like Sonkran and Loi Krathong remind us of Holi and Chatha Parva in India. On the occasion of Sonkran, which is celebrated in April every year, all the paraphernalia of Holi are followed. The only difference is that the Thais do not use coloured powder (*avir*), but they use water, mud, dust, and other things. The streets in Thailand are full of jolly boys and girls participating playfully in this festival. On the occasion of Loi Krathong, which is usually celebrated in November, little lamps are set afloat on the water in the canals and rivers with great pomp and show. In India too, on the occasion of Chatha Parva offering prayers to sun God in Bihar and Uttar Pradesh lights are floated on the river Ganga. In Bihar, the lights are found afloat even in small ponds. Patna's Chatha is famous all over India for its illuminations and general participation.

The Thais are very fond of seeing Indian movies, and they import Indian movies on a large scale. They translate the dialogue into the Thai language before screening them. Indian movies are popular and attract huge crowds.

Visit of Rabindranath Tagore to Thailand

Poet Rabindranath Tagore's visit to Thailand in 1927 is a landmark in Indo-Thai relations. Tagore felt very happy to find traces of Indian culture in Thailand, so much so that he wrote:

> I come, a pilgrim, at thy gate, O Siam,
> to offer my verse to the endless glory of India sheltered in thy home,
> away from her own deserted shrine,
> to bathe in the living stream that flows in thy heart,
> whose water descends from the snowy height of a sacred time
> on which arose, from the deep of my country's being,
> the Son of Love and Righteousness.[9]

During this visit, the Government of Thailand requested Rabindranath Tagore to send a scholar who could enlighten the Thai people on Indian civilization and literature. On his return to India, Tagore sent Swami Satyanand Puri, previously known as P.K. Sen, to Thailand. Swami Satyanand Puri was thereafter attached to Chulalongkorn University in Bangkok as Professor of Sanskrit. He wrote several books and articles in the Thai language and in English to promote understanding and goodwill between India and Thailand. He had personal rapport with Premier Phibun and was able to elicit his cooperation in organizing a front to support Indian independence. He was one of those who requested Netaji Subhas Chandra Bose to come to Southeast Asia and lead the Indian National Army (INA).

Satyanand Puri also founded an institution called Dharmashrama in Bangkok in 1930. This institution, known as the Thai-Bharat Cultural Lodge since 1940, has played an important role in the life of the Indians in Bangkok. At present the Lodge arranges religious meetings every Sunday. It runs a school where Indian and Thai children study together. The medium of instruction is the Thai language. The Thai-Bharat Cultural Lodge also has a library named after its founder, Satyanand Puri. The literature in the library is about ancient Indian and Thai cultures. Members of its staff help people (especially students) from India visiting Thailand and the Thais visiting India.

When Netaji Subhas Chandra Bose came to Southeast Asia in the early forties to lead the struggle for independence, he received invaluable organizational facilities in Thailand.[10] There seemed to be excellent rapport between him and the then Prime Minister of Thailand, Field Marshal Phibun Songgram. Thailand offered not only its land but also its information media to the INA to promote the cause of India's liberation. Thai Government broadcasts gave full publicity to the activities of the INA in all the major languages of India.[11] Netaji organized the INA from among the Indians in Southeast Asia. At the end of the Second World War, Burma fell once again into the hands of the Allied forces. On the eve of its fall, Netaji shifted the headquarters of the INA to Thailand. As the INA was running short of arms and ammunition, he then left for Singapore with a view to proceeding thence to Japan to obtain arms and equipments. However, the plane in which he was travelling crashed under mysterious circumstances, and he died *en route* to Japan. After his death the INA became defunct. In the same month (August 1945) the Second World War also ended. Thailand began to adjust its foreign relations according to the situation then obtaining in the region. It wanted to show that it had already abandoned its policy of helping the Japanese and sought to cultivate Britain, France, and the other powers dominant in Southeast Asia. INA volunteers were criminals in the eyes of the British government, and if Thailand had ordered their repatriation at that time, Britain would have been pleased. The Thai government, however, was kind and sympathetic to the INA. It granted political asylum to almost all the people connected with the INA. This gesture of friendship towards India provided solid ground for friendship between the two countries. India won its independence after two years in August 1947. It was natural to believe that Thailand's relations with free India would prosper rapidly, but it did not turn out that way in the years following independence.

Relations after 1947

During 1947-76, neither the King nor the Prime Minister of Thailand ever came to India on a State visit. In 1972, after twenty-five years of independence, President V.V. Giri of India visited Thailand. The Prime Minister of India went to that country on state visit in 1986 for the first time.

There were many reasons for the absence of warmth in Indo-Thai relations. First, there was a difference in the international outlook of the two countries. India became an ardent advocate of non-alignment and peaceful co-existence after getting independence from British rule. On the other hand, Thailand strongly supported US military presence in the region, especially after 1950. It also provided bases and manpower to the United States to put down Communist movements. From 1948 to 1973, Thailand remained under the dictatorship of three military strongmen—Field Marshal Phibun Songgram, Field Marshal Sarit Thanarat, and Field Marshal Thanom Kittikachorn. It became a founder member of the South-East Asia Treaty Organization (SEATO) in 1954. It even allowed Bangkok to be the headquarter of the SEATO. Through the SEATO it became an ally of Pakistan. Relations between Thailand and Pakistan were close as they were both under military dictatorships. On certain occasions Thai diplomats supported Pakistan at international forums. Indo-Pakistani relations were generally under strain, so much so that they fought three successive full-scale wars (1948, 1965, and 1971). India naturally suspected the friends of Pakistan. Thailand and Pakistan were allies, and Thai support for Pakistan was thus naturally something to be expected. However, Thailand gave definite support to India in 1971 by keeping itself neutral in the United Nations when Pakistan and the United States wanted to stop the Indian action in support of the independence of Bangladesh. As the SEATO was still in existence, and Pakistan had not formally withdrawn from it, it was assumed that all SEATO countries would take steps to prevent the dismember-ment of Pakistan.

Thai friendship can be useful to India in various ways. Thailand still produces a surplus of 1.2 to 1.8 million tons of rice every year. India, on the other hand, is always in need of rice. It is a fact that India could not buy Thai rice up to 1964. Since 1964, however, we have been buying it. India purchased 25,000 tons of rice in 1964; 150,000 tons in 1966; 80,000 tons in 1968; and 100,000 tons in 1969. In 1970 India signed an agreement with Thailand for the supply of 400,000 tons of rice every year for three years. Thai rice is of the best quality and has a world-wide market.

There have been some individual efforts in both countries to improve mutual relations. When the Supreme Patriarch of Thailand visited India in 1962, he expressed his happiness at the technological developments in India. Persons accompanying the Supreme Patriarch said that the Patriarch was trying to find ways to strengthen Indo-Thai friendship. The Supreme Patriarch said that Indo-Thai relations, already strong through the message of Lord Buddha, would become stronger in future.[12]

The Indian Press too has, on some occasions, tried to attract the attention of the Government of India to the need to improve relations with Thailand. *The Statesman* reported on 24 December 1969 that

> ... in spite of loud noises by the External Affairs Ministry, Thailand and some other countries of Southeast Asia continue to be neglected by New Delhi, clearly the habit of earlier years of refusing to give berth to any country unable to share the Indian policy of non-alignment. Not all Thai policies, domestic and foreign, can be to India's liking. But since when has it become the ruling dictum of diplomacy that a country should befriend only those nations which agree wholeheartedly with its world view? A more active policy of improving India's relations with Thailand will be in the best interests of both the countries. The geographical and political importance of Thailand cannot be gainsaid.[13]

Joint Venture

Joint venture projects, particularly those which have already gone into operation, have played useful roles in forging and promoting economic links. For one thing they enable Thailand to diversify its production structure and accelerate its economic and industrial development. They give India better access to the market of the host country for its products. They are, therefore, mutually advantageous.

India started a joint venture with Thailand in the field of steel mills and synthetic-fibre-spinning plants in 1969. When a delegation of the Engineering Export Promotion Council of India went to Bangkok in April 1972, it found that there was some prejudice against Indian products, partly because of certain faulty shipments in the past and partly because much of the latest advance in technology and expertise in India was not well publicized in Thailand. The delegation was told that the steel plant set up by an Indian firm had not done too well and had generated misgiving in the minds of entrepreneurs and Government officials.[14] If the members of the staff of the Indian Embassy in Bangkok take a keen interest, they can bring about better understanding between Thai businessmen and their Indian counterparts. It is found that the Embassy people can influence the Thais by speaking to them in the Thai language. But then, not many members of the Indian Embassy can speak the Thai language. In contrast, members of the staff of the Japanese Embassy in Thailand are very fluent in the Thai language and are thus able to influence the Thais easily although there is considerable resentment among the younger generation of Thais against Japanese business practices.

Indian Immigrants in Thailand

There are about 27,000 Indians in Thailand. More than half of these are settled in Bangkok. Most of the immigrants are from the Punjab and Uttar Pradesh. The immigrants from the Punjab are mostly traders and textile merchants, and those from Uttar Pradesh are generally milkmen, watchmen, news agents, and money-lenders. As watchmen, Indian immigrants are widely accepted; they are regarded as most trustworthy. Indian watchmen are often in charge of the keys to godowns stocked with goods of considerable value, and yet there is hardly ever a case where their reliability has been questioned.[15] On the other hand, there are some Sikhs doing a good job in the Thai armed forces.[16]

Indian immigrants are well-to-do, whether they have migrated from Punjab, Uttar Pradesh, or any other part of India. They are, however, criticized for not spending their money for the general welfare of the Thai people. The response of the Indians to appeals for contributions to relief funds or for charity is conspicuously lukewarm, if not poor. The main problem with the Indian immigrants in Thailand is that some of them have not been able to identify themselves fully with Thailand. They bear Indian names, eat Indian food, wear Indian dress, and stick to the Indian way of life. Most Indians marry only among themselves. On the other hand the Chinese minority has to a considerable extent been assimilated with the Thais. It is really difficult to distinguish between a Chinese and a Thai in Thailand.

Indian immigrants by and large seem to be conservative in outlook. They have their social and religious groups in Thailand on the pattern of India. The Hindus observe their religious rituals and ceremonies in such temples as the Maha Maya Mandir, the Vishnu Mandir, and the temple at the Thai-Bharat Cultural Lodge. The Muslims celebrate their festivals in the mosques and the Sikhs in the Guru Singh Sabha and the *gurudwaras*. The Indians continue to observe Diwali, Baisakhi, Holi, and Rakhi, as also Muslim and Sikh festivals. Some Indians have even retained their Indian nationality in Thailand. A child born to Indian parents in Thailand is a Thai citizen until the age of eighteen when he can make a choice between the Indian and the Thai nationality. So far the Thais have made no discrimination against Indian immigrants.[17]

In view of the new trend of nationalism in Asia and Africa, any rigidities maintained by the Indians are outdated and should change. Prime Minister Jawaharlal Nehru, in the course of a debate on foreign affairs on 17 December 1957, said:

> Indian settlers should associate themselves as closely as possible with the interests of the people of the country they have adopted, and never make it appear or to function in a way that they become an exploiting agency there.... If Indians are not friendly to the people of the country that they have adopted, they should come back to India and not spoil the fair name of India.[18]

Since 1972 India has taken some important initiatives to strengthen Indo-Thai friendship. The then President, V.V. Giri, visited Thailand from 27 to 29 March 1972. He was received enthusiastically by the King of Thailand. In his banquet speech on 27 March 1972 Giri underlined the good-will obtaining between the two countries. He said:

> There had been no conflict between the peoples of India and Thailand in the last 2,000 years of their contact. What better

conditions could there be between two countries and two peoples with this rich legacy to work together for our common good?[19]

During this visit there were talks between the official delegations of India and Thailand on internal matters and bilateral relations. Both sides discussed the means best suited to develop closer relations.

On a request from Thailand, G.D. Birla visited Thailand from 21 to 27 April 1974 and finalized a joint-venture project to set up a viscose rayon and staple-fibre plant at a cost of Rs 10 million.[20] It is interesting to know that the Birlas have already set up two factories manufacturing staple fibres and textiles in Bangkok.

In 1976 India once again manifested its eagerness to promote friendly ties. Government missions visited Thailand on two occasions to improve cultural and economic relations. India sent Bipin Pal Das, Deputy Minister for External Affairs, to Thailand from 15 to 17 June 1976. On the last day of his visit he said: "Thailand and India have decided to enter into formal cultural relations. Thai-Indian cultural agreement is ready for signature and will be signed at the earliest possible time."[21]

This visit was immediately followed in the next month by an Indian economic delegation led by India's Minister for Banking and Revenue, Pranab Mukherjee. Mukherjee had wide-ranging talks with Pichai Rattakul, the then Foreign Minister of Thailand, on 27 July 1976. Pichai said: "We are interested so much in India, but it does not seem we are co-operating that much."[22] He identified the areas of co-operation between the two countries, and agreed that three teams should go out to India to study the progress of rural electrification and power development, small-scale and agro-based industries and capital-goods industries, especially the machine-building industry like paper and paper pulp, sugar, textiles, and iron and steel.[23] The Deputy Minister for Industries in Thailand, Banharn Silapa Archa, drew the attention of Pranab Mukherjee to the need for India's assistance in strengthening the Thai economy, particularly in the field of rural electrification and machine-building.[24]

In recent years India's exports to Thailand have also increased. In 1976 India's exports totalled a little over Rs 120 million, which was an increment over the 1968 figures of Rs 80 million.[25] There is a feeling in the business circles in India that in some industries Indo-Thai collaboration can prove beneficial to both countries, e.g. in such industries as motor vehicles parts, tractor assembly or production of agricultural machinery, machine-tool building, hardware household appliances, electrical power generator and transmission pump centrifuges, chemicals, fertilizers, pulp and paper, food-processing, tanning, canning, taxtiles, and forest produce.[26]

Prospects for Indo-Thai Relations

Thailand has seen quick changes in its politics since October 1973. Between 1973 and 1976 it has had six Prime Ministers: some of these were advocates of friendship with the communist countries; others were opposed to such friendship; and yet others were either neutral or undecided. There have also been constitutional experiments. As stability is necessary for any initiative on the part of any Government, the Thai Government has not been able to take steps to strengthen Indo-Thai relations.

The emerging trends suggest that Thailand will improve its relations with India. According to a joint communique issued on 21 December 1976 in Manila, the Thai Prime Minister, Thanin Kraivichian, and the Philippine President, Ferdinand Marcos, agreed that a just balance among the Great Powers with legitimate interests in the region would contribute to the stability of Southeast Asia as a whole and that peaceful competition among the Great Powers would redound to the common benefit of Southeast Asia and the Great Powers.[27] This was repeated in the Marcos and Lee Kuan Yew communiqué of 19 January 1977. India's co-operation with the countries of Southeast Asia could be vital in this context. India has been keen to co-operate with members of the Association of South-East Asian Nations (ASEAN), of which Thailand is a member.

There is a military dictatorship in Thailand today, but this need not affect Thai relations with India. The existence of Communist regimes in the Soviet Union and other East European countries has not come in the way of India's good relations with those countries. On the other hand, although the

United States is democratic, India's relations with that country worsened when Richard M. Nixon was President. He even sent the US Seventh Fleet to the Bay of Bengal at the time of Indo-Pakistani War of 1971 to demonstrate his country's solidarity with Pakistan.

Closeness of relations between Thailand and Pakistan had been a matter of concern for our diplomats. In April 1975, when Cambodia and Vietnam fell into the hands of the Communists, there was a reappraisal of international politics by the Super Powers and their allies. There was a reappraisal of US Policy, too. In September 1975 the Foreign Ministers of the SEATO countries met in New York and announced the termination of that twenty-one-year-old organization. Pakistan had already terminated its membership of the SEATO in 1972, and, with that, Thai alliance with Pakistan, too, had ended. This had made Thailand free to lean towards India or towards Pakistan or keep a neutral stance as between the two. Moreover, Indo-Pakistani relations had shown some improvement after the signing of the Simla Agreement in 1972. Now it seems to us that even if Thai-Pakistani friendship is strengthened, it will not come in the way of Indo-Thai relations.

There is no evidence to suggest that in the past there were differences on a personal level between Jawaharlal Nehru and Phibun Songgram, but there certainly were a number of differences of outlook between them. These differences mattered in Indo-Thai relations because these leaders laid the foundations of the foreign policies of their respective countries and set the guidelines for their successors as well. Phibun wanted military alignments in region to suppress communism inside the country and in the region as a whole, whereas Jawaharlal Nehru advocated non-alignment to keep the Asian-African world out of the Cold War. Phibun supported Taiwan and was hostile to the Communist regime in the People's Republic of China. He advocated military alignments to save the Free World from communism. He was thus opposed to the policy of non-alignment. He shared the views of John Foster Dulles, the then US Secretary of State. He believed with Dulles that the policy of non-alignment was short-sighted and immoral. It is noteworthy that Phibun was one of those in the region of Southeast Asia who disagreed with India's point of view in the international field.

Happily, these differences are now things of the past. The present world is noticeably different from the world of the fifties. The concept of *detente* is pre-dominant today. The United States is improving its relations with the Soviet Union and strengthening its contacts with People's China. The Soviet Union and China are no longer spoken of as implacable enemies of the Free World. As for Thailand, it recognized People's China in July 1975. The contacts between the two countries are growing. If Thai relations with China can improve after their indulgence in polemics for more than twenty-five years, there is no reason why Indo-Thai relations cannot improve further.

As the birthplace of Lord Buddha India has a special significance in the minds of most Thais. It has recently attracted the attention of Thais for its technological advance as well. Thailand has very close economic ties with Japan, but it seems to be interested in diversifying its foreign economic relations. India could be of help to Thailand in this and other fields.

REFERENCES

1. In the part entitled "Kishkindha Kanda" of the Ramayana, Valmiki writes that after Sita was kidnapped, her husband Rama began a great search for her. In the course of that search he came across a person named Sugriva. Rama found in him a useful ally in tracing Sita. Rama helped Sugriva to become King, and in return Sugriva promised that he would offer all possible help to him in finding Sita. Sugriva ordered Hanuman to make a search for Sita at a number of places. These places included Suvarnabhumi and Yavadwipa (which is modern Java).
2. M.D. Luang Suriyawongse, 1955, *Buddhism in Thailand*, Bangkok, p. 38.
3. *Ibid.*
4. *Ibid.*
5. For a study of the cultural aspect of Thailand, reference may be made to the following books: Phya Anuman Rajadhon, 1953, *Loi Krathong and Sonkran Festival*, Bangkok, Charles Norton Edgecumbe Eliot, 1954, *Hinduism and Buddhism: An Historical Sketch*, New York, N.Y., 3 Vols., H.H. Prince Dhaninivat and

Danit-Yupho, 1958, *The Khon*, Bangkok, and Horace Geoffrey Quaritch Wales, 1931, *Siamese State Ceremonies: Their History and Function*, London.

6. Antony Bartlett, 1968, *Bangkok's Brahman Priests*, (n.p.), p. 13.
7. *Ibid.* At a meeting with the holy Phra Rajaguru Vama Depmuni Somchit Rangsibrahmanakul in Bangkok on 1 January 1974, the author received much valuable information on the Hindu influence in Thailand today.
8. Northern India Patrika Allahabad, 15 February 1969.
9. Rabindranath Tagore, "On Siam" (A monograph found at the Thai-Bharat Cultural Lodge, Bangkok).
10. A number of INA workers in Thailand, including C. Roy Narula, Harbanslal Sachdeva, Direk Kulasirisabat, and S.D. Archarjee, gratefully acknowledged Thailand's help.
11. Sunthorn Hongladarom, Information Minister of Thailand during the Second World War and now Secretary-General of the SEATO, told this to the present author in April 1974.
12. *Bangkok World*, 18 April, 1962.
13. *The Statesman*, New Delhi, 24 December 1969.
14. Delegates Report No. 48. Thailand, Malaysia and Indonesia, Engineering Export Promotion Council, World Trade Centre, Calcutta, pp. 4-5.
15. N.J. Nanporia, "The Overseas Indians", *Asia Magazine*, Hong Kong, 26 November 1967.
16. *Ibid.*
17. Tosh Desai, "Indo-Thai Ties," *The Times of India*, New Delhi, 19 November 1961.
18. Jawaharlal Nehru, *1971, India's Foreign Policy: Selected Speeches, September 1946-April 1961*, New Delhi, p. 131.
19. *The Statesman*, New Delhi, 28 March 1972.
20. *Sunday Standard*, New Delhi, 27 April, 1972.
21. *Bangkok Post*, 18 June 1976; and *The Times of India*, New Delhi, 18 June 1976.
22. *Bangkok Post*, 28 July 1976.
23. *Ibid.*
24. *Ibid.*
25. *Financial Express*, Bombay, 28 July 1976.
26. *Ibid.*
27. Derek Davies and Denzil Peiris, "ASEAN: Cooperation Is the Name of the Game", *Far Eastern Economic Review*, Hong Kong, Vol. 95, No. 7, 18 February 1977, p. 20.

11

Chatichai and Changing Dynamics in Indo-Thai Relations

Maj-General Chatichai Choonhavan's visit to India in 1989 was a landmark in the history of Indo-Thai relations because it was the first ever visit by any Thai Prime Minister to independent India. Accompanied by a high-level delegation, he came to reciprocate Prime Minister Rajiv Gandhi's visit to that country in October 1986. The deliberations covered resolution of Kampuchean crises and improvements in bilateral relations. Though both countries pursued foreign policies in the past four decades which were opposite to one another but changes in the international environment, Gorbachev's glasnost and perestroica, politics of structural reforms in Vietnam and ASEAN boom emboldened Thailand to take initiatives. Moreover, chartchai as Prime Minister wanted to promote business interests of the country. Vietnam and India were special areas of business interests for him.

It is worthwhile to say at the outset that Thailand (Siam) was the greatest supporter of India's war of Independence in the pre-1945 era. Thailand gave a strong support to Indian National Army (INA) of Netaji Subhas Chandra Bose. It offered not only men and materials to INA but also bases to prepare militarily to struggle for independence. Though Singapore was the headquarters of INA but majority of the armed forces were based in Bangkok and other areas of Thailand. Netaji had a personal rapport with the then Prime Minister Field Marshal Phibun Songgram, and his Cabinet Ministers, especially Pin Choonhavan and Mr. Sunthorn Hongladdarom. Above all Netaji was very near and dear to the Thais, who supported him overwhelmingly.

The visiting Prime Minister, the son of Mr. Pin Choonhavan, was a gifted leader to promote business environment in the region. He had a grand vision of India who showed keen interests to establish closer relations and friendship with India. He thought that geopolitically India was indispensable for peace and prosperity, stability and security of Southeast Asia.

Thailand during cold war years was often misunderstood because of its strong ties with the United States. A realistic appraisal of the developments at the end of the Second World War suggested that pro-Americanism was the easiest course to promote Thailand's national interests. Thailand was in the category of a war-criminal because of its support to Japan during the Second World war. Phibun, throughout the supporter of Japanese "co-prosperity sphere", came back to power in November 1947. Had he thought to remain neutral, it was quite possible that Thailand could be pressurized to pay compensation to Allied Powers. He did not wish to spoil country's resources to that end. Thus he sought legitimacy now as a partner of the free world. He envisaged that the friendship with the U.S. will serve his objectives better. He signed Economic and Military assistance agreement with the United States in 1950 and thus laid a solid foundation for Thai-American collaboration and friendship. Thai saying that "Like a bamboo, we bend with the wind", was successfully demonstrated in foreign policy and thus Thai interests were protected as the US did not support the resolution that Thailand was a war criminal.

Thailand became a member and headquarters of SEATO (Southeast Asia Treaty Organization) in September 1954 and proved to be an active collaborator of the Western countries in containment of communism. The United States constructed six air bases and one naval base on Thai soil to fight against communist activities. Those bases were continuously used during 1964-75 against communists in Vietnam, Cambodia and Laos. Thailand remained committed to support the US in pursuing anti-communist crusade in Indo-China.

Indian leaders were always opposed to violent means to attain any objectives in the post-independence era. Nehru was firm in his belief that violence will not deter the communists in Indo-China in pursuing their goals. India supported by Indonesia, Burma, Cambodia and others, were often vocal and critical not only of the US but also Thailand at international forums. Indian perception created irritations in Thailand, but this did not disturb our diplomatic relations. Being aligned to Pakistan through SEATO, Thailand did not indulge in anti-Indian activities. Thais paid due respect to India as the birth place of Lord Buddha and cherished undertaking pilgrimage to Bodh Gaya and Sarnath.

Nehru pursued a policy to promote Afro-Asian solidarity and Non-Aligned Movement (NAM). He was secular, democratic and internationalist. He wanted to support anti-colonial and democratic movements. Thai political system on the other hand, attached importance to nation, religion and the King and was always arguing that the governance cannot be effective without the participation of the King and the military. Thais are proud people with rich traditions. As they were never colonised, they have developed their indigenous pattern of government and polity. On the other hand, India adopted democratic government in 1947 and established institutions to promote democratic values.

On the other hand, Thai system is quite different. Though they also respect democratic system but they cannot envisage any system to be effective without the participation of the military. These are some of the intricacies of the Thai political system that becomes difficult to comprehend. Our first Prime Minister Jawaharlal Nehru did not go to Thailand on a state visit, though that country is one of our closest neighbours. His successors, including Mrs. Indira Gandhi too could not pay any state visit to Thailand. Moreover, her decisions to give full diplomatic relations to Democratic Republic of Vietnam in 1972 and People's Republic of Cambodia in 1980, were strongly disliked.

International politics and Indo-Thai relations are witnessing momentous developments since 1986. The euphoria for *perestroika* and *glasnost* in the Soviet Union, new developments in the concept of communism, modernization drive in China, the rapprochement between the two super powers, the impending Sino-Soviet rapprochement, etc. have impelled the leaders all over the world to review their policies and relations.

Mr. Rajiv Gandhi attached great importance to strengthening our Southeast Asian contacts. He was keen to retain the friendship of the Indo-Chinese countries and raise the relations with the ASEAN countries to the same level. He recognised the importance of Thailand in the ASEAN and paid a state visit to that country in October 1986. He received a tumultuous reception and held wide-ranging talks. Though bilateral issues were discussed but more attention was paid to listening Thai views on Kampuchean issue.

Thailand was the greatest opponent of Vietnam's military intervention in Kampuchea. Outside world projected it as a "frontline state" *vis-à-vis* Vietnam. Thailand was determined to compel Vietnam to withdraw from Kampuchea and in that endeavour it was supported by the ASEAN, China and the western world.

While in Thailand, Rajiv Gandhi had asserted that India could extend suitable proposals to solve the Kampuchean tangle. He and his diplomats were trying to search a compromise formula for conflict resolution and shuttled in several capitals to know views of the Kampuchean rebels and the government. India believed that the conflict resolution in Cambodia was issential for regional peace and stability.

The visit of Major General Chatichai to India just after China visit certainly threw new lights on the Kampuchean issue. He was closest to CGDK leaders and knew the Chinese and American perspectives. On the other hand, India was very close to Vietnam and People's Republic of Kampuchea. Thus the exchange of views between India and Thailand was bound to provide clues to solution of the Kampuchean crisis.

But Thailand's opinion was crucial to find any solution of the Kampuchean tangle. The CGDK, headed by Norodom Sihanouk in exile, depended on Thai assistance to pursue their activities. It was Thailand that gave them bases and sanctuaries. It was through Thailand that bases and sanctuaries of Cambodian rebels were protected. It was through Thailand that they got the Chinese and American supplies of strategic weapons. If Thailand was ready to resolve the Kampuchean dispute, all the contestants will be prompted to talk to each other and resolve the issue. The geopolitics in the region were changing and reconciliation looked better than confrontation.

The developments in Southeast Asia forced Vietnam to withdraw from Kampuchea. The worsening economic situation and international compulsions were against Vietnam's military presence in Kampuchea. On its part, Vietnam announced that it will withdraw from Kampuchea by 1990 but in reality the withdrawal was complete before 1988.

There were two contentious issues regarding Kampuchea that caused stalemate in the emergence of a consensus. Firstly, how to disarm the Khmer Rouge faction and secondly, how to assure security guarantees to the new government that may be established as a result of a compromise between PRK and the CGDK.

Norodom Sihanouk had advocated active role for India in solution of the Kampuchean crisis. Vietnam and the present government in Kampuchea also supported India's involvement in the resolution of the Kampuchean issue. Rajiv Gandhi was ready to play a political role in that direction, but Thailand was exploring business opportunities. When India gave importance to ideology, Thailand attached importance to economics.

Maj. General Chatichai Choonhavan hailed from one of the richest families in Thailand and had one of the most productive business talents. He was bound to apply his mind to promote our economic and trade relations. The Sixth Five Year Plan then in operation in Thailand was aimed at generating employment in the impoverished rural areas and reduce migration to urban areas. Thai Government had piloted several schemes for rural development. Thai Prime Minister therefore sought India's cooperation in that endeavour. There was a projection that Indo-Thai collaboration could prove useful in such areas as tractor assembly or production of agricultural machinery, machine-tool building, electrical power generator, chemicals, fertilizers, paper and forest products, etc.

India had been a major importer of Thai rice. In June 1988 India contracted for the import of five lakh tonnes of rice from Thailand and the contract was renewable. Thailand produced 3.7 to 4.5 million tonnes of rice every year and accounted for

40 per cent of world's rice exports. It had surplus sugar and other consumer items. It was also a major exporter of garments and frozen sea food. Chatichai's visit gave a solid impression that Thai expertise and experiences can be shared for our mutual prosperity. Fishing and agro-based industries are much more advanced in Thailand. Indian business can be benefited a lot if Thai technology is applied in Indian conditions.

12

Indo-Thai Relations: Retrospect and Prospects

Thailand, which is strategically located in Southeast Asia, used to be considered India's gateway to Far East during the colonial era.[1] The location advantage brought geo-political importance to it and Thai diplomats understood and used it meticulously to escape the yoke of western colonial masters. Thailand remained the only country in Southeast Asia, which was not colonized. France and Great Britain treated Thailand as a buffer zone between French Indochina and British Burma. Whenever serious threat to its sovereignty arose in the 19th century, attempts were made to resolve them through negotiated means. When France demanded territories on the eastern side of the Mekong river or when Great Britain claimed jurisdiction over Kedah, Perlis, Kelantan and Trengganu, there was resentment in Thailand. But the King of Thailand avoided going to war. He pleaded compromise with France and Great Britain in order to protect the sovereignty of the country. It was meaningless to fight a battle, if the adversary was very strong and also when the alternatives of battle were available.

In 1893, the French navy had attacked Thai positions at Paknam. It was meant to provoke Thailand to retaliate, but the king dissuaded its forces from retaliating. They understood that it was a meticulously laid French trap to colonize the area. Thailand agreed to vacate the areas on eastern side of the Mekong river as demanded by the French colonial masters.[2] Burmese, on the other hand, did not understand the meaning of British provocation. They decided to fight war against the British and ultimately lost the sovereignty of the country. On the other hand, Thailand was ready to concede, cooperate and compromise with the western powers in order to maintain and preserve the sovereignty of the country. They projected it by saying that "Like a bamboo, we bend with the wind". The astute conduct of Thai foreign policy established the wisdom and foresight of Thai rulers. It was successful in projecting that Thailand was peaceful and friendly towards western powers and ready to cooperate with western world. Its image as a friendly and cooperative Kingdom remained unalterable in Europe and thus the country was not colonized.

It was only during the Second World War that Thailand's role became adversarial to the western world. Thailand signed offensive defensive pact with Japan and supported the slogan of "Asia for Asians". It was also during that period that a strong foundation for Indo-Thai relations was laid. Thailand supported Netaji Subhas Chandra Bose and India's freedom struggle. It supported Indian National Army (INA) by providing facilities for base, propaganda channels, aid and assistance. The INA volunteers were kept in high esteem even after the end of the World War. Although Great Britain projected INA volunteers as war criminals and wanted their repatriation to India, Thailand did not oblige them.

When the Second World War was over, the international power equation was in favour of the US which had emerged the most powerful force in the region. Thailand understood this reality at a time when it was facing lot of internal and external problems, like anti-Chinese riots, the threat of communist subversion and the issues of economic reconstruction and to address them, Thailand decided to cultivate relations with the United States.[3] Americans on the other hand, had already started a containment drive and had evolved a grand strategic design for Southeast Asian region. They responded appropriately to Thai overtures and influenced Thailand to be a strategic partner. As Thailand was always independent and had not fought war against colonial powers, it kept herself open to the western world. Thailand agreed to be the headquarters of SEATO and strongly supported the containment policy of the US. Thus, the partnership with the US facilitated Thailand's building of the infrastructure, transportation network, port and airport in the country. The development of the country in terms of human resource development and external profile was impressive. Although Thai territories were used extensively in Vietnam War, in that process Americans also built an advanced infrastructure in the country. The US spent billions of dollars in establishing military and naval bases and all of them are now under the control of Thailand.

Although Thailand was on the opposite side of India during cold war years, it did not ignore India but attached importance to it as the cultural and spiritual centre. When ASEAN was born in 1967, Thailand wanted India also to be associated with it. India was not enthused to join it as the new organization was viewed pro-American. The ASEAN countries again tried to bring India into their fold in 1978-79, but again there were indecisiveness and debates about colonialism, anti-colonialism, idealism, etc. and India missed the opportunity. India began to attach due importance to the ASEAN region only after the termination of Cold War in 1991. Thailand was very happy to note the transformation in Indian policy perspectives towards eastern neighbours. It had been trying to cultivate India seriously ever since the visit of the Thai Prime Minister Chatichai Choonhavan to New Delhi in 1989, but the termination of the Cambodian conflict and cold war in 1991, offered new opportunities in regional politics. Thailand, then was enthusiastic in turning Indo-China from battleground to market place in the east but it was keen to explore markets and cooperation with India in the west, where it envisaged immense opportunities for business and trade.

Thailand while evolving new areas of cooperation, thought of involving India in establishing growth areas in Andaman's on the pattern of Bantam and Johore. India was not keen to explore Thai proposals instantly, as the intelligence report suggested that the smugglers and drug peddlers would get a free hand if government control of the area is relaxed. Moreover, government of India did not find the proposal fine-tuned to be suitably responded. But there was a new development in the post-1995 era that both Thailand and India began to attach importance to the opinion and proposals of one another seriously. The proposals for bilateral and multilateral collaboration were mooted and the two also agreed to establish BIMST-EC, the sub-regional grouping, to link South Asian countries with ASEAN for trade, investments and tourism.

BIMST-EC has proved an important instrument to understand culture and to promote socio-economic interaction and confidence building, but it has to attend to every delicate issue with caution. But before analyzing the achievements of BIMST-EC, it is necessary to examine Indo-Thai relations in retrospect.

Indo-Thai bilateral relations have witnessed different phases of ups and down ever since 1947 and they have not always been pleasant. However, in order to understand relations from proper perspective, it is necessary to analyze some of the major developments that shaped the foundation of our relations in the past and which very often influence the mindset of our decision-makers in the present.

During 1947-86, neither the King nor the Prime Minister of Thailand ever came to India on a state visit. In 1972, after twenty-five years of independence, President V.V. Giri of India visited Thailand. There were many reasons for the absence of warmth in Indo-Thai relations. First, there was a difference in the international outlook of the two countries. India became an ardent advocate of non-alignment and peaceful co-existence after getting independence from the British rule. On the other hand, Thailand strongly supported the US military presence in the region, especially, after 1950. It also provided bases and manpower to the United States to put down the communist movements. From 1948 to 1973, Thailand remained under the dictatorship of three military strongmen, namely Field Marshal Phibun Songgram, Field Marshal Sarit Thanarat, and Field Marshal Thanom Kittikachorn. It became a founder member of the South-East Asia Treaty Organization (SEATO) in 1954. It even allowed Bangkok to be the headquarters of the SEATO. Although the developments in the region and especially in Thailand were not positive for India, our diplomats worked hard to cultivate friendship.

India attached geo-strategic importance to Thailand and showed friendly gestures, on the eve of its independence. In February 1947, India's interim government extended a loan to Thailand, which was the first of its kind, given to a foreign country. The loan was Rs.50 million, to be paid in instalments. India on its part, adopted a very sympathetic attitude towards Thailand on the question of payment of reparation, which had been dictated by the British government. The war claims were $5,224,220 to be paid to Great Britain of which, India's share was one-fifth $104,484. On the other hand, Thailand adopted a very sympathetic attitude towards INA volunteers who preferred to stay back in Thailand, which facilitated their rehabilitation.

In December 1946, India appointed a consul general meant for Bangkok and one B. Dayal was deputed to go there. Thailand reciprocated this gesture by deputing Dr. Thanat Khoman to work as first charge affairs in New Delhi. Luang Pimitaksorn, as the first Thai Minister in New Delhi, succeeded Dr. Thanat, who later became the Foreign Minister of Thailand, and B. Dayal became his counterpart in Bangkok. Both the governments decided soon to upgrade diplomatic relations to ambassadorial level in 1951, when Thailand appointed Luang Wichitwadhakarn as the first ambassador. Though the diplomatic interactions were exchanged, the regional environment and the domestic developments in Thailand were not complimentary enough to boost Indo-Thai relations.

Thailand in the post-Second World War era, was witnessing the civil unrest. Thailand's ethnic Chinese were unhappy because of the communal riots in Bangkok and communist movements were picking up momentum. The communist takeover of power in China and their open support to Chinese population in Thailand, had created a hostile atmosphere. The Chinese had accelerated propaganda drives against military rule of Field Marshal Phibun Songgram in Thailand. On the other hand, there were disturbances in Patani, and the national security was a matter of prime concern for Thai decision-makers.

The United States well knew about the strategic importance of Thailand in the containment of China's propaganda drive and they had started showing common concern for Thailand. The US had appointed Edwin F. Stanton as an ambassador to Thailand, who astutely cultivated relations with military elites and thus, the two countries came closer to each other. Thailand and the US, signed military assistance agreement in 1950 and they founded SEATO in 1954 and became allies. Thailand became the headquarters of SEATO and thus, contributed in terms of contingents of armed forces in Vietnam War. Thailand gave its air and naval bases to the US and American air force regularly used those bases to bomb the communist belts in Vietnam. When the war finally came to an end in 1975, Thailand became a frontline state to prevent Vietnam from expanding and consolidating its influence in the region.

However, a number of economic reforms (Doi Moi) in Vietnam since 1986, the signing of the Cambodian Peace Accord (1991) and the disappearance of the Soviet Union (1991) changed the global security and economic environment. The Uruguay round of talks, WTO, human rights issues and the rise of Islamic radicalism, generated new challenges and this diverted the opinion of the countries in the region to attend the issues of regional concern.

In retrospect, we find that the cold war of the two super powers had intensified the disputes in the region, wherein the ideological and strategic issues predominated the deliberations at the regional and global level. The China factor and Cambodian crisis were the preoccupations of nations in the Asia-Pacific. The end of the cold war in 1991, although offered some new opportunities, some new challenges also emerged. Accordingly, the countries of the region began to review their old policies and alignments. Indo-Thai relations, which had been marginalized as a consequence of the cold war, got new life and meaningful dimension in the post-cold war era. Both understood the importance of one another and took initiatives to make the relations more vibrant and beneficial.

Indian Premier, Rajiv Gandhi had done some necessary homework when he had gone to Thailand on an official visit in October 1986. This was surprisingly, the first visit of an Indian Premier to Thailand, after independence in 1947. Prime Minister Rajiv Gandhi tried to provide economic dimensions to existing relations and thus the Indo-Thai Joint Business Committee (JBC) was established to explore the possibilities of promoting trade, cultural and educational interaction. This committee suggested some measures to promote bilateral trade and both sides showed keenness to implement them.

Thai Premier Chatichai Choonhavan, later took an initiative to strengthen ties. He reciprocated the visit of Indian Premier and came on a state visit to India in 1989. Being an astute business-man, he admired the role of JBC and wished to upgrade it. Hence the JBC was renamed as Indo-Thai Joint Business Council/Indo-Thai Joint Trade Commission and entrusted with the task to promote trade on the lines suggested earlier by the JBC. Premier Chatichai took personal interests in the success of the JBC and so, the business targets for 1990-92 were fixed in New Delhi. The bilateral trade picked up momentum, and both sides felt happy about the satisfactory progress.

It is interesting to know that the trade turnover was quite encouraging. According to Joint Trade Commission spokesman, the trade plan projected for 1991-92, had been achieved in 1991 itself. The target of US $1 billion was reached within 18 months and there were prospects of boom. India exported gems and precious stones, cotton and fabric, machinery and parts, urea and fertilizers to Thailand, while imported pulses (Moong and Urad), rubber, machinery, synthetic fibres and inorganic chemicals. The export of gems during 1989-91, rose from 10 per cent to 75 per cent and earned India about $600 million, cotton and fabric about $60 million and Leather and fodder about $40 million in 1991. Joint Trade Commission in the meanwhile explored avenues of trade in other sectors like textiles, machinery, pumps, diesel engines, vehicle parts, organic and inorganic chemicals, dyes and hand tools.

India's investment relations with Thailand also started growing. Being ranked as the 13th largest investor in Thailand, India involved itself in 20 joint venture projects in the fields of textiles, rayon, chemicals, dyestuffs, iron and steel products. India and Thailand agreed to expand collaboration in fishing, including joint ventures in deep-sea fishing, fresh water and brackish water prawn farming, fish processing and study of tuna in the Andaman Sea.

In retrospect, we find that two-way trade between India and the ASEAN countries has grown at a fast rate in the post-1991 period. India's exports to ASEAN-9 (excluding Cambodia) had grown from US $1.38 billion in 1990 to US $4.31 billion in 1996. On the other hand, India's imports from ASEAN-9 had grown from US $1.38 billion in 1990 to US $3.97 billion in 1996. The two-way trade between India and ASEAN as per Indian official data, has grown more rapidly in the period 1993-94 to 1996-97. The relevant trade turnover has been more than doubled from just over US $2.5 billion in 1993-94 to 1996-97 (up from 6 per cent share in 1993-94). Considering this healthy trend, India has set an ambitious target of US $15 billion trade with the ASEAN countries for the year 2000-2001.[4]

The major exports from India to ASEAN countries currently comprise of agro-based products such as oil meals; edible nuts (ground nuts); sesame seeds; meat and meat products; textiles including cotton yarn, fabrics and ready-made garments; drugs and pharmaceuticals; chemicals including inorganic, organic and agro-chemicals; primary and semi-finished iron and steel; machinery (including textile machinery) and transport equipment; and processed minerals. Apart from expanding India's exports of the above major items of ongoing exports, the following goods and services have tremendous potential for giving further push to India's exports to the ASEAN countries. These include sugar processing machinery; railway rolling stock; electrical equipments and machinery; gem and jewellery; automotive components; and above all, information technology including software development consultancy and training in both hardware and software; construction; health and educational services, and processed fruits and vegetables.

Apart from bulk imports of palm oil and other metals, minerals and primary articles, India can profitably expand its imports from ASEAN countries of electronic items, computer hardware, electrical equipment, and most importantly services for the construction, maintenance and upgrading of ports, airports, telecommunication centres, roads, bridges, and power stations.

Despite the satisfactory incremental growth of India's growth of two-way trade with the ASEAN countries during the post-1991 period, the basic asymmetrical nature of this two-way trade has not yet materially changed. Thus, viewed from the ASEAN perspective, India still accounted for only

1.17 per cent of ASEAN's worldwide exports in 1996. Similarly exports from India had amounted to just 1.05 per cent of total imports of ASEAN in 1996. Clearly, ASEAN's trade relations with India are still much below their potential, commensurate with their economic strengths (comparative advantage) and considering the areas still untapped.[5]

Mr. P.V. Narasimha Rao gave a new thrust to India's "Look East" policy and incidentally attached great importance to partnership with the ASEAN.[6] He, was also interested in improving the investment climate and thought that Thailand could play a key role in this respect. He, therefore, decided to pay a state visit to Thailand coinciding with the meeting of Indo-Thai Joint Commission in Bangkok in April 1993. He eloquently underlined the significance of a new orientation in India's foreign policy, in which Thailand occupied a key position as a close and contiguous maritime neighbour. Thailand was indeed regarded as one of the gateways to the expanding trade, investment and tourism ties with the ASEAN. It had been admired as India's major trade partner and Mr. Rao showed his eagerness for further cooperation and collaboration.

Indo-Thai Joint Commission, which was scheduled to meet for setting up the target for 1993-95, tried to turn Thailand as one of the largest trade partners of India. New areas of cooperation were being explored and suggestions were given. Thailand has already emerged as the sixth largest foreign investor in India. In 1993, Thailand had approved of the investments worth $120 million in areas like fisheries, chemicals, air-conditioning systems, hotel and tourism. Thai companies have also signed agreements with Indian companies for joint ventures in the telecom sector.

As Thailand attached importance to growing relations with India, it sent its Foreign Minister, Prasong Soonsiri to India in November 1993. Besides meeting the business people, he met Prime Minister Rao. He discussed the issues of cooperation in the area of nuclear energy, business exchanges, fisheries and agriculture. Thailand also accepted India's offer of technology transfer of areas like fibre optics electronics including computer software and hardware.

Innovative ideas were evolved to boost the investment ties and in this connection, the proposal of a "growth triangle", is quite interesting. In October 1994, Mr. Surin Pitsuwan, Thai Deputy Foreign Minister, visited India and proposed "growth triangle" amongst Sri Lanka, Thailand and India for business and trade. Such a tie is expected to augment the supply of raw materials, financial goods and high technology. India, however, was not enthusiastic enough to respond.

Thailand reinforced its suggestions for "growth triangle", when Supachai Panitchpakdi, Deputy Prime Minister of Thailand, visited India in January 1995. He discussed the proposal with Indian businessmen and exposed the idea in detail at Secretary level talks. This proposal envisions the building of a four-lane highway between Andaman Sea and the Gulf of Thailand. The projection is to construct deep-sea ports, refineries and industrial ventures, alongside the highway.

In fact, India is unable to take a decisive step in the direction of establishing a "growth triangle". When Prasong Soonsiri had met Rao in November 1993, he had himself suggested that India and Thailand should cooperate in business ventures in Third World countries, such as Vietnam. This proposal, later known as "Troika", could involve partnership of India with various partners of the ASEAN and could produce items required outside the region, but this is yet to be taken up seriously.

In fact, India has suggested Troika to Singapore also for collaborative efforts and business in Vietnam. Though they have welcomed Indian proposals they involved India in business ventures in the SAARC region, namely Sri Lanka, Bangladesh and Nepal.

"Growth Triangle", or "Troika", both aimed at the collaboration involving three countries of the region but "growth triangle", has assumed some meaning in the ASEAN countries. They have established this at Johore and Bantam and the three countries—Singapore, Malaysia and Indonesia—have been benefited with this venture. However, the meaning and scope of Troika is yet to be explored.

Indonesia, the biggest country of the ASEAN, has also expressed its intentions to be a partner in the "growth triangle" in the Andaman regions with India and Thailand. They emphasized the importance of our collaboration through meetings of the India-Indonesia Friendship Association. India is an important dialogue partner of ASEAN, in which Thailand is a member. The relations with ASEAN countries are improving and Thailand has facilitated India's playing its legitimate role in the region.

Dr. Surin Pitsuwan, Foreign Minister, led a delegation including senior officials and representatives from the private sector to visit India during 8-10 July 2000. Members of the private sector accompanying the Thai Foreign Minister were representatives from the Thai Chamber of Commerce, the Thai Bankers Association, Fishery Association, Thai Computer Association and the Thai businessmen with Indian origin. The Thai delegation held talks with Indian leaders such as the President, Prime Minister, Foreign Minister, Agriculture Minister. Foreign Minister Surin also took the opportunity to meet Indian businessmen and delivered an address at the Confederation of Indian Industry.

During his talks with Indian officials, both the sides explored the opportunity to increase the amount of two-way trade. At the moment, the average annual trade volume is only US $846 million. The Thai side also proposed to the Indian side its plans for enhancing cooperation in the area of fishery, investment, education, information technology, and culture, and will review the progress in cooperation every three years. Thailand expressed its particular interest in investing in the Indian infrastructure projects and invited Indian companies in the information technology (IT) and food sectors to invest in Thailand.

The Thai side also proposed to enhance cooperation with India in international and regional organizations such as UN, BIMST-EC, IOR/ARC and ASEAN. And, Thailand being the chairperson of ASEAN Standing Committee, the Foreign Minister Surin invited India to increase its participation in ASEAN, especially in IT, human resources development, Mekong development, and the "Great Wonders of Subarnabhumi" project.

On behalf of the Royal Thai Government, Foreign Minister Surin Pitsuwan concluded two agreements with the Indian government, which were the Agreement on the Promotion and Protection of Investment and the Agreement on Joint Cooperation for the Peaceful Use of Energy.

Members of the private sector accompanying the Foreign Minister Surin had an opportunity to meet their Indian counterparts at Indian Chamber of Commerce and Industry, the Federation of Indian Industry, and importers, to explore business opportunity in areas such as computer, banking and finance, IT, automotive parts, and agro-industry.

Bilateral trade between India and Thailand amounted to US $248 million in 1991, rising to US $644 in 1995-99 and remained the same in 1996-97. Indian exports to Thailand have gone up steadily in the 1990s, as have Thai exports to India. Exports to Thailand rose to 58.6 per cent in 1993, went up by 18 per cent in 1995 and registered a growth of 16.2 per cent in the first half of 1996. Thai exports increased 12.6 per cent in 1993, went up phenomenally by 159 per cent in 1994, rose to 49.3 per cent in 1995 but dropped by 16 per cent in the first six months of 1996. The decline was in keeping with the general decline in Thai exports. The major items of Indian exports to Thailand are diamonds and stones, primary and semi-finished steel, plant solvent extracts, chemicals, dyes, raw and finished cotton, drugs and pharmaceuticals and machinery. Thai exports to India comprised pulses, rubber products, electrical machinery, tools and metal scrap and gems and ores, including rice at certain times.

Investment proposals from Thailand in the fields of fisheries, chemicals, air conditioning systems, hotel and tourism, were approved of, in 1994-95. Indian investment of US $25 million in Thailand was registered in the same period. In 1998, there were 27 Indian joint ventures in Thailand involving about US $16.5 million. Total approved investment from Thailand for the 1991-98 period was, Rs.24517.21 million.

However, Thailand and other ASEAN partners are presently interested in economic relations and in exploring South Asian market. They may like to expand their economic influence through India in South Asia and treat India as the gateway to enter into the SAARC market.

Thailand is a key regional actor. It has been taking landmark steps in the promotion of business and trade. It tried to turn Indo-China into a market place and facilitated the construction of Lao-Thai Friendship Bridge. Now it is giving new thrusts to "Look West" policy and in that connection, they attach prime importance to India for its success.

Thailand has evolved "Look West" policy to compliment India's "Look East" policy. Thailand's Foreign Affairs newsletter stated that the conceptual basis of the Look West policy for Thailand is to cope effectively and efficiently with the rapid changes in the international political and economic environment in accordance with the reality of the post-cold war era. The Look West policy is also derived from the fact that Thailand recognizes promising economic potential of other regions beyond Southeast Asia. The main objectives of the Look West policy as they summed up are as follows:

1. To strengthen the existing bilateral relations with the target states.
2. To seek potential markets and investment opportunities overseas, and to promote foreign investment in Thailand.

Target states are countries in South Asia, Middle-East and Africa. But South Asia is a gateway to the Middle-East and Africa. In that connection, there is a special reference to India, where they find promising economic environment, vast economic potential, cheap labour and an abundance of natural resources. "Look West" policy of Thailand, as explained by Pitak Intrawityanunt, Deputy Minister of Foreign Affairs, on 27 May 1997, in New Delhi, was to strengthen and expand the economic, political and cultural cooperation between India and Thailand. The ministerial visit to India was projected as part of the "Look West" policy, and both the sides agreed to expand trade from $900 million to $2 billion by 1998. Thai products with high market potentials in India, were electronic devices and plastic goods and Thailand assured to explore ways and means of increasing her investment in India. It was during this visit that India agreed to consider the issues of expanding of cooperation in fishery around the Andaman and Nicobar Islands and the release of the 16 Thai fishermen who had been detained.[7]

In fact, Thailand had taken an initiative in 1995, to establish a sub-regional grouping involving India for greater cooperation in the name of BIMST-EC, and this evoked a positive response. On June 6, 1997, this sub-regional grouping was formally launched and the main areas of cooperation included trade, investment, industry, transportation, infrastructure, science and technology, human resource development, energy, fisheries, agriculture, natural resources and tourism.

A special meeting of the BIMST-EC hitherto known BIST-EC took place in Bangkok in December 1997, where Myanmar too was admitted into the grouping. Hence, BIST-EC was renamed as BIMST-EC and it decided to establish an Economic Forum with both private and public sector participation from member countries.

Again Economic and Trade Ministers of BIMST-EC met at Bangkok on August 7, 1998, where India was represented by Commerce Minister R.K. Hegde. This meeting underlined BIMST-EC's substantive economic agenda and marked a significant step towards further institutionalizing BIMST-EC cooperation. A BIMST-EC Senior Economic Officials Committee (SEOC) was established and the responsibilities for the various sectors identified for cooperation were delegated amongst the five countries as follows:

County		*Sectors*
Bangladesh	—	Trade and investment
India	—	Technology
Thailand	—	Transport and Communication
Myanmar	—	Energy
Sri Lanka	—	Tourism and Fisheries

Although the "Look West" policy of Thailand, is meant for promoting the relations with India in cultural, political and economic areas, the cooperation in strategic/security areas are growing. There is convergence of interests between India and Thailand in strategic areas, which had not been properly understood in the past. There are non-traditional security threats such as terrorism and spread of small arms, drug trafficking, maritime piracy, money laundering, illegal migration, environmental degradation, growing scarcity of energy resources and spread of infectious diseases. These matters are of great concern in South and Southeast Asian region. Therefore, both Thailand and India have been struggling to evolve policies to ward off the non-traditional security threats, but both have failed in that attempt. An effective coordinated action plan is needed to address various issues and Thailand and India can contribute significantly especially to controlling drug trafficking, maritime piracy and terrorism.

Drug trafficking is a serious problem and both India and Thailand are interested in curbing it. The Golden Triangle, which includes the territory of Laos, Myanmar and Thailand, is the largest producer of opium. The opium producers have their transit points through India or China and through them it is illegally transported in the outside world. Drug trafficking generates narco-terrorism, crimes, aids and other infectious diseases. A large number of people in Thailand and India are the victims of drug abuse and drug-trafficking. Both Thailand and India can coordinate their activities in the Gulf of Thailand and Andaman Seas to contain the activities of drug lords and smugglers. As far as maritime piracy is concerned, there are reports of attacks by the pirates in Malacca and Sunda straits. The pirates are always violent and unscrupulous and they target only small local vessels, tugs, supply ships and fishing trawlers, and attack their targets for stealing the cargo or kidnapping the crews for ransom.[8] However, the most disturbing issue for both India and Thailand is the rise of terrorist outfits in the region. Islamic fanatics are engaged in violent activities and Muslim fanatics in Patani (Thailand) have definite links with Jemmah Islamiyah. On the other hand, India is witnessing violent activities in northeastern states, especially in Nagaland, Mizoram and Manipur, which have impinging impacts on broader issues of regional cooperation.

Again, terror attacks in the US on 9/11, serial bomb blasts in London on 7/7, and bombing attacks in Bali, Jakarta, New Delhi, Patani and Mindanao, have disturbed the security environment. India and Thailand, sharing common maritime borders, are cooperating under the framework of ASEAN Regional Forum (ARF) and have signed several agreements against terrorism in the region. However, it can be stated that terrorism and other issues of non-traditional security matters are sensitive issues and demand utmost care and urgent attention to handle. It is a complex exercise and demands a dynamic approach. The western panacea, as witnessed in Iraq and Afghanistan are counterproductive. A regional consensus and solution are required and as a Centre of Buddhist learning and civilization, Thailand is expected to play an enlightened role in that direction.

There is scope for cooperation and coordination in security and defence matters in the present dispensation and the ARF is exploring them. The cooperation in strategic areas between Thailand and India, was dismal before 1991. Both were patrolling their maritime frontiers individually and in isolation of each other. However, they were arresting fishermen trespassing into each other's territory. Thailand was strategic partner of US and so was the case of India *vis-à-vis* the Soviet Union. The smugglers and pirates were active in the region and they were treating Andaman as an important channel for narcotics and drug supplies. The smugglers exploited the differences in the attitudes of the two countries and branded both India and Thailand as soft *vis-à-vis* drug mafias. But now the situation has changed. India and Thailand are associated with ARF and they discuss their problems and policies. Again, China's strategic presence in Myanmar, especially in Coco Island and Haingyi, was a matter of concern for all of us. The countries in the ASEAN region, concerned at China's sovereignty claims over the Spratlys and incidents of skirmishes at Mischief Reef. Hence Thailand also began to review its strategic perspective and found Indian opinion sharing Thai concerns.

Kavi Chongkittavorn who has been writing about Thai strategic thinking in the leading national daily newspaper Nation, noted that the opinion of Thai Armed Forces towards India started changing after 1992, which became clear after the exchange of visits by senior army officers and defence personnel to India. Thus, the army officers from India also reciprocated and the growing interaction showed areas of cooperation. India and Thailand are the only two Asian countries, which possess aircraft carriers. Thailand has Spanish built Chakri Naruebej aircraft carrier based at Phuket. India has its naval presence at Andamans. India has missile technology and potentials to assist Thai navy's modernization plans.[9] India has conducted nuclear tests and its missile technologies are advanced. If Thailand and India will coordinate their strategies in the region, it will prove beneficial for both. Thailand and India through their joint exercises, joint patrolling and coordination, can ensure the safety of the international waters, especially in the Gulf of Thailand and Andaman regions from maritime piracy, illegal poaching of fish, and unauthorized extraction of various types of marine resources. Thailand shares 10,000 nautical miles of common maritime boundary with India in the Andamans.[10] If the two agree to have joint patrolling and surveillance, it will prove useful for both the countries. If they ensure cooperation in that area, they will significantly and substantially contribute to the safety of the international sea-lanes of communication in the straits of Malacca, Lombok and Sunda.

Thus we find that Indo-Thai relations are on the right track. In the economic or security matters, both of them have similar views. They are evolving common stand in WTO and on free trade. However, it can be found that all these matters are constantly in a flux and the business is much below the target. What binds India with Thailand on permanent basis, is culture and Buddhism and therefore, we must attach importance to cultural interaction, and use that feedback for regional cooperation.

To sum up, it can be stated that the status of relations with Thailand is a decisive factor in promoting our ties with Asia-Pacific. Thailand continues to remain an important gateway to promote our partnership with ASEAN and East Asian countries. Thailand had played a key role in promoting the bonds of regionalism in the past. The idea of establishing ASEAN had emanated in Thailand. Thai Foreign Minister, Thanat Khoman, had played a pivotal role in bringing Indonesia and Malaysia on a common platform to work for regional cooperation and forget the policy of confrontation. The confabulation amongst Thailand, Malaysia and Indonesia paved the path for cooperation and thus, ASEAN had been evolved. Although ASEAN had a slow progress, in due course of time it substantially contributed to the boom of the region.

Thailand has been given credit for evolving the policy of changing Indo-China from battleground to marketplace. It has given its own interpretation of democracy and human rights, free trade and fight against terror as an alternative to western views. Its support of regional cooperation especially in the post-cold war period, is appreciated. But the attitudes and mindset of the leaders cannot be changed abruptly. It takes time to evolve a common vision and strategies. We understand that India and Thailand have immense scope of cooperation in mining, fishing, IT, BT, science and technologies. The economic thrust in relations is indeed rewarding, but in our assessment, the relations with Thailand are symbolic of our friendship with Southeast Asia. Whenever Thailand solidly supported India in any regional trials, it was successful. Whether it was the subject of spread of Buddhism in the ancient past, INA struggle against colonial rule in India or the establishment of BIMST-EC in the recent past, Thai support proved to be crucial. If India is willing to contribute to Asian resurgence, and if it believes that Asia-Pacific must be given a priority in trade and investments, it has to give attention to clearing India's gateway to Asia-pacific. In that attempt, it can be stated that with Thai support, cooperation and coordination, we can handle the situation effectively. Although the support of Myanmar and Bangladesh is important, the making of cooperative environment is possible.

India has been pursuing "Look East" policy and has attached priority to the ASEAN region for economic and strategic partnership. It has cultivated strategic partnership with Indonesia and Singapore. It has helped in reviving nuclear plant in Ho Chi Minh City under international supervision. Its credentials as a responsible important power in the region are recognized. However, geo-politics of the region suggest that Indians can achieve their objectives in the Asia-Pacific, if there is peace in the northeast, coordination with Bangladesh, and complete solidarity with Myanmar. Thailand is the only country in the region, which can act as a facilitator in that process, to provide new thrusts to regional cooperation and integration.

Thailand finds convergence of interests with India and "Look West" policy is intended to create conditions for better relations. It is aimed at evolving a new mindset, new environment and new incentives conducive to promote relations.[11] India is slowly framing suitable rules and regulations to exploit growing opportunities. The "Look West" policy explored avenues to establish contacts for mutual benefit and regional prosperity and India reciprocated them by actively supporting their proposals both for strategic and economic cooperation. Both sides have exchanged high-level visits for complete understanding and solidarity and ASEAN partnership facilitated these exercises.

However, the trade and investment figures indicate that it is far less than its potentials. There is lot of scope for improvement. Various issues like the cold war mindsets, standards of production, business environment and bureaucratic loopholes etc. very often come in the way of cooperation. Those issues spoil the rhythm of cooperation and various elements to promote cooperation get "misplaced". It is the need of the hour that all the elements of cooperation are fine-tuned with sincerity, understanding and urgency. The respective Prime Ministers of Thailand from Chatichai Choonhavan (he was the first Prime Minister of Thailand to come to India on a state visit in 1989) to Prime Minister Thaksin Shinawatra are highlighting the importance of India in the contemporary world and their views are suitably reciprocated by India. Indian Prime Ministers from Rajiv Gandhi (he was the first Indian Prime Minister to visit Thailand on a state visit in 1986) to Prime Minister, Manmohan Singh, tried to remove negative mindsets persisting in both the countries, but the transformation is gradual. Both India and Thailand are trying to expand areas of cooperation in economic, cultural and strategic areas. Thai perspective of India can be understood in the words of Field Marshal Phibun Songgram, the architect of modern Thailand, who spoke the following words, years ago:

> India is the mother country of religion, culture, arts and sciences, as she has been the world teacher from olden times. The light of Indian soul has therefore never been extinguished, but henceforth shine gloriously brighter, fanned by the unity, endeavour and perseverance of all of us.[12]

REFERENCES

1. For an understanding of Thailand's Strategic importance, see K.M. Panikkar, 1943, *The Future of Southeast Asia: An Indian View*, New York, and Donald E. Nuechterlein, 1965, *Thailand and the Struggle for Southeast Asia*, New York and Ganganath Jha, 1979, *Foreign Policy of Thailand*, New Delhi.
2. Prince Chula Chakrabongse, 1960, *Lords of Life: A History of the Kings of Thailand*, London, pp. 197-201.
3. To know in detail, about this aspect, see Frank C. Darling, 1965, *Thailand and the United States*, Washington D.C., and Ronald W. Pruessen, "John Foster Dulles, and Decolonisation in Southeast Asia", in Marc Frey et al. (eds.) 2004, *The Transformation of Southeast Asia*, New Delhi, pp. 226-40.
4. S. Pushpanathan, 2003, "ASEAN and India: A Partnership for Success", Jakarta, *ASEAN Secretariat*, pp. 32-34.
5. *MEA Annual Reports, 1995 to 2005*, New Delhi.
6. A.N. Ram, "India's 'Look East' Policy" in Raja Reddy (ed.), 2005, *India and ASEAN: Foreign Policy Dimensions for the 21st Century*, New Delhi, pp. 1-11.
7. *Outcome of Deputy Foreign Minister's visit to India, Crystal Lotus*, Bangkok, Information Department, Ministry of Foreign Affairs, April-June 1997, p. 16.
8. For a better understanding of this aspect, see P. Chalk, Grey-area Phenomena in *Southeast Asia: Piracy, Drug Trafficking and Political Terrorism*, Canberra papers on Strategy and Defence, No. 123, Canberra, 1997. (Prime Minister, P.V. Narasimha Rao in his famous Singapore Lecture on September 8, 1994 had spoken about security threats in the following words, "India has in fact been subjected to considerable burdens on account of migrations of populations, terrorist attacks and smuggling. Our interests lie in peace and harmony which will enable us to improve our standard of living".)
9. *The Nation*, Bangkok, 1 August 1997.
10. Kavi Chong Kittavorn, "Thai-India Security Ties Enjoy Peace Dividend," *The Nation*, 1 August 1997.
11. Rita Patiyasevi, "Video-Conference opens India Link", *The Nation*, 1 August 1997.
12. Quoted by Ranjit Gupta, "Indo-Thai Relations", *The Nation*, 1 August, 1997.

13

India's Vietnam Policy in Regional Perspective

India had been consistently viewing Vietnam as one of the pre-eminent powers in Southeast Asia.[1] It backed the anti-colonial struggles launched by the Vietnamese people against France and the United States. It opposed containment policy of the US and the formation of Southeast Asia Treaty Organization (SEATO). On the other hand, it advocated the need for conducive and proper environment, democratic dialogues and peaceful means to resolve the emerging conflicts. As it perceived natural role of Vietnam in regional politics, it wished its attachment or integration with Southeast Asian regionalism. The Association of Southeast Asian Nations (ASEAN), which had emerged as a regional bloc in 1967, did not see eye to eye with Vietnam initially. It took almost 28 years to the ASEAN to extend membership of the association to Vietnam.

India supported Vietnam ever since its independence in 1947. Whenever India perceived that Vietnam was cornered, attacked or isolated, it came forward with moral and diplomatic support. Vietnam had emerged the decisive factor in India's Southeast Asian policy for some decades. It refused to participate in Southeast Asia Treaty Organization (SEATO) despite the persuasion of leaders like President Eisenhower or Secretary of State John Foster Dulles.

India believed SEATO to be ill-timed and ill-conceived. Prime Minister, Jawaharlal Nehru, in course of a debate in the Lok Sabha on 29 September, 1954 said:

> "I feel that its (SEATO) whole approach is wrong and dangerous from the point of view of any Asian country. I realize that the motives might be quite good but countries in Asia as well as

> outside may have certain justifiable fears. But, I say, the approach of this treaty is wrong and may antagonize a great part of Asia.[2]

He again said that:

> Whether in Indo-China or elsewhere, peace can only come if we endeavour to establish a climate of peace. It is not by condemnation or mutual recrimination that we shall achieve this goal. We must forget past conflicts and past grievances and decide to make a new approach to each other in a spirit of tolerance and forbearance with charity towards all and malice to none.[3]

India believed the emergence of SEATO as a negative development directed against Vietnam exclusively. Hence, it was always critical against the role of SEATO. In fact, the SEATO alliance was adversely affecting four basic principles of Indian foreign policy. That was to promote the causes of decolonization, detente, disarmament and development at the international level. The Western alliance in the name of "Containment of Communism", focused their fire and fury against Vietnam and caused immense hardship to the common people by choosing military means to crush communist movements.

India believed that Vietnam did not deserve such a treatment. It thought in terms of enlisting Vietnamese cooperation and consent for regional harmony and cohesiveness. It regarded confrontation and war undesirable and counter-productive. It believed indigenous solution superior to imposed and imported ones.

India supported Hanoi's "Four Points" as a basis for resolution of the conflict in Vietnam. They were (*a*) an end of attacks on North Vietnam, (*b*) the withdrawal of foreign troops as provided by the Geneva accords, (*c*) continued temporary partition of Vietnam, and (*d*) a political settlement in the South in accordance with the programme of National Liberation Front (NLF) or the people of Vietnam.

In fact, Hanoi's Four Points were based on actual interpretation of the Geneva Accord (1954). This ultimately became the basis of Paris Peace Accord (1973), but Saigon regime and the US never relied on letter and spirit of those treaties. They continued their crusades till April 1975, when they were finally defeated.

The year 1971 was crucial in the politics of the region, when Dr. Kissinger started visiting China on secret missions. In 1972, President Nixon visited China and signed Shanghai communique. According to Sino-US understanding, China was to forget its fraternal ties with Vietnam and the US was free to attempt winning the war in Vietnam. Hence Vietnam was subjected to reinforce indiscriminate bombing without any fear of Chinese intervention. The ASEAN was a benevolent spectator, but India ploughed a different furrow. It regularly expressed its concern and sympathies for the Vietnamese people. There were hundreds of demonstrations and public meetings in important Indian towns condemning American intervention in Vietnam War. The opposition to American war in Vietnam were so vocal that it annoyed influential section of American decision-makers. The pressure of strong public support compelled Government of India to upgrade its diplomatic relations with North Vietnam in 1972 and establish full ambassadorial ties. It did not extend similar treatment to Saigon regime. It appointed Prof. Sisir Gupta as its first ambassador to Vietnam. At the same time, India renewed its demands for an end to US air raids over North Vietnam, withdrawal of American forces from South Vietnam and political settlement on the Geneva Model, leading to a peaceful Vietnam without foreign troops and alliances.[4]

Finally, when Vietnam war came to an end in April 1975, reconciliation and reconstruction were the needs of the hour. India wished Vietnam to be integrated into the regional order, but the ASEAN countries perceived threat to their stability and system from that corner. The ASEAN, which had become friendly with China, the US and the EC, adopted a cautious approach *vis-à-vis* Vietnam. As the three countries of Indo-China embraced communism in 1975 and projected the formation of "Indo-Chinese Federation" for the time being, such apprehen-sions of the adversaries were natural. Again the unification of North and South Vietnam in 1976, and its intervention in Cambodia in 1978, created lots of misunderstanding. The ASEAN as a group, felt real security threat from Vietnam and, therefore, concentrated on economic developments, i.e. joint ventures, free trade, tourism and democratization to improve their socio-economic system. Japan, Taiwan, the US and the EC came forward with generous aid and assistance to boost ASEAN economy. The Bali Summit (1976) and Kuala Lumpur Summit (1977) subsequently gave new direction, new vigour and enthusiasm to the ASEAN and opposition to Vietnam provided them a rallying point to be united.

In 1979, the US pursued a policy of "bleeding Vietnam white", and China marched on a punitive mission "to teach Vietnam a lesson". They succeeded in isolating Vietnam at the international level. They projected Vietnam as a major culprit in the Cambodian tangle but India perhaps believed that regional environment was responsible for Vietnamese intervention in Cambodia. The feeling of insecurity and insensitivities of the Khmer Rouge regime in Cambodia were responsible for Vietnamese intervention in Cambodia. The Khmer Range policy of resettlement, anti-Vietnam crusades, concentration of forces on Vietnamese frontiers were provocative for Vietnam.

In the face of the Cambodian crisis, India did not condemn Vietnam. It thought isolation of Vietnam to be counter-productive. It advocated accommodation of Vietnamese interests and its due honour in the power politics of the region. That perspective was to open the gateway to peace and development. India has had great regards for Vietnamese nationalism and it aspired Vietnam's constructive role in regional politics. It maintained cordial relations with the latter despite international opposition and advocated needs for creating peaceful environment for lasting peace in the region. Premier Narasimha Rao had referred to the need for peace and stability as a precondition for economic development and welcome the emergence of "a new climate of mutual trust in Southeast Asia.[5]

India had strongly opposed the Chinese aggression on Vietnam in 1979 and raised its voice at the United Nations. President N. Sanjiva Reddy and Premier Morarji Desai expressed shock and distress and Mr. Rikhi Jaipal, India's Permanent Representative at the UN, urged the Security Council to demand total withdrawal of the Chinese forces from Vietnam. He said that "it cannot but be a matter of concern and regret that Vietnam and Kampuchea should have been subjected to armed conflicts involving outside forces. We hope the Security Council will take steps to ensure the independence, and territorial integrity of the states in Indo-China." He further added that India was totally opposed to the concept of "punitive military action". It was fraught with great peril for stability in international relations.[6]

Though there was a ceasefire after two months of warfare, but guerrilla warfare between the Khmer Rouge and the Vietnamese forces continued unabated till the end of 1986. Vietnam was not getting an opportunity to retreat. However, when Vietnam adopted doi moi and pursued the policy of disengagement from Cambodia, the situation started changing. In 1988, when China used its naval powers to subdue Vietnam, the ASEAN sensed security threat from other corners and thereby started changing its approach towards Vietnam. As soon as Vietnam perceived positive reactions in the ASEAN region, it rapidly withdrew its forces from Cambodia and it paved the way for Jakarta Informal Meets, followed by other international meetings to settle the Cambodian tangle. The changes in the international system and disintegration of the Soviet Union posed new challenges and opportunities and Vietnam and ASEAN both tried to exploit it to their advantages. Democracy, free trade, human rights, ecological protection, environment and nuclear non-proliferation, etc. were given new emphasis in the emerging world order marking the end of the Cold War. As a result, the ASEAN began to think of Vietnam in terms of partnership and cooperation. They began to show their confidence and goodwill and enlisted Vietnamese support for regional development. The ASEAN postures gave birth to a new thinking and spirits that was not only desirable but needs of the hour.

The present attitude of the ASEAN towards Vietnam is aimed at strengthening regional security and prosperity and it was this state of affairs that India dearly espoused for Vietnam *vis-à-vis* ASEAN. However, Indian policy towards Vietnam was by and large misunderstood in the past. Now the ASEAN is perceiving the constructive role of Vietnam and they are saying the same things about Vietnam that India had been advocating. Thus Indian perspective of Vietnam has now been vindicated by the ASEAN and this is bound to augur well for regional integration and harmony.

Vietnam joined ASEAN on 28 July 1995. Thus a new era dawned on the horizon of regional politics in Southeast Asia. Vietnam, which perceived ASEAN as a "trojan horse" of the United States in 1967 and maintained adversarial relations with the latter for over two decades, now became a partner and a cherished destination for friendship and cooperation.

With Vietnam's inclusion in the ASEAN, the association became broad based and assumed a new meaning. The image of the ASEAN as an anti-communist and anti-Vietnam forum was diluted and this phenomenon opened the path of integration of the remaining three southeast Asian states--Myanmar, Laos and Cambodia—into the ASEAN. Thus the realization of the vision of "ASEAN-10" became a distinct possibility.

The ASEAN membership of Vietnam has negated the myth that Vietnamese culture, nationalism and ideology, being different from other ASEAN states, is alien and unfit to be included into non-communist forum of the ASEAN. This has also demonstrated that ideological differences cannot inhibit any Southeast Asian countries to be a member of the ASEAN.

It is understood that Vietnam's integration would help ASEAN in resolving security and political matters. The association has offered opportunity for Vietnam to concentrate on development activities and broaden the horizon of *doi moi* (Renovation). ASEAN partnership have instilled new confidence, motivation and enthusiasm and this has opened avenues for greater trade, investment and tourism in the region.

Vietnam's partnership with the ASEAN would greatly assist the goals *"to turn Indo-China states from battleground to a market place."* Momentous changes can be expected of more democracy, freedom, economic liberalization and globalization of Vietnam under the new dispensation.

Thailand, which had originally come out with the idea to turn Indo-china into a market place, may be affected adversely if Vietnam develops leaps and bounds. If Vietnam is in a position to compete with Thailand in business and trade; which is a distinct possibility, they may feel uncomfortable.

Thailand has been a major exporter of rice, gems, garments, fish and textiles. It has been innovative in tourist industries and growth rates are nearing the proportion of NIEs. On the other hand, Vietnam has potentials to concentrate on production of those very items. It has an added asset of offshore oil, gas, natural resources and cheap labour. They are entering the international market with a big bang and is projected as an emerging "Asian tiger".

On the other hand, China may not rejoice that their historical adversary had been a partner of the ASEAN regional grouping. It was possible for China to assert its views bilaterally to resolve border conflicts, but now Vietnam is an ASEAN partner and it would support multilateral approach to settle multilateral disputes. Its bargaining powers are improved and its opinion cannot be ignored even on bilateral matters. China and Vietnam faced territorial conflicts at the Guangxi border and Vietnamese grievances were given peripheral importance.

However, the important cause for concern is that not only Vietnam, but the frontier of the ASEAN became contiguous to China as soon as Vietnam joined the association. This may not be portrayed auspicious, because historically China has a tendency to be aggressive and assertive *vis-à-vis* immediate neighbours.

Nevertheless Vietnam's integration is aimed at resolving regional disputes and clear the path for peace and development. It may help not only in the conflict resolution of the Spratlys but also of the demarcation of ocean boundaries in the South China Sea. It is likely to assist in establishing 200-mile exclusive economic zone as well as free-trade zone under its jurisdiction. Above all, Vietnam would be helpful in improving the strategic environment in Southeast Asia.

The ASEAN states are committed to support the sovereignty and territorial integrity of its partners. They are opposed to hegemonistic manoeuvres of its neighbours and it was, therefore, that they opposed Vietnamese intervention in Cambodia in 1978. China then actively supported ASEAN endeavours to isolate Vietnam.

The ground realities have been reversed now as China is in the dock for its assertive and aggressive movements in the

South China Sea. China does not recognize the territorial rights of Vietnam, Brunei, Malaysia and the Philippines in the Spratlys despite the actual possession of the latter four. China is acting against status quo and is forcing its way to assume command of the Spratlys in toto.

Vietnam is an important contestant on the Spratlys question and committed to abide by the regional consensus, which negates Chinese stand. The Chinese march for expansion in the South China sea are to be checked and Vietnam as a frontline state, has to assume special responsibilities. Thus, Vietnam is enabled to return some of the gestures to the Chinese that they were subjected to at the time of Cambodian crisis (1978-1989).

Vietnam is occupying a significant corner of the Spratlys and their sincere efforts in coordination of the ASEAN for amicable and reasonable solution would be liked and encouraged. However, there is a possibility that such moves might turn counter-productive if the "adversary" is provoked to take retaliatory steps.

It is a reality that the conflict over the Spratlys have caused headache to the ASEAN partners. They have increased their diplomatic parleys over the issue since 1992. Most of them are procuring sophisticated arms to strengthen their security system. But their combined strength is much more inferior compared to China.

The ASEAN is devoted to promote economic developments in the region and avoid the possibilities of a war. They are trying for early settlement of the conflict and would appreciate Vietnamese contribution in that direction. However, there is a catch that the Chinese might feel base motives if Vietnam assumes a pivotal role.

If the endeavour is to check Chinese advance towards Southeast Asia, Vietnam's role is bound to prove strategic. Besides that, the deliberations of the ASEAN Regional Forum (ARF) and regular discussions with the Dialogue Partners would definitely deter China to play any destabilizing role in the Spratlys.

The integration of Vietnam in the ASEAN has recognised Vietnam's role in regional politics of Southeast Asia. It is yet to be watched whether it would continue to symbolize Third

World nationalism through this integration or play a secondary role in regional politics. Whatever happens, the integration is a realistic step with positive consequences. Such a move was overdue to heal the wounds that were inflicted on Vietnam in course of the Cold War.

India believes that Vietnam's partnership of the ASEAN would help the latter achieving both short-term and long-term interests. In short-term, the integration is projected to act as a deterrence to restrain China and other regional powers. It is aimed at promoting regional stability and existing order that contributes to continuing economic boom of the region. However, the integration in the long-term would certainly help the evolution of democratic order in the region, whereby human rights, free enterprise, free trade and market economy would gain utmost importance.

India has been attaching importance to Vietnam and to the ASEAN as one of the cardinal principles of its foreign policy. To recall Premier Rajiv Gandhi, who often praised the Vietnamese people for their extraordinary contribution to history, said in course of his visit to Vietnam that:

> "We were with you during your struggle for freedom, we are with you in your efforts for development and reconstruction and we shall be with you in any problem that you may face in future."[7]

His Vietnamese counterpart Nguyen Van Linh reciprocated his feelings by saying that:

> "India had always come to Vietnam as a friend while many others had come as invaders or marauders. Vietnam appreciated India's sincerity of purpose and its role at significant times in world history. This proved that the policies laid down by Nehru and Ho Chi Minh were correct. We seek closest possible relations with India."[8]

Subsequently, when Vietnam signed the ASEAN Treaty of Amity and Cooperation and gained observer status in the ASEAN, India projected it as a new and important development in international relations. It believed that such an association would contribute to the endeavour for making Southeast a zone of peace, friendship, cooperation and development. Indian Premier, Narasimha Rao welcomed Vietnam's growing links with the ASEAN and said that "India, having become a sectoral dialogue partner of the ASEAN, looked forward to closer cooperation with the countries in Southeast Asian region".[9] Mr. Rao, in course of his visit to Hanoi in September, 1994 said that the world is looking at Vietnam with new eyes as it goes through momentous changes in economic orientation. He welcomed Vietnam's forthcoming membership of the ASEAN as a positive and significant development and said India was determined to promote good neighbourly relations and expand the process of cooperation in the region. He emphasized once again that the initiatives taken by Vietnam for creating a climate of trust and understanding among the countries of the region were extraordinary. He believed that closer interaction between Vietnam and the ASEAN is an important component for peace and stability in the Southeast Asian region and thus he welcomed Vietnam's membership of the ASEAN.[10]

Indo-Vietnam bilateral ties, which is not under the scope of this study, needs to be mentioned here in the context that investment ties are getting new dimension. Indian entrepreneurs are exploring "troika" approach with the support of some ASEAN countries. The confederation of Indian industries in association with Singapore Manufacturers Association, have given their proposals of "troika", for investments in Vietnam. Initially they are willing to focus their investments in infrastructural sector in Vietnam for markets in African and other developing countries.[11]

Thus Vietnam's integration in the ASEAN may prove useful to India strategically, politically and economically. India has an impression that under the new dispensation its interests in Southeast Asia would be protected and promoted. To conclude in the words of a Vietnamese diplomat:

> "While liberalizing the economy, diversifying and multilateralizing the external economic ties, the task of strengthening and developing the traditional friendship and multi-sided cooperation with India always occupies a special place in the foreign policy formulation of Vietnam.... We are optimistic about the bright perspective of our relations, particularly in the field of economic cooperation".[12]

Since Vietnam has chosen the path of market economy and democratization, their paradigms ultimately would determine the quality of relations in coming decades.

REFERENCES

1. Mohammed Ayoob, 1990, *India and Southeast Asia: Indian Perceptions and Policies,* London, p. 35.
2. Jawaharlal Nehru, 1971, *India's Foreign Policy, Selected Speeches,* New Delhi, p. 89.
3. *Ibid.,* p. 401.
4. Paul, F. Power, "India and Vietnam", *Asian Survey,* Vol. 7, No. 10, October 1977, pp. 744-5.
5. *The Times of India,* 9 September, 1992.
6. *The Times of India,* 26 February, 1979.
7. Premier Rajiv Gandhi at a banquet hosted by Nguyen Van Linh in Hanoi on 17 April, 1988, *The Times of India,* 18 April, 1988.
8. *Ibid.*
9. P.V. Narasimha Rao on the eve of the state visit of Do Moi to India, *The Times of India,* 9 September, 1992.
10. *The Hindustan Times,* 6 September, 1994.
11. Sri Subodh Bhargava, President of Confederation of Indian Industries is quoted regarding the Troika approach in *The Hindustan Times,* 9 September, 1994.
12. L.K. Tran, 1995, "Vietnam-India Multifaceted Cooperation for Development and Prosperity", *Vietnam: September 2, 1945-September 2, 1995,* Embassy of the Socialist Republic of Vietnam, New Delhi, p. 18.

14

India and the New Order in Cambodia

India has been deeply concerned about the plight of the Cambodian people. Indeed, in its own modest way, India has done its lot towards resolving the crisis in that country. In July 1990, it was instrumental in arranging a meeting between the two adversaries, Prince Norodom Sihanouk, then head of the exiled government and Hun Sen, head of the Phnom Penh government—a meeting which, by all accounts, was momentous. It broke the impasse and cleared the way for working out mutually-acceptable solutions. Besides India has also had a hand in working out compromises at various peace talks and helped in the signing of the Cambodian Peace Accord in Paris, on 23 October 1991.

The Cambodian peace accord was signed by nineteen nations along with the leaders of Phnom Penh government, Funcinpec, Khmer Rouge (KR) and the Khmer People's National Liberation Front (KPNLF). Following which the Cambodian Supreme National Council (CSNC) has agreed to work collectively as a team. (The CSNC was to remain in power till the end of the general elections in Cambodia.) CSNC invited the United Nations Transitional Authority in Cambodia (UNTAC) to come and supervise free and fair elections. The CSNC however was to continue as a symbol of Cambodia's sovereignty and occupy the country's seat at the UN. The CSNC comprised twelve members from Hun Sen's People's Party, the KR, KPNLF and the Funcinpec. As chairman of the CSNC Prince Norodom Sihanouk was to receive the UNTAC team—though even before the arrival of the UNTAC, new equations and permutations were being worked out, with serious consequences to the resolution of the conflict and establishment of peace.

Prince Ranaridh, the Funcinpec leader, was busy forging close ties with the Hun Sen group and it was understood that they will support each other at the time of the UN-supervised elections. The two were projecting Norodom Sihanouk as a Presidential candidate, with Hun Sen agreeing to play a secondary role.

The KR ideologue, Khieu Samphan, was unfortunately attacked and injured when he came to attend a meeting of the CSNC scheduled to be held in Phnom Penh on December 2, 1991. The situation became so grim that Khieu Samphan had to be summarily sent back to Bangkok and Sihanouk changed the venue of the CSNC meeting to Thailand, specifically to facilitate KR's participation in the meeting.

The attack on the KR leader was interpreted differently in various countries. China in particular, was very unhappy, and asked Cambodian leaders to tighten their security arrangements. Sihanouk was sharp to retort while responding to the idea of a US Congressman and others for measures to stop the KR's return to Cambodia. To prove his neutrality Sihanouk was trying to distance himself from the People's Party of Hun Sen. Although a coalition between Funcinpec and People's Party—to contain the KR—had been accepted a week earlier, Sihanouk had gone on record to say that the proposal has been dropped.

According to the terms of the Cambodian Peace Accord, The CSNC chairman was to remain neutral and impartial. The ground realities in Cambodia were however forcing Sihanouk to adopt a more flexible stand. A large section of the people were unhappy at the prospects of the KR working as a component of the CSNC. And they hinted at the harsh measures they may adopt against the KR leaders, which is why the KR had requested for UN forces to monitor the law and order situation in Cambodia. And it was likely that they on this pretext would oppose the complete demobilisation of their guerilla forces.

India was watching these developments with concern. On December 12, 1991 it sent Eduardo Faleiro, Minister of State for External Affairs to Cambodia to explore the possibilities of defusing the crisis. The Minister assured the CSNC leaders that India would provide inputs necessary for the implementation of the peace accord. He pledged India's support for the reconstruction of Cambodia and, in his press conference at Phnom Penh, he said that India was prepared to send a contingent of soldiers to join the UNTAC.

India had already contributed personnel to the UN advance mission in Phnom Penh and was prepared to add more. It had deputed a representative to the CSNC. And, in its keenness to participate in the peace-keeping operations, it was only following a historic precedent. It had in 1954-56, as chairman of the International Control Commission had worked for the delimitation of boundaries between the three Indo-Chinese countries. Its efforts to implement the terms and conditions of Geneva Accord had won accolades and its peace-keeping role in Cambodia had been admired by Prince Norodom Sihanouk also.

There are three aspects of the Cambodia Peace Accord that require Special attention. First, the CSNC takes charge of the Phnom Penh government. Second, the CSNC remains neutral and impartial, and third, the UNTAC will wield administrative powers till a representative government is formed in 1993.

The concept of the UNTAC take-over is new. Indeed, it is for the first time in the history of the United Nations that it is to exercise such wide-ranging responsibilities. This exercise is expected to cost a minimum of US $ two billion. The funds are being raised by contributions from Japan, France, Australia, the US and the ASEAN six, namely Thailand, Singapore, Malaysia, Indonesia, Brunei and the Philippines.

The UNTAC is empowered to take all such necessary measures that will ensure the implementation of the comprehensive agreement, including those related to conducting the general elections and other relevant aspects of administering Cambodia. In effect, it has to play both civil and a military role. In its latter role it will keep an eye on peace and supervise, monitor and verify that there has been no breach of ceasefire. The mandate requires it to demobilise 70 per cent of the troops of all four contending groups. The other 30 per cent are to be put in UN-supervised camps and their arms in storage. The KR guerillas still number around 30,000 and they are heavily armed.

Again, the UNTAC is to supervise defence, foreign affairs, public security, finance and information. A number of great powers, keen to share the burden of the UNTAC with men and material, are sending their advance teams to help the UN endeavour. They are interested in Cambodia not only because the cold war is over and there is a detente in Sino-Vietnam relations, but also because of economic considerations.

Cambodia is endowed with a vast reservoir of natural resources and fertile soil. It has rich deposits of phosphates, high grade iron, gold and gems. Almost half the land area is covered with forests and there is tremendous scope for expanding the fishing and tourist industries. Of the 44 million acres of land available, more than 20 million acres are cultivable with increased production. It has the prospects of re-emerging as the rice bowl of Southeast Asia. Australia, Singapore, Japan and Thailand are willing to make large investments in the reconstruction of that country. Thailand is even interested in restoring rail links.

Briefly, the signing of the peace accord is welcome, not only for the sake of national reconciliation in Cambodia, but also for the peace and harmony of the region. The establishment of peace will automatically end the international isolation of Vietnam. It will close down an ugly chapter of internecine fratricidal war which had resulted in the installation of the Heng Samrin regime on 7 January 1979.

Vietnam's dispute over Cambodia in December 1978, was the direct result of the clash between Vietnam's regional ambitions and China's quest for supremacy in the neighbourhood. Subsequently, the fight between the KR guerillas and Vietnamese forces became a proxy war. The government of Heng Samrin, backed by Vietnamese forces, was not recognised by the UN and the Cambodian issue became one of the destabilising factors for the region. The accord is therefore a happy augury for national reconciliation and regional prosperity.

It is difficult though to condone the misdeeds of the KR between April 1975 and December 1978. The KR indulged in genocide, killing at least one million of the six million people. Many people were driven out of their houses during the implementation of the resettlement plan and subsequently perished. The KR did not even spare Sihanouk's family members. Five of his children and fourteen grand children are believed to have been massacred. The KR had also abolished the currency system and adopted a hostile attitude against Vietnam. Is it any surprise if a large majority of people in Cambodia are sore with the leaders of the KR? And there is fear of their security, despite promises by Hun Sen and Norodom Sihanouk to provide government quarters to KR leaders. The Phnom Penh army and police force too have been instructed to ensure the safety and security of the KR leaders.

India's endeavour is to cooperate with the UNTAC. It is willing to assist the UNTAC in disarming the guerilla forces, maintain law and order and conduct elections.

India has long term interests in Southeast Asia particularly in Cambodia. For one, it would like to retain the age old cultural links between the two countries. The Archaeological Survey of India has already undertaken the task of renovating Angkor Wat and is willing to restore other damaged monuments.

India has also to keep an eye on her economic interests if she is to compete with the outside world. For which the help of the NIRs in Southeast Asia, particularly of Thailand, can be of immense help. India's commercial contacts with Cambodia have been quite significant since July 1980. Both countries can profitably increase cooperation in the agricultural and technological fields.

15

India's Relations with Laos

Laos and India are fraternal countries and they have had similar cultural and historical experiences. Both had supported Non-Aligned Movement (NAM) and actively opposed colonialism and the armed external intervention of great powers. Both struggled hard for their independence against Western colonial masters. During the nationalist movement, India actively campaigned for freedom of Indonesia, Burma and Indochina. India considered the nationalist cause of Southeast Asia as its own and therefore Indian National Congress passed resolutions for decolonisation of Indochina states through its annual meetings from 1937 onwards. It repeatedly urged France to concede freedom to Laos, Cambodia and Vietnam. The multi-ethnic Lao people and India felt the sense of fraternity and displayed similar perspective in the realm of foreign policy and relations.

India is geopolitically linked with Southeast Asia and particularly with Laos. When freedom dawned, India cherished the emergence of a zone of peace and prosperity in the Indochinese region. But the US, which emerged as the most influential country at the global level, started a crusade against communism and focused its attention on developments in Indochina states. It tried to enlist regional support to contain communism and turn Southeast Asian strategic environment in its favour. It propounded "domino theory", to say that if Vietnam ever falls to communist forces, the rest of Southeast Asia would follow the suit. This thesis was rejected outrightly by India, Indonesia and some others.

Always articulating Third World interest, India differed with the question of containment drive. It opposed the contents of "domino theory" and refused to be a part of anti-communist alliance system. In fact, India opposed SEATO from the very beginning. However, SEATO was formed just after the conclusion of Geneva Agreement in 1954. The signing of this treaty and the provision for unilateral inclusion of any country under its "protective umbrella", proved the genesis for American military intervention in Laos subsequently.

Laos was subjected to the "protective umbrella" of SEATO without its consent. The government of Laos which had a neutralist posture during the period opposed the extension of protective umbrella to that country and in fact the issue became so controversial that Laos began questioning the very legitimacy of SEATO. The protective umbrella for Laos was withdrawn in 1962, but by then enough damage had been done. The US had managed to establish its foothold in Laos.

India as chairman of the International Control Commission (ICC) opposed the extension of protective umbrella at the cost of greatly annoying the Americans. India's first Prime Minister, Jawaharlal Nehru, unequivocally criticized SEATO under which protective umbrella was extended. In his own words,

> "There is constant reference in the SEATO to its defensive area. This area does not comprise merely the territory of the countries which are parties to that treaty but goes beyond it. This, I submit, is a dangerous extension of the idea of defence".[1] He further said that "Manila Treaty is an agreement about dividing the countries in sphere of influence. It is inclined dangerously in the direction of spheres of influence to be exercised by powerful countries."[2]

India supported the non-aligned and neutral position of Laos and viewed Pathet Lao movement positively. To quote Nehru, "Pathet Lao is not communist, but has communists in it and is an extreme nationalist force."[3] But the Americans viewed Pathet Lao as communist movement and tried to contain them by any means. They propped up the rightist forces led by Phoui Senanikone, Kong Le, Phoumi Nosavan and Boun Oum at the beginning of 1960s and aided and abetted them to subdue Pathet Lao forces. These endeavours proved disastrous and led the country to the grip of civil war."[4] The situation proved so grim that the 14-nation conference on Laos was called in 1961-62. India was one of the participants in this conference, through which the great powers declared that they would refrain from all direct and indirect interference in the internal affairs of Laos and also assured not to establish any military bases in that country. It was also decided that the warring factions—the rightists and leftists—would join together to form a coalition government and would desist from becoming a part of the military alliance.

This agreement was a blueprint for reconciliation but there were violations of its letter and spirit. The US continued to pursue its clandestine operations in Laos. It built an airstrip at Long Cheng and organised Thai and Meo irregulars to fight against Pathet Lao. Hmong tribesmen under Vang Pao were organised to fight against the leftist forces. Laotian territories were also used in fratricidal war in Indochina states by the Americans during 1964-75. The then Prime Minister of Laos, Souvanna Phouma had either no knowledge of it or it was beyond his control to stop this.

India disliked all these developments and continued to bestow support on the nationalist forces led by Pathet Lao. Indira Gandhi was one of the admirers of Pathet Lao movement. She established full diplomatic links with communist forces in Vietnam (1972) and when Paris Peace Accord (1973) was signed and a provisional government of national union for Laos was envisaged, she was happy that the socialist forces led by Prince Souphanouvong would share power at equal level with the rightists. However, the rightist forces were not sincere in implementing the accord. The morale of the rightist forces was shattered finally in the following years and Americans withdrew lock, stock and barrel in 1975. Hence the system of constitutional monarchy was abolished and Lao Peoples Democratic Republic (LPDR) came in its place.

The credit for victory of the Pathet Lao over the Americans goes to its leaders but it proved generous enough to pay tributes to its friends who stood by it at the time of the struggle. India was one of those along with the Soviet Union and Vietnam to be acknowledged by the Laotian leaders. In the political report of the third national party congress of Lao People's Revolutionary Party (LPRP), Keysone Phomvihane, Prime Minister and General Secretary of LPRP, said: "We express high appreciation for India's role and her contribution to the

Non-Aligned Movement to world peace, especially in South and Southeast Asia. We have treasured our friendship with India and Burma as well and will spare no efforts to consolidate and strengthen these ties".[5] Again India was admired for economic ties about which Keysone Phomvihane remarked: "We should expand economic relations with and secure assistance from India, from other countries and international organisations which are sincere in helping our country".[6]

Again Prince Souphanouvong the Laotian President attached due importance to India for friendship and cooperation and he paid a state visit to this country after the establishment of LPDR. Indian media gave lot of focus on his visit and President of India, Fakhruddin Ali Ahmad hosted a banquet in honour of Laotian leader. In his address, the Indian President extended warm welcome to the Laotian counterpart and said: "India was aware of the Lao people's great struggle for national liberation and we are extremely happy that the long dark night of fratricidal conflict has ended in your country, and a new, stable and united Laos has now emerged at the dawn of another day."[7]

President Souphanouvong reciprocated it by saying that "for our country and people throughout our armed struggle against imperialist aggressors for national liberation, India has consistently been most helpful".[8] He admired India's role in ICC in the past and emphasized that good relations between Laos and India have grown harmoniously to the satisfaction of both sides. The joint communique stated that not only the government and people of India had lent support to Laos and showed sympathy during the protracted and relentless struggle which the Lao people had waged against foreign colonialists and imperialists, but also in the post-1975 era aided the reconstruction and development. The joint communique laid the foundation for all-round beneficial cooperation between the two countries.[9]

In 1977-78, when Laos was struck by drought, India dispatched relief assistance in the form of rice, medicine, clothing and electric pumps. In 1980, India sent 100 buffaloes and veterinarians to improve the dairy farming in Laos. In 1985, India sent a number of high capacity water pumps for irrigation purposes. Indian companies-BHEL and CIMMCO-evinced interest in investments in Laos. Admitting our closeness Souvanh Srithirath noted: "The countries of Indochina and India have a long standing tradition of friendship and mutual help. India has played very appreciable role vis-a-vis Indochina. Her role in the ICC had greatly contributed to the stabilization in the region. Even in the difficult and delicate times, when India is the object of destabilization, encirclement and subversion by imperialist, expansionist and reactionary forces, she does not lack in bringing her valuable contribution to the countries of Indochina and for their political stabilization".[10]

In 1984, when Mrs. Gandhi was assassinated, Laotians felt grief and shock. The Laotian newspaper, *Passason* reported, "this news have caused shock and pain to our government and people because Mrs. Gandhi was the outstanding leader of the entire Indian people and a steadfast friend of Laos. Mrs. Gandhi had actively supported just struggle for liberation of Laotian people and continued to support in the new phase of national reconstruction as well, which made friendly relations and cooperation between Laos and India further consolidate and strengthen."[11]

It is a fact that India always considered Laos to be its equal partner and trustworthy friend. When M. Gorbachev emerged in the Soviet Union and advocated *glasnost* and *perestroika*, Vietnam adopted the path of Doi Moi (renovation) and Laos evolved New Economic Mechanism (NEM) in 1986 and apprehensions were raised about the continuity and future of our fraternity, particularly after 1991, when the Soviet Union was dissolved. But Lao-Indian ties continued to remain strong in the post cold war era also. Democracy, free trade and human rights are presently receiving new emphasis in the new world order, in the absence of which punitive actions are envisaged. Laos and India are striving to liberalise and adjust with the existing order. Hence they are faced with common challenges of liberalisation and globalisation.

Laos has adopted the policy of economic reforms under the agenda of NEM which have proved extremely successful. In fact, NEM is aimed at market-oriented reforms. It is planned towards decentralization of economic decision making, more accountability for public enterprises, fiscal and financial reforms, deregulation of prices, removal of trade barriers, implementation of new investment laws and overall greater reliance on market forces.[12]

The economic reforms have paid rich dividends. Laos is prospering and its industrial and agricultural output has increased. Foreign investors are satisfied with the pace of reforms. Initially, the investors concentrated their attention on tourism and textiles, but now their attention is diverted towards mining, logging and hydro-electric power generation.

The number of joint ventures with the outside world are increasing rapidly. The projects approved for foreign investments were 69 in 1991, 102 in 1992, and 79 in 1993; but by the end of 1996, the total projects sanctioned were more than 600. In 1996 the Western investors were for investments in mining and the ASEAN investors for hydro-electric power generation.

Laos became a full fledged member of the ASEAN in 1997 and it is destined to be a part of ASEAN-free-trade-area. It has allowed the passage of the ASEAN goods towards China and vice versa. China is reported to have developed two northern provinces of Laos for commercial purposes and the accord on Sino-Laos economic relations is already concluded.

On the other hand, India is also trying to liberalise and is doing all the needful to cope with globalisation. It has said good bye to the system of controlled economy and opted for the course of market economy. It has opened the country for commercial interactions at the international level. It offers a huge market of large middle class population. The changes in the economic policy are appreciated globally but the pace of reforms is cautiously initiated. In the realm of foreign policy, it lays emphasis on "Look East" policy and accords high priority to ASEAN with which it is associated as a "dialogue partner".

Thus, both India and Laos are witnessing transition phase in the politico-economic sense and both find convergence on major issues of international concern and under the existing dispensation, both have wide scope for cooperation in economic, strategic, political and cultural spheres. The Committee for Investment and Foreign Economic Cooperation (CIFEC) of

Laos has stated that the sectors of cooperation of collaboration are transport, energy, environment and natural resource management, human resource development, trade, investment and tourism.[13]

However, the key sectors for private investment are mining (gold, tin, lead and zinc, precious stones, coal, iron, limestone and gypsum), energy (hydro-power), agro-business (palm oil, coffee, cotton, sugar, fruits, vegetables and flowers) and wood-based industries.[14] Attractive incentives in the investment guidelines allowing 100 per cent foreign owned investments, repatriation of capital and profit, and legal guarantees against nationalization of private property, indicate high degree of liberalization in that country. It is understood that there is rich potential for foreign investments in the mining sector. Laos has over 500 recorded mineral deposits, of which most have yet to be exploited. Notable mineral deposits are iron ore, gold, coal, copper, potash, limestone, antimony, manganese, lead, gypsum, bauxite and tin. There is wide scope for trade and investments relations and only opportunities need to be exploited for mutual advantages.

Again Laos is situated in the middle of ASEAN countries and China, and it has special obligations to protect regional security interests. It is an important partner of the ASEAN Regional Forum (ARF) with which India is associated. ARF is for confidence-building and for ensuring regional political and security cooperation. However, the strategic development in South China Sea on the one side and Indian Ocean on the other side of Southeast Asia, are disturbing. The Chinese assertion of sovereignty in those areas is substantial. The naval installations at the Paracels, the Spratlys, Coco and Hainggyi by the Chinese are matters of concern and their hidden agenda are the subject of speculation. India and Laos have similar perspectives regarding security scenario in the region and they have substantial scope for cooperation.

Besides, the issues of democracy, human rights and environment are getting new definitions for negative purposes. Some of the Western countries are advocating sanctions for the absence of democracy and human rights; and the advocacy of their sanctions is to bulldoze dissent in the Third World. This is a dangerous idea and is to be tackled collectively. Laos and India are the supporters of ZOPFAN and they are unwilling to be dictated about their policies by the external powers.

Finally, we have wide scope for cultural cooperation. Being a Buddhist country, Laos has cultural similarities with India. Ton That Thien, in his famous study, *India and Southeast Asia*, has observed: "Of the three states in Indochina, namely Cambodia, Laos and Vietnam, the first two are closest to India. Culturally they belong to the Indian world, while Vietnam belongs to the Chinese world. In philosophy and religion, in literature and arts, in political and social organization, Cambodia and Laos have been strongly influenced by India, while Vietnam has been strongly influenced by China."[15]

It is interesting to find the images of Hindu deities in Buddhist temples of Laos along with Lord Buddha and architecture of Pagodas or temples, and works of art are in tune with Hindu and Buddhist traditions. In one of the major archaeological findings in the southern Champassak province, Hindu religious relics and symbols (Shiva Lingam) were discovered in September 1998 reinforcing the strong cultural and civilizational links between the two countries between 5th and 17th Century AD.

Again Laotian language has a lot of Sanskrit words and their epic, music, dance and festivals have striking similarities with those of India. All these are indicators of our cultural affinities which have flourished in the past for several centuries. All those are valuable assets which need to be nurtured and they would open the path for diverse areas of beneficial cooperation between the two countries.

However, the important aspect of bilateral relations lies in enhancing our commercial relations. The leaders of the two countries are aware of it and ministerial visits have been accelerated in the recent past and in that connection the official visit of Laotian Prime Minister to India in 1997 was important. Prime Minister, Khamtay Siphandone, visited India on May 1-5, 1997 to give new thrust and direction to our bilateral relations. He held extensive discussions with the Indian leadership reiterating the continued support of Laos to India on regional and global issues. During his visit a Memorandum of Understanding (MoU) on cooperation in the field of agriculture and allied sectors was signed and accordingly, an agreement for setting up of a joint commission on trade, economic and scientific cooperation was finalised. Subsequently, Lao Foreign Minister, Mr. Somsavat Lengsaved visited India to co-chair the first session of the India-Laos joint commission in New Delhi on July 6-11, 1997. The two sides resolved to find ways and means to increase their bilateral trade, which merely amounted to Rs.1.4 crores in 1996-97.[16]

India's relations with Lao People's Democratic Republic continued to be close and cordial with Laos showing considerable understanding in matters of importance to India. Dr. Souli Nanthavong, Vice-Minister of Science, Technology and Environment of Laos, visited India on April 1-4, 1998 to participate in the Global Environment Facility Conference at New Delhi. Shri S.T. Devare, Secretary (ER) visited Vientiane on July 5-6, 1998 and had detailed discussions with the Lao Deputy Prime Minister, Vice Minister of Foreign Affairs and other officials. Lao Vice-Minister of Commerce, Mr. Siaosavath Savengsuksa visited India on November 15-17 to attend the India-G77 and China Trade Conference.

Bilateral trade with Laos during 1997-98, while remaining at a modest level, showed a healthy increase, at Rs.2.9 crores compared to Rs.1.3 crores in 1996-97 and maintained the trend during 1998-99. Several Indian companies such as Kirloskars, Tatas, BHEL, PEC, etc. evinced keen interest in exploring the Lao market. Kirloskar Bros. Ltd. which exported irrigation pumps worth about US $30 million to Laos, set up a showroom-cum-service centre in Vientiane.

As part of 50th Anniversary Celebrations of India's Independence, an exclusive Indian Photo Exhibition was held at Savannakhet on July 24-26, 1998 a Seminar entitled "India and Laos: Areas of Understanding and Cooperation", was held in Vientiane on July 27-29, 1998, in which academics, industrialists and businessmen participated. They emphasized the need for more initiatives to promote our relations. As part of the cultural exchanges, 21 officials of the Lao Government attended training courses in India under ITEC and Colombo Plan in 1997-98.

Smt. Vasundhara Raje, Minister of State for External Affairs, visited Laos on January 17-20, 1999, to co-chair the Second Meeting of the India-Laos Joint Commission (JCM) held in Vientiane on January 18-19, 1999. The Lao delegation was led by H.E. Mr. Phongsavath Boupha, Vice-Minister of Foreign Affairs of the Lao's People's Democratic Republic. In their discussions at the JCM, the leaders of the two delegations reviewed the overall state of bilateral relations and agreed to further strengthen and upgrade the existing economic and cultural relations which will be commensurate with the excellent political bilateral relations. During her visit to Laos, the Minister of State for External Affairs called on the President and the Deputy Prime Minister and the Foreign Minister of Lao PDR. An Agreement for US $2 million soft credit to Laos and a Protocol to renew the Cultural Exchange Programme for another three years (1999-2001) were signed during the visit.

The main concern of the leaders of the two countries, however, is how to promote our commercial interaction. The general understanding is that there is enough scope of expanding our trade and investment ties. An account of our existing trade shows that items exported to Laos in 1995-96 fell under seven product categories. Of these drugs, pharmaceuticals and fine chemicals accounted for 53 per cent, and paints, enamels and varnishes accounted for 41 per cent. The demands for Indian cotton yarn and fabrics and engineering goods in Laos are decreasing. On the other hand, India imports metal scrap, consisting of copper and copper ore scrap, valued at Rs.4.8 million in 1990-91. The occasional paper of the Export-Import Bank of India stated in 1997, that Indian exports to Laos and Cambodia are gradually decreasing. In 1995-96, the total value of Indian exports to Laos and Cambodia aggregated to Rs.80.92 million, which was a minuscule 0.01 per cent of total Indian exports in the year.[17]

India and Laos are interested in promoting our traditional friendship and cooperation in the agricultural sector. India is providing many new hybrid crop species, such as sugarcane, mungbeans, soyabeans and rice. India is also trying to upgrade irrigation system in Laos by providing diesel water pumps and electric water pumps. The efforts are made to promote exchange of crop seeds between the two countries and as a beginning, mango production in Laos and in India have been initiated. Besides, India is also cooperating in human resources development by providing its expertise and scholarships. India has been awarding 32 to 37 scholarships to Laotian students every year and more than 300 Laotians have already availed themselves of this opportunity.

Finally, it can be observed that Laos has certain advantages, i.e., low labour costs, relative political stability and a commitment to economic reform. But it suffers from poor and limited transport infrastructure. In fact this is a stumbling block in the way of the country achieving its goal of emerging as a regional hub. The mountainous nature of northern Laos has isolated it from the rest of the country. On account of poor transport linkages and poor intra-regional transportation, Laos has yet to develop a railway network and thus infrastructure sector is poor. India's Birla group has signed a MoU with the Laotian government to refurbish the Vientiane airport and to build a cement plant in Laos.

To conclude, it can be stated that although India and Laos trust each other, and live in the heart and minds of each other, they are unable to exploit opportunities because of certain developments beyond their control. India is facing political turmoil ever since the end of the Cold War and it is unable to take any firm steps in the realm of economic liberalisation or foreign policy. In view of the plethora of political parties, each party is concerned about the vote banks and acts merely as pressure group. Thus, they ignore larger national interests. Various short-lived coalition governments have come and gone eluding stability, and economic developments are disrupted. On the other hand, Laos has political stability and the leaders are concerned about the welfare of the people. They have successfully undertaken the programme of economic reforms, and the investors are coming without much hassles. There are many East Asian and Western investors in the pipeline and they have certain advantages over India. Naturally, it can be predicted that Indo-Laotian trade and investment relations would remain low in the near future.

REFERENCES

1. Jawaharlal Nehru, *India's Foreign Policy*, New Delhi, Publication Division, 1971, pp. 88-89.
2. *Ibid.*
3. *Ibid.*, p. 406.
4. For further details, see Usha Mahajani, "US intervention in Laos and its impact on Laotian relations with Thailand and Vietnam", in Mark Zacher and Stephen Milne (eds.), *Conflict and Stability in Southeast Asia* (New York, 1974), pp. 237-74.
5. *Kaysone Phomvihane's Report on the Political Situation at the Third Congress of the LPRP*, Vientiane, Ministry of Foreign Affairs, 1982, p. 36.
6. *Ibid.*, p. 26.
7. Sudhasattwa Ghosh and Tridib Chakraborti, "Indo-Laos Relations in Retrospect", *Socialook*, special supplement on the Occasion of 10th anniversary of the founding of the Lao PDR, New Delhi, 2 December 1985, p. 24.
8. *Ibid.*
9. See the text of the joint communiqué between India and Laos, *ibid.*, p. 20.
10. Souvanh Srithirath, "Laos and India: A Common Cause", in T.N. Kaul (ed.), *India and Indochina: Perspective of Cooperation* (New Delhi, 1987), p. 24.
11. *Passasson* (Vientiane), 2 November 1984.
12. Richard Vokes, "Laotian Economy", *Far East and Australasia* (Hong Kong, 1995), p. 493.
13. *Brief Introduction on Lao PDR* (Vientiane, 1997), p. 6.
14. *Investing in Laos: Opportunities and Options*, Office of Foreign Investment Management (Vientiane, 1997), p. 2.
15. Ton That Thien, *India and Southeast Asia* (Geneva, 1963), p. 185.
16. Ministry of External Affairs, Government of India, *Annual Report*, 1997-98, p. 32.
17. Export-Import Bank of India, Occasional Paper No. 58, *Vietnam-Cambodia and Lao PDR* (New Delhi, 1997), pp. 63-65.

16

A Brief Survey of India-Indonesia Relations

In recent years, India and Indonesia have taken important initiatives to strengthen their level of co-operation and partnership. Both countries support economic liberalization and perceive scope for expansion of bilateral trade and investment. The article analyses the various factors that had created misunderstanding between the two countries in the past and emphasizes the importance of both to each other in the present. Finally, some tentative projections for future bilateral co-operation are essayed.

India and Indonesia are currently engaged in increasing dialogue intended to bring a new dynamism to their bilateral relationship. Both countries find a growing convergence of interests in diverse areas in an era of global economic liberalization. Indonesia opted for economic liberalization in the mid-seventies, but India did so only at the start of the nineties. The two countries had suffered a stagnation of their economies in the past and both are now trying to overcome that condition. Indonesia, however, has a comparative advantage over India, because it had liberalized its economy two decades ago and has a lengthy head-start. India has showed interest in Indonesia's developmental experiences, while the latter has indicated interest in the resources and vast market India can offer. Both countries are willing to learn from each other and have expressed their wish to enhance the level of their existing relationship.

Indonesia, with more than 17,600 islands and 187 million people, is the largest country in Southeast Asia, while India with 1,261,810 square miles of territory and a population of 950 million, is the largest country in South Asia. The two nations share a contiguous maritime boundary between Great Nicobar and Sumatra, and along the Andaman Sea and the Indian Ocean.[1]

Geographic proximity, cultural similarities, anti-colonialism, and the spirit of Afro-Asian solidarity, were common factors that brought India and Indonesia to see eye to eye on the eve of their independence. Relations developed so deeply that New Delhi preferred the Indonesian embassy to be located as near as possible to Teen Murti, the then Prime Minister's residence. The well-known Indian defence analyst, K. Subrahmanyam, has noted the bilateral Indian-Indonesian security collaboration of the past, which existed during Indonesia's liberation struggle in the forties and continued up to the beginning of the sixties.[2] There was close military co-operation between the armed forces of the two countries. Each country's army, navy and air force had signed separate co-operative agreements.[3] But the relationship faced some setbacks and in the mid-sixties the two countries started drifting in opposite directions.

The differences in attitude between India and Indonesia arose as a result of the nature and future role of the Non-Aligned Movement (NAM), "Ganjang Malaysia", and the perception towards China and Pakistan. Indonesia, during 1961-65, wanted to project NAM as a forum for confrontation against colonialism and neo-colonialism in the Third World. President Sukarno believed in revolutionary ways and exhorted the Afro-Asian world to confront the western powers. India, on the other hand, supported a neutralist posture and a middle path. New Delhi perceived dangers in the adoption of a confrontationist stance in relation to the west.

In fact, President Sukarno and Prime Minister Jawaharlal Nehru were charismatic leaders in their respective countries. They had great influence in decision-making and definite views about power politics at the international level. Initially, they saw eye to eye and worked jointly for the resurgence of nationalism in the Afro-Asian world. Both held a positive view of the role of communist China, but India had to change its perception after its war with China in 1962. On the other hand,

Indonesia changed its perception three years later after Suharto ascended to the presidency.

Indonesia, under the leadership of President Suharto, tried to improve relations with all those whom Sukarno had offended but, in so far as India was concerned, the timing was not propitious. Domestic developments in both countries and the politics of the Cold War were largely responsible for this. Suharto replaced Sukarno and endeavoured to establish a "New Order". He banned the Communist Party of Indonesia (PKI), viewing it as a destabilizing factor. Thousands of PKI members were persecuted and a significant number of activists fled to China. Beijing expressed solidarity with the PKI cadres and allowed them to indulge in anti-Indonesia propaganda. Indonesia felt outraged and broke off diplomatic ties with China in 1967. Thus, India after 1962 and Indonesia after 1967 had strained relations with China, but this common denominator between the two countries was not sufficient for them to come closer together. The role of the military in Indonesian politics, and increasing proximity with the American cold warriors were inhibiting Indo-Indonesian relations for decades.

Both India and Indonesia supported rapprochement with China in an effort to evolve collective strategies for peace and development. Accordingly, India restored its diplomatic relations with China in April 1976, while Indonesia's resumption of relations with China occurred fourteen years later, in August 1990. Both New Delhi and Jakarta believed that Chinese partnership was desirable for resolving regional disputes. On the other hand, China too was introducing economic reforms whilst breaking off fraternal ties with communist parties in Southeast Asia. China also established new economic zones and started evolving trade and business ties with South and Southeast Asia. It made friendly gestures to the two regions and this had a positive impact on its external image.

Clearly, for several decades, the China factor was an important element in the conduct of India-Indonesia relations. It was because of China that India and Indonesia opposed the formation of the Southeast Asia Treaty Organisation (SEATO), and evolved policies to stay away from the western-inspired drive to contain communism. Both countries disliked any effort towards the regional isolation of China and welcomed China into regional groupings. However, for different reasons (and as intimated earlier), both countries changed their attitude towards China in the mid-sixties.

After assuming power, President Suharto attached importance to stability and economic development in Indonesia. He supported the crusade against communism at the national level and accelerated privatization of the economy. He retained the 1945 Constitution but empowered the military to uphold the system. India, on the other hand, under the leadership of Indira Gandhi, supported a socialist approach, in terms of nationalization, land reform and industrialization. Prime Minister Mrs. Gandhi enlisted the support of the Communist Party of India and pursued assimilation of the communists into her party. In the realm of foreign policy, she was closely identified with the Soviet Union. Indonesia, on the other hand, had discarded the socialist ideals of the Sukarno era and established the "New Order" in which relations with the west, and the United States in particular, were attended to with great care. Thus, the two leaders supported different ideologies, political systems and foreign policies. It was for these reasons that both countries could not remove the misunderstanding between themselves. The basic differences in their systems and moorings in the post-1966 era allowed very little scope for reviving the fraternal ties of the fifties. Instead, the mass media of the two countries viewed each other through cold war lenses and, thus, biased propaganda against each other became a regular phenomenon.

Despite this, India did support Indonesia's integration of East Timor. New Delhi pleaded the Indonesian case forthrightly at the United Nations. India was also one of the few countries to send an observer to the specially convened People's Representative Council in Dili on 31 May 1976 which legitimized Indonesia's integration of East Timor. It is noteworthy that many countries, including two ASEAN states and the United Nations, boycotted the invitation to send observers to that event.

India has always felt that Indonesia has a major role to play in promoting stability and development in the Asia-Pacific, but the dynamics of the Cold War did not allow for a proper understanding between the two countries. India's conclusion of a treaty of peace and friendship with the Soviet Union, and New Delhi's support for "socialist" regimes were considered by Jakarta as unhelpful to Asia-Pacific stability. When India gave recognition to the Heng Samrin regime in Kampuchea in July 1980, it was opposed by the ASEAN states. The view of Indonesia, the unofficial leader of ASEAN, was that the installation of the Heng Samrin regime as a result of Vietnamese aggression was an instance of interference in the sovereign affairs of another country and therefore, the international community should take a principled stand to invalidate it. Indonesia advocated a collective strategy to deal with the Kampuchean crisis.

The most important issue that adversely affected India-Indonesia relations in the eighties was pertaining to the activities of the Indian Navy. In 1986, when it was reported that India was planning to build a major naval base at Great Nicobar, Jakarta expressed its concern.[4] Though the plans to build the base were finalized, India had to shelve them as a result of adverse regional reaction. However, India, under the stewardship of Rajiv Gandhi, tried to enhance its navy's sea control capabilities with the backing of the Soviet Union. In 1988, the Indian Navy acquired a Charlie-class nuclear-powered submarine on lease from the Soviet Navy. Again, serious concerns were expressed by the ASEAN states, particularly Indonesia. India subsequently found the procurement of that submarine a liability, and in 1990 returned it to the Soviet Union. While India retraced its steps, China raised New Delhi's ire by building naval bases at Coco island and Hainggyi in Myanmar. The Chinese also strengthened their foothold in the South China Sea after a March 1988 naval clash with Vietnam, and asserted claims of sovereignty over the entire South China Sea. These moves became a matter of concern to the Southeast Asian states and helped to shift the spotlight of regional anxiety from India to China.

Imperatives for Change

Southeast Asia faced new challenges of a regional and international dimension at the beginning of the 1990s. As a result of the eruption of Mount Pinatubo and the actions of the Philippine Senate, the United States lost two of its largest overseas bases, Clark Airfield and Subic Bay. This aroused widespread fears of a power vacuum in Southeast Asia. Though the Cambodian problem was resolved, the question of sovereignty over the Spratlys Islands emerged, which then involved three ASEAN claimants. The dissolution of the Soviet Union, the emergence of China as a great power and the passage by the Japanese Diet of legislation for peacekeeping operations, gave birth to new imperatives for change. New diplomatic paradigms, therefore, emerged in which India and the ASEAN states had identical viewpoints. Under the new conditions, the ASEAN states reviewed their policies towards India and offered "sectoral dialogue partnership" status to the latter in January 1992. India and ASEAN thereby began to identify areas of co-operation in trade, investment and tourism. Later, they embraced co-operation in science and technology. The isolation of India *vis-à-vis* ASEAN began to wither away. India with a middle-income population of 250 million people with a craze for foreign goods, offered a big market which the ASEAN states began to exploit. Delivering the Annual Singapore Lecture in 1994, Prime Minister P.V. Narasimha Rao called for a larger role for India in the Asia-Pacific region in the coming years and assured that, in return, the countries of the region would find in India a reliable partner and a vast market. He also referred to reforms in the Indian economy and pledged that there was no question of the government slowing those reforms down as they were irreversible.[5]

Notwithstanding India's overtures, some constraints remain. Despite identical goals in the post-cold war era, India was overlooked when APEC (Asia-Pacific Economic Co-operation) and the ARF (ASEAN Regional Forum) were established. This showed the continued existence of the residual impact of the cold war among decision-makers in the Asia-Pacific. Similarly, when Dato Ajit Singh, Secretary-General of ASEAN, visited New Delhi in February 1995 to broaden the scope of trade and investment ties and to announce the removal of non-tariff barriers over the next five years to facilitate Indian firms to take advantage of this provision, it received hardly any coverage in the Indian media.[6]

Indonesian Overtures

Against the foregoing, there were other, brighter spots. Indonesia gave due importance to India at the time of the Jakarta Informal Meetings (JIM) on Cambodia. India was considered useful in mediating and bringing together the warring Cambodian factions. As India was the only country from the region to have good rapport with both Hun Sen and Sihanouk, it was suitably placed to work as a middleman between the two. It was through Indian persuasion that both Hun Sen in Phnom Penh and Norodom Sihanouk in Beijing agreed to join the peace talks. When the United Nations Transitional Authority in Cambodia (UNTAC) undertook the task of reconciliation and peace, India assisted it by sending an engineer company (200 troops), a medical field ambulance force (300 troops) and an infantry battalion (840 troops) to Cambodia. India's support of this U.N. undertaking was appreciated by Yasushi Akashi, the head of UNTAC.[7]

India had thus demonstrated its willingness to participate in regional peacemaking and peacekeeping. It has given top priority to improving relations with the ASEAN states, and Indonesia, as the largest country of ASEAN, has been given due attention. The two countries have been holding bilateral seminars and have activated meetings of a joint business council. No one is interested in listening to views on political matters on such occasions, yet the polemics of the past do surface during such gatherings. However, the overwhelming number of the participants at such seminars tend to arrive at a consensus that suggests transforming and upgrading the present level of bilateral relations.

Trade and Investment Relations

India and Indonesia presently give utmost emphasis to trade and investment ties. India's basket of exports to Indonesia include cotton, iron ore, chemicals, textile machinery, machine

Table 17.1: India's Major Exports to Indonesia
(US $ thousand)

	1992-93	*1991-92*	*1990-91*
Oil meals	36,257	28,884	948
Engineering goods	23,135	28,600	37,904
Dyes intermediaries and coal-tar chemicals	11,602	10,629	8,64
Cotton raw, including waste	7,769	7,951	10,201
Iron ore	7,528	10,751	7,581
Processed minerals	7,182	8,722	16,276
Inorganic/organic chemicals	6,146	5,761	6,522
Shellac	3,557	1,988	1,505
Drugs, pharmaceuticals and tine chemicals	3,384	1,866	117
Cotton yarn, fabrics, made-ups, etc.	3,188	3,651	6,636
Manmade yarns, fabrics, made-ups etc.	2,590	4,200	669
Primary & semi-finished iron & steel products	2,244	41	72
Electronic goods	2,486	1,339	1,394

Source: P.K. Sandell, "New Dimensions of Business and Trade Relations between India and Indonesia" (paper presented at the India-Indonesia Seminar, 3 September 1994), p. 12.

Table 17.2: India's Major Imports from Indonesia
(US $ thousand)

	1992-93	*1991-92*	*1990-91*
Cashew nuts	10,773	13,306	1,895
Organic chemicals	7,838	10,426	3,623
Inorganic chemicals	10,256	17,160	346
Non-ferrous metals	3,798	89	390
Pulp and waste paper	3,453	2,191	5,741
Chemical materials and products	3,103	3,083	6,299
Coal, coke and briquettes	2,037	0	6,187
Dyeing, tanning, colouring materials	1,234	771	836
Paper board and manufactures	1,174	1,298	948
Synthetic and regenerated fibres	1,140	292	0
Artificial resins, plastics, etc.	1,001	1,582	3,679
Edible oil	656	5,152	37,291

Source: *Foreign Trade Statistics of India* (Calcutta: DGCI & S, various years).

tools, automobile components, and engineering products[8] (see Table 17.1). For its part, India has been importing spices, vegetable oil, leather and coal from Indonesia (see Table 17.2).

It would appear then that overall trade between the two countries is largely of the traditional type and is meagre. Trading volume could be increased by greater interaction through trade fairs, workshops, commodity buyers' and sellers' meetings as well as subcontracting and ancillary exchange programmes. P.K. Sandell, Director of the Indep Group of Companies, has recognized some core areas for business, such as computer software, processed foods, telecommunication products, chemicals—methylene chloride, ethylene glycol, phosphate, soda ash, caustic soda, sulphide salts—steel cables, tanned leather goods, textiles, machinery, woven fabrics, soyabean oil-cakes, wheat and iron oxide.[9] Sandell has surveyed the position of these commodities and has found that Indonesia would have a comparative advantage in dealing with India, relative to other countries.

Table 17.3: India-Indonesia Two-Way Trade
(US $ million)

Year	*India's Exports*	*India's Imports*	*Balance of Trade*	*Total Trade*
1987	29	63	-34	92
1988	35	67	-32	102
1989	79	51	+28	130
1990	149	59	+90	209
1991	226	56	+170	282
1992	216	70	+146	286

Source: Indonesian Trade Figures, Embassy of the Republic of Indonesia, New Delhi.

As shown in Table 17.3, Indonesia's trade with India has been increasing but it has yet to pick up significant momentum. Indonesia's exports to India increased marginally from US $46 million in 1980 to US $60 million in 1990, declined in 1991 to US $56 million, and rebounded slightly to US $59 million in 1992.[10] Imports went up from US $43 million in 1980 to US $151 million in 1990, US $226 million in 1991, US $253 million in 1992, and US $335.39 million in 1993.[11] Thus, after a surplus in the bilateral trade balance of $31.5 million in 1988, Indonesia suffered trade deficits of US $29.9 million in 1989, US $89.6

million in 1990, US $170.18 million in 1991, US $145.92 million in 1992, and US $235.47 million in 1993.[12]

There are some constraints in the way of trade expansion between India and Indonesia. The India-Indonesia Joint Business Council, in a recent report, recognized five constraints, as follows:[13]

1. Doubts regarding India's reliability as a business partner persist. The apparent problem relates to India's inability to stick to delivery schedules, after-sales service, poor quality of goods and so on;
2. Lack of direct shipping links between India and Indonesia and delays and expenses involved in transhipment via Singapore, as Indian exports meant for Indonesia are first shipped to Singapore;
3. Indian exporters provide only limited amounts of loans or concessional credit to Indonesian importers;
4. India's export of capital goods to Indonesia has suffered a decline since the mid-eighties; and,
5. Both countries produce similar agricultural goods, such as tea, coffee, cashew-nuts, pepper, spices, fruit and vegetable, and thus there is limited scope for expansion of two-way trade.

These constraints suggest a need for diversification of exchanges in traditional items, and policy-makers on both sides are attending to this problem with due care.

In the area of investment ties, Indians were collaborating with Indonesian counterparts in eleven joint ventures in producing cotton and synthetic yarn, engineering files, billets, furniture, steel pipes, rubber rollers, tubes and rayon well before 1990; but after 1992 the number of joint ventures increased only marginally to fourteen (see Table 17.4). When Indonesian Minister for Industries Hartato visited New Delhi in March 1992, the three new joint-venture agreements were signed to manufacture paper and rayon. Indonesia has sufficient raw materials for the production of paper and rayon and it attracts a global market. Mr. Hartato envisaged great scope for Indian joint ventures in Indonesia, particularly in forest-based industries (including pulp for rayon, and paper), marine-based

Table 17.4: List of Indian Joint Ventures in Indonesia
(As at December 1992)

S/No.	*Name and Address of the Applicant*	*Name and Address of the Joint Ventures*	*Field of Collaboration and Year of Approval*	*Indian Equity (%)*
1	2	3	4	5
1	M/s. The Raymond Woollen Mills Ltd. JK Building N Marajee Marg Ballard Estate Bombay	PT Jaykay Files Indonesia Hotel San Pacific JI MH Thamrin No. 6 PO Box No. 31 Jakarta	Engineer's Steel Files and Rasps 1974 In operation	30
2	M/s. Eastern Spinning Mills Industries Ltd. 24, Parganas West Bengal	P.T. Elegant Textile Industry G7, Jalan Haji Agun Salim Jakarta	Teaxtile Yarn 1973 In operation from December 1976	5.73
3	M/s. Bharat Commerce and Industries Ltd. Surya Kiran (5th Floor) 19, Kasturba Gandhi Marg New Delhi	PT Horzon Syntex Radung Baruk Rungkutt Surabaya	Textile Yarn 1977 In operation	42.5
4	M/s. Ispat Projects Ltd.	PT Ispat Indo	Wire rods for round steel bars, etc.	19.32

(Contd....)

1	2	3	4	5
	M/s. Aso Engineers and Allied Industries Ltd. Chatterjee International Centre 19th Floor, 33A, Jawaharlal Nehru Road Calcutta 700 071	Jalan Jaksa No. 2 Jakarta	1977 In operation from October 1978	
5.	M/s. Kusum Products Ltd. Bombay-Mutual Bldg, 9 Bruborne Road Calcutta 700 001	PT Godrej Indonesia, 23-25 Jalan Kapi Jakarta	Solvent extraction 1975 In operation	47.47
6.	M/s. Godrej and Boyce Mfg. Co. Ltd. 44, Homy Modi Street Bombay 400 001	PT Godrej Indonesia Jalan Kapi Jakarta	Steel Furniture Security equipment, etc. 1975 In operation from August 1980	60
7.	M/s. Bombay Dyeing & Mfg. Co. Ltd. Neville House JN Heredia Marg Ballard Estate	PT Five-Star Industries Ltd. 184 Cipaganti Eandund	Textile Mills 1978 In operation from February 1981	40
8.	M/s. Goka Patel Volkart Ltd. Forbes Building Charanjit Rai Marg Bombay 400 001	PT Gokak Indonesia Wisma Kosgoro Jalan MH Thamrin Jakarta	Textile Mills 1979 In operation from December 1980	44

9.	M/s. Garsim Industries Ltd. Industry House 1st Floor 159 Churchgate Bombay	PT Indo-Bharat Rayon Jalan Johar 24 Jakarta	Viscose staple Fibre 1978 In operation from April 1982	10
10.	M/s. Birla Bombay Pvt. Ltd. Industries and Zenith Ltd. 103, Walkar Town Secunderabad 500 025	PT South Pacific Voiscose, Jalan Cik Ditiro, 42 Jakarta	Viscose Staple fibre 1979 In production from December 1982	25.70
11.	The Standard Mills Co. Ltd. Mafatlal Centre Industries Nariman Point Bombay 400 021	PT The Standard Mills Indonesia Jalan Suelen Jakarta	Machinery & equipment for textile and industries 1981 In operation from July	40
12.	Ispat Alloys Ltd. Room No. 511 and 512 Prakash Deep 7, Tolstoy Marg New Delhi	Indonesia	Ferro Alloys 1991 Under Implementation	24.62

Source: Indian Investment Centre, New Delhi.

industries, oil and gas industries, the textile sector, and small-scale industrial plants (including for handicrafts). He invited Indian entrepreneurs to take advantage of the growing capital goods import market in Indonesia—which amounts to US $4-5 billion annually—by setting up joint ventures in Indonesia for the manufacture of equipment required by that country. Indian Minister of State for Industry, P.J. Kurian, and Hartato also agreed to sign a Memorandum of Understanding (MoU) to co-operate in the fields of small-scale industries, capital goods and the newsprint sector.[14]

Indian investment in Indonesia is ranked seventeenth in that country and was worth US $247.6 million in 1994.[15] The quality of Indian products is appreciated by Indonesians and new areas of growth are being identified for greater investments. On the other hand, Indonesian investment in India up to the end of 1994 was negligible. Indonesia is, however, cautiously moving to explore investment opportunities in India where reforms have been introduced to attract foreign investments. India is interested in evolving a healthy external economic environment and is gearing up its economy to the challenges of the global market-place. It is moving step by step. It has already reduced requirements for obtaining an industrial licence for manufacturing activity to only fifteen sectors of strategic, social and environmental concerns. It has allowed full foreign equity in certain sectors, and foreign investments are trickling in. There are some investors who would like to see more transparency in investment procedures and these are now being paid utmost attention. The liberalization has popular backing, and major political parties, including the ruling Communist Party of India (Marxist) in West Bengal, are supporting it. For example, West Bengal signed seventeen MoUs in 1994 for foreign investments, and more are likely to be signed.[16]

It is heartening to note that sectoral dialogue between India and ASEAN has been accelerated. The first sectoral dialogue between India and the ASEAN states took place in Bali in 1994, during which the emphasis was on boosting trade and investment relations. It stressed the need for scientific and technical co-operation in such fields as non-conventional energy sources, fibre optics, laser technology and tourism. It was agreed that the dialogue should tackle trade promotion, trade facilitation and industrial co-operation. The ASEAN countries are gradually easing their barriers to trade and removing regulatory restrictions and other non-tariff barriers. They are also discussing trade incentives and have set up an ASEAN Information Centre in India. Thus, understanding of each other is developing and a better environment is emerging. Dato Ajit Singh, Secretary-General of ASEAN, on the eve of the establishment of ASEAN-India sectoral relations said in New Delhi on 17 March 1992 that:

> "The sectoral dialogue provides us with the opportunity to make ASEAN-India relations more meaningful and substantive. These relations will also carry us to a higher plane of understanding and co-operation. We in ASEAN look forward very much to working closely with you as we deepen and strengthen our relations."[17]

Future Projections

Though economics have assumed prime importance in bilateral relations, new vistas of friendship and co-operation are emerging in India-Indonesia relations. These developments are evaluated below:

Firstly, Indonesia can provide immense support to India in the success of its economic liberalization programme. Both countries have faced similar problems of development after discarding the socialist path. Indonesia made its currency fully convertible at the beginning of the "New Order" and subsequently simplified investment procedures. Presently, Jakarta has placed emphasis on structural diversification of the economy to reduce dependence on crude oil and, in particular, on the development of export-oriented and labour-intensive industries, in the agricultural and manufacturing sectors. On the other hand, New Delhi is encouraging foreign investment through a tax holiday on income in certain sectors and has announced depreciation allowances, customs and excise concessions, while also trying to simplify investment procedures.[18] Proposals for investment ventures involving 51 per cent foreign equity require only the Reserve Bank's approval. As a first step towards the privatization of 248 state-owned corporations, selected public sector enterprises are being allowed to raise funds through equity issues. In short, India and Indonesia might find complimentarities in their economic objectives.

Secondly, India and Indonesia are leading exporters of textile goods and close co-operation between them could result in evolving joint strategies which could prove mutually advantageous. Furthermore, India is interested in the joint exploration of oil and natural gas in the Andaman Sea, and might benefit from Indonesia's experience in oil exploration and exploitation. Moreover, Indonesia's success in family planning has been phenomenal, and India might learn from the Indonesian experience in that area.

Thirdly, India has certain advantages in science and technology and it is not averse to transferring its knowledge. India has nuclear know-how and, in the field of missile technology, has intermediate range ballistic missiles, the Nag anti-tank missile, and surface-to-air Trishul and Akash missile systems. There is, therefore, wide scope for interaction in scientific and technological collaboration. In this context, a cultural agreement between India and Indonesia, which lapsed in 1991, needs to be renewed in the present context of a world-wide perception that cultural interaction is crucial in facilitating economic co-operation.

Fourthly, India is interested in the various "growth triangles" in the ASEAN region. Again, the "growth triangle" hub of Riau in Indonesia is particularly instructive. This raises several questions pertinent to India's intentions to establish similar "growth areas", particularly in the Andaman and Nicobar islands, and to promote intercourse with Southeast Asia. As Indonesia is contiguous and likely to benefit equally, its interests in influencing India and clearing doubts could prove advantageous to both.

Fifthly, India and Indonesia have identical perceptions on the question of human rights. They are equally concerned about reports of international agencies—Amnesty International, Asia Watch, and so forth—who are monitoring the human rights conditions and passing judgements without assessing the impact on people. Indonesia views the problems of human rights in an Asian context to be different from that of the West. President Suharto has observed:

> "It is our firm conviction that the objective of human rights is the realization of full potential of human beings. But human potential is not confined to political aspects only. The fundamental rights to economic and social development, for example, cannot be separated and cannot be treated separately from other categories of human rights."[19]

Despite facing domestic unrest in certain areas, Indonesia has established a national Human Rights Commission to safeguard the human dignity of its citizens, but it prefers to distinguish it from western norms. India, on its part is also trying to improve its human rights record and has established a Human Rights Commission to prevent gross human rights violations.

Sixthly, India and Indonesia face similar security threats in the post-cold war era. They have expressed similar concerns about a power vacuum in the event of a precipitous U.S. military withdrawal. They are disturbed about the future security situation in the South China Sea and the Indian Ocean. India would prefer collective strategies with ASEAN in general, and Indonesia have been participating in joint naval exercises since 1992, but serious efforts are needed to enhance defence contacts. If the two countries could establish a "hotline" and accelerate strategic co-operation in the spirit of *Gotong Royong* (mutual help), it would promote better understanding between each other.

Finally, Indonesia's role as a regional peace broker has been unique in the recent past. Its roles in the resolution of the Cambodian conflict, moderating Moro Muslims in the Philippines, and highlighting the complexities of the South China Sea, have been pioneering. India is faced with the problem of Islamic insurgency in Kashmir, and Pakistan has been constantly supporting terrorists there. If Indonesia takes a similar interest in Kashmir as it did in resolving the problems of the Moro Muslims in the Philippines, it would contribute to resolving a conflict that has the potential to turn into a major conflagration. That contribution to peace could be the capstone to improving relations between New Delhi and Jakarta.

REFERENCES

1. India and Indonesia have signed agreements relating to the delimitation of the continental shelf boundary on 8 August 1974 and 14 January 1977, respectively. For the text of the treaty, see *Law of the Sea: Maritime Boundary Agreements, 1979-1984* (New York: Office of the Ocean Affairs of the Law of the Sea, United Nations, 1987), pp. 230-35.
2. K. Subrahmanyam, "Security Cooperation Between India and Indonesia" (Paper presented at the India-Indonesia Seminar, 3 September 1994 and 22 January 1995), p. 1.
3. Three separate security agreements were signed. First, the agreement between the Indian Air Force and AURI was signed on 28 February 1956 allowing exchange of pilots, training of air-force officers and the sale, loan and exchange of air force spares. The second agreement was signed between the Indian Navy and Indonesian ALRI on 3 December 1958 for co-operation in the cross attachment of officers, combined naval training exercises, and mutual naval visits. The third agreement was signed between the Indian army and ADRI on 3 June 1960 for co-operation in training, exchange of personnel, and supply of modern arms. For details, see Dipankar Banerjee, "India-Indonesian Relations: Partners in an Era of Cooperative Security" (Paper presented at the India-Indonesia Seminar, New Delhi, 3 September 1994), pp. 3-4. For a period of past constraints see, Mohammed Ayoob, *India and Southeast Asia: Indian Perceptions and Policies* (London: Routledge, 1990), pp. 40-41.
4. Mohan Ram, "Ruling the Waves: New Indian Base Extends Move Towards More Sea Power", *Far Eastern Economic Review* (Hong Kong), 15 May 1986, p. 30.
5. *The Times of India*, 9 September 1994.
6. For this, see "Business News", *The Times of India*, 18 February 1995.
7. *The Times of India*, 20 April 1993.
8. *Hindustan Times*, 17 March 1992.
9. P.K. Sandell, "New Dimensions of Business and Trade Relations Between India and Indonesia" (Paper presented at the India-Indonesia Seminar, New Delhi, 3 September 1994), pp. 15-18.
10. C.P.F. Luhulima, "Dynamics of Economic Cooperation Between India and Indonesia" (paper presented at the India-Indonesia Seminar in New Delhi, 3 September 1994), p. 3.
11. *Ibid.*

12. *Ibid.*
13. Background Paper, Fourth Meeting of the India-Indonesia Joint Business Council and Seminar on Trade and Investment Opportunities Between India and Indonesia, New Delhi, 18 November 1993, pp. 17-18.
14. *Hindustan Times,* 17 March 1992.
15. Luhulima, *op. cit.,* No. 10, p. 4.
16. Somnath Chatterji, Chairman, West Bengal Industrial Development Corporation (WBIDC), on 7 February 1995, said that they on their own had entered into seventeen MoUs involving a total investment of 250 crore rupees in the past five months. Singapore, Malaysia and the United States are the major investors. For further details, see *Hindustan Times,* 8 February 1995.
17. Text of the speech by Dato Ajit Singh. See also *The Times of India,* 19 March 1993.
18. Sujatha Singh, "India's Economic Reforms and Opportunities for Malaysian Businessmen", *Strategic Analysis* 17, No. 1, April 1994, pp. 45-54.
19. Text of President Suharto's speech at the 47th session of the United Nations General Assembly in New York, 24 September 1992, issued by the Embassy of the Republic of Indonesia, in New Delhi, No. 12/92, pp. 8-9.

17

The Philippine-India Relations in Retrospect

The Philippines and India have had similar historical experiences as they were both under colonial rule for centuries. The Philippines was under Spain for about 400 years followed by the United States for 48 years and India was under British colonial rule from 1757 to 1947. The Philippines declared independence in 1898, but the US forces intervened to civilise and train the Filipinos in self-rule till 1946. India became independent in 1947. Both adopted democratic polity in the republican mould.

The Philippines has 300,000 square km. of territory and 7,107 islands of which only 3114 are named. India has 31,65,956 square km. of territory, and a large population. Both India and the Philippines are strategically located and cannot be overlooked in the politics of their respective regions.

India has a parliamentary form of government based on the Westminster model and the people are provided right to equality, religion, and freedom to speech, expression, association and free press. On the other hand, the Philippines has a Presidential system which provides for a separation of power. Under its constitution, executive powers are vested with the President and the cabinet, the legislative powers with the elected National Assembly (a Senate and a House of Representatives) and judicial powers with the Supreme Court and lower courts.

The Philippines and India struggled very hard to throw out the colonial rulers and they discovered common links in the course of their nationalist struggle. India always attached importance to the Philippines because of the latter's contribution to the anti-colonial struggle. The Philippines started Asia's first nationalistic revolution in the 19th century and fought several wars against the Spanish colonial masters.

Jose Rizal (1861-1896), a renowned poet, writer, sculptor, doctor and a political activist played an exemplary and catalytic role in the launching of the anti-colonial struggle. He symbolised India's Rabindranath Tagore in the intellectual sense and Bhagat Singh in the revolutionary sense. He had the combined qualities of both nationalists, who aroused public opinion against the Spanish colonial system. The Spanish rulers became annoyed with his activities and thus framed charges to kill him. He was hastily executed in 1896 and ever since he is regarded as one of the most important martyrs of Asia.

Jose Rizal had inspired the formation of Katipunan a secret revolutionary organization in 1892 under the leadership of Andres Bonifacio and Emilio Jacinto to fight for independence. This organisation which believed in revolutionary methods, organised soldiers, and the Filipinos enthusiastically volunteered to fight. Colonial Spain was angry with his activities and thus targeted him as the main enemy. They conspired to kill him for his betrayal to the Spanish cause. The situation became surcharged in the wake of the execution of Jose Rizal and thereby the Spanish rulers unleashed a reign of terror.

The martyrdom of Jose Rizal worsened the situation for the Spanish rulers. In 1897, a revolutionary assembly of the Philippine people at Tejeros announced the promotion of a government under the leadership of Bonifacio. But he could not lead the struggle for long as he was executed that year. Thereafter Emilio Aguinaldo assumed leadership of the revolutionary movement. He sought assistance of the Americans to defeat the Spaniards and in the process he faltered.

It is astonishing as to how the Philippines was placed under the American colonial rule after they ousted the Spanish. It is understood that the nationalist leaders in the Philippines were determined to throw out the Spanish colonial rulers and in that endeavour while seeking support from the US they did not distrust the American intentions. The US had been sponsoring its support to the Philippines since 1892 and which was taken in 1898. The American fleet under the command of Commodore Dewey came and defeated the Spanish forces in May 1898.

Thus the Philippines announced their independence on 12 June 1898 at Aguinaldo's headquarters at Kawit, Cavite. Aguinaldo became the President of the revolutionary government and a constitution was drafted. There were celebrations of independence everywhere and it was at the end of 1898 that the Americans announced their hidden agenda. They decided to stay back and assume the burden to civilise and train the Filipinos in self-rule. In that endeavour they took decades and the Philippines was given political independence only when colonial rule in Southeast Asia became unsustainable after the end of the Second World War.

In retrospect, we find that the dedication, sacrifice and heroism of Bonifacio and Aguinaldo and the intellectual tradition established by Jose Rizal still inspires patriotic elements in Asia. Rizal's contribution to nationalist movement can be compared with Ho Chi Minh of Vietnam. It was because of the betrayal and collection of the colonial powers, that Philippines was subjected to colonial rule once again under the new colonial master.

India has been full of praise for the contribution of the Philippines in the anti-colonial struggle. Mahatma Gandhi and Jawaharlal Nehru attached due importance to that country in the post-independence era. Nehru always expressed appreciation for Philippine history and invited their representative to the Asian Relations Conference (1947), The Conference on Indonesia (1949) and Bandung Conference (1955). Again the Philippines was one of the three Southeast Asian countries besides Burma and Indonesia, with which India signed a Treaty of Friendship on 12 July 1952. This treaty affirmed their faith in perpetual peace and everlasting amity, besides granting nationals of either country reciprocal rights to acquire property and to travel, reside and engage in trade and industry in the other.

However our endeavour of perpetual friendship was obstructed due to cold war dynamics. The Philippines joined in the American alliance system—SEATO—and pursued anti-communist drives. It supported the US sponsored containment policy in the region. While India opposed the formation of SEATO as well as the containment drive.

However, with the end of the cold war, the international situation changed and a new configuration of powers emerged. Both India and the Philippines are facing similar challenges and, there is convergence of interests. Here it is important to mention some areas where we have common concerns and convergence of interests:

(*i*) Regional security threats,
(*ii*) Economic challenges posed by globalization
(*iii*) Trade and investments
(*iv*) Human rights.

The security challenges to the region are of common concern to both India and the Philippines. The Chinese are rapidly strengthening their military profile and have claimed sovereignty rights over South China Sea including Paracels and the Spratlys along with other countries in the region. On the Indian side, China has been occupying a big chunk of territory in NEFA (Arunachal Pradesh) since 1962 and now it has established its strategic presence in the Indian Ocean with the support of Myanmar. It has its naval outpost at Coco Island near the Andamans and has increased surveillance over the Malacca Straits after the establishment of a powerful radar station at Katran Island. This is a cause of concern not only to India but to all the countries in South and Southeast Asia.

India and the Philippines are cooperating very closely to address regional security issues as both are active participants in the ASEAN Regional Forum (ARF) process. The main objective of the ARF is to promote stability and security in the Asia-Pacific region through dialogue, confidence-building measures and preventive diplomacy.

The second issue which affects us collectively is the assertion of dominance of developed countries. The western world is technologically advanced and superior to the Third World. They tend to treat us as their markets and sometimes articulate laws through financial institutions, that restrict our economic freedom. Their role to resolve the Asian economic crisis 1997-98 of Asian tigers have been far from satisfactory and their suggestions as forecasted, would promote control of the western world. The conditions suggested for releasing bail-out funds have caused closures of banks, industrial enterprises and development projects in Thailand, Korea and Indonesia. Millions have lost their jobs and there are price rise and currency shortages.

Again the World Trade Organisation (WTO) favours the developed countries by declaring patent laws. For example, the US has patents to produce Basmati rice and Neem-related products. The western world would like to retain Third World as their markets perpetually and India and the Philippines feel common concern on this issue.

Thirdly, India and the Philippines do perceive common interests in trade and investment. The main Indian exports to the Philippines in the era preceding independence were shellac, jute manufactures, leather, cotton twit and yarn, and vegetable oils, and it imported tobacco, raw hemp, cordage, ropes and metals. Presently, India is exporting engineering goods, oil meals, cotton yarn fabrics, paints, enamels and varnishes, leather and leather manufactures, primary and semi-finished iron and steel. It imports project goods, cashew nuts, organic chemicals, inorganic chemicals and manufactured fertilisers. Besides it has also been importing vegetables, textile fibres (other than cotton and jute, and copra.

India has joint ventures with the Philippines to manufacture transmission line materials, diesel engines and yarn. They are also collaborating to develop cashew plants and dairy products. Efforts have also been made to establish joint ventures for rubber manufactures (automobile tires), gems and jewellery, cement, pulp and paper, etc. They would also like to collaborate in project exports, such as the construction of rail bridges, road bridges, tunnels and flyovers, and open new vistas of co-operation to tap the vast potential for commercial relations.

Fourthly, India and the Philippines have similar views on the question of human rights. Both have faced insurgencies in certain areas of their countries—India in Kashmir and the Philippines in Mindanao. The opposition in both areas are based on religion and ethnicity who question the right of the other religious groups inhabiting these areas. Thus the insurgents terrorise the people who do not obey their dictates and create a situation in which the law and order situation worsens.

Various peace agreements have been signed in India and the Philippines to restore peace and stability in insurgency afflicted areas. The governments have given various concessions to fulfil the legitimate aspirations of the people, but the intermittent cases of skirmishes and guerrilla warfare continue, thus provoking authorities to retaliate and in the process violate human rights of other communities in the area. Government forces, in order to restrain and contain the insurgents, very often commit acts of omission and commission, and allegations of human rights violations are reported by the international media whose reports often ignore crimes committed by insurgents. India and the Philippines have confronted similar situations in their efforts to resolve the insurgency problem.

The issue, however, is too complicated as the Philippines and India have democracy and free press, where politicisation of every matter makes the issue debatable. For instance, family planning programmes which are the desirable goal in both countries, are not rigorously implemented because of the intervention of certain religious groups. In early 1993, there was a difference between the government and church in the Philippines after the Catholic Bishops Conference issued a pastoral letter attacking the governments promotion of condoms as part of a "safe sex" campaign. They insisted that chastity and monogamy were the only moral ways to control growth of population and sex-related diseases.

India on the other hand, faced serious problems in enforcing family planning programmes during the emergency period (1975-77) and the government was voted out because of the alleged excesses committed. There are some strong religious organisations in India which are opposed to family planning and most of the national leaders are unwilling to do anything that would disturb vote-banks.

India and the Philippines are committed to protect human rights, democracy and development, and there are many other pressing issues to be attended. The Philippine President, Fidel V. Ramos in his address to the Tenth Congress on 24 July, 1995 enumerated six major tasks of his administration, namely:

(*i*) Adapt to the competitive world economy,
(*ii*) Reform of the electoral system,
(*iii*) Stamp out crime,
(*iv*) Prevention of rising poverty,
(*v*) Capability of self-reliance,
(*vi*) Improving the quality and integrity of administrators.

If we analyse the aforementioned six issues, it becomes obvious that the first and most important challenge in making the Philippines globally competitive, can only be effectively met if at least four of the five other tasks are accomplished. The Philippines can be more competitive in the world economy if criminality is controlled, mass poverty reduced, self-esteem enhanced and quality and integrity of governance raised. On the other hand similar situations prevail in India. In order to be globally competitive, self-reliant and prosperous, it has to control the evil of corruption, criminal-politician nexus, poverty and population growth.

Thus both countries are finding similarity of views on domestic and international matters, and interactions have increased in the recent past. Bernardo M. Villegas, Dean of the University of Asia-Pacific, visited India and opened fruitful dialogue at government and academic levels. Again the Philippine Agriculture Minister, Roberto Sebastian visited India in 1993 and emphasised the importance of Philippine co-operation with India in various agricultural and allied fields such as fisheries, animal husbandry, dairy farming and horticulture. The interaction is also taking place through ASEAN and various joint working groups and the avenues of co-operation are being expanded.

For the last three years, we witnessed a considerable increase in bilateral trade and investment relations. The first Philippine Trade Mission to India was dispatched in 1995 with the then Under-Secretary of Trade, Cesar B. Bautista as head of delegation. He was accompanied by high-ranking government officials and private sector representatives. The Mission explored possibilities for expanding two-way trade and investment activities. The setting-up of the Joint Working Group (JWG)—a high-level policy body and the Joint Business Council (JBC) greatly facilitated interaction between the government and the private sector groups at various levels. The bodies also served as mechanisms for addressing barriers to trade and investments.

The high-point in bilateral relations was the historic 1997 state visit by H.E. Fidel V. Ramos, the first by an incumbent Philippine President. He was accompanied by a high-powered business delegation. President Ramos held high-level meetings with government officials and captains of Indian business and industry. He witnessed the signing of two landmark agreements: the MoU on Scientific and Technological Cooperation in the Field of Pharmaceuticals and the MoU on Small and Medium Enterprises (SMEs) Cooperation. During a dinner tendered in his honour by FICCI-Assocham, President Ramos challenged the private sector of both countries to increase two-way trade to at least US $500 million by the turn of the century. The President's historic state visit has yielded in the following results: the implementation of the Indo-Philippines Textile and Design Complementation Programme (a fashion show presentation dubbed "Passage to India" was staged at Pragati Maidan, New Delhi January 1998 show-casing Indian fabrics using the ingenuity and creative design of four top Filipino designers); setting-up of three joint venture projects between Filipino and Indian companies engaged in food and beverage, telecommunications and petroleum. A number of Indian companies have also expressed interest in establishing joint ventures especially in the fields of power generation, computer software, garments and food processing among others.

However, an area of co-operation which needs to be explored is our common cultural heritage. It may be recalled that Pandit Jawaharlal Nehru, who had sentimental attachment for the Philippines, stated in a letter to his daughter Indira Gandhi, the following:

> Today they (The Philippines) have a Spanish-American appearance, but the whole background of their old culture came from India. Indian culture travelled to them via Sumatra and touched almost every aspect of life; social, religious and political. Old Indian myths and stories and part of our literature reached them. Their languages contain many Sanskrit words. Their art is influenced by India. So are their laws and handicrafts.

Presently, we are trying to rediscover the essence of our age-old cultures and civilisations, which were inadvertently destroyed or diluted by colonialism. We have not attached much importance to recognise them but as and when it is done, our relations will flourish. India and the Philippines have immense scope of cooperation in human resource development, information technology, drugs and pharmaceuticals. The Indian diaspora in that country are active in business and trade and if a suitable networking is established and the input of the Indians are considered, the Philippines as a partner, is bound to prove of crucial importance in the 21st century.

18

Indian Diaspora in Myanmar

Indian started going towards Burma (Myanmar) centuries ago. Sharing a common frothier, Burma was a part of Subarnabhumi and an important segment of Indian civilization. When India was colonized, Burma too was colonized by the same colonial power. The Britishers used Indians in their army to subdue the Royal Forces of the Burmese. After defeating the Burmese, it was placed under the administration of British India. Calcutta, the then capital of British India, became the capital of Burma as well. Thereafter Indians were appointed massively in Burmese bureaucracy, police and military. When the Britishers started exploring production of oil, rubber, teak, timber, sugar, rubies and rice, they needed skilled labourers and encouraged large-scale migration of labourers. As situated on the eastern frontier, it was easy for the Indian to go there.

Burma lies between longitudes 92 degree and 102 degree east of Greenwich and latitudes 100 degree and 28 degree north, and its area, 230, 800 square miles, more or less equals that of Spain. Three main rivers cross it from north to south. The Irrawaddy, with its two upper tributaries rising in the ramparts dividing Tibet from Burma is about 1500 miles long and runs through the heart of the country. It swells in the rainy season and subsidies in the dry season, while its current, like its width, varies correspondingly. It is navigable for about 800 miles, from Bhamo (with difficulty at the end of the dry season) to the Andaman Sea, and has always been and remain Burma's main artery of commerce and communication.

Another river, the Chindwin drains the ranges bounding the Hukawng valley, then cuts a gap through them and flows on until it joins the Irrawaddy near temple sites at Pagan. It is navigable for about 400 miles. Yet another river the Salween rises in central Tibet and runs at furious speed over cataracts and through deep gorges for most of its long route to the sea, entering Burma at the northeast corner of Shan State and providing an imposing natural barrier behind which hill peoples such as the Kokangs, Was, Akhas, Lahus, Karens and Mons have sheltered almost entirely free of external interference for most of Burma's recorded history. Navigable only for the last 90 miles before it reaches the Gulf of Martaban, it has little commercial but great political and military significance.[1]

The new Indian migrants who started going there after 1986 proved very enterprising, affluent, efficient and successful. They were very hard working and as a result Burma became one of the richest nations in Southeast Asia. Many Indians prospered much to the envy of indigenous people and this in due course became a serious matter against the diaspora. The diaspora was engaged in agriculture, retail shop, service sectors and various professions. They excelled in all the areas with the support of British colonial masters. The Burmans disliked that Indian migrants were trusted and supported by the colonial masters at the cost of the indigenous people. They became critical about the economic influence of the Indian diaspora and started opposing it. The propaganda was launched that Indian migrants were projected as a part of British exploitation and campaign was launched to equate with the Colonial exploitation. Anti-Indian sentiments became high and the slogan: "Burma for the Burmans", raised by the nationalist forces, were directed mainly against the Indians.[2]

It will be in order to analyse how Indian migrants went there on a large scale and how they became a powerful force. The Britishers as colonial masters attached emphasis on agricultural and industrial production in Burma. They decided to expand the agricultural land for rice cultivation and they needed labourers on a large scale to make the land cultivable. In that endeavour they looked towards India for both labour and capital. There were overgrown jungles to be cleared for rice cultivation but the Burmese farmers had no money to pay to the labourers. The Britishers encouraged Indian chettyars, the money lenders to go there to assist the cultivators. At the same time European exporters agreed to provide money in advance to boost agricultural production. The policy was successful in expanding the agricultural areas and boost production. But the ownership of the land rapidly changed from one hand to another and within two decades Indian traders, brokers and money lenders purchased a large chunk of the cultivable lands.[3]

The increasing demand for labour and capital in Burma and increasing profits in the investments became the main reason for the large scale migration all over to Burma. Indians had lower standard of living and after arrival in Burma they made profits and competed against the indigenous people for land tenancy and other endeavours. Between 1915 and 1930, the native owners lost no less than 1,300,000 acres of land and the small Burmese rice millers were driven out to their business as the large steam driven mills were introduced.[4]

In the beginning of the 20th century, Indians were arriving in Burma at the rate of 250,000 a year. In 1927, it reached the peak figure of 480,000.[5] The majority came over only for seasonal occupations on the land and returned home afterwards. But at the same time many stayed back to excel in agriculture and business. Indians invested their surplus money in paddy cultivation and export business. The opinion of the indigenous population against the Indians started growing after the end of the First World War. In 1930, there was an outbreak of anti-Indian riots in Rangoon, when 120 Indians were killed and 900 were wounded. They thought that action against Indian will be considered action against colonial rule.

After 1930, a vicious campaign was launched against Indians. They were projected as exploiters and more dangerous than the Britishers. Although the teak woods of Burma were increasingly used by the Britishers for the railway network in the region, but Indians were targeted as exploiters of forest resources of Burma. Besides teak, Burmese bamboo, cutch, lac, firewood used in steamers, mills and railway engines and charcoal had large demands in the areas administered by the Britishers. Burma was also producing petroleum of good quality. Although the final management was controlled by the Britishers, but the impression was that Indians were constantly misappropriating them with the support of the bureaucracy, which had significant representation of the Indians.[6] The British government, on the other hand, allowed the situation to deteriorate. They were unhappy with the Indians in Burma during the second world war. Indians, by and large, were supporting freedom movement in India. They had been funding either Indian National Army (INA) of Netaji Subhas Chandra Bose or Indian National Congress of Mahatma Gandhi. They refused to support British war efforts against the Japanese. So the Britishers in return treated them in unfriendly manner. Indians were indeed considered as a liability. Indian diaspora in Burma and Fiji have suffered mainly because of the negligence and apathy of the former colonial rulers. The Britishers were angry to find that the immigrant Indians were supporting anti-British crusades in India.

Burmese leaders acted in vengeance on the eve of independence. They did not confine to limiting rights of Indians over the land, but their existence in the country also. Burmese government passed a Citizenship Act in 1948. Accordingly every Indian migrants in Burma were required to have a certificate of citizenship. The process of extending citizenship in Burma was made cumbersome and complicated to such an extent that only 7994 Indians out of 740000 got this certificate.[7] The rest of them were declared illegal migrants and stateless. Indians in Burma have been suffering ever since.

It is surprising that Indian National Congress was strongly backed by overseas Indians in Burma. They generously funded the activities of Indian National Army (INA) of Netaji Subhas Chandra Bose and mobilized volunteers to fight. They celebrated every success of Indian nationalists. They expected substantial improvement in their conditions in the event of British withdrawal, but their conditions rapidly deteriorated in the post-independence era.

India was more concerned about happenings in Indonesia and was calling conferences and seminars to highlight Dutch atrocities. It was sponsoring the dispatch of planes in Indonesian space to rescue Indonesian nationalists. It generously contributed its troops to protect the sovereignty of South Koreans and wanted to do the same for the Vietnamese. It was helping formation of various provisions in the Universal

Declaration of Human Rights (1948) but it was lackadaisical about the plight of Indian in Myanmar. What was happening against Indians in Burma never became a big issue for Indian government. It did not speak strongly against various acts in Burma as it could jeopardize the support of Burmese government in the NAM. It merely sent some officials to convey the problems of stateless Indians in Burma and never took a firm stand. A large number of Indians were thrown out of Burma and Indian government remained a mere spectator, although India was in very strong position in 1948 to restrain the Burmese in protecting Indian lives and properties, and restraining them in anti-Indian activities, it remained " soft" and vacillating. Thus the problems of Indian population in Burma complicated.

After getting independence, Burma made it difficult for Indians to continue their service in the bureaucracy. About 3000 Indians in the government service and 8500 in Burma Railways were dismissed in 1953.[8] The government of Burma passed Immigration Act, which imposed restrictions on the movements of Indians. The government discouraged all the foreigners to retain properties in Burma and it mostly affected Indian landlords and businessmen. Ethnic Indians were viewed to bring about India's imperialist domination over Burma and the fear was expressed that Burma may be swamped by Indians if the status quo was maintained. The campaign was launched to pursue the policy "Burma for Burmans" and in that endeavour socialistic drives were launched.

Burma passed a Tenancy Standard Rent Act for possession of land in Burma followed by a Land Alienation Act, which forbade the sale of land to non-Burmese nationals. Again they passed Land Nationalization Act. Accordingly a person could possess only 10 acres of land. Again Burma passed transfer of Immovable Property Act, which forbade property owners from selling, mortgaging or leasing their property to non-Burmese citizens. Again Burma Company Registration Act was passed which restricted the business of Indians in Burma.[9]

Burma took systematic steps to hurt Indians. Wherever they worked i.e. in administration, business, medical and engineering services, they were compelled to resign. Indians owned 2.5 million acres of land out of 11.25 acres in Burma. South Indian chettyars were landlords. Indians comprised 80% in textile business, 90% in rice business and their overall share in other businesses were dominant. The Burmese leaders started taking strong measures against Indian as soon as they were separated from India in 1937. It was surprising that Burma signed an agreement with colonial Great Britain to give financial concessions but remained unhappy with Indian Diaspora. Indians were subjected to harsh treatment. Burmese displayed friendly gestures to Britishers and unfriendly and unjust gestures to Indians. Discriminatory practices were pursued for the Indians, and there were none to stop this injustice. In fact, this was the major reason for the downfall of Burmese economy in 1960's.

In 1962, General Ne Win came into power. As he was opposed to democracy and followed a policy of "socialism in one country," suppression of ethnic minorities and the policy of pro-china, he was ruthless against Indians. Ne Win was a dictator, who introduced structural changes to remain in power permanently. While analysing this aspect Shelby Tucker has observed, " dictatorial regimes use various means of deflecting criticism from themselves. Some (such as Enver Hoja in Albania) raise spectres of imagined enemies plotting to destroy the State. Some (various African dictators) blame past exploitation of colonial powers for present hardships. Some (propagandists of the Soviet Comintern) fantasize ever-receding future utopias to relieve present hardships. Rangoon has used all these tactics to manipulate the Burmese. The politicians fostered a number of myths—that the diverse peoples of Burma were one, and Britain destroyed that unity in order to conquer and rule them; that the British deprived the 'national races' of their freedom; that British administrators regarded Burmans as their inferiors; that Burma's poverty was due to British exploitation; that independence would deliver Burma from the disunity, bondage, indignity and poverty imposed on them by the British. When the Burmese wearied of the false hopes the politicians aroused, the military took over and added another myth, that the politicians ('the enemy within') were colluding with Britain and the 'neo-colonialist' Americans ('the enemy without') to keep

Burma in bondage. Such myths become self-proving, tautological substitutes for the truth, and we do not help the Burmese people by pondering to them. We merely help the autocracy deceive the people".[10]

India viewed Ne Win as a symbol of authoritarianism without any mandate to introduce structural changes in Burmese socio-economic life. But Ne Win remained in power from 1962 to 1988 and during that period cultivated special strategic ties with Peoples Republic of China. Although he advocated isolationist policy but China was an exception. He established one party rule of Burma Socialist Programme Party and its loyal followers were awarded key positions in the cabinet, bureaucracy and business. He was the epitome of corruption who turned Burma as one of the poorest countries of the world. Indian Diaspora was subjected to feel suffocation during his stewardship.

Ne Win was dictatorial against the minority population in general, but he was very keen to weed out any groups that had any connection with India in the past.[11] Thus Rohingyas were targeted, who were regarded as Bengalis and aliens. The word "Rohingya" is derived from Rohang, the ancient name of Arakan. Situated on Burma's Southern border with Bengal (India) and now Bangladesh, Arakan (Rakhine State), have a population of five million, 40 per cent of whom are Muslims.

Burma has different ethic groups and majority of them wanted autonomous status on the eve of independence, Burma adopted a democratic constitution in 1948. The nationalist leaders were concerned about the trends for fragmentation. At that time numerous ethnic groups were active for gaining autonomy. Shans, Karens and Kachins were very well organised and hopeful that the government will give a sympathetic consideration to their demands. Arakanese were also thinking that their problem will be solved if they get autonomy. They had been different from the Burmans in terms of religion and culture. However democracy was short-lived and the Ne Win Administration had ignored this area for development. When some Muslim fanatics advocated violence, the entire area was treated sensitive. In the beginning, Muslim Mujahid insurgents advocated guerrilla activities for autonomy. They, however, could not attract popular support and they went underground. In 1974, an Arakan Liberation Party was founded under the leadership of Khaing Mo Lin, who was subsequently killed by the government troops while fighting. Thereafter the Burmese authorities expressed concern that some Rohingyas were working for destabilizing the state. The government instituted cases for treason against some lenders harbouring and shaping the idea of autonomy in Arakan areas. The treason trials began on 8 September, 1977 and death sentences were pronounced against some prominent leaders, i.e., U Mhan Ngwe Aung, U Mhan Dar Waik, Maung Kyaw Htto and U Htein Lin and which was carried out subsequently. These four leaders were alleged to be involved in conspiracies to establish a separate independent state of Arakan. But questions were raised against the fairness of those trials. For example, during one of the trials, it was stated by a prosecution witness that U Mahn Ngwe Aung and U Htein Lin had early in 1976 been in contact with Colonel Amin, the military attache at the Embassy of Bangladesh who was declared persona non grata by the Burmese government.

The death sentence to Rohingya leaders surcharged the atmosphere. The military began to undertake stern action to keep Rohingyas under control, and unleashed reign of terror. An official report issued in Burma on 29 April 1978 revealed that in a census operation begun in 1977 and known as Naga Min, it was found that there had been an alarming rate of illegal entry of Bengalis in Arakan. The author ties felt that they must be repatriated. Thus several thousand prosecutions had been instituted against Muslim Rohingyas so that they are evicted. The Muslim Rohingyas started deserting their homes in search of a safe sanctuary and Burmese authorities alleged that 19,457 Bengalis had "absconded", leaving their homes to the Burmese.[12] On 2 May, 1978, Burma regime announced that in Buthidaung, 198,431 persons had been interrogated; legal action had been taken against 643; a total of 35,596 persons had been "absconded" and 6,294 houses had been abandoned. According to Burmese sources, a total of 101,048 persons had left Buthidaung and Maungdaw to escape an immigration check by May, 1978. These Rohingyas stated their arduous journey across Naaf River to reach Bangladesh for their safety and security. This river forms part of the two nation's 285 Kilometre long border, interspersed by forests and hills. The authorities asserted that they were carrying out a routine check on illegal immigrants and that a few Bengalis who had no citizenship documents left the country. However, the refugees claimed to have been forced to leave the country as a result of killings, rape, pillage and arson committed by the armed forces.[13]

Thus a conflict arose between the government of Burma and Bangladesh as a result of the arrival of a large number of Muslim refugees. The vast majority of these refugees consisted of women, children and elderly people to whom the authorities regarded as citizens of Bangladesh, whereas the latter considered them to be Burmese. The Muslim refugees comprised three groups, the largest of them being the Rohingyas from Arakan, the second group were the Kamanchils and the third group were Bengali farmers and fishermen. The first two groups had gone to Burma in the historical past and were unable to communicate in Bengali, but the third group who had settled in Myanmar during the British colonial period could communicate in Bengali language quite well.

The Military rulers in Burma regarded the Rohingya refugees as absconders but in fact nobody likes to desert their homes without a substantial pressure. Bangladesh began to take up the issue of Rohingyas at the international level. It said that thousands of Burmese Muslim nationals had been expelled to Bangladesh by Burmese law enforcement officers, being evicted from their homes which had been theirs for generations, and forced the border at gun point. President of Bangladesh, Ziaur Rahman openly accused Myanmar of inhuman eviction of Muslims and demanded the repatriation of Rohingya refugees to Myanmar.[14] His accusations were officially denied in Burma on 10 May, 1978, when it was reaffirmed that those had fled across the border were Bangladeshi nationals who had been illegal immigrants.

Bangladesh was really alarmed with the massive arrival of the refugees. Being impoverished, it was not easy to look after thousands of refugees coming everyday. The situation compelled Bangladesh to refer the matter to the UN. Prof.

Shamsul Huq, then President Ziaur Rahman's advisor on foreign affairs appealed to the UN Secretary General, Dr. Kurt Waldheim, for international assistance for the refuges to whom Bangladesh had offered temporary shelter for humanitarian reasons. The Secretary General felt concerned and thus directed the UN High Commissioner for Refugees to coordinate relief for the Rohingya refugees. The World Food Programme sanctioned US $2,000,000 for food distribution, while World Health Organization (WHO) and the UNICEF gave US $3,000,000 for relief operations. On the other hand, Britain gave 750,000 pound sterling in addition to 30,0C0 pound sterling emergency aid for Rohingya refugees.[15]

These developments had international ramifications. International media began to highlight the plight of Rohingya refugees. The prestigious French weekly *Le Nouvel Observer*, in its issue of 19 May, 1978, carried a story by Francois Hauter under the caption, "Massacre in Burma". The article gave details of the massacre perpetrated by the Burmese army on the refugees. He wrote that on 23rd April, when he was in a refugee camp at Tampru on the Burmese side, 30 Burmese soldiers appeared at the top of the hill which overlooked the camp. Everything happened very fast. They loaded their machine guns, opened fire and aimed into the crowd. The refugees fled towards the Naaf River. Those who fell were trampled. Some who carried invalids sunk into the mud. He revealed that the Arakan province have for the past several months lived in the throes of a genocide that has no equal except in Cambodia. He also stated that the Karens and Rohingyas were deprived of their civil rights if they do not Burmanize their names and if they do not renounce their customs.

Another paper, *Le Quotidien de Paris* carried a four column photograph of a man killed by the Burmese soldiers on 12 May, 1978. It also carried a six column under the headline "A million Muslims in the Danger of Death" were being pushed into Bangladesh, killed and raped. To justify this genocide, the Burmese pretext is that they illegally entered the country several years ago. But the Rohingyas have been in Burma since the 12 century. It appears that the Burmese policy is to wipe out the Rohingya race and therefore rape, poisoning and mutilation are taking place.[16]

This is in the backdrop of the problem of Rohingyas. Needless to emphasize that the Rohingyas have been unhappy with the prevailing system in Myanmar. They are interested in maintaining their separate identity and have been advocating that Islam should be treated at par with Buddhism. If not, their life style and customs should not be disturbed. As Arakan province is contiguous to Bangladesh, an Islamic state, the military administration has been over-sensitive to react against any opposition. The government has tried to change the existing demography of Arakan state. It was probably therefore that the Muslim Rohingyas were evicted from their homes for rehabilitation elsewhere. It is reported that there has been new settlements of Mogh tribes in the area, whose religion is Buddhism.[17] Abdul Hashim, a refugee, has been quoted as saying that "thousands of Mogh families have occupied land and property of the Muslims in Bithidong, Maungdaw and other towns where Muslims predominated. Our houses, bullocks and ploughs were taken by the police and the soldiers and were given to Mogh settlers. Moghs were permanently settled in areas where Muslims were being uprooted. While evicting us, the police and troops told us, "you Rohingyas do not belong to this soil."[18]

In fact there are many factors for the conflict between the ethnic Burmans and the Rohingya Muslims. Socially Rohingyas could not integrate with the Burmans because of historical and religious differences. They do not inter-marry and usually live in segregation. They do speak different languages, though Burmese language can be understood in the area. Arakan province has been traditionally under the impact of Bengali culture and civilization. They have consistently opposed their Burmanization and are keen to maintain their lifestyle distinct from the mainstream. Rohingyas are proud of their Islamic heritage and culture and are willing to see them reflected in the political culture of the country. One of their organizations, Ommar Liberation Front, had articulated the grievances of the Rohingya Muslims by cataloguing 23 specific complaints, including the denial of rights to political activity, employment and educational opportunities and religious observation etc.[19]

There had been efforts during the Ne Win era to Burmanize the names of the Rohingya Muslims as happened in case of Thailand *vis-à-vis* ethnic Chinese. The authorities also used to insist that the Rohingyas should renounce their cultural customs so that they may join in the mainstream. But the methods that were adopted by the authorities were crude and it did not get the support of the people in the state of Arakan.[18] Most of the initiatives undertaken by the government aroused apprehensions in the minds of the people and it caused tensions at the social level.

Again Burma had been a great centre of Buddhist learning and civilization for centuries. It said that Lord Buddha himself used to visit Mandalaya hills and there are several anecdotes and tales regarding Lord Buddha in Myanmar. J.A.F. Dalal while reporting about Mandalay Hills in *Hindustan Times* on 8 October, 1978, said that Mandalay Hill mount had for long been visited by Lord Buddha, who once preached his favourite disciple Anand that "this hill was my abode in my many lives—as an elephant, a lion, a stage, a iguana, a quail, and a hunter—this spot so fair in its formation, possesses every quality that is good, and it is fit as the abode of kings, etc. Thus we find the important places, customs, and traditions have been influenced by Buddhism and the political masters cannot ignore this reality.

Buddhism has been the state religion right from the period of U Nu (1948-1962) and majority of the people in Burma have reverence for Lord Buddha and they believe in the Buddhist faith. But the Rohingyas are by and large Muslims. They are the original inhabitants of that area and believe that Arakan had a separate culture, history and identity in the past, because they believed in the Islamic faith. Islam is their way of life and their behaviour, customs and traditions have been moulded accordingly. Thus there is no compromise on the question of religion and therefore there is a latent feeling of ethnocentricism which divides the people of these two religions—Muslims and Buddhists—into two parts. Again Rohingyas have historical interaction with the Arab and Persian traders, who came to the area during 9th and 15th centuries and some of them settled there and married local woman. Islam was a great force in the sub-continent during the Mughal period and thereafter Sultenate of Bengal became very powerful to protect the interests of the Muslims in the area. As Arakan was contiguous to Bengal, the Nawab of Bengal promoted socio-economic interaction of the people of that area with Arakan and the various kings in Amarapura were restrained to do anything against the Rohingya Muslims. When the Britishers came as rulers in the 19th century, they also protected the existing social life of the people in Arakan and tried to extend the frontiers of its colonial rule by defeating different rulers in Burma. But after gaining independence and subsequently after introducing Buddhism as the state religion, the situation started changing. When U Nu was overthrown and the military came into power in 1962, it evolved the policy of "Burmese way to Socialism", whereby the ideals and fantasies of General Ne Win became the order of the day.

Ne Win propagated centralization, nationalization and Burmanization of the political system and there was no room for dissent within the establishment. He undertook some socio-economic measures that proved retrogressive, which subsequently led towards economic mismanagement and disgrace. The country became least developed and one of the 10 poorest countries in the world. The attempts towards ethnic harmony which were the hallmark of U Nu period (1948-1962) were sacrificed. The various ethnic groups, i.e., Karens, Shans and Rohingyas began to feel uncomfortable and restive. Some of them adopted a militant posture and supported insurgency against the state. The military thus came into the picture to restore law and order and suppressed the opposition with an iron hand. When the authorities began a search for citizenship documents in April, 1978, they wanted to transmit a fear psychosis as well as their power potentials. In that process, the army became crazy and the Rohingyas became the victims. At least 130,000 Rohingyas deserted their homes initially, and went as refugees to Bangladesh.

The developed and civilized countries of the world expressed their shock and concern for the Muslim minorities in Burma and some of them strongly condemned the policies of the then regime in Myanmar. Thus the international pressure against Ne Win's administration grew. Myanmar agreed to negotiate repatriation of Rohingya refugees from Bangladesh. As a result, Tabarak Husain, Secretary of Bangladesh foreign ministry came to Yangon on 6 June, 1978 and had talks with U Thin Ohn, Myanmar's deputy foreign minister. After this meeting, Tabarak Husain said that "Burma recognised the seriousness of the situation and keenly desired to maintain good relations with Bangladesh".[20] U Thin Ohn paid a return visit to Dacca on 7 July, 1978 and signed agreement on repatriation of all the refugees. It was subsequently officially announced in Rangoon that in the first phase those person would be repatriated who held national or foreigners registration cards together with the member of their families mentioned on the lists kept by each household and endorsed by the local Burmese registration authorities.[21]

Though the agreement was signed, but due to rainy season, the repatriation work was delayed. The refugees started returning to Myanmar after August, 1978 and thus the situation was normalized for the time being. However the Rohingyas did not feel comfortable to return back home. The political system had not changed and the authorities were not sensitive to their grievances. The rulers officially promoted the resettlement policy in 1980s, to move the people into new satellite towns, apparently as a means of imposing more effective military controls over the people.

It was after one decade that the Rohingyas got an opportunity to be active once again. There was a civil unrest in Myanmar in April, 1988 for the restoration of democracy and fresh elections. Ne Win, who had been in power for more than 26 years, subsequently resigned on 25 July, 1988, The National League for Democracy (NLD) which had come into existence, was effectively leading the opposition for termination of the military rule. There were political instabilities and two successors of Ne Win , Sein Lewin and Maung Maung resigned between 25 July and 18 September, 1988. NLD was temporarily commanding the political situation. It was during the period of civil unrest that various ethnic organisations extended their support to the NLD and cooperated fully so that democracy would be restored. Like other ethnic groups, Rohingyas also extended support to the NLD, but the latter could not be successful in its endeavours.

The military under the leadership of General Saw Maung and General Khin Nyunt staged a coup d'etat on 18 September, 1988. They created Law and Order Restoration Council (SLORC) and declared martial law. There was a crackdown on the opposition. More than 3000 students had been gunned down and most of the NLD leaders were jailed and immobilised. They promised to hold elections and they did so on 27 May, 1990 whereby NLD won 392 seats out of 485 and the governments's National Unity Party got merely 10 seats. All the parliamentary seats from Yangon went to the NLD and so was the situation in Arakan. Rohingyas had enthusiastically supported NLD, Arakan League for Democracy and other opposition parties campaigned against the SLORC. Again when NLD and other ethnic organizations announced the formation of a provisional government—National Coalition Government of the Union of Burma—from Manerplaw on 18 December 1990 under the leadership of Dr. Sein Win, the Rohingya leaders had extended their support. Dr. Sein Win exhorted his followers to form liberated areas and establish the government to eliminate SLORC.

These developments naturally annoyed the military rulers who wanted to stick to power. They had already negated the result of the general election after passing order 1/90 in July, which stated that the junta would continue as the de facto government until a constitution was drafted. It also threatened party members with arrest if they refused to comply.[22] In the meanwhile the regime made strategic preparations to face the turbulent situation. It purchased medium sized tanks, anti-aircraft guns, petrol boats, short range F-7 jet fighters and a variety of missiles and howitzers from China. It also procured MIG-19 from China to subdue the insurgents. These purchases were aimed eliminating the internal opposition. At the same time it forged security links with China by offering Hainggyi for naval base. Again it cultivated economic contacts with Thailand by signing an accord to sell its teak woods at the cost of one million US dollar.[23] These resource mobilization were aimed at procuring arms and containing insurgency for good. The regime targeted wrath particularly against NLD leaders, the Karens, and the Rohingyas.

Bangkok Post reported on 22 February, 1991 that 17 out of 19 central committee members of National Coalition Government of the Union of Burma (NCGUB) had been arrested. NLD members of parliament were also detained and immobilised. The next target was the Karen insurgents, active on Thailand's border. Jeremy Wagstaff had very well explained their fears in *Bangkok Post* on 14 February, 1994. He surveyed the area and quoted Major Than Maung saying that the government intended to wipe out the Karens, who comprised 10 per cent of the total population of Burma. SLORC was particularly unhappy with the Karens because they had offered their capital, Manerplaw, for the headquarters of the NCGUB. The regime was offended because Karen leader, Bo Mya played an important rôle in supporting anti-establishment forces. It had sheltered many NLD leaders and were aiding and abetting them.

Besides Karens, the SLORC was biased against the Rohingyas and it was this reason that they succeeded in completely mauling the citizens.[24] This time the authorities came out with an allegation that the Rohingyas in general were aiding, abetting and hiding the insurgents, active for creating an independent state of Arakan. There were some illegal migrants at Arakan from Bangladesh and they must go back. On the other hand, they found the activities of Muslim students to be questionable. They were believed to be either the supporter or sympathizer of Rohingya solidarity organization or Arakanese Rohingya Islamic Front, advocating separate homelands for Rohingya Muslims at Arakan. Thus the authorities issued arrest warrants against 10,000 Muslim students for an alleged insurgency plot against the state in November 1991. Contingents of Myanmar troops moved to arrest those student leaders. In the process army terrorised Rohingya populace very ruthlessly. First of all, they arrested 2800 Muslims and detained them in crowded storehouses in northern Arakan. It was later revealed that 700 of those detained died due to suffocation.[25] The brick and concrete warehouse, normally used for storing rice, had been converted into detention camps. The situation deteriorated rapidly for the Rohingyas and fears gripped them so much that once again they started deserting their homes to save their precious lives. Thus streams of people moved towards Bangladesh and the story of 1978 was repeated once again. Thousands of refugees gathered on the Myanmar side of the Naaf River en route Bangladesh.

Bangladesh, being impoverished, was alarmed about the massive influx of Islamic refugees. In December, 1991, the relation between Bangladesh and Myanmar further chilled, because a Myanmar patrol police attacked Bangladesh border outpost, killing two soldiers and wounding 22 others. Thus both began to prepare for the worst and increased the presence of the soldiers on the common frontiers. In the meanwhile the influx of refugees to Bangladesh continued. *Times* (London) reported on 26 January, 1992 that "Burma's xenophobic junta, the SLORC, has embarked on a campaign to subdue the Muslims, known as Rohingyas and drive them into Bangladesh. It appears that the junta is about to send Buddhists into Burma's western state of Arakan, a rugged, jungled terrain that was once an independent Muslim homeland.[25] It was reported resettlement campaign had been accelerated to settle Buddhist Rakhines in the predominantly Muslim areas of the state.[26]

In the meanwhile, a serious indictment of the SLORC regime came from *Amnesty International* (London), which called on Burma's rulers to halt the campaign of terror and violence against Muslims that has caused thousands to flee the country. An amnesty fact finding team, sent to interview Burmese refugees in Bangladesh, confirmed reports of widespread human rights abuses, including torture and murder. Muslim men have been rounded up in large numbers into forced labour of the military, often as porters. They are ill-fed and abused . Many are reported to have been beaten to death when they became too weak to carry their loads. Muslim women have been raped in their homes, others have been held in army barracks and repeatedly raped.[27]

It further said that "the Myanmar authorities are believed to have militarized the border areas along Bangladesh border and here are reports of forcible action of the military to remove the populace to make way for military projects. Three additional battalions of government troops are deployed and thousands of civilians from ten-year old boys to elderly men are forcibly conscripted as unpaid labour for the construction and maintenance of a new military camp and other border development projects in the area, including major new roads being constructed through the state and helicopter landing pads."[28] The armoured vehicles always patrolled the area. These activities unleashed reign of terror for the Rohingyas and the UN felt concerned. Finally Javier Perez de Cuellar, the Secretary General of the UN expressed his personal shock about human right abuses in Myanmar.

In his February, 1993 report to the United Nations Commissions on Human Rights, the UN special Rapporteur on Myanmar concluded that Muslims in the state were at high risk of being taken by the army for use as porters or forced labour. They were tortured if they tried to return.[30] Again the reports of the Amnesty International, which visited refugee camps in February-March, 1992 were critical against military rulers in Myanmar. It confirmed the reports of the UN Special Rapporteur and added that most male members were in effect completely at the disposal of the troops because they might be arbitrarily seized at any time. They are carrying heavy load of food, bricks or ammunition for troops, working on road construction projects, digging trenches and moving earth; constructing or improving military camps; of acting as servants for troops in army camps. They were also forced to build new villages for the Buddhist Rakhine settlers whom the Myanmar armed forces moved into the area.[31] They were given either no food at all or a small amount of rice a day. Amnesty International documented reports from Muslim refugees of torture and ill-treatment having been carried out in a number of circumstances: if Muslims tried to protest when security forces attacked other Muslims; if they object on their own behalf or if they were suspected of opposing the government. Forms of ill treatment included slashing with bayonets, beatings with sticks and kicks with heavy boots.[32]

These reports indeed moved the conscience of the humanity. Besides the United Nations, the Organization of Islamic

Conference (OIC) expressed grave concern for the Rohingya Muslims. However, the regime in Myanmar paid very little attention to what the leaders in the Western world were saying. They were also not much concerned about the feelings of the organization of the Islamic conference. But the most crucial factor which restrained Myanmar was the opinion of the ASEAN countries. Myanmar is keen to maintain "constructive engagement" with the ASEAN and its trade links with Thailand. Malaysia and Singapore are quite strong. It would be unrealistic to offend the opinion of those countries without whose support, its economic lifeline would be chocked. The ASEAN countries wanted SLORC regime to be diplomatic to deal with its ethnic minorities. As far as Rohingyas are concerned, they are Muslims and there are Muslim countries in the ASEAN. These factors influenced Myanmar to listen to the advice of the ASEAN countries and negotiate on the repatriation of Rohingyas with the government of Bangladesh and the agreement between the two countries was signed on 29 April, 1992. Again the UNHCR was authorised to coordinate the repatriation work but this time it proved an arduous task. The UNHCR which was to ensure the safe return of the refugees, tried to obtain an assurance from Myanmar regarding safety of the returning refugees. On the other hand, Bangladesh wanted immediate return of the refugees to Myanmar. But the refugees were not so eager to return without guarantees of safe return. Rohingya refugees were reluctant to return because of the continuing refusal of the Myanmar authorities to allow the UNHCR to monitor their return and reintegration. As the prevailing political system were totally authoritarian and were biased against them, the Rohingyas were very hesitant to return.

Ne Win's successors have not yet proved better, although they attach importance to business and trade. They have to cope with large number of Chinese presence in economic and strategic spheres. State Peace and Development Council (SPDC) besides advocating the role of military in politics, are also taking measures for globalization, development and regional integration. Official policy is not to support crusade against Indians but to support BIMSTEC process, which is bound to facilitate better relations and integration.

The Government of India under the stewardship of Atal Bihari Vajpayee supported the policy of globalization, free trade and regional integration. He knew the importance of overseas Indians in improving the economic profile. He instituted a high-level committee on Indian Diaspora under the chairmanship of L.M. Singhvi to study the entire range of issues and recommendations on a variety of issues such as dual citizenship, cultural promotion, economic ties, tourism and education, etc.

The people of Indian origin in Myanmar are 2.9 million and they comprise 5% of the total population. According to Singhvi Committee Report, 2 to 4 lakh persons of Indian origin are stateless. They have no documents to prove that they were born in Myanmar.[33] Sharing a common maritime and land borders of 1600 kms., Myanmar had been a favourite place for Indian immigrants in the past. Their greatest concentration has been in Yangon areas and economically they are poor now. They are engaged in domestic services, mechanics and construction work.[34]

Indian Diaspora was denied admission in universities and professional courses during 1964-1988 and therefore, their education and representation in the academic institutions is dismal. The government of India introduced PIO card on payment of US $1000 for NRIs but Indians in Myanmar did not utilize it. It is understood that Indians in Myanmar cannot help in promoting trade and investment as their position is marginalized. If they are empowered once again, the economic prosperity of Myanmar will improve and the entire scenario would change.

Vajpayee and his successors have been pursuing the policy of "Look-East" and in that endeavour, attach importance to Southeast Asia. He knows that the person of Indian origin, numbering about 4.5 million in the ASEAN countries can greatly facilitate India-ASEAN relations and overall objective of integration with Southeast Asia. Indian Diaspora had played decisive role in the success of INA under Netaji Subhas Chandra Bose. INA was based in Southeast Asia with headquarters in Singapore.

Now there is an effort to revive economic resurgence of India in association with the ASEAN region. This is complimentary for both India and the ASEAN. Southeast Asian NRIs can play an important role in bringing India and the ASEAN closer to one another. They can fill up the vacuum of linguistic, cultural and political barriers. They may assist in proper understanding of the attitudes of their host countries with the country of their origin.

Myanmar is the hub of India's economic diplomacy in East Asian region. It figures prominently in BIMSTEC, Mekong-Ganga Project, Highway and Railway projects linking India to ASEAN, ARF and Anti-terrorist drives. The two, being the partners in regional and sub-regional groupings have succeeded in forging understanding and confidence. This has salutary impact on the status of the people of Indian origin in Myanmar. Myanmar gives an impression that very few people of Indian origin are still stateless and the ban on their socio-economic life have been lifted. However internal dynamics of the problem are difficult to understand.

The Burman regime's human rights abuse, and especially the ethnic cleansing occurring in Shan, Kayah and Karen states in the name of maintaining Burma's unity, are an outrage to mankind, and condemnation of these practices are taking place.[35] The campaigning for civil rights however tend to divert attention from the corruption and involvement in the drugs trade that underpin the regime's hold on power.

Shelby Tucker has further stated that "On May, 1990, the military regime allowed a general election in Burma, believing, that it would demonstrate popular support for its National Unity Party (NUP). To improve its chances of victory, it disqualified Aung San Suu Kyi from standing as a candidate, for having conceived children by a British father, prevented her from campaigning (indeed, kept her under house arrest), orchestrated a media campaign vilifying her as a Mrs. Race Destructionist", accused the NLD of colluding with Burma's 'enemies', disenfranchised voters living in insurgent-controlled areas, relocated voters in widespread gerrymandering, restricted political assembly, limited political broadcasts to one pre-censored, 10-minute television statement and one pre-censored, 15-minute radio statement per party, forbade reference in campaign speeches to Ne Win, the army, the

SLORC and the economy, and opened the context to more than three dozen parties, one supporting the SLORC and all others the opposition. Nevertheless, the NLD won 392 of the 485 seats contested, against 10 for the NUP—a preponderance of 40 to 1. If 83 seats won by other opposition parties are included in the tally, the preponderance of support for the opposition was 47 to 1".[36]

To conclude it can be stated that although Myanmar government advertently reduced the socio-economic existence of the Indians, made their life miserable, and forced them to immigrate elsewhere, yet they remain significant today. Indians in Burma had played powerful role in economic spheres as well as in anti-colonial struggle. Burmese thought that Indians rather than the Britishers were the root cause of all their problems but they have realized now that depriving Indians of their properties and citizenship could not help them in the economic arena. Moreover the Chinese entrepreneurs are advertently supported and they have tried to fill up the absence of Indian entrepreneurs and it is difficult to say who is more exploitative. History says that Burma became the richest in Southeast Asia with the support of Indians but today in the absence of Indians, Myanmar has miles to go to gain that status. They cannot ignore the enterprising skills of the Indian Diaspora and the realities demand a communion of Indo-Burman spirits for regional integration and prosperity.

REFERENCES

1. Shelby Tucker, *Burma: The Curse of Independence*, New Delhi, 2001.
2. Ton That Thien, *India and Southeast Asia, 1947-1960*, Geneva, 1963, pp. 150-84.
3. V. Suryanarayan, "Indian Communities in Southeast Asia", *Dialogue Quarterly*, Delhi, September 2003, pp. 105-18
4. *Ibid.*
5. *Ibid.*
6. *Ibid.*
7. Ton That Thien, *India and Southern Asia, 1947-1960*, Geneva, 1963.
8. *Ibid.*

9. *Ibid.*
10. Shelby Tucker, *Burma: The Curse of Independence,* New Delhi, 2001.
11. *Ibid.*, also see Martin Smith, *Ethnic Groups in Burma: Development, Democracy and Human Rights,* London, 1994.
12. *Observer*, London, 4 June, 1978.
13. *Bangladesh Time,* 25 June, 1978.
14. *Ibid.*, 9-10 July, 1978.
15. *Asia Week*, 4 January, 1991, pp. 16-18.
16. "Road to Manerplaw", *Asia Week,* 4 January, 1991, p. 17.
17. *Time of India,* 21 January, 1992.
18. *Ibid.*
19. John Swain, "Muslim Refugees Flee the Terror of Brutal Burma", *Times, London,* 26 January, 1992.
20. See the Report of Amnesty International, *"Union of Myanmar: Human Rights Violation Against Muslims in the Rakhine (Arakan) Sate"*, AI Index: ASA, 16/06.1992, London, May, 1992.
21. *Times*, London, 21 March, 1992, for a better understanding, see Bertil Lintner, Outrage: Burma's Struggle for Democracy, Hong Kong, 1989.
22. *The Times of India,* 24 March, 1992.
23. Inder Malhotra, "Unending Brutality in Burma", *The Times of India,* 19 March, 1992.
24. *Times*, London, 21 March, 1992; also see Amnesty International, *"Myanmar: No Law At All, Human Rights Violations Under Military Rule"*, All Index: ASA/16/11/1992, London, October, 1992.
25. *Myanmar Muslims from Rakhine State: Exit and Return,* New Delhi, Associated Press, 25 November, 1992, p. 5.
26. *United Nations,* 17 February, 1993, E/CN.4/1993/37, p. 27.
27. *Muslims from Rakhine State,* New Delhi, Associated Press, p. 5.
28. Amnesty International, May 1992, pp. 15-16.
29. Muslim from Rakhine State, No. 27, p. 13 (by August, 1993, only 33,000 refugees had returned to Burma, but the vast majority, about 217,000 remained in camps in Bangladesh).
30. Amnesty International, No. 24, p. 15.
31. *Ibid.*
32. Muslims from Rakhine State, No. 27, p. 8.
33. Singhvi Committee Report, New Delhi, 1998 and see V. Suryanarayan, "Indian Communities in Southeast Asia," *Dialogue Quarterly,* Delhi, September, 2003, pp. 105-18.
34. *Ibid.*, p. 115.
35. Shelby Tucker, No. 1, p. 212.
36. *Ibid.* After its defeat, the regime claimed that the election was to

a constituent assembly for the purpose of drafting a new constitution, and not a legislature. However, Chapter II, Article 3 of Phithu Hluttaw Election Law No. 14/89, 31 May, 1989, ordained that a Parliament (Hluttaw) would be formed of representatives 'elected in accordance with this law from the Hluttaw constituencies', and ten days after promulgating election law No. 14/89, the regime stated, 'If [the elected representatives do] not like the two existing constitutions, they can [draft] a new constitution. Neither the Defence Forces nor the State Law and Order Restoration Council will draw up a new constitution.' 43rd News Conference organized by the Information Committee of the SLORC in Rangoon on 9 June, 1989; quoted in Article 19 (Venkateswaran), 1996: 13. Moreover, three weeks before the general election, the regime stated that 'the drafting of a constitution should be discussed and decided by elected representatives in the [emerging] assembly'. Press Conference, 11 May, 1990, Rangoon, *ibid.*

19

Indo-Myanmar Relations: An Overview

Myanmar (Burma) is the only ASEAN partner with which we share both land and maritime frontiers. Burma was the constituent part of British India till 1937 and our economic, social and constitutional system had common features. When Myanmar became independent in 1948, it adopted a parliamentary system and both U Nu and Jawaharlal Nehru had similar perspective about world politics. Although there were some outstanding issues to be addressed—such as the question over the citizenship of Indians in independent Myanmar, the compensation over their land and properties and their overall existence—those issues were left on the wisdom of Burmese leaders to be resolved. India tried to project herself as a friendly neighbour in the hope that such a feeling will be reciprocated. In that endeavour, India felt frustrated ultimately. Burma passed a Union Citizenship Act (1948) and made it difficult for Indians to get a certificate of citizenship. Getting citizenship of Burma was so difficult that thousands of Indians in the Burmese Civil Service, government offices and railways lost their jobs in the absence of citizenship in post-1948 era. Indian diaspora in Burma suffered setbacks and their role in the economy which was dominant during the colonial era were usurped advertently to contain Indian influence on society and politics of Burma. This was the achievement of the democratic era in Burma before 1962.

Burma came under military dictatorship of General Ne Win in 1962. He strongly believed in the philosophy of "Burma for the Burmans". He had great dislikes for Indian Diaspora in Burma and envisaged no role for them in business, trade and farming. He pursued policy of nationalization of the properties of the Indians and was biased against the performance of

Indian labourers as well. Indian Diaspora—who had made large investments in Burma and had dedicatedly worked to make Burma a prosperous nation during the colonial era—found no future in the country and they were compelled to migrate elsewhere. This had devastating impact on Burmese economy and Burma turned into one of the poorest country of the world during Ne Win era (1962-1988). Although there were several other reasons for poor economic conditions—such as isolationism, nationalization, corruption, omission and commission of BSPP officials—but the vacuum created by the absence of trained manpower in bureaucracy, farming and business after the forced migration of Indians to go out of Burma were responsible for poverty and mismanagement.

Although Indian government always displayed subdued opinion about its concerns for Indians, but it was one of the major constraints in the bilateral relations of the two countries. Burma was not sufficiently sensitive about Indian concerns and similarly our leaders also were not much bothered about the plight of its people in the country. Both ignored economic and strategic implications as a result of the absence of entrepreneurial class of Indians and both suffered in the process.

In retrospect, we find that India and Myanmar are natural partners. Myanmar is dominated by the people of Buddhist faith and India is emotionally and culturally linked to that country. Besides, there are a number of ethnic groups in India's north-east, who have their counterparts in Myanmar. Nagas, Mizos, Bodos, Ahoms and Meitzis have their ethnic counterparts on the other side of the frontier and their social interactions have been continuing from time immemorial. In order to promote the feeling of Indian nationhood and creation of peaceful environment in the region, it is of great importance that we support the policy of people-to-people contacts and that can be possible if we pursue the policy of good relations with Myanmar. The peaceful environment and economic prosperity in India's northeast will certainly prove beneficial for the people on other side of the frontier as well.

Myanmar is a gateway for India to enter into ASEAN market through roadways and railways. When the ASEAN car rally was held in Kolkata, it had passed through Tamu-Moreh border road to other parts of Southeast Asia. In fact, Myanmar occupies one of the most important land routes for China also. *'The Burma Road'*, also known as *Silk Route,* has been historically important for business and trade in Southeast Asian region. A hostile power in control of Myanmar could threaten India's security through land, sea and the air. It can paralyse shipping in the Bay of Bengal and play havoc in the movement of ships in the Malacca Straits. A dominant hostile power in control of Myanmar can prove disastrous for the nations in South and Southeast Asia. Both ASEAN and SAARC knows the strategic importance of Myanmar and adopted the policy of "constructive engagement" to maintain constant interaction. Myanmar is an important partner in ASEAN Regional Forum and confidence building measures are taken to enhance the level of regional cooperation. However, neither ASEAN nor the SAARC members are sufficiently satisfied about political and strategic developments in Myanmar.

Although officials of the regional groupings, or the heads of governments, do not speak openly, but they do display queries about growing Sino-Myanmar strategic connections. They do speak about evolving constitutional roadmaps or the house arrest of Aung San suu Kyi. On the other hand, the US and the EU have openly raised the issue of military dictatorship, human rights and democracy in Myanmar and they are prescribing punitive actions to transform the attitudes of military to go back to the barracks. The Western attitudes vis-a-vis Myanmar has been so critical that even those who do not have any sympathies for the military rulers start opposing US prescriptions. Malaysia, Indonesia and India are interested to see the rapid developments in the political "roadmaps" that Myanmar leaders are articulating, but they dislike outside intervention or dictates that the Americans are fond of suggesting.

A history of Myanmar suggests the Burmans are very proud of their cultural history. They believe that although Lord Buddha was born in India, but He had chosen Burmese jungles and forests as His favourite place. The king of Burma was so proud of Burmese culture and traditions, that he did not allow the British emissary to have an audience without removing his shoes and court customs. The situation worsened to such an extent that the British Empire felt offended and decided for military intervention in 1824. The Burmans fought bravely and courageous acts of Commander Budela are still remembered through short stories, anecdotes and poetries. Although the Burmans lost their war and the system of monarchy ultimately, they preserved their culture.

In the conduct of foreign policy, they have proved trustworthy to their allies. Though they supported the policy of non-alignment in the first decade of its independence, but subsequently they cultivated People's Republic of China as the closest partner. It abstained to choose either of the two super powers—the US and the USSR—but chose a neighbour with which it shared border and culture. Consequently, Myanmar's economic and strategic connections with China have increased rapidly. Chinese goods are coming to Myanmar through "Burma Road" and other routes. Myanmar has become a major destination for Chinese goods and through Myanmar; it is supplied into ASEAN and SAARC markets. However, the matter of great strategic significance is the construction of certain strategic outposts/facilities on two banks of the Irrawaddy River and the Indian Ocean. China has established a Signals Intelligence (SIGINT) facility at Coco Islands, 30 nautical miles from the Andaman Islands. The projection is that the Chinese SIGINT facility can enable China to monitor Indian missile tests off the Orissa Coast. Besides Coco the Chinese have also developed Hanggyi as an important port and facilitated communication through Bassein River. The Chinese collaboration in opium industry has also been well known. Myanmar is an important part of the golden triangle and drug syndicates in the area have evolved networks for production, sale and illegal trade of narcotics. In that endeavour, there has been collusion amongst opium growers, military elites and the smugglers. The Chinese collusion in opium business in Myanmar has been historically deep-rooted. India is concerned about it because there is growing abuse of drugs in the seven states of Northeast and the source of supply is by and large through Myanmar. Yet another issue which disturbs India is the nexus of Pakistan's ISI supported by China in Myanmar, which fomented insurgency and terrorism in India's northeast. Despite India, China, Pakistan and others along with the ASEAN states, are the aligned partners through ARF, the consensus over certain matters of economic and security concern for amity and cooperation have yet to emerge. Although "ASEAN way", mutual consultation, dialogue and cooperation have given birth to strong faith in regionalism in Southeast Asia, South Asian political masters have yet to understand the ethics of peace and development. This is not to suggest that their mindset is static, they are changing; but the pace is so slow that it is hardly visible.

Situated between India and China, the projection was that Myanmar would maintain equidistance in relations to both. If China is important strategically, India cannot be ignored. India is important enough for Myanmar for strategic and economic considerations. For most of the 1990s it has been Myanmar's largest export market, importing pulses, timber, rubber, leather and spices. It has also provided major assistance in building a 170-km road by the Border Roads Organisation, from Tamu, opposite Moreh in Manipur, to Kalemyo, which is connected to Mandalay. The road is completed and it provides an important passage for India into ASEAN market and vice-versa. The opening of the road has facilitated tourism and made it possible to expand trade. The opening of the road made it easier for Burmese Indians to visit their relatives. Most of them have suffered from the general impoverishment of the country since the army took it over in 1962 (when the better-off Indians and Chinese left, after their assets were nationalized by General Ne Win). It may not be fanciful to even look ahead to the days when Tamu becomes one of the land entry points for tourists, along with similar crossing points from Thailand and China. Discussions have also been held on Indian assistance in building a second road, connecting the border near Champhai, in Mizoram, with existing road networks further inland. India could also become a useful source of investments, although the largest Indian investment approved so far has been a proposal by Kolkata firm to invest $4.5 million in rebuilding, maintaining and leasing Caterpillar tractors. India accounts for about two-thirds of Burma's pharmaceutical imports.

Myanmar understands the importance of cultivating good neighbourly relations with the countries in the ASEAN. Besides China, it tried to cultivate ASEAN. It approached Thailand, Malaysia, Indonesia and Singapore in particular and it found a good response. The ASEAN, which was witnessing a booming economy, was trying to expand cooperation in the neighbourhood. Indo-China states and Myanmar were being assiduously cultivated to be partners of ASEAN regionalism.

In 1994, when the Americans tried to isolate Myanmar and projected it undemocratic, underdeveloped with potential to poison the region with narcotics, ASEAN leaders retorted that they will not deviate from the policy of constructive engagement with Myanmar. US Under Secretary of State, Madeleine Albright emphasized on taking strong stand against human rights abuses in Myanmar, but ASEAN stood firm on the policy of constructive engagement and integration of Myanmar in ASEAN activities.

This had positive impacts on the creation of positive environment for regional cooperation. Myanmar had already de-linked political from economic liberalization. The result was an economic boom. In September 1988, responding to the severe shortages, the government had opened the rice trade to the private sector, and followed this up by liberalizing internal trade in other commodities as well as allowing the private sector into foreign trade (except in teak, natural gas, petroleum, pearls and gems). This included legalization of the black-market trade in goods across the Thai border. When Thai logging operations were officially allowed, the Government of Thailand, in order to take full advantage for their logging companies of this profitable business which, hitherto, had been largely in the hands of the insurgents, began to clamp down on Myanmar insurgents operating from Thai territory and not to look too hard if Myanmar troops crossed the border, while campaigning against them.

Encouraging foreign investment, Myanmar adopted in November 1988 a foreign investment law allowing full foreign ownership of companies in certain areas like export expansion and the mining of natural resources, while joint ventures were encouraged in other areas. For both, a generous tax exemption regime was added to other incentives including guarantees against nationalization. In January 1993, private banks were allowed to function, and then licenses were issued to foreign banks; in three years 20 foreign banks, mainly from Thailand and Singapore, were operating.

It was Southeast and East Asia that particularly welcomed the opening of the economy. Singapore, Hong Kong and Thai companies were among the earliest to sign joint venture agreements in light industry, the retail and service sectors, hotel and tourism development. In 1993, for instance, Singapore companies signed hotel and tourism investment deals worth US $465 million. In 1995, a subsidiary of the Thai Petroleum Authority, together with a US and a French company, signed a deal worth US $1 billion to build a 416-km. pipeline from the Gulf of Martaban to Thailand. But Western companies, initially reluctant due to political pressure from their governments, also came in; in fact, by 1996, the British were the largest investors of all, while the French and Americans were among the top five. By 1996, a total of 169 foreign investment projects had been signed involving a foreign investment of US $3.23 billion.

The economic boom was seen in domestic as well as trade growth. The four-year plan ending March 1996 saw an average annual GNP growth of 8.25 per cent. Helped by good rice crops, the liberalization of the rice trade, a rapid rise in tourism, and large remittances from Burmese abroad, exports rose 50 per cent from 1992 to 1995, and by 1996, foreign exchange reserves stood at nearly US $600 million.

The Chinese Prime Minister, Li Peng paid a visit to Myanmar in 1994 and signed some agreements for providing soft loans for building infrastructure, which included construction of airbase at Mandalaya, a highway to connect Mandalaya to Yunnan (China), a port at Hanggyi and a passage through Irrawaddy delta to Bay of Bengal. The Chinese were already supplying strategic weapons to Myanmar ever since they signed agreements for $1 billion arms deal. In 1994, the two countries signed another agreement worth $400 million for naval frigates, jet aircraft, tanks, APCs, etc. Both countries displayed understanding for each other's concerns but it was after this visit of Li Peng that apprehensions about the nature of Sino-Myanmar strategic nexus were expressed at the regional level.

Hence India became important to balance the situation. India was given status of full dialogue partnership of ASEAN in 1995 and the membership of ARF in 1996. The ASEAN desired that India should promote the objective conditions for peace, stability, security and prosperity of the region. Pursuing the policy of Look East, India entered into dialogues with Myanmar to strengthen economic and strategic ties. India wanted to enlist the cooperation of Myanmar to address the threat of insurgency and terror in the northeast. Myanmar agreed to exchange information on insurgents and help India in tracing their hideouts. Myanmar also offered support for India's bid for permanent membership in the UN Security Council. It evinced interests in maintaining Indian Ocean as a zone of peace. General Malik visited Myanmar on goodwill missions (2000) and he was satisfied with the positive response. He was trying to get Myanmar's deeper level of cooperation to address the problem of cross border insurgency and drug trafficking. General Maung Aye, Myanmar's Army Chief, listened to General Malik's views and desired to extend cooperation as a good neighbour. General Than Swe also expressed support for India and serious dialogues have started ever since to counter cross-border subversion and insurgency. There is a constant effort to promote understanding. India's Foreign Minister, Pranab Mukherjee, visited Myanmar recently and was happy with the outcome. The *Time of India* (22 Jan. 2007) reported that :

> "In what may be a breakthrough of sorts in the drive to close in on secessionist outfits engaged in terror against India, Myanmar has agreed to India's proposal to institutionalize cooperation between their armies for operations against ULFA and other insurgent groups in the North-East. The understanding was reached at a meeting where India's foreign minister Pranab Mukherjee also agreed to Myanmar's pending request for supply of military equipment. While Myanmar has been cooperating with India's drive against insurgency in the north-east and has even taken action on the basis of information provided by New Delhi, it has not been enough to prevent insurgents from crossing over the Myanmar."

During his meeting with Mukherjee, General Maung Aye, vice senior general and vice chairman of the Myanmar's ruling State Peace and Development Council, said that he would pass instructions to his commanders to work out with their Indian counterparts on how to operationalise the understanding. General Aye, the number two in the Junta there, did not, unlike Bangladesh, dispute Mukherjee's contention that north-eastern insurgent groups were using sanctuaries on the Myanmarese side of the border to engage in anti-India activities. For his part, the Indian foreign minister showed appreciation of General Aye's plea that lack of infrastructure was hindering his troops from extending full cooperation to India. Mukherjee offered to help with cost of infrastructure development in the densely forested and inhospitable terrain. North-Eastern insurgent groups—ULFA, Khaplang faction of National Socialist Council of Nagaland and secessionist outfits from Manipur, have taken shelter here and procure arms from Myanmar's ethnic rebel groups like Karens and Kachins to attack Indian targets. Pleased with the outcome, Mukherjee, told reporters that Burmese authorities were "very receptive and responsive" to India's concerns.

Officials were tight-lipped about the military equipment Myanmar is keen on sourcing from India. Independent sources, however, said that the wish list of the chief of Myanmarese army, General Thura Shwe Man who visited New Delhi in December 2006, consisted of 35 MM field guns, helicopters, mortars, submarine-detecting Sonar's, Islanders aircraft and spares for MiG fighters.

In fact, China, Pakistan and Israel were supplying arms in the past, but now Myanmar is trying to diversify it. It is reported that India and Myanmar have decided to promote constructive engagement and establish cooperative mechanisms between the navies of two nations. Their agreement for joint exercises and exchange of intelligence would help the drive against sea piracy and smuggling of narcotics. India is pleased to transfer two BN-2 Defender Islander maritime aircraft to Myanmar and there are positive signals for better understanding of our security concerns.

India and Myanmar are evolving cooperative mechanism through ASEAN, ARF, BIMST-EC and Mekong-Ganga project to promote economic and strategic interaction. But there is another area, which needs to be addressed properly. Myanmar is richly endowed by nature in terms of oil and natural gas. It was a huge supplier of oil through Burmah Shell to the sub-continent in the historical past, but today most of the energies are going in the Chinese direction. Always hungry for oil and natural gas, the Chinese succeed in getting contracts in Myanmar. Pranab Mukherjee discussed the issue of energy supplies from Myanmar with General Maung Aye and with Brigadier General Thura Myint Maung on 20 May 2007. The deliberations also focused on India' desire to tie-up energy supplies from Myanmar, with Mukherjee raising the issue of a pipeline to ensure uninterrupted supply of natural gas to India with General Aye. But it was clear that progress could be made only if India matched the price quoted by aggressive competitors and if A-3 block, in which India wants to take a stock, yielded enough gas to be economically feasible. A Belgian consultant engaged by the Government of India has estimated that a pipeline must carry a minimum of five lakh million cubic feet of gas to be feasible.

India and South Koria, which had invested in Rakhine offshore area to explore and to extract oil, were disappointed when Myanmar signed a MoU with China, committing all gas from Block A-I and A-III to China. The gas is to be wheeled through a 2,380 km pipeline connecting Myanmar's Kyakphyu in the Bay of Bengal to Rili in China's Yunnan. China agreed to pay an annual transit fee of $150 million for 30 years to Myanmar.

Two Indian owned state companies—ONGC Videsh and GAIL—alongwith South Korean Daewoo had made investments and they were expecting a better price and deal. India was planning to build a pipeline through Bangladesh to bring energy to India, but could not succeed. Due to non-cooperation of Bangladesh, and astute business sense of the Chinese, India faced setbacks.

The regional environment is however changing rapidly and East Asians are interested in Indian markets. East Asian

Community (EAC) which has emerged recently is going to create a cooperative environment. India, China, Myanmar and Japan have to play major role for community building in the region. Free trade, common currency, people-to-people contacts are on the agenda of the future. Myanmar has to act as an important hub of economic activities between SAARC and ASEAN and has to dilute its tendency of over-dependence on China. That would be appreciated not only by China but by the international community in general. In that scenario, India's position for collaboration and integration with Myanmar will certainly improve.

20

Struggle of Malaysian Indians

Malaysian Indians are regarded as a deprived community politically and economically. Most of them are working for palm oil estates and rubber plantations and their educational and employment opportunities are shrinking in independent Malaysia. The ethnic Malays who comprise 60 per cent of the total population are the dominant force in the socio-economic and political spheres. The ethnic Chinese who comprise 25 per cent are powerful in business and trade. Indians comprising eight per cent of the total population are increasingly marginalized due to several reasons.[1] First of all they are mostly the labour force. Secondly the majority of the two million Indians are Hindus and they observe Hindu way of life. On the other hand, Malaysia gives emphasis on Malay Muslims and the government tend to support Islamisation programmes at the national level. Various government institutions, banks and universities are given Islamic names to satisfy Islamic leaders. However, the policies which have proved most discriminatory are the affirmative action for the Bhumiputra (Sons of the Soil), which makes provision for reservations only for ethnic Malays, the majority community of the country. This is a unique arrangement rarely to be found elsewhere in the civilized world.

The new generation of Indians born and brought up in Malaysia are unhappy with the present dispensation. Although they had never raised their voice against the government policies in the past, but now they are restless to convey their grievances. There is growing feeling of alienation and marginalisation and they think in terms of "do or die". They have thus formed an organization, called Hindraf (Hindu Rights Action Force) in which 30 Hindu organizations have joined their hands.[2] They are demanding reforms in the system, repeal of Article 121 (IA) which says civil court has no jurisdiction on matters under the purview of Sharia, and review of affirmative action of the privileged Malays. The prominent leaders of Hindraf are Waytha Moorthy Ponnusamy and P. Udhayakumar, who articulated the grievances of ethnic Indians.

Although there has been phenomenal economic development in Malaysia under New Economic policy (1970-1990) and subsequently National Development Policy and the country got Newly Industrialized Economy (NIE) status long ago, but ethnic Indians remained marginalized and poor. Whereas ethnic Malayas prospered, the fruits of modernization and development could not percolate down to better the socio-economic life of the Indians. The political system supported the policy of affirmative action for the Malays exclusively and some opportunities in education and bureaucracy which were available to Indians in the past were stopped. The ethnic Chinese, which comprise the largest minority group in the country, has somehow managed to maintain their influence in the economic and commercial fields.

The ethnic Malays do believe that Malaysia is their land, and its privileges cannot be shared with ethnic Chinese or Indians. The rules governing the citizenship laws are biased in favour of the Malay Muslims. Indians may be staying in that country for generations and may know the culture and customs of the Malays, but they are not considered Bhumiputra. Indians are settled in different parts of Malaysia, and they have lost their touch with the country of their origin. They have nothing left in India to come back as they left their homes centuries ago. They were 'have-nots' when they had left as contract labourers and now if they have anything, it is at the place of their inhabitation. They have nowhere else to go. They don't see future outside Malaysia as most of them are semi-literate. The government of Malaysia always tend to support Malay Muslims and its citizens. If there is a person of Malay origin in Java, Sumatra or Luzon for citizenship, their cases are sympathetically considered. They are also extended facilities under Bhumiputra policies. The critics hold the view that if indigenous people are entitled to Bhumiputra privileges, it should be extended to Orang Asli, who happen to be the original inhabitants of Malaya, and not the majority community. These are some of the anomalies of the system that have been highlighted by the Hindraf in the recent past. Despite the ban to discuss Bhumiputra policies by the government, the issues have been raised and the officials have to cope with it.

The ethnic Malays were favoured as a group by the British colonial masters during the Second World War. They were unhappy with Indians because of their support to India's freedom struggle. The Malayan leaders gave a slogan of 'Malaya for the Malays", and it had the approval of the Britishers. The Malay leaders were apprehensive against ethnic Chinese who were disliked both by the Japanese invaders and the ethnic Malays. Malayan Communist Party (MCP) had a strong cadre and they had occupied some territories in course of the Second World War. They were posing serious challenges to the evolving nationhood under the leadership of United Malay National Organization (UMNO) led by Dato Onn bin Jaafar.[3] After the end of the Second World War, the western nations including Great Britain was supporting containment drive and they were strongly opposing the Chinese communists. Britain signed even a defence pact (FPDP) with Malaysia and Singapore against the Chinese insurgents and enlisted the cooperation and support of ethnic Malays. Although Malaysia got a democratic constitution but advertent efforts were made to evolve Bhumiputra concept (Sons of the Soil), which is the root cause of inequality and discrimination in Malaysian society. The ethnic Chinese and Indians are deprived of the privileges of Bhumiputra policies and only Malay Muslims are the privileged group.

It is understood that the ethnic Malays were apprehensive about maintaining their dominance permanently as their majority status were evenly balanced. There was substantial presence of the Chinese population in that country in 1957. It was only when Singapore separated from Malaysia in 1965 that majority status of the Malays became unquestionable and the leaders began to think in terms of Bangsa Malaysia (The nation for Malayan race). The ethnic Chinese had faced reverses in the past because of racial riots and MCP insurgents. On the other hand, Indonesia had complicated the situation because of "Crush Malaysia Plan". Sukarno had viewed that the emergence of Malaysia was a colonial plot to destabilize political stability of the region. He thought that Malaya and Singapore were integral part of the Indonesian archipelago. He had envisaged military solutions to integrate Malaya, but could not succeed. His hostile statements against Malaysia and Great Britain however helped Malaysia to gain western support. It also helped Malay leaders, namely Tunku Abdul Rahman, Tun Abdul Razak and others to consolidate the support of their countrymen in facing the threat of external aggression.

The downfall of Sukarno and subsequently the butchering of thousands of Indonesian Communist Party (PKI) members ushered into an era of New Order in Indonesia which discarded "Crush Malaysia Plan". They made friendly overtures to promote cultural and economic relations and enabled Malaysia to evolve developmental policies. But Malaysia still felt that People's Republic of China and Malayan Communist Party (MCP) had potentials to foment trouble in the country. They gave importance to attending the issues of reconciliation especially after 1969 race riots. As Indians were mostly the labour force, they were mostly ignored by the new leaders. The Indians continued to remain poor, which is the genesis for the feeling of deprivation and alienation.

The government of Malaysia has kept Indians suppressed. Waytha Moorthy says that after 50 years of independence, Indians own 1.5 per cent of the country's national wealth.[4] Their representation in civil services are merely two per cent, which was 40 per cent in 1957. Most of their schools are privately run, which were funded by the government during the colonial period. They have limited educational & professional opportunities in independent Malaysia as most of them are reserved for the Bhumiputras. They are convinced that their marginalized status cannot change unless they raise their voice, and the endeavour of Hindraf is to work in that direction.

It was after 50 years of independence that Indians decided to raise their voice. They organized a rally in Kuala Lumpur and simultaneously filed a lawsuit in London on 25 November 2007. Waytha Moorthy Ponnusamy went to London and filed a class action suit at the Royal Court of Justice after paying 2000 British pounds as court fees. The lawsuit was to sue the British government for US $4 trillion, because it held the British responsible for migration and exploitation of Indians for 150 years. Majority of Indians had gone to Malaya as indentured labour or Kangani system. They had dedicated their services not only in the agricultural development but also in rubber plantations. The bulk of the indentured labourers stayed back as most of them were "have-nots" in India. As India and Malaya both were under British colonial rule and the work was available, it was a privilege to work for British masters even outside the country.

After the Japanese aggression on Malaya in 1942, the Britishers had taken the strategic support of Malayan People's Anti-Japanese Army (MPAJA) but after the end of the war Britishers began to favour UMNO. It was discovered that MPAJA was overwhelmingly supported by the Chinese but the British tended to support pro-Malay parties. They changed their rhetorics and policies. Now they began to support the popular slogan of "Malaya for the Malays". When the new constitution was framed by a commission under Lord Reid, it made provisions for an elective monarchy, a conference of rulers, a cabinet responsible to a bicameral legislature and a judiciary independent of the executive. It was this constitution which incorporated Bhumiputra policies (Article 153) and thereby depriving ethnic Chinese and Indians to be treated at par with ethnic Malays. The British attitude in determining the future norms for independent Malaysia was somewhat similar to what they did in Burma in 1948 or Fiji in 1970. They generously supported the interests of the majority and forgot that they had some obligations towards Indians also to whom they had taken to Malaya under the indentured labour system. Indians have suffered traumatic experiences in Burma and Fiji but they did not sue Great Britain. However Malaysian Indians proved different and sued Britain for their deprivation, alienation, and exploitation.

It is interesting that Malaysian Indians filed a lawsuit against the former colonial master, and attracted their attention about Indian miseries. Malaysian authorities, however was much disturbed by the rally of 20 thousand people near the Petronas Twin Towers in Kuala Lumpur. The rally wanted to submit a petition to the British High Commission signed by thousands of ethnic Indians. The petition urged Queen Elizabeth to appoint a consul to represent the case of Malaysian Indians in the class action suit for compensation. The lawsuit is holding Britain responsible for bringing Indians to Malaya and leaving them behind to face inequality and sufferings.

Malaysian police has taken stern action against Hindraf's anti-government rally. They did not give permission either to hold the rally or to submit the petition to British High Commission. The leaders of the rally were arrested and charges were framed to prosecute them. The rally was considered unlawful, provocative and violent. Although the rally was peaceful carrying the life-size photographs of Queen Elizabeth and Mahatma Gandhi, but their organised show of strength despite the ban irked the authorities. The police used tear gas and chemical laced water to disperse them. Prime Minister, Abdullah Ahmad Badawi himself warned the protesters and threatened to invoke a security law allowing indefinite detention without trial to punish them.

Reporting about the rally, Charles Santiago said that three important leaders of Indian community were arrested for seditious speeches in Tamil and 31 on attempted murder charges. The rally was projected as an illegal assembly for creating mischiefs. The Police inspector general, Musa Hassan was so annoyed that he accused the protesters of seeking help from terrorists. The attempts were made to link Hindraf with Sri Lanka's Tamil Tigers (LTTE) and Jemaah Islamiyah. The allegations were astounding and unbelievable. However the wisdom prevailed on the authorities. Attorney General of Malaysia, Abdul Gani Patail favourably argued the case of ethnic Indians and most of the accused were subsequently released.

The November rally in Kuala Lumpur exposed the myth of communal harmony in Malaysia. It was clear after the rally that Indians were unhappy with the prevailing system. They roundly criticized the Bhumiputra policies, which promotes the interests of Malay Muslims and promotes the belief of Ketuanan Melayu, which means "Malays are masters of Malaysia."

Reid Commission had inserted Article 153 in Malaysian constitution (Bhumiputra Policy) as a temporary arrangement and was to be reviewed after 15 years but instead of reviewing it, National Operation Council (NOC) of independent Malaysia made it a permanent arrangement. NOC introduced some amendments in the Sedition Act in 1970, which mentioned that it was illegal to question Bhumiputra Policies. This amendment was passed by Malaysian parliament in the same year. It was thereafter that various programmes for National Economic Policy under Mahathir Mohamad were evolved which favoured ethnic Malays in all aspects of the economic life including the industrial and entrepreneurial sectors. Mahathir had been a strong supporter of affirmative action for Malays as expounded in his book, *The Malay Dilemma*. He always argued that strong measures were needed to improve economic conditions of ethnic Malays. They were the rightful owners of Malaysia, which entitled them to their privileges and reservations. Mahathir did his best to safeguard the rights of Malay Muslims for decades and he succeeded in that endeavour. His successor Abdullah Ahmad Badawi wanted to prove different and had talked about reforms on the eve of elections in 2004. But after getting a massive mandate, he forgot to fulfil his election promises. He did not do anything for reforms or to assuage the grievances of the minorities.

Indians are feeling insecure about their religious rights also. The reports are that some of their temples have been bulldozed. The implementations of Sharia laws are such that Hindu women's right to divorce are rejected. The Hindu husband has the right to convert himself and be Islamic, but if the wife wants to divorce him on that ground, it is not allowed, as has been in the case of Sarvanan Thangthoray alias Muhammad Shafi Abdullah in 2008. The Indians are thinking that under the present dispensation their socio-economic and natural rights will continue to be ignored unless they use legitimate initiatives to convey their grievances.

It is noteworthy to point out that Indians had never raised their voice against the government in the past. Although the Chinese had very often been vocal and violent against affirmative action for Malays, but their efforts had never got the support of the Indians. Singapore separated from Malaysia basically over the differences regarding Bhumiputra policies. Indians did not do anything to support the Chinese, who demanded equal rights and opportunities. Instead Malaysian Indian Congress extended full support to the Barisan National Coalition. However the situation has changed now after the emergence of Hindraf. The hostile statements and persecution of Indians after the November rally in Kuala Lumpur have given support to a new brand of politics, which is termed racial activism and it is a matter of concern for the exponents of Bhumiputra policies.

An understanding of 2008 election results, clearly indicate trouble for ruling Barisan National Coalition. Although they have got simple majority to form the government in the centre but they have lost powers in majority of states. The ruling party was always getting more than two third seats in the parliament and in state assemblies ever since independence, but polarization of the voters in 2008 were against the government. The Prime Ministership of Abdullah Ahmad Badawi has been questioned and the debate for reforms accelerated because of electoral reverses to the ruling coalition. There is interesting polarization in different constituencies in which new equations and combinations are defeating the veterans and challenging the myth of permanent dominance of UMNO.

The election result of 2008 is projected as a political upheaval. It was for the first time that ruling coalition lost two thirds majority in parliament. They got merely 139 seats out of 222. The opposition which used to win dozen seats or so have got 82 seats. The increasing presence of the opposition in parliament are positive for democratic polity and the debates in the new parliament are bound to be vibrant. However this is giving sleepless nights to UMNO leaders.[5]

Another outcome of the election has seen the defeat of leaders who were considered sycophants and least bothered about their constituencies. S. Sami Vellu, head of the Malaysia Indian Congress and a minister in the cabinet lost the elections because he was consistently vocal against Hindraf. On the other hand, a detained Hindraf leader, M. Manoharan won the election with a massive support. Had Waytha Moorthy fought the election, he would have been a legislator but he chose to stay out of the country after filing a lawsuit in London. He came to India to enlist the support of Indian leaders and in the process made some statements linking the conditions of Malaysian Indians with Tamils in Sri Lanka which may prove counterproductive, but his credentials as a fighter cannot be ignored.

The election process has shown that Bhumiputra policies are not supported by all the sections even within the Malay community. For instance Parti Islam se Malaysia (PAS) which has been a party of conservative Muslims has been critical against it. They hold the view that such a policy cannot help Islamisation process in the long run. It is believed that Bhumiputra policy is short-sighted and it has simply promoted corruption, favouritism and cronysm. PAS which was aligned to UMNO in the past, has changed its strategies and is seeking new alignments. It is cultivating Democratic Action Party (DAP) and Keadilan party and thus the support of ethnic Chinese and Indians are solicited. In short we find that after 2008 elections, a new combination of political groupings have emerged, which is a development of great concern for the protagonists of Bhumiputra policies.

As a result of new alliances, the ruling coalition has lost elections in various states. Kelantan had been under the governance of PAS for years and if the national coalition lost the elections in that state this time also, there was nothing to feel surprised. However the defeat in Penang, Perak, Kedah and Selangor was surprising. The defeat in Penang was shameful. Barisan national coalition was in power in that state uninterruptedly since 1969. It had won 38 parliamentary seats out of 40 in 2004 also but in 2008 they could not get even a single seat. As far as state assembly was concerned, DAP and Keadilan Party of Anwar Ibrahim got majority of the seats in 2008 and they decided to form a coalition government.

Thus political polarization finds Indian at the centre stage and their support is demanded by smaller parties against the national coalition. This may prove useful for racial harmony in the long run but presently the protagonists of Bhumiputra policy have targeted them as a disturbing element for national unity and solidarity. Thus Indians have to choose their strategies very carefully so that the majority of Malays do not perceive them hostile for future reconciliation and integration. Though power is the most important cementing force, but leaders have to be sensitive and dynamic to understand the concerns of Islamic forces who think in terms of Kafirs and Jehad.

The political development in Malaysia is keenly watched by the outside world. Although the government of Malaysia has been talking about the policy of multiculturalism, but their policy of affirmative action has been reserved for the majority community, especially for those who are close to power centres. The government policies have neither promoted assimilation of the ethnic groups nor national integration. What Kernial Singh Sandhu had written decades ago about the challenges of the new nation is still relevant. He said:

> "The ethnic, cultural and economic differences among its inhabitants have often led people to describe Malays as a country with a 'cleaved plural society'. To weld this plural society of Malays, Indians and the Chinese into a unified and loyal Malayan citizenry—with a Malayan consciousness—is probably the major problem of the society. Assimilation is the most perplexing and pressing issue in Malaya today".[6]

Professor Sandhu further said that "the Chinese and Indians are discriminated against in almost every field of government employment and yet they are taxed more heavily, proportionately speaking, then the Malays. Jus Soli is denied to them, but they are called to give all their loyalties to the Malays cause. Furthermore, they fear that their very linguistic and cultural affinities are threatened through strongly biased Malay-language educational policy".[7]

Ethnic Indians are not happy with the prevailing situation and they have started looking beyond UMNO to fulfil their ambitions. They have opened their dialogues with smaller political groups in the country so that they may get equal opportunities. They also try to attract external support and in that endeavour, they tend to enlist Indian support. Hindraf is a facilitator in that endeavour. It is known that India had supported Tamils against Sinhals in the past and Tamils have sympathies for fellow Tamils at the global level. However the government of India had never supported its diaspora strongly.[8] Whether it was the plight of Burmese Indians (1948-62) or Indo Fijians (1987-89), the support was nominal and moral. In case of Malaysian Indians recently, External Affairs Minister, Pranab Mukherjee displayed a subdued response by saying that Indian problems in Malaysia were related with internal affairs of Malaysia. India is a dialogue partner of ASEAN and a member of ARF. It can articulate its opinion about the plight of its diasporic community, but it does not want to raise any controversial issues lest it may be criticised to flaunt the Treaty of Amity and Cooperation (TAC) that it has already signed with ASEAN. The most important factor which is given importance in the present dispensation is to promote business relations and India and Malaysia have a strong trade, investment and tourism ties. India has been importing palm oil, tin, petroleum, rubber and wooden products from Malaysia on a large scale. Malaysian timber, tin and palm oil have great demands in India. On the other hand, India had been exporting meat and its preparations, vegetables and fruits, machinery including transport equipments, non-metallic manufactures and textiles to Malaysia. The food products include a variety of meat and fish products. India's buffalo meat has great demands in Malaysia.[9]

India-Malaysia trade picked up momentum in the post-Cold War era when Malaysian side agreed to invest in wood based industries, ceramics, chemicals, pharmaceuticals, value added automotive accessories, rubber related products, tourism and hotel industries. Collaborations in software, cellular mobile phones, IT, BT, tele equipments and electrical goods etc. were welcomed. The trade volume has increased and India's imports from Malaysia amounted to US $2,415.61 million in 2004-05, while exports were US $1,161.86 million, but it increased by 5.75 per cent to US $3,383.07 million to US $3,577.47 million in 2005-06. Both sides especially petronas of Malaysia and Cairn India have decided to invest facilities to promote regional trade. Needless to say that, India attaches great importance to Malaysia for bilateral ties.

India has been pursuing Look East Policy and ASEAN region is giving utmost importance to strengthen ties. Malaysia is an important ASEAN partner and of great geopolitical significance to India because it is located at the banks of Bay of Bengal and Malacca Straits. Malaysia had supported India *vis-à-vis* Pakistan in 1965 and has been vocal to articulate ideas for Asian values, Asian democracy and Asian century. Moreover as India's Sujatha Singh has stated that India's foreign policy have two important economic objectives, (a) creating a framework conducive for the economic wellbeing of its people by encouraging a healthy external economic environment and by cheering up the Indian economy to the challenge of global marketisation, (b) through active political and economic diplomacy to contribute to peace and stability in Asia.[11] The ideological postures of the Cold War era have no relevance now and the leaders are trying to cope with the challenges of globalization. Again as Indian leaders have time and again advised its overseas population to adjust and accommodate with the people and politics of the countries that they inhabit, there is very little scope to extend active support to its diasporic population.

It is no exaggeration to say that India has been unable to evolve a clear cut policy regarding support to Indian diaspora. China on the other hand has a clear policy to support its diaspora. When there was an exodus of Hoas from Vietnam (1978-81), China expressed its anguish by sending its armed forces to teach a lesson to Vietnam. When there were anti-Chinese riots in Thailand (1945), Malaysia (1969) or Indonesia (1998), China actively and strongly argued the case of its diasporic population and it had its salutary impact. The United States also has a clear policy to support its citizens outside the country. The US government is authorized by law to march its troops in any part of the world if the life of an American is endangered there. Again when there was a bomb blast in Bali (2002) and hundreds of Australian tourists were killed, Australia expressed its strong support for its citizens and talked about "pre-emptive strikes" to punish the terrorists in Indonesia. However, Indian policy has been very soft and has been of wait and watch without asserting its viewpoints. Indian diaspora has seen the dismal support of Indian government when Prime Minister Mahendra Chaudhry was ousted from power in Fiji illegally or when Indians were deprived of their natural rights in Burma or Uganda. It has been found that the outside world takes no interests in resolving the crisis relating to Indian diaspora except to express sympathies.

Malaysian Indians will have to fight their case at the domestic and international level without any support of the government of India. It is believed that 90% of Malaysian Indians are Tamils and they have their kith and kins in Tamil Nadu, Karnataka, Andhra Pradesh, Kerala and Sri Lanka. Ethnic Tamils may have emotional connections with their counterparts everywhere but Indian Tamils cannot extend support to Malaysian Indians as the government of India will not permit it. Above all exploring the support of India is not productive or useful.

To conclude, it can be stated that the struggle of Malaysian Indians are difficult because there is lack of unity amongst the community in Malaysia, that MIC always failed to articulate its grievances before top UMNO leaders, that there is a divide between ethnic Malays and Indians, that majority of Indians are plantation workers and poor, yet there are rays of hopes which will help the Indian activists to attain their objectives. The Malays may be parochial *vis-à-vis* Indians but they have a civilization of their own. They have adopted a democratic framework and they know the parameters of power politics. None will like to lose power and in order to enjoy the perks and privileges of power, certain adjustments are indispensable. The Malays will never support a policy of ethnic cleansing because of economic and political compulsions. Hence they will compromise with major minority groups and Indians have to keep their channels open. Elections of 2008 have clearly indicated that UMNO is losing the grip over power. Election has also taught lessons to sterile Indian leaders who did not actively nurture or support their community needs. Their sycophancy were disliked by the people. The Hindraf highlighted their omissions and commissions and they had their downfall. There is a need of dedicated leaders who can speak the truth to the authorities without adopting the art of sycophancy. If Indians will work unitedly and honestly, if they adopt a dynamic approach without any inhibitions, and if they link themselves with affluent diaspora outside—the US, the UK, Singapore and Hong Kong—the solution to their problems will automatically emerge. Religion may be inhibitive but developmental factors are more important in Malaysia. Thus democracy and development will take care of the system's anomalies in coming decades.

REFERENCES

1. Waytha Moorthy Ponnusamy (10 Dec. 2007), "Indians weakest section in Malaysia", *The Times of India*, for an understanding of the issues in socio-economic conditions of Malaysian Indians, see V. Suryanarayan (1982), "Indians in Malaysia—The Neglected Minority", in I.J. Bahadur Singh (ed.), *Indians in Southeast Asia*, New Delhi, Sterling, pp. 34-51.
2. Charles Santiago, "Malaysia Feels Racial Heat", *The Times of India*, Kolkata, 27 November, 2007.
3. D.G.E. Hall, *A History of Southeast Asia*, London, Macmillan, 1968, pp. 885-88.
4. Moorthy, No. 1.
5. *The Times of India*, 9 March, 2008.
6. Kernial Singh Sandhu, "Communalism: The Primary Threat to Malayan Unity", *Asian Survey*, Vol. 2, No. 6, August, 1962, p. 33.
7. *Ibid.*, p. 34.
8. Manmohini Kaul, "Indians in Southeast Asia", in I.J. Bahadur Singh (ed.), *Indians in Southeast Asia*, New Delhi, Sterling, 1982, pp. 29-31
9. Charan, D. Wadhva, "India-Malaysia Trade: Problems, Opportunities and Strategies", *IDSA*, March 1988, pp. 13-14.
10. Sujatha Singh, "India's Economic Reforms and Opportunities for Malaysian Businessmen", *Strategic Analysis*, Vol. 17, No. 1, April, 1994, p. 53.
11. *Ibid.*, p. 46.

21

Recent Developments in Indo-Thai Economic Relations

Business and Culture had been the essence of Indo-Thai relations in the ancient past. When Sona and Uttara went to Nakhon Pathom (Subarnabhumi) to spread the gospel of Buddhism, they were accompanied by Indian Traders acquainted with the area. The cultural interaction between India and Thailand were never disrupted but commercial interaction faced setbacks in the post-1947 era due to certain ideological and political reasons. However the situation have changed now and there is a upswing in the economic ties. The endeavour of this paper is to analyse the recent developments in economic relation and project future trends.

Thailand is an important gateway for India to interact with ASEAN and the Asia-Pacific region. It is a key actor to facilitate the success of BIMSTEC and Mekong-Ganga Project. It is the first country in the ASEAN to sign bilateral free-trade-agreement with India. It is the first country in the ASEAN to sign bilateral free-trade-agreement with India. It is the first to evolve "Look West Policy" to reciprocate India's "Look East Policy". Again Thailand is one of those countries, which had proposed the establishment of growth triangle in the Andaman region. It had worked for turning Indo-China from "battleground to market place" in the east and introduce dynamism in economic relations with India in the West.

There has been landmark developments in the promotion of trade and investment ties in the past few years. Although during 1947 to 1988 the relations were limited to purchase of rice and exchanges of some agro-based products and capital goods, but after the visit of Thai Prime Minister Chatchai Choonhavan in 1989, serious efforts were made to enhance economic ties. Thus joint commissions and Business councils were established to suggest constructive suggestions to promote bilateral economic relations, including the proposals for avoidance of double taxation. The thrust on economic ties proved beneficial eventually after the end of the Cold War in 1991. India became a sectoral dialogue partner of ASEAN in 1992 and under its framework trade, investment and tourism were the important sectors of cooperation between the two. Thailand began to pay greater attention to India because the latter had offered a big market for the Asian neighbours.

Strategically located, Thailand had been playing pivotal role in promoting trade through roadways, railways and airways in the ASEAN region. Now it is possible to go through roadways directly from Bangkok to Kunming (China) and to Hanoi (Vietnam) or Singapore. Chuan Leekpai (1997-2001) and Thaksin Shinawatra (2001-2006) took innovative decisions to promote free-trade in the region and accordingly developed infrastructure to facilitate it. Although the agreement for free-trade in the area has been signed (AFTA) in 1992, but it was slow to develop satisfactorily. Prime Minister Chuan Leekpai began serious discussions for free-trade agreement with Australia and New Zealand in 2001 at the bilateral level and now the FTA has already been signed between Thailand and several important countries in the region, namely India, China, Japan, Australia, and the US. Kozo Kiyota (2006) has noted that Thailand redirected its major target countries in the post 2001 era from developing to large/or developed countries in response to shifts in both its domestic and foreign economic and political forces. The foreign forces included issues involving the formation of an AFTA, the implementation of new WTO rules and policies, and competition with Singapore and China to attract new Foreign Direct Investments (FDIs).

Hence India could not be overlooked. India-ASEAN summit which was initiated in 2002, supported the quest for free-trade in the region. The Nation (BKK) reported that "India and Thailand are natural partners, but somehow they have failed to connect with each other both in regional and global arenas even though no actual barriers exist to keep them apart." It further noted that "India has in recent times adopted a more outward-looking foreign policy, which looks beyond the traditional realm of South Asia and developing countries.... India is a genuine regional power, with the potential to become a global power."

India's Prime Minister, Atal Bihari Vajpayee (1999-2004) was keen to evolve a comprehensive economic cooperation agreement with ASEAN and he used to say very often that the role of his government was that of a facilitator and promoter of liberalized trade regime. He had supported a target of $30 billion for Indo-ASEAN trade by 2007 and he had gone to attend Indo-ASEAN summit at Bali (2003) with a comprehensive package. Each country of the ASEAN were equally important to India. Thailand proposed to sign FTA with India on the eve of the Bali summit and FTA was signed with Thailand for setting up of a free-trade-area covering goods, services and investments in 10 years. The Indo-Thai FTA covered as many as 84 items and several areas in the first phase including services, investment, economic cooperation in goods like food items, tourism, auto-parts and electric goods. (See Appendix)

As per the early harvest scheme (EHS) under the agreement, a common list of items for exchange of tariff concession at 6-digit level and tariff on these identified items was slated to be phased out by 1 March, 2006. However the negotiation on various aspects of FTA which started in 2004 are yet to be concluded. The negotiation are continuing on the framework of "Rules of Origin". Although the bargaining has not been fully conclusive, but the volume of trade is increasing. Indo-Thai trade which was worth $606 million in 1990 increased to $1.22 billion in 2000 and $2.2 billion in 2003. Indian companies in gems and jewellery sectors earned a good reputation in Thailand and it became an important item for foreign exchange earning.

The volume of Indo-Thai trade increased further to $3.4 billion in 2006 and proposed target for 2007 is $4 billion (*The Nation*, 28 June, 2007). Foreign Ministry source in Bangkok says that Thailand's exports to India include plastic pellets, radios, televisions and parts, steel and iron products plus automobile accessories, while Thailand imports diamonds and jewellery, silver ingots, gold, ore, metal and chemical products from India.

The FTA has facilitated environment for bilateral trade. Thailand, China and India are negotiating FTA in order to remove trade barriers earlier than envisaged through agreements with ASEAN. Thailand sees not only a first mover advantages but also real progress in negotiations of ASEAN-China and ASEAN-India FTAs. Negotiations with the two countries are accelerating based on the "early harvest" concept, which allows for a reduction of import tariffs on selected items before the formal negotiations begin (Kozo Kiyota, 2006).

EHS under which common items of export interest to the two sides have been negotiated for elimination of tariffs on a fast track includes auto parts, electronic goods, and fruits. India has sought tariff concessions on items such as marine products, chemicals (including drugs and pharmaceuticals) and iron and steel. Prime Minister of Thailand, General Surayud Chulanont on a visit to New Delhi in June, 2007 said that "we very much look forward to concluding regional FTAs in the framework of ASEAN and BIMSTEC which will benefit the regional economy as a whole, and to concluding mutually beneficial agreements such as bilateral FTA with India which will further energize our trade and investment."

Thai Prime Minister also announced that India-Thailand FTA roadshow will be staged in major Indian cities which will explain new business opportunities upon the coming into effect of the Indo-Thai FTA. (*Times of India*, 27 June, 2007). Kolkata, Chennai, Mumbai, New Delhi etc. were chosen as venues for roadshows and the endeavour was to explain the advantages of FTA on trade and investment relations.

The contents in FTA are constantly reviewed and monitored. On 30 August, 2004, India and Thailand signed a protocol to amend the framework agreement and dropped two items from the original 84 items for EHS. The Thai Commerce Minister, Watana Muagsook hoped that there will be successful implementation of FTA even before 2010. According to the amended framework both parties decided to reduce their applied tariff by 75 per cent in the period between September 1, 2005 to August 31, 2006 and by 100 per cent by September 1, 2006. The caution has been taken to avoid bringing sensitive agro-commodities under the EHS scheme of FTA. Thai textile yarns, fabrics and made up articles which currently consists of 5.31 per cent of India's imports, do not figure in the list. Vegetable oil and natural rubber are other sensitive commodity not included in the list. Vegetable oil from Thailand consists of 3.56 per cent of India's import while natural rubber consists of 2.26 per cent. The agro-products included in the list of commodities are fresh mangosteens, mangoes, apples, durians, rambutans, longans, pomegranates, durum wheat, salmon, sardines, rardinella and bristling or sparts, macherel, crab, pure sodium, table and denatured salt. These commodities are not likely to pose any problem in implementation of the bilateral trade agreement. Only thing required is to work out acceptable quarantine and sanitary and phytosanitary standards for these commodities (Ashok B. Sharma, 7 September, 2004).

The areas of cooperation between India and Thailand are increasing. Former Foreign Minister of Thailand, Surin Pitsuwan, who had visited New Delhi in July, 2000 had envisioned immense potentials for economic relations in future especially in the areas of computer industry, IT, E-Commerce, agriculture, construction and tourism. In the computer and software industry, India had highly skilled personnel in software development, while Thailand excelled in hardware production. So it was complimentary. The Prime Minister of Thailand, General Surayud, while on a visit to New Delhi in June, 2000 stated that "Thailand regards India as one of the most important partners. Our growing partnership is the outcome of synergy between India's Look East and Thailand's Look West Policies. Thailand sees India as a key engine of the rising Asian economy, a dynamic force for enhanced economic interaction within Asia and indeed globally. We see in India a vast reservoir of skilled personnel and entrepreneurs to help drive a knowledge based Asia" (*Bangkok Post*, 27 June, 2007).

Trade relations are indeed improving satisfactorily, and at the same time initiatives have been taken to improve investment relations. Although Indian investments in Thailand were in the synthetic fibre spinning plant, steel mill and cotton industries, but Thai investments in India till the beginning of 1990s were dismal. This anomaly has been rectified now. Thai companies rank 19th in the list of countries in terms of cumulative

FDI approved in India during 1991-2006. The total number of approvals from Thailand are 144 with an equity participation of US $0.83 billion. The FDI inflows from Thailand are about US $67.8 million, and it is the third largest investor in India from the ASEAN region. Top investing companies from Thailand are M/s. Fascel Ltd., Interglobe Hotel Ltd., Charoen Pokphand Seeds, Thai Summit Neel Auto Pvt. Ltd., Tigar Jewellery, Holley Meters and Ajinomoto etc. Telecommunications and fisheries account for the chunk of Thai investment in India. Besides that we find Thai investments in tourism sectors, light engineering industry and food processing and they trust each other to undertake bigger projects.

Indian companies have invested in areas that are relatively high technology and even capital-intensive, which cover a broad range of products and activities, including production of rayon fibre, steel wires and rods, paper-grade pulp, chemicals, drugs and pharmaceuticals, nylon, tyre cord, real estate, etc. Two Indian companies, NIIT and APTECH have their operational bases in Thailand in software development and computer education. Besides Aditya Birla Group, Tata Steel, Tata Motors, Indo-Rama Group, Ranbaxy Laboratories, Baroda Rayon Group, Ballarpur Industries, Dabur, Usha Martin industries, etc. have invested for different products. According to Indo-Thai Chamber of Commerce, the potential areas for Indian investment in Thailand include IT, pharmaceuticals, herbal based medicines, cosmetics, diary development, space technology, bio-technology and bio-mass projects, manufacturing of machine tools, medical supplies and instruments, transport and equipments.

The investment relations are in diversified areas. A bilateral agreement on non-conventional energy are being worked out. There are natural gas in the Gulf of Siam and the projected reserves are estimated at 172,000 million cubic meters. There has been onshore discoveries in the Nam Phong areas of Khon Kaen province and petroleum in the north central plain of Kampaongphet. Besides there are resources of hydro-electric power in Thailand, which may get a passage in the South Asian region. Simultaneously there is a proposal for transportation link from India to Thailand's Mae Sot district in Tak province

Via Myawadi in Myanmar to facilitate the transport of goods. The commerce Minister of Thailand Krirk-Krai Jirapaet has spoken of the project to construct roads in the eight northeastern states of India, costing $15 billion in the next five years. The endeavour is to promote trade, investment technology and entrepreneurship between the two. It has also been decided to establish an institute in the northeast to teach Thai language. (Huma Siddiqui, 23 June, 2007).

India and Thailand are taking important initiatives to promote tourism. The developments in Tourism infrastructure at Bodh Gaya can attract tourists from Thailand, and other Buddhist Countries. It is reported that 250,000 Indians visit Thailand every year, but the number of Thai tourists are less. There is also a proposal to develop the ancient sites of Nalanda with international assistance, in which Singapore also will play a major role. Thailand is assisting in the construction of hotels and roads at the places connected with Lord Buddha, but lots are needed to attract tourists at the global level. Thailand offers many different landscapes and stylish resorts, a lively night life and a depth of culture and adventurous pursuits. This established tourist market is one of Asia's most popular destinations, with endless opportunities for new and exciting adventures such as hyking, jungle tracks, scuba diving, bird watching, white water raffling and rock climbing. India has yet to develop as a model tourist destination.

Thai Prime Minister General Surayud Chulanont in his recent visit to India has stated that "India has become a dynamic market place and investment destination, meaning bright prospects for our bilateral trade and investment. India has become Thailand's new major market, our largest trading partner in south Asia, and 16th largest trading partner...." Thailand now accounts for around $830 million dollars of approved foreign direct investment in India, ranking 18th in India's total FDI, top investment sectors include food processing, telecommunications, trading and transportation. India's FDI in Thailand has also increased, with the first quarter of 2007 seeing an increase of 110 per cent over the same period last year. (Keynote address of Thai Prime Minister at Indo-Thai Business Summit, New Delhi, 26 June, 2007).

To conclude, it can be stated that the prospects for Indo-Thai economic relations are bright and its success will pave the path for India's greater integration with ASEAN. Although bargaining over certain aspects of FTA are endemic and arguments over "who gets what, when and how" are continuing, but the observers are convinced that the commercial issues are on the fast track, and ultimately both sides will be benefited because of the vibrancy in economic relations.

India's bilateral trade with Thailand (in US $ million)

	Exports	*% Change*	*Imports*	*% Change*
1997-98	344.90	–22.92	233.60	18.36
1998-99	320.92	–6.95	273.05	16.89
1999-00	449.92	40.20	328.17	20.18
2000-01	528.69	17.51	314.97	–4.02
2001-02	634.73	20.06	424.49	34.77

Source: CMIE date.

Department of Commerce: Export Import Data Bank

Export: Country-wise

Dated: 10/07/2007

Values in US $ Millions

S. No.	*2006-07 (Apr.-Dec.)*	*Country*	*2005-06 % Share% Growth*	*% Share*
1.	Thailand	1,075.31	1.0431 1,022.55	1.1192
	India's Total Export	103,090.54	91361.25	

Exchange Rate:
2005-06: 1 US $ = 44.2735
2006-07 (Apr.-Dec.): 1 US $ = Rs.45.6086

ANNEXURE-I

India-Thailand Consolidated List of Items for EHS

No.	*HS*	*Descriptions*
1.	080450	Ex. Fresh Mangosteens, Mangoes
2.	080610	Fresh Grapes
3.	080810	Apples
4.	081060	Ex. Fresh Durians

No.	*HS*	*Descriptions*
5.	081090	Ex. Fresh Rambutans, Longans, Pomegranates
6.	100110	Durum Wheat
7.	100190	Other Wheat and Meslin
8.	160411	Salmon, Whole or in Pieces but not minced, prepared or preserved
9.	160413	Sardines, Sardenella and Brisling or Sprats, Whole or in pieces but not minced, prepared or preserved
10.	160415	Mackerel whole or in pieces but not minced, prepared or preserved
11.	160510	Crab prepared or preserved
12.	250100	Salt (Incl. Table Salt & Denatrd Salt) & Pure Sodium Chloride W/N AQS soln sea Wtr
13.	261000	Chromium Ores & Concentrates
14.	281119	Other Inorganic Acids
15.	281820	Other Aluminium Oxide
16.	281830	Aluminium Hydroxide
17.	291739	Other Armtc Plyscrboxylc Acids thr Anhydrds Halides Peroxides Peroxyacds & Thr Drvtvs
18.	390210	Polypropylene, in Primary Forms
19.	390690	Other Acrylic Polymers in Primary Forms
20.	390710	Polyacetals in Primary Forms
21.	390730	Epoxide Resins in Primary Forms
22.	390740	Polycarbonates in Primary Forms
23.	390760	Polyethylene Terephthalate in Primary Forms
24.	390799	Saturated Polyallyl Esters and Other Saturated Pol
25.	390810	Polyamide –6, –11, –12, –6, 6, –6, 9, –6, 10 or –6, 12, in primary forms
26.	390890	Other Polyamides in Primary Forms
27.	390950	Polyurethanes in Primary Forms
28.	391990	Other self-Adhesive plates, sheets, film, foil, tape, strip and other flat shapes of plastics
29.	441219	Other plywd comsstng only shts of wood of thickness of each sheet nt excd 6 mm
30.	710310	Precious stones (Other than Diamonds) and semi-precious stones, Unworked or simply sawn or roughly shaped
31.	710490	Other synthetic or Reconstructed Precious or Semi-Precious stones
32.	710510	Dust and Powder of Diamonds
33.	711319	Articles of Jewellery and Parts thereof, of other

No.	*HS*	*Descriptions*
		precious metal, whether or not plated or clad with precious metal
34.	720150	Alloy Pig Iron: Spiegeleisen
35.	720711	Prdcts Contng By wt <0.25% CRBN of Rctnglr (Incl Sqr) crs-Sctn; Wdth < Twice the Thckns
36.	720719	Othr Prdcts Contng By Wt <0.25% of Carbon
37.	722619	Flt-Rold Prdcts of Silicon Electricl Stl Othr Thn Grain-Oriented
38.	722990	Other wire
39.	730792	Threaded Elbows, Bends and Sleeves of Iron or Steel
40.	732020	Helical Springs, of Iron or Steel
41.	732690	Other Articles of Iron or Steel Wire, Not Forged
42.	760110	Aluminum, Not Alloyed
43.	760120	Aluminum Alloys
44.	840490	Parts of the Items of 840410 & 840420
45.	840991	Parts Suitable for use solely or Principally with spark-ignition internal combustion piston engines
46.	841360	Other Rotary Positive Displacement Pumps
47.	841381	Other Pumps
48.	841451	Table, Floor, Wall, Window, Ceiling/Roof Fans, With Slfcntnd Elctrc Motor of Outpt < = 125 W
49.	841459	Other Fans
50.	841490	Prts of Air/Vacum Pumps, Cmprssrs & Fans
51.	841510	Window/Wall Types Self-Contained Air Conditioning Machines
52.	841821	Compression-Type Refrigerators, Household
53.	841990	Prts of Mchnry, Plnt/Lbrtry Eqmpmnt Etc of the items of HDG 8419
54.	842199	Othr Parts of Fltrng/Purfyng Mchnry
55.	842390	Weighng Mchn Weights & Prts of the Mchnry
56.	842549	Jacks, Hoists, of a Kind used for Raising Vehicles
57.	843221	Disc Harrows
58.	543780	Other Machnry For clng, Srtng/Gradng Seeds
59.	844820	Prts & Accssrs of Mchns of Hdg. No. 8444/Of Their Auxlry Mchnry
60.	844833	Spindles, Spindle Flyers, Spinning Rings and Ring Travellers
61.	847141	Othr Dgitl Automatic Data Procesng Machns Comprisng in samehousing a centrl procesng unit & Input & output Unit, Wh/Not Combind

No.	*HS*	*Descriptions*
62.	847190	Other
63.	847290	Othr Office Machines
64.	847751	Mchnry Fr Mouldng/Retreadng Pneumtc Types or Fr Mouldng/Othrwse Formng Innr Tubes
65.	847989	Othr Mchn & Mchncl Applncs of Hdg 8479
66.	847990	Parts of Machines of HDG 8479
67.	848079	Othr Moulds for Rubber/plastics
68.	848180	Other Appliances for pipes, Boiler shells, Tanks, vats or the like
69.	848210	Ball Bearings
70.	848350	Flywheels and Pulleys, Including Pulley Blocks
71.	850431	Othr Trnsfrmrs Hvng a Pwr Hndlng Capacity Not excdng 1 KVA
72.	851220	Other Lighting or visual Signalling Equipment
73.	851711	Line Telphon Set wth cordless hand sets
74.	851790	Parts of Telephonic/Telegraphic Apparatus
75.	852390	Other Prepared Unrecorded Media
76.	852812	Receptn Aparts for TV etc colour
77.	852910	Aerials & Aerials Reflectors of All kinds Prts suitable Fr Use Therewth
78.	853400	Printed Circuits
79.	854011	Cathode-Ray TV Picture Tubes, Including Video Monitor-Cathode-Ray Tubes-Colour
80.	870840	Gear Boxes
81.	903289	Othr Atmtc Rgl Tng/Cntrlng Instrmnts & Apprts
82.	903290	Parts and Accessories of Instrmnts of 9032
83.	910211	Wrst-Wtchs, Electrly Operated, W/N Incrprtng Stop-Wtch Fclty With Mchncl Display only
84.	940190	Parts of Seats, Whether or Not convertible into beds

22

India and ASEAN—Evolving a New Culture

India and ASEAN—geopolitically linked to one another are constantly expanding the areas of their cooperation, but they have miles to go to fulfil their vision of "Asian Century". Their urge to have common concern for emerging challenges are successful in certain areas but the problems of sustainable development, environmental pollution and terrorism are rising. The theories of peace and conflict are discussed at the academic level and in the meanwhile, radical elements are actively supporting unrest and turmoil. The terror groups are determined to sabotage the gains of the civilized world in South and Southeast Asia. Besides the threat of terrorism, rising population, hunger, and illiteracy have contributed to erosion of social values. Hence the countries in the region have to give their attention on building a common consensus to work together in the broader interests of humanity. India and ASEAN are keen to work for regionalism, peace and development and in that endeavour, a renewed feeling of brotherhood with new inputs are required. This requires evolving a new culture of universal brotherhood and humanitarianism of high order. There is a need to evolve a system in which each partners are trusted and the scope of violence minimized.

India adopted the policy of Look East in 1992 and extended the hands of cooperation with eastern neighbours. Although it was deeply embroiled in attending its economic and security problems, India's initiative of Look East enthralled ASEAN and the response was to offer Sectoral partnership. This event proved a landmark in creating new spirits for regional cooperation. The ASEAN has been working for community building and the Treaty of Amity and Cooperation (TAC),

ASEAN Concord I and ASEAN Concord II are aimed at minimizing the scope of conflict and creating a common approach. Every partner of the ASEAN are required to make commitments to TAC, but the question is to what extent, those resolutions impact the attitudes of terrorists? What needs to be done for peace and prosperity? There is a need to generate new ideas, which may help in building creative and positive environment for peace and prosperity. The concept of universal prosperity and happiness as propounded by Vinoba Bhave (Sarbodaya) for example, is an ideal worth considering, but to implement them needs vision and charisma, which is rare.

Talking about Mahatma Gandhi or Vinoba Bhave in the present day world may not look realistic in market-worshipping western world and community minded Islamic world. The developments since 9/11 have alarmed the international community. Al Qaida in the Arab world and Jemaah Islamiyah (Ji) in Southeast Asia are supporting Islamic terror. Jehad is foremost in their agenda. The realists led by the US tried to subdue Al Qaida Jehadis through military means in Afghanistan and Iraq and that proved counter productive. Hence cultural approach assumes importance. China used its traditional wisdom to cement ties with ASEAN in the post-financial crisis era. It diluted its usual assertiveness and adopted accommodation with the crisis ridden ASEAN countries. It showed enormous supports for ASEAN and shared the problems. It adopted a cultural approach with a touch of Buddhism and Confucianism to provide help to crisis resolution. China's humanitarian attitude endeared ASEAN Partners. This helped the evolution of a culture of Sino-ASEAN cooperation which ultimately assisted China to emerge as the largest trading partner in 2006. ASEAN successfully recovered from the crisis and gave fitting answer to all those who criticized ASEAN model and "Asian values" in the aftermath of the crisis.

Asia is richly endowed with resources and manpower. It has natural rights to be on the top of the development index, but unless a culture of cooperation and accommodation is evolved in South Asia, the projection of "Asian Century" will remain elusive. The eminent persons, comprised of Ban Ki Moon, Lee Kuan Yew, Mahathir Mohammad, Thaksin

Shinawatra and Manmohan Singh are endowed with ideas and vision and they can provide necessary input for the agenda of Asian Century. Ban Ki Moon is experienced and renowned for his opinion on Asian community building. Although Mahathir's anti-West rhetoric's may look negative but he is charismatic. Lee as an architect of Singapore has exceptional qualities. His advice has helped Vietnam's boom in recent years. Again Thaksin's rural development ideas have popular support and Manmohan Singh as an architect of India's economic liberalisation, have put India on development path. They are exceptionally qualified but when and how they can work in a team and support effective governance for development and unleash a new culture are hypothetical projections. The establishment of common currency, common parliament, common markets etc. are required for the development of Asian nations and that can be possible only if the regional leaders work out consensus, plans and programmes for collective and common good.

In 1992, when India joined ASEAN as a sectoral partner, it was a step in the right direction. For decades before 1992, India and ASEAN indulged in polemics and this situation was fully exploited by China. The US ever since the signing of Shanghai Communiqué (1972) extended tacit support to China in expanding influence in the ASEAN region. India's economic and security relations remained dismal. However, when the sectoral partnership started, India's trade, investment and tourism ties immediately picked up momentum. Both took important steps to boost economic and cultural ties. This event induced Pakistan to seek ASEAN partnership. In 1993, Pakistan was also offered sectoral partnership but it took years between Pakistan and ASEAN to choose the sectors of cooperation. Pakistan was also restrained by ASEAN to keep its bilateral disputes with India outside the preview of the sectoral partnership. This was frustrating for Pakistan because they tend to use every international fora—the United Nations (UN), Organization of Islamic Conferences (OIC) or South Asian Association for Regional Cooperation (SAARC)—for India bashing. The SAARC proved a failure for regional cooperation because of India-Pakistan disputes. Kashmir remained volatile and trans-border terrorism was supported by one against another. The ASEAN leaders knew it and therefore opposed their entry in any form in the ASEAN. But when India was accepted as a sectoral partner, it was difficult to ignore the case of Pakistan. It is understood that before offering the partnership, Pakistan was categorically told that the association is exclusively for economic cooperation, and contentious bilateral disputes are not within preview of sectoral partnership. Pakistan accepted the conditions of the ASEAN and have not raised its voice against India through ASEAN forum. It is neither satisfied with trade and investment relations, because it is far less compared to India.

India is geopolitically connected with ASEAN states with land borders of 1600 kilometres with Myanmar and maritime borders of thousands of kilometres with ASEAN states in the Indian Ocean along the Bay of Bengal. India's trade with ASEAN countries are increasing because of our contiguity with Myanmar, Thailand and Indonesia. The fixed targets for Indo-ASEAN trade are US $50 billion by 2010. India's trade volume with ASEAN was US $38 billion in 2007. Pakistan's trade with ASEAN shows upward trends particularly with Malaysia and Indonesia, but overall volume was merely US $342 million (2004). Although the trade volume marginally increased thereafter but it is around one billion US dollars only. (Shivpuri Singh, 2005). Although Pakistan had been aligned partner of Southeast Asian states through SEATO in the past, it could not expand its economic influence in the region to overtake India. What is disturbing the countries in the region today is Pakistan's role in supporting Taliban and Mujahideen violence to spread the gospel of Islam.

ASEAN's policy to cultivate relations with India proved a landmark step because it facilitated India to prove a worthy partner for regional cooperation. The sectoral partnership proved so rewarding that ASEAN decided within two years to upgrade it into full dialogue partnership in 1995. This enabled India to participate in ASEAN Post-Ministerial Conferences and also got the membership of ASEAN Regional Forum (ARF). This event proved catalytic for improving ties as it laid the solid foundations to promote economic, cultural and strategic linkages. ASEAN-India working group looked for cooperation in new areas such as health and pharmaceuticals, social security and rural development in addition to trade, investment, tourism science and technology. The development in relations created a new ethos and culture of cooperation, which was missing during cold war years.

The ASEAN in the post cold war era took another landmark decision to cultivate Vietnam and other Indo-Chinese neighbours and tried to bring them to the ASEAN fold. It was not an easy decision because Vietnam had been isolated for its actions in Cambodia (1978). It was projected hegemonistic and hostile for decades. The US had evolved "domino theory" for its crusade against Vietnam and the ASEAN was projecting it as a common threat and an exporter of violent revolution in the region. But after the demise of the Soviet Union, ASEAN found convergence of interests with Vietnam, as the globalisation and the emerging new world order posed challenges to both ASEAN and Vietnam without discrimination. Thus there was a consensus that Vietnam should not be further isolated, that both Vietnam and ASEAN should face the challenges of globalisation collectively. Vietnam welcomed the gestures of the ASEAN leaders and took necessary steps to reform the system and accommodate the grievances of adversaries. ASEAN was satisfied with the reforms in Vietnam and thus offered its membership. Vietnam was ready and thus it was integrated with the ASEAN in 1995. Vietnam proved a trustworthy partner of the ASEAN ever since, and has shared responsibilities with other partners. It is devoted to turning impoverished Indo-China region into a market place and supporting growth triangle proposals. Vietnam is in the forefront of Mekong Basin Development initiative, East-West Corridor or any projects connected with developments of Cambodia, Laos, Myanmar and Vietnam (CLMV). All this has been possible because of the change in the attitudes of ASEAN and the end of the policy of "bleeding Vietnam White". Vietnam has signed ASEAN Treaty of Amity and Cooperation, Free trade agreements and all conventions to combat terrorism. These developments have given birth to a new culture of Southeast Asian fraternity and cooperation, which is a necessary condition to build environment for "Asian Century".

Another area of relief is the suspension of polemics over South China Sea. There were overlapping sovereignty claims in the Spratlys region and China had used its military to throw out Vietnamese from Truong-Sa (1988) and the Philippines from Kalayaan (1992). In 1995 when Vietnam joined ASEAN and China became the dialogue partner, cooperation was explored amongst the contestants. Several conferences on the problems of South China Sea in Jakarta conveyed ASEAN concern and Track II diplomacy had moderating impact on China. The ASEAN claimants were not averse to joint exploration and exploitation of resources in the contested areas and they were not interested in doing anything detrimental to Chinese interests. ASEAN established a special committee to formulate a code of conduct for the South China Sea to be observed by all claimants to the Spratlys islands. A draft code of conduct was approved in 1999 which had the approval of the majority. China, insisting that it would adopt the proposed code only as a set of guidelines and not as a legally-binding document, resolved not to strengthen its presence on the islands. However in November 2002, ASEAN and China's foreign ministers adopted a Declaration on the conduct of Parties in the South China Sea agreeing to promote a peaceful environment and durable solutions for the area, to resolve territorial disputes by peaceful means, to refrain from undertaking activities that would aggravate existing tensions, and to initiate a regular dialogue of defence officials. Sinologist, Bronson Percival (2007) has explained this phenomenon by saying, "China has thoroughly adjusted to the 'ASEAN way". It places contentious issues (such as conflicting claims in the South China Sea) temporarily to the side, places process before product, and welcomes efforts to build an East Asian community".

China adopted a benevolent attitude towards ASEAN in the post-financial crisis (1997) era. The crisis had devastating impact on Indonesia, Thailand and other countries. China preferred the policy of accommodation with ASEAN in place of assertiveness. It refused to devalue its own currency, and contributed to IMF rescue plans. It agreed to provide additional financial support to Thailand. It did not attach any conditions for its financial contributions whereas the US did so while contributing to the IMF.

Again the ASEAN exports to traditional markets which had stagnated due to the financial crisis, needed outlets. China provided them outlet and support and thus there was a rapid rise in China-ASEAN trade which ultimately helped in pulling the region out of the crisis. China bravely faced the challenges posed by the financial crisis and endeared herself with the ASEAN countries with generosity and overtures. Its role during the crisis indeed paved the path for establishment of China-ASEAN Free Trade Area, which is destined to remove all tariff barriers by 2015. This will cover the area of 2 billion people with a combined GDP of $3 trillion and a trade of over $1.5 trillion.

In 2004 the trade between ASEAN-China was of $103 billion and that of the US $136 billion. However the ADB reports in 2006 suggested that China surpassed the US and became the largest trading partner. The trade volume then was $189 billion which increased further to $202 billion in 2007. This is the figure of China and Hong Kong taken together. ASEAN-China trade has suggested that they have taken proper steps to create a common market, which is necessary for the rise of Asia, but correspondingly the progress in creating proper conditions for trade and investment in South Asia is abysmal. The insurgency in Mizoram, Nagaland, Manipur and Assam are being abetted by the political leaders for petty gains and divisive elements are more prominent. It may be easy to blame New Delhi for disturbances in the country but it is simplistic. The ethnicity, religion, culture and history of the people in Northeast differ. They are sensitive about their identity and ethnocentricity. Thus we find that the gateway which geographically connects India with Southeast Asia are disturbed.

Again Bangladesh, which is adjoining Southeast Asia via Northeast is witnessing the growth of Islamic fundamentalism. They too are busy in tirade against India and restrained from doing anything, which is advantageous to India. Besides geopolitical factors, there are some infrastructural gaps on India-ASEAN frontiers. India in comparison to Japan and

China, was much late in taking initiatives to strengthen transportation linkages with Southeast Asia. It began to do so only after 1991 but Japan started its friendship drives just after the Fukuda doctrine (1976). China initiated programmes to cultivate ASEAN as soon as it adopted the policy of Four-Modernization (1978). India was late in establishing its infrastructure for cooperation with ASEAN. Satu, P. Limaye (2003) has rightly observed that "India's economic ties with ASEAN are in their infancy partly because India's trade liberalization started recently and is far from complete. Moreover, India-ASEAN trade has been growing steadily—30 per cent in the past three years". Indo-ASEAN trade stood at $10 billion in 2002. On the other hand, ASEAN trade with the United States stood at $120 billion, with Japan $116 billion, with China $70 billion, and with Korea $32 billion in that year.

It is interesting that Pakistan which continues to remain the sectoral partner of ASEAN is keen to strengthen its ties. Pakistani leaders are visiting ASEAN countries and negotiating free trade agreement and Malaysia and Singapore have been supporting Pakistan in the association. Pakistan has come out with its policy initiatives in the name of "Strategic Vision East Asia Initiative" (2003) and is trying to send its overtures. It is pleading for full dialogue partnership status. However, the main hurdle in that endeavour is that the level of trade relations are so low (less than one billion) that ASEAN has delayed its decision.

The ASEAN countries are interested in South Asian markets and that can be secured if there is peace and stability in the region. If there is rapprochement between India and Pakistan, it will offer huge and secure market to ASEAN. It will provide master key to conflict resolution in different parts of South Asia. Naturally it will suit the interests of the region and our East Asian neighbours. It will open vast opportunities for trade and investment. The normalization will require Pakistan's acceptance of existing frontiers with India and adherence to the principle of non-interference in the affairs of a neighbouring country. India and Pakistan both would be benefited if the relations become cooperative. This point has been very well illustrated by Business Times of Singapore, which stated that "a booming economy and improving ties with India will help Pakistan build bilateral alliances in Southeast Asia."

Pakistan is at a crossroad today. The political turmoil after the exit of General Parvez Musharraf and split between Nawaz Sharif and Asif Ali Zardari indicates political instability in that country. We cannot expect any visionary initiative of Pakistan towards India in the present dispensation. However if there is confidence building and cooperation between India and Pakistan, it will prove path breaking not only for conflict resolution of Kashmir but also for prosperity of South Asian region, which is most impoverished.

Indian profile in the ASEAN region is satisfactory because we have been taking initiatives to evolve culture of cooperation under Look East Policy. The concept of Look East was advocated by P.V. Narasimha Rao, I.K. Gujral and Atal Bihari Vajpayee, the three Prime Ministers of India respectively. Although Sukarno, Phibun and Roxas also advocated "Look East" in 1940's but their emphasis and objectives were different from India. 'Look East' for an Indian is connected with their traditions that their Sun God is in the East, and if they will offer prayers to the rising sun in the morning everyday, they will be healthy, wealthy and wise. Southeast Asia is geographically located in the East and an important component of our traditional folklores. It was identified as central to India's foreign policy in the entire Asia-Pacific. India's Look East had three-pronged approach. First to renew political contacts with the ASEAN partners; second to increase economic interaction (trade, investment, science and technology, tourism etc.) and third to forge defence links with ASEAN partners as a means to enhance political and strategic interests and understanding. Indian think-tanks are reviewing the notion of economic security, self-reliance and national interests in light of developments in the post-cold war era. As a nation of one billion people, India cannot afford to remain a marginal player in the global economy, as measured for instance by our share in world trade or income. Commensurate with her size and civilization characteristics, India is willing to assume greater role in global affairs and world economy. Look East policy is endeavoured to fulfil those aspirations and it has evoked positive response in the ASEAN region.

The meaning and contents of Look East policy was explained by Narasimha Rao himself during his tenure as the Prime Minister of India (1991-1996). His speech delivered on 8 September, 1994 in Singapore was a milestone to influence the opinion of Southeast Asians where he spoke about endogenous and exogenous nature of the problems, which were a matter of common concern and common interests and they were:

(a) interpretations of sovereignty, whether over the oceans, in outer space, over territory, resources etc.,
(b) frictions arising out of differing cultural perceptions—as we witnessed in the case of Michael Fay;
(c) massive needs and demands of relatively under-developed populations and migratory tendencies, with no respect for national boundaries;
(d) confrontational postures on a broad range of fundamental issues related to trade barriers, currency stabilization, international aid and investment flows;
(e) intensification of the debate over linkages between issues such as human rights, labour-laws, environmental protection and resource management, liberal information flows etc., in political and economic relationship.

Southeast Asian countries were also looking for suitable answers to afore-mentioned issues but Indian premier pointedly articulated "the increasing tendency on the part of dominant powers to assume that they cannot only define the means, but even the ends, of collective international endeavour. This has been revealed in the form of intrusive prescriptions in the areas of social regulation, dissemination of knowledge, technological development and even domestic administration. The worst part of this tendency is that on closer scrutiny, it can be easily shown to be based on unsympathetic half-knowledge. Indian Prime Minister's speech was widely applauded because he pleaded for combining synergies between India and ASEAN and spoke about the broad parameters of cooperation in diverse areas.

In retrospect we find that both India and ASEAN broadened the scope of their cooperation and have gained from their interaction. When India had become the sectoral partner of the ASEAN in 1992, the mindset of bureaucrats in ASEAN and mandarins in Ministry of External Affairs had not sufficiently changed, but the developments in the years following proved positive. It is heartening to find broader understanding on matters of regional concern whereas we failed to generate similar response through SAARC. It is very difficult to evolve consensus within SAARC whereas ASEAN has a consensus over matters of regional concern and stringent punishment may be given to the culprits. Here however India's strategic and economic cooperation with ASEAN will be evaluated, and it is in order to mention about institutional arrangements which have placed the relations on the right track.

India and ASEAN have set up a number of institutional mechanism to facilitate economic relations. Joint trade committees which had come into existence after 1992 has been renamed as Joint Business Commissions. Besides ASEAN-India Business Council and ASEAN-India Joint Management Committee are coordinating economic exchanges. ASEAN-India Trade Negotiation Committee, and ASEAN-India Economic Minister's Meetings have been providing inputs for fruitful economic contacts. After the elevation of India into a dialogue partner status, ASEAN-India Joint Cooperation committee and India-ASEAN Working Group on Trade and Investment had been established. They provide suitable advice about various areas of economic relations with positive results. There is Indo-ASEAN Fund also, which support the lectures of important ASEAN leaders in India and that of Indians in the ASEAN region. It has been supporting exchange programmes and track II process to strengthen relations so that India ultimately becomes an integral part of proposed ASEAN Economic Community.

The ASEAN has been a dynamic regional grouping and has been incorporating new ideas to strengthen the feeling of togetherness in economic and security matters. Although ASEAN objectives were enshrined in the Bangkok declaration (1967) but on the eve of ASEAN summit meeting in 2003, they adopted a declaration, known as "Bali Concord II,' which committed signatory states to the creation of an ASEAN Economic Community, an ASEAN Security Community, and an ASEAN Socio-cultural Community. They affirmed commitments to existing economic cooperation frameworks, regional plans of action and Initiatives for ASEAN Integration (IAI), and outlined plans for the creation, by 2020, of an Integrated ASEAN Economic Community (AEC) entailing the harmonization of customs procedures and technical regulations by the end of 2004, the removal of non-tariff trade barriers and the establishment of a network of free-trade-zones by 2005; and the progressive withdrawal of capital controls and strengthening of intellectual property rights. ASEAN economic and trade ministers worked closely to produce a 'roadmap' for the integration of 11 sectors identified as priority areas in the AEC plan of action, namely agriculture, air travel, automotive, electronics, fisheries, healthcare, information technology (IT), rubber, textile, tourism and wood.

In order to prove useful for the grouping, the dialogue partners were expected to facilitate the endeavour of community building. India always keen to act as a relevant partner began to articulate through various forums some valuable inputs. It is understood that Indian leadership wanted to fortify relations with ASEAN and the latter wanted to actively engage India *vis-à-vis* China to develop a more balanced relationship. (Rahul Sen and Mukul, G. Asher, 2004). It was also believed that India's economic structure was largely complementary (service oriented) to ASEAN economic (light manufacturing) and if the level of relation are enhanced, both sides would be benefited (Mukul, G. Asher, 2003). Indian Prime Minister, Vajpayee had noted that the ASEAN countries have begun to develop regional dominance in certain areas of technologies and wished India and ASEAN to exploit their respective synergies. As a market, ASEAN is attractive for Indian exporters because of its geographic proximity, resulting in shorter delivery schedules and lower freight costs. With a sizable population of people of Indian origin, and a shared sense of historical, cultural and religious commonalities, the emerging economic linkages between India and ASEAN are bound to be multifaceted and in-depth. Moreover the new breed of Indian migrants to Southeast Asia are likely to be software engineers, financial analysts and management professionals who will increasingly play an influential role in connecting ASEAN with South Asia.

(Faisal Yahya, 2003). With this projection in mind, both decided to hold India-ASEAN Summits every year. The first Summit was held in Phnom Penh (2002) and the second Summit was held in Bali (2003). Prime Minister Vajpayee attached great importance to addressing the agenda of those meeting and took initiatives to fortify relations. He wanted to break new grounds of cooperation besides approving the recommendations of ASEAN-India working Group (2001) to pursue cooperation in new areas, such as health and pharmaceuticals, social security and rural development.

After India-ASEAN Summit at Bali in 2003, India signed Treaty of Amity and Cooperation and thereby signed a joint Framework Agreement for comprehensive economic co-operation and supported the establishment of an Indo-ASEAN regional trade and investment area including the setting up of an ASEAN-India Free Trade Area in goods, services and investments. The objective of the framework agreement included (a) strengthening and enhancing economic, trade and investment cooperation, (b) liberalizing and promoting trade in goods and services and (c) facilitating economic integration within ASEAN. Various new issues of cooperation were discussed in the field of agriculture, biotechnology, and human resource development and both sides adopted the joint declaration for cooperation to combat international terrorism. The framework agreement also provided agreement on trade in goods towards progressive tariff reduction in 105 agreed items. Tariff reduction for ASEAN-6, namely Brunei, Indonesia, Malaysia, Philippines, Singapore and Thailand were to be completed by 2007 and for the CLMV by 2012. The idea of a FTA with a ten-year time frame was mooted by India during the first summit. However the idea of FTA have certain issues of negative listing, rules of origin and the level of tariff reduction on agricultural commodities. Those issues are yet to be resolved.

A framework agreement for the creation of FTA with Thailand was signed in 2003, under which 84 items could be imported from Thailand at 50 percent of the normal rate of duty prevailing in India. Similar agreements were signed with Singapore. The framework agreement to be signed with CLMV countries, MGC and BIMST-EC also. India took active interests in Thailand's initiative for Asian Bond Fund and provided $ one billion as a modest contribution to consolidate India's partnership with the ASEAN. The framework agreement for comprehensive economic cooperation is indeed a landmark document through which India provided "fast-Track" tariff concessions to ASEAN partners. The proposal was to achieve US $30 billion target for India-ASEAN trade by 2007 which stood merely at $10 billion in 2003. India also offered to run daily flights to major Indian cities including New Delhi, Kolkata, Mumbai and Chennai. The proposal to hold Car Rally had also been made on the eve of India-ASEAN summit which was flagged off from Guwahati in the following year. This Car Rally proved the geographic connectivity of India with Southeast Asia through a land route.

The third India-ASEAN summit was held in Vientiane in 2004. The participants signed a partnership pact for Peace, Progress and Shared Prosperity containing a long-term vision for boosting trade, investment, tourism, culture, sports and people to people contacts. It also included Action Plan touching upon the entire gamut of political and security cooperation, including food, human resources, energy, finance, science and technology, IT, communication technology, health and agriculture. Prime Minister Manmohan Singh on the eve of the summit said that a "long-term partnership agreement with ASEAN world provide a new dimension to our relations. He said that new India is on the horizon and the future lies in working together with our neighbours in the East, with whom we have profound civilization ties" (2004) At the same time, he spoke about linking East Asia with ASEAN for the community building. This was an idea which was meant to give an Asian touch to the existing regional arrangement. Whether it was proper to be revealed at ASEAN-India summit, is an issue to be debated.

India's trade relations with ASEAN are expanding. From US $2.4 billion in 1991-92, it reached US $23 billion by 2005-6. It is understood that as and when FTA will be implemented in letter and spirits, the volume of trade will exceed the targets. The Chinese have already signed FTA with the ASEAN and with this they have established a combined market of 1.7 billion people, regional GDP of $2 trillion and international trade worth $1.2 trillion. China's trade with ASEAN in 2004 was about $70 billion and now it is increasing rapidly. They have certain advantages over India in the ASEAN region, but it is suggested that if FTA with India becomes operational, it would also be a market of 1.5 billion people and regional GDP of $1.5 trillion. If the agreement is signed, it may complement India-ASEAN tree-trade proposals. At the same time, it will brighten the prospects for better economic and security understanding and confidence building. It is interesting to note that the Communist Party leaders in China are solidly supporting new economic zones and FTA. They are the important partners of Manmohan Singh led government and have been playing the obstructionist role ever since 2004.

India's major export items to the ASEAN market are gems and jewellery, machinery and instrument, dyes, semi-finished iron and steel, oil meals, drugs, pharmaceutical and fine chemicals, transport equipments, electronic goods, inorganic/ organic/agro chemical, non-ferrous metals, plastic and linoleum products, manufacture of metals, man-made yarn fab and made-ups, meat and preparations, cotton yarn, fabrics and made-ups. India's major items imported from ASEAN are electronic goods, vegetable oils, organic chemicals, wood and wood products, coal, coke and briquettes, non-electrical machinery, transport equipment, metal ferrous ores and metal scrap, artificial resins, plastic materials, printed books, pulses, electrical machinery, and non-ferrous metals, etc. India's trade with ASEAN countries is hovering around 7-9 per cent of its total every year (Bhattacharya, 2006).

Bilaterally, the trade between India and Singapore have been increasing. From $6.6 billion in 2004-05 it has reached $8.7 billion in 2005-06. India's trade figures with Thailand have increased from $1.22 billion in 2000-01 to $3.9 billion in 2004-05 to $4.3 billion in 2005-06. Similarly trading figures with Malaysia have increased and it is one of the top ten investors in India. Again the trade between CLMV countries and India are increasing substantially. However, it is investment relations which has to be attended with utmost care. The environment has been disturbed especially after the suspension of Tata-

Singapore Airline project and that of special economic zone at Nandigram, Haldia, where Indonesia's Salim Group has lot of stakes. Despite obstacles, avenues are explored to strengthen investment relations. Malaysia and Singapore are major investors in India. Malaysia has made substantial investments in expanding capacities in selected infrastructural areas such as logistics, highways, and ICTs in India. On the other hand, Singapore has made investments in health care, real estate and tourism. Their technology park in Bangalore has created a positive environment for investments in India.

There are several areas of collaboration between India and ASEAN countries which can prove mutually beneficial. For example, energy, edible oil, pharmaceuticals, IT and BT are prospective areas of joint ventures. It is commonly understood that India Origin entrepreneurs owns the largest palm oil refinery in Malaysia, the largest carbon-black manufacturing units in Thailand and a large number of textile factories in Indonesia (Yahya, 2003). On the other hand, Tata, Reliance, Birla and Ranbaxi are noted Indian companies which are potential investors in the ASEAN region. Indian companies are ready to invest in auto-components sector in Thailand, for motor vehicles and energy sector in Indonesia and Vietnam, and for Information and Communications Technology (ICT) in the Philippines.

In food processing, forest products and cooking oil, there are abundance of scope for collaboration with Indonesia, Malaysia and Myanmar. Malaysia and Indonesia are major palm producers and Thailand has much expertise in food processing industry—particularly in deep sea fishing and other marine related activities. The information technology (IT) is an area where India has advantages and Singapore's Info-Comm Development Authority has signed an MoU with NIIT. Entertainment and multi-media especially films and TV programmes of India are popular in the ASEAN region. The collaboration in those areas could be fruitful to both sides. Both India and ASEAN can be benefited if there is investments in drugs, pharmaceuticals and human resources.

Foreign Direct Investment (FDI) from the ASEAN region are trickling in slowly in limited areas and they are mainly for infrastructure building, hotels and tourism services, heavy industries, chemicals, fertilizers and food processing. Total Indian FDI in the ASEAN region are merely $225 million and that of ASEAN in India are $2 billion (Shekhar, 2007). India has attached importance to infra-structure development to connect India with ASEAN. They intend to build railways and roadways from New Delhi to Hanoi and Kolkata to Singapore directly. Tamu-Moreh road connecting India and Myanmar through highways are to be expanded to facilitate trade and people-to-people contacts. This is intended to facilitate greater movement of people from across the eastern borders and wants to welcome tourists and pilgrims visiting Sanchi, Sarnath, Bodh Gaya, Nalanda and other parts of India.

We find landmark developments in economic relations with ASEAN and similarly India's linkages in the security matters have witnessed positive developments. When SEATO or Five Power Defence Pact were signed, it had cold-war parameters. However when ARF was established (1993), it reflected regional concerns of security. Brunei meeting of the ARF (1995) defined a framework for the future of ARF. It was to be evolved in three stages (a) the promotion of confidence building (including disaster relief and peace keeping activities), (b) the development of preventive diplomacy, and (c) the elaboration of approaches to conflict resolution. In 1996, India got the membership of ARF and it has been participating in its activities. The ASEAN wanted India, China and other actors in the Asia-Pacific to engage in regional security matters and build a consensus on broader issues of common concern. Indian participation in ARF can be understood in the following areas:

(a) Confidence Building,
(b) Maritime Cooperation, and;
(c) Combating Terrorism.

For confidence building, India regularly participates in ARF Senior Officers' Meetings (ARFSOM) and Inter-Sessional Support Group Meeting for confidence Building Measures (ISG on CBMs), the Council for Security Cooperation in Asia-Pacific (CSCAP) and other forums. The participants deliberate on trans-national organized crimes such as drug trafficking, terrorism or counter-terrorism, maritime piracy, and illegal movement of nuclear, chemical, biological and other materials. There is greater understanding of India's security concerns in the ASEAN region and Pakistan has been deterred in taking Kashmir dispute in the deliberations of ARF. The advertent support of ASEAN was tacit when India went for Pokharan II as most of the states did not join Japan or Australia for trade embargo. Although Western reactions were vociferous, ASEAN did not pass any resolutions against India. The US, the UN, the EU, Australia and Japan indulged in strong criticism of Indian experimentation and called for adherence to non-proliferation, but majority of ASEAN partners felt that if China can experiment its nuclear weapons or North Korea can do so, why not India?

Pokharan II was a clear indication of India's emerging status as a nuclear weapon state and its potential to influence strategic developments in the region. The nuclear testing was not viewed as a threat, but as an asset. The countries in Southeast Asia could find India's contribution in a more positive perspective as far as fighting against terror compared to the United States, for example (Acharya, 2006). Equally important is the fact that India has been able to assure the regional states on its manifest neutrality and its desire to keep South Asian issues out of the ambit of ASEAN or ARF. Although India has refused to sign the Comprehensive Test Ban Treaty (CTBT), but as a nuclear-weapon state it was willing to respect the nuclear-free status of Southeast Asia by converting this recognition into a de jure commitment. ASEAN states appreciated Indian gestures in strengthening their security profile. India's substantive role in preventing sea piracy and terrorism have been appreciated.

India has established a naval base at Andaman Islands, called Fortress Andaman (FORTAN). This is strategically located in the waterways that pass through Southeast Asia connecting Bay of Bengal to East Asia. This waterway connects Indian Ocean with the Pacific and thus FORTAN has lot of implications on the politics of Malacca Straits. The maritime threats, sea piracy, smuggling and terrorism—in the region are matters of common concern and both India and Southeast Asia cooperate to grapple with those threats. India welcomed Indonesia, Malaysia and Singapore to have joint naval exercises at Andamans in the post-Cold War era (1991). This proved a good exercise for confidence building between India and the ASEAN states. India was encouraged to establish defence ties with some of the ASEAN states and Malaysia was the first to sign MoU for defence cooperation in 1993. This was for training Malaysian air force personnel and at least 100 pilots came for training. (Naidu, 2006). In the same year, India and Singapore made arrangement for training and joint exercises of their naval personnel with Indian counterparts. India had agreed to provide anti-submarine warfare training to Singapore's naval personnels also. Thailand has availed the strategic expertise of the Indians after acquisition of an aircraft carrier. On the other hand, Vietnam is trying to build up its navy with Indian expertise, and seeking technological support for upgradation of MiG-21 fighters. Similarly defence cooperation with Indonesia, Laos and Myanmar have also started. India had supplied anti-insurgency defence equipments to Myanmar and has transferred two BN-2 Defender maritime aircraft to Myanmar (2007). There is coordination of search and rescue operations at sea and establishment of inter-operability with navies of other ASEAN states. The most important aspect of Indian navy's role is the protection of sealanes of communication in the Indian Ocean region. As articulated in India's Naval Doctrine of April, 2004, India's maritime policies has been made clear. The doctrine is premised on the necessity to build cooperative maritime security with the countries on the shores of the Indian Ocean with regard to challenges encompassing safe flows of trade and energy as well as threats of terrorism. (Acharya, 2006).

After ASEAN-India summit in 2003, both sides have given focused attention on security cooperation. They agreed for joint operations to protect sealanes and pooling resources in the war against terrorism. The military contacts and joint exercises that had already started in 1991, was expanded into full fledged defence cooperation. India has got access to various ports in Southeast Asia for enhancing the level of cooperation. India and ASEAN have signed a joint Declaration for Cooperation in combating international terrorism (October, 2003) and accordingly they have agreed for (a) exchange of information (b) legal and enforcement matters (c) institutional capacity augmentation and (d) training. India has also signed

Treaty of Amity and Cooperation in 2003 and repeated its commitments for peace and stability of the region. The ASEAN countries convinced about India's role in the region and they have looked for complimentarity to support one another.

However, combating terrorism is a difficult task. The terrorists have their concealed network and websites and they are active in India and Southeast Asia. In certain cases they have popular support also, and it is difficult to contain them. India has a long history of fighting terrorism, but they have succeeded only in few cases. Kashmir, for example, has been a centre of terrorist activities led by Laskar-e-Toiba (LET) and Harkat-ul-Jihad-al-Islami (HUJI) and their political settlements is not in sight. They get regular supply of arms and ammunitions from across the border and Pakistan has been supporting them at the international fora without any hesitation. It is understood that Al-Qaeda had funded the establishment of training and indoctrination centres for the spread of terrorism in Afghanistan, Pakistan, the Philippines and Indonesia to create jihadi forces. They were also supported by the government in Pakistan and Bangladesh initially. Abu Sayyaf group (ASG) and Moro Islamic Liberation Front (MILF) in the Philippines had Al Qaeda connections. Jemaah Islamiyah (JI) in Indonesia was also inspired by Al Qaeda, which had several groups to spread terror in different parts of Southeast Asia. Again Kumpulan Militant Malaysian (KMM) and Majelis Mujahidin Indonesia (MMI), Pattani National Liberation Front (Thailand) had jihadi squads, suicide bombers and indoctrinated fanatics to be sacrificed in the name of Islam.

Following 9/11, Asia became the main focus of counter-terrorism, and the terrorists began to retaliate. Their attacks on Indian Parliament (2001), suicide attacks at the tourist resort in Bali (2002), the bombing of Marriot Hotel (2003) and Australian Embassy (2004) in Jakarta, the explosion in Super Ferry 14 in the Philippines (2004) and various suicide attacks on security establishments in Kashmir, Jaipur, Bombay, Bangalore and Delhi are big challenges for the security establishments. The threats of trans-national terrorism and the imperatives for global coordination have been a challenging task. The terrorists in the ASEAN region have revealed that they were trained in

Afghanistan, Pakistan and Bangladesh. Whether it is JI, LeT or HUJI they have got specialized training and at present most of them are based in SAARC countries. On the other hand, the intelligence reports suggest that criminal groups in Southeast Asia do supply arms and ammunitions to insurgent groups in India's northeast such as ULFA as well as to the Liberation Tigers of Tamil Elam (LTTE) in Sri Lanka (Acharya, 2006). The ULFA in Assam and other separatist groups are using sophisticated weapons which is regularly supplied through the porous borders at the Myanmar frontiers. It is difficult to recognize various criminal outfits which supply arms to rebels. Again the countries in the region have not been able to stop the sources of their funding, which very often comes in the name of welfare activities from inside and outside the country. There are a number of West Asian countries which have been sending assistance to promote Mosque and Madrasah activities and it is difficult to exercise surveillance over its expenditure and place them for audit.

Terrorism is against the ethics of civil society. It attempts to destroy business centres, communication channels and sabotage every infrastructure of growth. It is barbaric in approach against its adversaries and intends to restructure society to promote hatred and terror. Although the terrorists try to take the help of religion to attain their objectives, but it is a retrogressive development to be grappled. India and ASEAN are committed to combat terror, but till the combating is sincerely coordinated by India, Pakistan, Bangladesh and ASEAN and effectively by the appropriate agencies without fear or favour, the endeavour will remain incomplete.

Finally we find that the balance sheet of economic relations are satisfactory. Although negotiations over FTA are still in the bargaining process, but the fact that China and Japan are going to implement FTA proposals in near future, will surely have positive impact on Indian decision makers. India has a vision to emerge as a developed nation by 2020 and this objective will automatically pave the path for mutually beneficial economic cooperation with ASEAN and other partners. However security cooperation is not satisfactory. The ASEAN may be actively trying to nab their terrorists and cooperating with one another in tracing the hideouts of Jemaah Islamiyah or Abu Sayyaf or remnants of Al Qaida supporters, but there are certain pockets in South Asia, where the terrorists have got the protection of state in the name of religion. There are some who for the sake of "vote bank politics" argue protection to certain religious or fanatic groups irrespective of whatever they do. There must be a regional consensus over certain issues of regional concern and regional actors should try to spell out those norms in this age of globalisation. The developments in South Asia have impinging impacts on the overall situation of Southeast Asia and vice versa and the matters of grave security and economic implications should not be overlooked.

ASEAN has evolved sophisticated mechanism to resolve separatist movements and a reference to them would be in order here. They at the outset tried to understand the genesis of secessionist movements and tried to effectively contain them through a coordinated action in which national efforts were supported by regional initiatives. Again, acceptance of the principles of non-interference in the internal affairs of neighbouring countries desisted all the partners from supplying weapons to insurgents or provide sanctuaries. In this context, the reference to ASEAN's two important a resolutions, namely, "Declaration of ASEAN Concord", and the "Treaty of Amity and Cooperation in Southeast Asia" (1976) is important.

The ASEAN Concord (1976) observed that the stability of each member state and of the ASEAN region is an essential contribution to international peace and security. Each member state resolves to eliminate threats posed by subversion to its stability, thus strengthening national and ASEAN resilience. Again it has observed that the member states, in the spirit of ASEAN solidarity, shall rely exclusively on peaceful processes in the settlement of intra-regional differences. Again the Treaty of Amity and Cooperation (TAC) evolved code of conduct to minimize scope of conflict. Article 2 stated that in relations with one another, the high contracting parties shall be guided by the following fundamental principles:

(a) Mutual respect for the independence, sovereignty, equality, territorial integrity and national identity of all nations;

(b) The right of every state to lead its national existence free from external interference, subversion or coercion;
(c) Non-interference in the internal affairs of one another;
(d) Settlement of differences or disputes by peaceful means;
(e) Renunciation of the threat or use of force;
(f) Effective cooperation among themselves. (TAC, 1976).

The Treaty of Amity and Cooperation further resolved that "in the event no solution is reached through direct negotiations, the High Council shall take cognizance of the dispute of the situation and shall recommend to the parties in dispute appropriate means of settlement such as good offices, mediation, enquiry or conciliation. The High Council may, however, offer its good offices, or upon agreement of the parties in the dispute, constitute itself into a committee of mediation, enquiry or conciliation when deemed necessary, the High Council shall recommend appropriate measures for the prevention of a deterioration of the dispute or the situation.

Besides passing these resolutions they tried to cultivate ASEAN spirit of cooperation and sincerely worked for confidence building. They expressed their strong faith in ASEAN partners and kept vigil on their borders. When Vietnam militarily intervened in Cambodia, the ASEAN partners rallied their support to the de jure rulers to oppose Vietnamese occupation. Whatever compulsions or motive that Vietnam had in deciding military intervention to overthrow genocidal Khmer Rouge from power, it was a case of interference in the internal affairs of a neighbouring country. Vietnam's action did not get ASEAN approval. In 1986, Vietnam reviewed its policy and in 1988 withdrew from Cambodia which paved the path for reconciliation and cooperation with ASEAN.

To conclude it can be observed that the ASEAN has evolved mechanism for conflict resolution and confidence building, which works. They have consensus over matters of regional concern and for issues of sustainable development. South Asians, on the other hand, are left far behind in that endeavour. They always take one step forward and another backward, and hence there is stagnation and under-development. The endeavour to bring gas pipeline from Myanmar to India via Bangladesh or Iran-Pakistan and India gas pipeline proposal proved a failure due to the opposition of one or other SAARC partners. The endeavour of free trade, upgrading of roadways, highways and railways and other communication network amongst SAARC countries are delayed because of political and strategic differences.

Singapore's Prime Minister, Goh Chok Tong once portrayed India as one Wing of ASEAN's jumbo jet and China and Japan as the other Wing (2002). It was generous on his part to project India equally important as East Asian neighbours despite India's low ranking in development matters. Although India has immense resources, vast expertise, and manpower, it has suffered due to faulty management, corruption and socialist drives. It is universally recognized that India has appropriate scientific and technological expertise, keen to offer their services for India's modernizations, but they are not mobilized properly. India has a huge market with approximately 500 million middle class population, who believe in free market system. Its potential to act as an effective wing of ASEAN is possible, but this objective is interlinked with issues of regional understanding, peace and prosperity.

The ASEAN has played important role in integrating India and strengthening the ethos of regional cooperation, which is bound to pay dividends in future. Singapore's role to campaign for India's sectoral partnership in 1992, Thailand's role in supporting India in BIMSTEC or ASEAN's tacit support for Pokharan II were crucial developments in confidence buildings in India-ASEAN relations. The arrival of Salim Group of Industries from Indonesia, and the involvement of Singapore, Malaysia and Thailand in joint ventures have increased our mutual confidence in each other. Again the increasing cooperation in traditional or non-traditional security matters, joint exercises and sharing of military intelligence have been of high order. The increased level of cooperation in political, economic, security and cultural areas have generated new spirits. We have faith in "ASEAN way", and if it is accepted as a norm, it will certainly help in community building in the SAARC region. Both India and ASEAN are advertently working in that direction and the projection is that we will be an integral part of a common market by 2020.

REFERENCES

Satu, P. Limaye (2003) "India's Relations with Southeast Asia Take a Wing", *Southeast Asian Affairs*, pp. 39-51.

Frederic Grare and Amitabh Mattoo, (2001), *India and ASEAN: The Politics of India's Look East Policy*, New Delhi.

G.V.C. Naidu (2006) "India and Southeast Asia", *World Focus*, pp. 16-20.

Swapan, K. Bhattacharya, (2006) "India's Economic Relations with the ASEAN Countries," *World Focus*, pp. 28-32.

Faizal Yahya (2003), "India and Southeast Asia: Revisited", *Contemporary Southeast Asia*, pp. 79-103.

Arabinda Acharya, (2006), "India and Southeast Asia in the Age of Terror: Building Partnership for Peace", *Contemporary Southeast Asia*, pp. 297-321.

Sudhir Devare, (2006), *India and Southeast Asia: Towards Security Convergence*, Singapore.

Rahul Sen, Mukul, G. Asher, Ramkishen S. Rajan (2004), "ASEAN-India Economic Relations", *Economic and Political Weekly*, pp. 3297-3307.

Vibhanshu Shekhar (2007), "India-ASEAN Relations: An Overview", *IPCS*, pp. 4-7.

K.S. Nathan (2000), *India and ASEAN: The Growing Partnership for the 21st Century*, Kuala Lumpur.

Ganganath Jha, "India's Relationship with Southeast Asia", *Dialogue Quarterly*, (2004), pp. 157-68.

The text of the Speech delivered by Prime Minister P. V. Narasimha Rao, 8 September, 1994 at Singapore.

Text of Treaty of Amity and Cooperation in Southeast Asia, 24 February, 1976, Bali, Indonesia.

Text of Declaration of ASEAN Concord, 24 February, 1976, Bali, Indonesia.

Saeed Ahmed Rid, Pakistan's Look East Policy: Opportunities and Constraints, *Regional Studies*, Winter, 2006-07, pp. 64-92.

The Times of India, 29 August, 2008.

Aparna Shivpuri Singh, *Business Times*, 23 June, 2005, Singapore.

Bronson Percival (2007), The Dragon Looks South: China and Southeast Asia in the New Century, *Praeger Security International*, Westport, p. 9.

Satu, P. Limaye is Director of Research, Asia Pacific Centre for Security Studies, Hawaii, USA.

Satu, P. Limaye (2003) "India's Relations with Southeast Asia Take a Wing", *Southeast Asian Affairs*, p. 43.

Goh Chok Tong (2002), Text of his speech in the first ASEAN-India Summit, Phnom Penh.

Index